# DESERT SUMMITS

## A CLIMBING & HIKING GUIDE
## TO CALIFORNIA AND SOUTHERN NEVADA

## BY ANDY ZDON

Phil Gonzalez on the summit of Manly Peak in the Panamint Range, Death Valley National Park
Photo: Andy Zdon

# DESERT SUMMITS

### A CLIMBING & HIKING GUIDE
### TO CALIFORNIA AND SOUTHERN NEVADA

## BY ANDY ZDON

Spotted Dog Press, Inc. • Bishop, California

Desert Summits: A Climbing and Hiking Guide to California and Southern Nevada
By Andy Zdon

For updates on this and other Spotted Dog Press books, please visit our website:
www.SpottedDogPress.com

If you have comments about the information found in this book or any other book published by Spotted Dog Press, please let us know.  Contact us by FAX at (760) 872-1319, or by mail at: Spotted Dog Press, Inc., P.O. Box 1721, Bishop, CA 93514, or e-mail: spdogpress@qnet.com
Please include your name, mailing address, and a daytime phone.

Spotted Dog Press, Inc., First Edition 2000
ISBN   1-893343-02-2

Cover photograph: The author descending Pyramid Peak (6,703'), Death Valley
Back cover: On the ridge between Boundary Peak (13,140', high point of Nevada) and Montgomery Peak (13,440') in background.  Photos: Wynne Benti
Maps ©2000 Spotted Dog Press, Inc.
Printed by Central Plains Book Manufacturing, Winfield, Kansas

Library of Congress Cataloging-in-Publication Data
Zdon, Andy, 1960-
Desert Summits: a climbing and hiking guide to California and Southern Nevada/by Andy Zdon--1st ed.
        p. cm.
Includes bibliographical references (p.) and index.
ISBN 1-893343-01-4 (alk. paper)
1. Mountaineering--California--Guidebooks. 2. Mountaineering--Nevada--Guidebooks. 3. Hiking--California--Guidebooks. 4. Hiking--Nevada--Guidebooks. 5. California--Guidebooks. 6. Nevada--Guidebooks. I. Title.

GV199.42.C2 Z36 2000
917.9404'54--dc21

Printed in the United States of America

*To Margaret O'Brien Zdon,
who inspired my love of books.*

# Safety in the Desert

A climb in the desert by an experienced mountaineer in the right state of
mind using the right gear, is a safe and enjoyable venture.
Without the proper equipment and preparation, climbing or traveling in
the desert can be a dangerous activity, so it is reasonable to assume that
certain risks and hazards are associated with traveling and hiking in the
remote desert regions of California and Nevada.  Some of these hazards
include, but are not limited to:  adverse weather conditions, unpredictable
flash floods, stream crossings, sand drifts, loose rock and rockfall, rugged
terrain, potential for insect, snake or animal bites, hypothermia, heat stroke
and heat exhaustion, hyponatremia and dehydration.
Carry plenty of water; let someone know your travel plans, where you are
going, and when you plan to return. Make sure your vehicle is in good
running condition, with at least one good spare, and a basic tool kit. Stay
on established roads.  In Nevada, it is possible to travel a main highway
and not see another car for an hour or more, even days, on some state
routes. The author and publisher of this guide make no representations as
to the safety of any driving or hiking route described in this book.  Always
check ahead for pertinent information, as conditions are constantly
changing.  There is no substitute for knowledge of safety procedures
and a little common sense.

## A word about archaeological sites and artifacts

Archaeological sites and artifacts are protected by the Antiquities Act of
1906 and the Archaeological Resources Protection Act of 1979.
All historic and prehistoric sites on federal lands are protected and
defacement, removal, excavation or destruction of such antiquities
is prohibited by law.

# Acknowledgements

The author would like to acknowledge those who have joined him on many a desert summit and wanderings, including Dave Clegg, Phil Gonzalez, Russ White, Bob Whitney, Danny Zampirro, Bruce Garbacchio, Pete and Punkin' Tresselt, Campy and Ski Camphausen, Walt and Bettie Hines, Ella Power Wheelock, the entire Zdon clan including, Ed, Sr. and Ed M. Zdon, and Wynne Benti.

In addition, thanks are expressed to those who knowingly and unknowingly contributed to this book, and to the literature of the region, through their additions. Their names are listed throughout the book and in the reference section.

Tina Bowman next to Winnedumah Paiute Monument, Inyo Mountains.  Photo: Doug Bear

# Table of Contents

## List of Maps

Limber pine on Wilfred Peak in the Benton Range. Photo: Wynne Benti

## Foreword

# A Place of Inspiration
## Edmund Benti

The moment you step from your vehicle onto the desert firmament, you exit the modern world of convenience and luxury and enter an ancient place of eternal moments, encapsulating and, at rare times, entombing that which strays within. The expectation of "the thrill of the climb" now, here in the presence of the thing, pales somewhat, surpassed by a sense of mystery and foreboding. You may find this sensation, however, irresistible, as much so as what you thought had brought you here in the first place, the climb.

The adventurous spirit is drawn to mystery and danger as surely as the predator is drawn to the kill. The very names with which humankind has adorned these places of the world evoke that sense of the unknown, awe and dread; names such as Kalahari, Takla Makan, Kara Kum, and Death Valley.

Great places of inspiration, the world's deserts play an indispensable role in our human heritage. Those who take on and conquer these lands find themselves in the company of legendary figures. Caressed by the nourishing waters of the Tigris and Euphrates rivers, the very cradle of western civilization evolved from the bosom of a desert oasis. From this same oasis came the exultant voice of Old Omar and his Rubayat fired in to the psychic kiln of humanity. Moses led the Israelites through the great Sinai desert for forty years, his climb resulting no less in the law of God and man! Alexander marched his antique army throughout the deserts of the Persian Gulf, on foot, for little else than the unquenchable desire to explore and conquer the ends of his earth. Genghis Khan's army burst from the frigid desert wastes of the Mongolian steppes, destroying and then rebuilding Chinese civilization into the largest land empire of all time. T.E. Lawrence discovered his heroic role in the Arabian desert and, as legend has it, Antoine de Saint-Exupery met his Little Prince while awaiting rescue from a plane wreck in the Sahara.

When the frozen body of George Leigh Mallory was revealed to climbers on the icy slopes of Mt. Everest, preserved in its failure and aspirations so near heaven, where it fell to the elements, and hubris, some eight decades past, there lay a moral of sorts to the climber: The icy elements of the great alpine ranges preserve and retain in their cold hearts. What the desert mountaineer will find in the furnace fires of the great American desert peaks covered by this work is not a rigid experience frozen in time, but, rather, a purification, a catharsis of body, mind and soul. From this a certain wellspring of inspiration may be revealed, a clarification of purpose and place, a distillation as only fire can produce. And, too, of course, the thrill of the climb.

The deserts of the deep American southwest have only recently revealed themselves to examination by the Anglo-Saxon explorer, the result of the process of expansion driven by a religious belief system historians refer to as Manifest Destiny. Some consider the land you have come to enjoy, an occupied war zone. For thousands of years, trails, padded soft and swept clean of stones by bare feet, crisscrossed the desert. Only as recently as 1847, as an access route to join in the Mexican-American War, was the first road into Southern California hewn from rocky canyons and arroyos of the Anza-Borrego desert, one of the truly demanding, inhospitable and sublimely beautiful places on this earth. That accomplishment fell to Mormons, one people of many claiming a divine right to some part of the American west. They were fleeing brutal religious oppression, seeking a homeland. A familiar human tale.

What turned out to be one of the longest military marches in history, portions of the trail built by the Mormon Battalion can yet be seen less than an hour's drive from San Diego. When one gazes upon that small, primitive highway, in that scorched, unforgiving terrain, seemingly in the midst of nowhere, that 2,000 mile sacrifice made by those men and women staggers the imagination even now, just a mere fifteen decades past.

Yet the human saga played out upon these lands stretches far beyond the dim historical horizon marked by the last century. Telltale markings, grinding mortars, wall paintings and carvings exist here, pointing to an even more obscure past. There were people living here long before the "pioneers"; the Washoe, Paiute and Shoshone scratched out an existence centuries past where one seems so unlikely. While there were only some 7,000 or so Mexican citizens in California at the outbreak of the Mexican-American War, an estimated 75,000 Native Americans prospered here. The folk legends of the Mechica warriors tell of an ancient homeland from which their ancestors came, and to which they shall once again return to claim. That is the land of Aztlan, roughly what is now known as the American southwest. That a great warrior nation emerged from the place in which you now find yourself echoes, does it not, somewhat familiarly? Make no mistake: the arid panorama presenting itself to you, is one of great human inspiration. And you now come to match yourself to these elements too. Consider this while following a climb provided in this guide.

As you stand beside the ruins of a long forgotten prospector's cabin, pause a moment from the heat of day, to take a breath, to sip some water. A warm, drying wind sweeps past, brushing across the wavering vista before your eyes, a silent jagged landscape folded and unfolded for you to the horizon. Visible far down below, a dust cloud kicks up behind the vehicle of another temporary visitor scurrying along a desert road to reach some other place. Alone, perhaps lonely, vast and deceptively empty, the ancient desert land holds and fills you with its quiet solitude. You've come to climb, yet a glance at the map reveals only tantalizing clues as to the nature of this mysterious place. Names like Coffin, Funeral, Last Chance, Scattered Bone and Devil dance off the page and into the imagination. This is a land of spectacular scenery, vibrant, unique life forms and an obscure past. The desert reveals itself to the visiting climber only reluctantly, incrementally.

The ranges covered here by Andy Zdon's text, the product of twenty years of desert mountaineering, though regarded less seriously by many mountaineers, do possess everything necessary for the "thrill of the climb," like those of the world's greater ranges. The region itself can be so challenging as to test the best climbers. Climbing opportunities span the spectrum in this land of extremes. From the hot, searing sands and sun-bleached alkali of valley basins, to the spring-blessed alpine summits of its highest mountains, the demands of mountaineering found here are as varied as the terrain. From the rugged limestone of Death Valley's Eagle Mountain to a quiet walk up Sagehen Peak in the Benton Range, the peaks described herein provide a complete experience. The fact that most are accessible to those simply possessing strong legs, healthy lungs and a dose of stoic determinedness makes desert mountains appealing to a broader range of climber. Many who came before would be surprised at the simple reason behind this guidebook. However, the inspiration between the early visitors and today's mountaineering explorer are really not so different. Every person who has come here has chosen to leave somewhere else, to seek the challenge of the unknown, to succeed that challenge, to survive.

# Introduction

## Andy Zdon

It was on a camping trip to the sage-covered Bodie Hills, that Walt Wheelock first talked about updating his desert guide books, *Desert Peaks Guide, Part 1, and Desert Peaks Guide, Part 2* (La Siesta Press). These books were desert climbing classics, understated and inexpensive, usually tucked away on the bottom shelf of the local sporting goods store to make room on the higher shelves for more costly titles. For me and many others, the *Desert Peaks* series was our first introduction to the concept of desert peaks and desert climbing. And, they seemed to accomplish what a guidebook should accomplish; they left the reader with a curiosity and desire to get out there and explore the desert. Just enough information was provided to send the reader in the right direction, without lessening the challenge of exploration or even reaching a desert summit.

Walt had traveled through the California desert as early as 1929, beginning with a high school trip in a Model T Ford to Death Valley. At that time, all roads to Death Valley were dirt. Most followed old wagon routes. In any event, they were not the well-traveled paved roads of today. That first trip to Death Valley made an impression that would last a lifetime; Walt spent the next seventy years traveling the deserts of the southwest. Visiting the desert, and all things related, was his first love.

*Desert Peaks Guide 1* was first published in 1962, followed by the second guide in 1975. When Walt reprinted a book, the only text he updated was the year in which the book was printed. He rarely if ever revised text. A book would remain in print, essentially unchanged, for thirty years. Rarely did he get complaints from readers, perhaps because a La Siesta Press book was a real bargain, costing only a dollar or two. When

Walt Wheelock and Andy Zdon at camp in the Bodie Hills. Photo: Wynne Benti

he did get complaints, he'd scan the letter for the general gist, then toss it in the circular file.

The desert always seems to remain the same, a vast arid plain of sage, scrub and creosote, where time stands still. But, time doesn't stand still there. Since Walt first wrote and published his desert guide books, conditions have changed, radically in some cases. New highways have been built; older roads have been abandoned or renamed; mining operations have removed parts, if not all, of some peaks that Walt wrote about; flash floods, erosion, abandonment, or neglect have caused some routes to revert back to nature. Passage of the California Desert Protection Act changed the access to many peaks by creating new wilderness boundaries.

Walt Wheelock intended for his *Desert Peaks Guide* series to consist of several parts. *Part 1* covered the peaks lying immediately east of the Sierra Nevada including the Benton Range, the Inyo and White Ranges, the Coso and Argus Ranges. *Part 2* consisted of what was termed the "Death Valley Country." Walt dreamed of completing other volumes that would cover additional desert peaks in California, Arizona, Nevada, and Utah. While this guide does not take on such an ambitious scope, it does encompass a variety of areas that will be of interest to the desert mountaineer, including peaks in the newly established Mojave National Preserve, the expanded Joshua Tree and Death Valley National Parks, Lake Mead National Recreation Area, and other areas in Southern Nevada and California. Additionally, peaks with restricted access due to their inclusion in military bases, or on private property, and peaks that have been mined away, have been removed. When we first discussed updating and expanding his guides, Walt was keen to the idea that his works would be continued. Some of his historical sketches (for the Mono Peaks, White-Inyo Range and Death Valley) live on in this book. It is with sorrow that Walt is not here today to see the finished work.

The following sections, originally included in *Desert Peaks Guide 1,* answer the questions, "What is a desert peak?" and "Why desert peaks?" Edmund Jaeger, head of the Department of Zoology and Professor Emeritus at Riverside College, and author of "What is a desert peak?" was a noted desert biologist who wrote such classic desert works as, *The California Deserts, Our Desert Neighbors, Desert Wildflowers,* and The *North American Deserts.* Randall Henderson, publisher of *Desert Magazine,* and author of "Why Desert Peaks?" wrote several books describing his desert experiences.

## What is a Desert Peak?

The term "desert," applied to any place, implies that certain climatic conditions prevail in the area, first in importance being meager, often erratically distributed, rainfall (ten inches or less per year, its effectiveness depending on many local and general conditions, such as soil porosity, amounts of wind, exposure, etc.). Second, the term implies a total evaporation rate especially high in summer and adverse to all but specialized plants.

Few mountain peaks 6,000 feet high or over satisfy these requirements for being called "desert peaks." Their elevation induces too large an amount of precipitation, and there is coolness both by day and night that keeps the evaporation rate low.

The vegetational cover is one of the best indicators of true desert conditions. In the southwestern United States, the pinyon-juniper-sagebrush association may be present at the very upper limits of desert but the growth is sparse. Really good stands of juniper, pinyon and yellow pine suggest a rainfall greater than 10 inches and up to 20 inches or more. Therefore, we can immediately rule out any mountain peak with thick stands of these trees as a true desert peak.

The Spring Mountains of Southern Nevada, while wholly surrounded by desert, can hardly be called desert mountains according to this criterion. Telescope Peak in the Panamint Range is not essentially different unless we change our definition and call a desert peak any eminence partly or wholly surrounded by desert. Because of the strong up-sweep of hot dry winds on both western and eastern sides of these highlands, the summer evaporation is unusually high, and true desert conditions prevail farther up the slopes than usual, but certainly not at their tops. In lower California, El Picacho del Diablo, in the Sierra San Pedro de Martir, satisfies the requirements for being a desert peak unusually far up one slope (the eastern), but certainly not on its western flank facing the nearby Pacific Ocean.

Outstanding true desert peaks of rather high elevation, worthy of the mettle of desert peak climbers, come to mind: Baboquivari Peak in southern Arizona, the summits of the Coxcomb, Granite, Kingston, Old Woman and Grapevine Mountains in the Southern California deserts, the Virgin of Guadalupe and El Capriote and several other lower but very steep eminences on or near the eastern slope of the Sierra Juarez in Baja California, all enticing to climb because of the magnificent desert views they offer.

– *Edmund Jaeger*

## Why Desert Peaks?

From my window in Palm Desert, California, I look up every morning to the 8,705-foot summit of Toro Peak in the Santa Rosa Mountains. Toro Peak is not a high peak compared with Charleston or Boundary Peaks of Nevada, the San Franciscos in Arizona, or a score of others in the Southwest. For me, Toro Peak symbolizes the challenge that all desert mountains hold for those stout-hearted folk who know that exhilarating moment when after many hours on the trail, or perhaps without a trail, they have stood on a summit they have conquered by sheer hard work.

There was no forestry road to the high ridge on the Santa Rosas when I first climbed Toro in 1933, not even a trail at the higher elevations. The temperature on the desert below was 116 degrees on that August day, and the springs are far apart on these mountains, but all these are the obstacles that challenge the climber. It would be no fun to walk up a mountain on a stairway, or climb one where there is a lemonade stand every half mile.

Desert peaks are unique in that those that tower above the 7,000-foot level virtually are forested oases in a vast expanse of arid terrain. The charm of these high-altitude oases is that they combine the most favorable elements of both mountain and desert. The air is dry, but the altitude insures against unbearably high temperatures. It is always cool in the shade of the pine, fir or cedar trees that grow at these high elevations. Although they receive more rainfall than the floor of the desert below, the air is generally clear and the summit of a desert peak is a grandstand seat for a vast panorama that extends for a hundred miles or more in all directions.

The life zones in the world of botany and zoology are more clearly defined on desert slopes than in the more temperate regions, and for any students of nature these are never-ending sources of delight and informative observation. On many desert peaks, the sturdy climber may ascend from the creosote or larrea of the Lower Sonoran zone, to the hardy shrubs of the Arctic in a single day, from the sand-dune home of the sidewinder, to the rocky burrow of the marmot.

Because this is a land of little rainfall, the peaks that crown the desert landscape are generally landmarks visible for long distances. What is more important for the perennial mountaineer, there are not many days in the year when impossible weather closes the route to the top, nor the downed wood too damp to provide quickly the warm glow of a campfire (*where permitted! - editor*) that relaxes tired muscles, refreshes the spirit, and makes the tasks of today and tomorrow so worthwhile.

Civilization, in its frantic quest for new resources to exploit has so far found most of the desert peaks too inaccessible or too barren to yield a profit. May this always be true. May these high oases of the desert land be reserved always for you and me and those other nature-loving humans who seek not profit only in the whirl of the wheel and the clang of steel, but in those remote high places known only to those valiant souls who climb mountains for the pure joy of climbing mountains.

– *Randall Henderson*

# Using this Guide

Anyone who climbs or just travels to the desert should carry a bevy of road maps, and there are a few highly recommended ones. The Automobile Club of Southern California produces a series of road maps that are free to Auto Club members, or can be purchased at an Auto Club travel center by non-members. Recommended for this book are: Eastern Sierra, Death Valley Area, Colorado River Area, San Bernardino County, Riverside County, and San Diego County. In addition, the DeLorme Company publishes a series of road atlases known as the "Atlas & Gazetteer" series. They include topography, landmarks, and other useful information. Purchasing their Southern California, Northern California, and Nevada atlases is highly recommended. These maps are required reading for anyone heading out to the desert.

7.5-minute (1:24,000 scale) topographic maps prepared by the U.S. Geological Survey are as necessary as a good road map. The topos needed for each peak are listed. Copies of the topographic maps have not been included. Frequently, guidebooks will include a portion of the topographic map showing only the summit and the immediate area around the summit, while a publisher's disclaimer advises not to use the maps provided, but everyone does. The author has done this many times. The problems with this practice are two-fold. First, the very small area covered on these maps, when reduced to fit on one page, remove or distort potential points that could be used for navigation purposes. Second, straying either on purpose, or accidentally from the map's plotted route will likely leave the hiker without any map coverage, making additional navigation very difficult.

Buying the maps for every peak in this book will make for a hefty investment. The U.S. Geological Survey has developed a series of metric, pre-folded, 1:100,000 scale maps which may be an economical alternative, primarily for those peaks with easy route-finding. In either case, the dollars spent on these maps are small in comparison to the cost of the transportation to get to the climb itself. Road and climbing route conditions can change completely as a result of changes in access policy by the local land management agency, conversion to private property, or any number of natural events including flash floods, earthquakes, landslides, and other inconveniences. Snow on any of the routes and roads can turn a rather simple approach and climb into an epic adventure, so be prepared. A list of agency addresses, phone numbers, and web site information is provided in the Appendix A, and essential equipment is listed in Appendix B.

Each writeup contains the following information: the peak's name and elevation (in feet), followed by the 7.5-minute (1:24,000 scale) quadrangles needed for the ascent, the U.S. Geological Survey 1:100,000 scale metric topographic map covering the area, the Automobile Club of Southern California (AAA) road map as appropriate, the best season for climbing the peak, descriptions of the approaches and routes, and any alternate routes of interest. Peaks with quotation marks around their names, are those peaks for which the name is unofficial, and does not show up on the topographic maps. All peak elevations are given in both feet and meters, as numerous topographic maps have been created in a metric format. There seems to be no geographic rhyme or reason as to which maps will be metric. Metric elevations have been provided in the trip write-ups where landmarks are needed and a quick field reference to the map should not include solving a math equation to figure out which point is which! Just for reference, to convert feet into meters, divide the elevation in feet by 3.28.

Climbing difficulty can be assumed to be Class 1 or 2 on the Yosemite Decimal System unless otherwise noted. For those not familiar with this grading system:

Class 1 - trail walking or otherwise easy walking routes (for example Telescope, Charleston and Wildrose Peaks, Borrego Mountain)

Class 2 - off-trail hiking with some use of hands for balance possible (for example Glass Mountain, Corkscrew Peak, East Ord Mountain, Indianhead)

Class 3 - easy climbing with hands needed, some climbers may need a rope (for example Casa Diablo Mountain, Eagle Mountain, New York Mountain, Clark Mountain).

Class 4 - moderate climbing with rope recommended and possible use of anchors (for example Umpah Point, Thumb Peak)

Class 5 - technical rock climbing (for example Winnedumah Paiute Monument, Old Woman Statue, Dyadic Peak)

Throughout the book, the age of the rocks encountered on the peaks is discussed in terms of their geologic age, such as Cambrian or Tertiary. For those unfamilar with the geologic time scale, one is provided in Appendix C to give the reader relative and numerical ages with which to associate these terms.

Every day, more desert land, especially in Nevada and the high desert on the outskirts of Los Angeles County, is permanently closed to the public. Open land once freely walked upon and explored, is now covered with houses, private resorts and roads. Not too long ago, there was plenty of space between the Desert National Wildlife Range and the outskirts of Las Vegas. That open space, that natural buffer zone, has all but vanished. Where the night was once dark and full of stars, city lights illuminate quiet canyons and mountain tops. It is our hope, that people will take this book and explore the desert's natural beauty; learn what's out there, and become a voice for desert protection.

Lastly, once out in the desert, the hiker will find scores of peaks, named and unnamed, worthy of ascent, but not included in this guidebook. There is no way for any guidebook to cover every desert mountain worthy of ascent. Besides, part of the joy of mountaineering is to discover your own peaks and ranges that no one has written about, and exploring them on your own.

# Preparing for the Desert

For every mountain climbed with the aid of a rope, a hundred are climbed by trail or good old-fashioned cross-country scrambling. Most of the desert peaks in this guide fall into the latter class. Relatively little if any technical ability is needed, except perhaps the coordination and ability to hike down loose, steep slopes, and maneuver through cactus. A summit crag may call for some third class climbing, while a few peaks do require technical rock skill. This guidebook assumes that the reader has studied some standard works on climbing, and is capable of doing easy friction climbs or bouldering. A list of essential items can be found in Appendix B. They include a basic first aid kit, topographic map, compass, flashlight with spare batteries, food and water, extra clothing as appropriate, pocket knife, matches in a waterproof container, sun glasses, sun screen, a hat, and a cell phone.

Planning a desert climb begins with the right equipment, and proper physical and mental preparation. Responsible climbers realize that their pursuit is inherently risky; they do not climb beyond their ability, and they do not let their personal desires, ego or goals outweigh good judgement. Those who choose to head out into the desert environment will constantly be faced with decisions that ultimately affect their well-being, perhaps even their lives. In doing so, they must accept complete responsibility for their decisions and their actions. For those who have little or no experience hiking in desert terrain, the book *Desert Hiking* by Dave Ganci is a highly recommended read. Also, joining a desert hiking group, such as the Sierra Club's Desert Peaks Section (based in Los Angeles, California), is an excellent way to become trained in the ways of the desert mountaineer.

Desert mountaineering presents certain problems not commonly associated with alpine ascents. Among them are:

## Temperature

Deserts can have an enormous temperature range within a twenty-four hour period. Under certain conditions, a few hours may be the difference between a freezing dawn and a 100-degree day in a shadeless canyon exposed to the direct rays of the sun. Long-sleeved, wind proof garments should be carried, and may be needed to protect the climber from the cold, wind, or direct rays of the sun. Take short but frequent snack breaks every forty-five minutes to an hour of hiking, and wear a light-colored broad-brimmed hat. During late spring, summer, and early fall (in the lower elevations) hike when the trails and canyons are shaded, usually from dawn to late morning or from late afternoon to dusk. Avoid hiking in the sun, and in particular, avoid hiking uphill during the hottest part of the day. When we climbed Avawatz Peak in the Mojave Desert (during early summer), we started hiking around four in the morning, making for some very pleasant hiking. By the time we reached the car shortly before noon, the temperature had risen to over 100 degrees. If there is water to spare, dousing the top of one's head every forty-five minutes can be very refreshing on a hot day.

## Heat-related Illness

Heat exhaustion is a serious heat-related illness that occurs when the body rate of heat gain is greater than the rate of heat loss. The best way to avoid heat exhaustion is to drink adequate water with electrolyte additives. Several factors can cause heat exhaustion, dehydration and over exertion when it's hot are the two biggest causes. Symptoms include physical weakness, dizziness, nausea, vomiting, minimal or no urination and headache. When symptoms are identified, the victim should move (or be moved) out of direct sunlight, sit or lie down (preferably with feet elevated somewhat), and slowly drink a fluid such as water with electrolyte replacements. Future movement should be limited until the body's fluids are restored.

Heat stroke occurs when the body's internal temperature rises above 105 degrees, and results in death if not treated immediately. Hikers or mountaineers who are not used to hot temperatures like those found in the desert, may suffer from "exertional heat stroke" if they prolong their activity. Their initial symptoms will include pale, damp, cool skin even when their internal temperature has reached dangerous levels, followed by confusion, irrational, even aggressive behavior and physical collapse. Others will exhibit symptoms of classic heat stroke in which their skin will be hot and dry to the touch. In both cases, the goal of treatment is to reduce the body temperature quickly. The victim should be placed in the shade, tight clothing removed or loosened, and cooled by swabbing with water-soaked cloths or bandanas, and fanning. If the victim is conscious, have them drink water in sips. The victim must be carried out and hospitalized.

## Hypothermia

During the winter, or at higher elevations, during any time of the year, hypothermia can be one of the principal hazards to the desert climber. Hypothermia occurs when the body experiences heat loss causing the body's core temperature to drop, impairing brain and muscular functions. The most common way for the desert climber to become hypothermic is by not dressing warmly enough to insulate the body from the cold environment. Initial symptoms may include feeling very cold, numbness of skin, and minor muscular impairment. As the body temperature drops, the muscles become increasingly uncoordinated, there is mild confusion, slowness of pace, apathy or amnesia. If not treated immediately, it can progress to unconsciousness and eventually death.

Preventing hypothermia requires warm dry clothing, food and water. Again, drinking water and snacking on foods high in carbohydrates at frequent intervals will provide energy supplies for physical activity and production of body heat. Most important, dress in layers. Wool and polyester are the best insulators. A layer of polypropylene long underwear, tops and bottoms, followed by wool or synthetic sweater and pants, topped off with a waterproof, breathable layer of nylon, jackets and pants that can double as rain and wind protection. The final critical item is a wool or polyester weave hat since most heat loss occurs from the head. Include on the list, a warm pair of gloves and socks. If a person comes down with hypothermia, removing wet clothes and warming them with another human body can be a lifesaver. If a sleeping bag is handy, climbing into the sleeping bag with them can help restore their body temperature.

## Dehydration

Low humidity, high temperatures, and brisk winds draw water from a person at a rate that seems impossible to climbers not familiar with the desert's arid environment. Streams seldom exist; desert water holes are far apart and easily missed by those not versed with the desert landscape. A climber who boasts that he never carries a water bottle will find that he may need as much as a gallon of water under certain circumstances. Dehydration and heat-related illnesses account for most of the injuries and rescues throughout the year in desert terrain. Muscle cramps in the legs or the abdomen can result from the loss of water and electrolytes. Certainly, no attempt to climb a mountain should be made with less than two quarts of water or other liquids combined with an electrolyte replacement supplement. With temperatures exceeding 100 degrees in canyon floors, and humidity dropping below 10%, twenty-four hours without water can be fatal to an inexperienced hiker. The author commonly carries up to four liters of water for a full day's outing on a warm day.

The flip side of dehydration is "hyponatremia" or water intoxication. Hyponatremia occurs when a person drinks an excessive amount of water without replacing lost electrolytes either by not eating or not including an electrolyte replacement supplement in their water. Initial symptoms are similar to those of heat exhaustion–physical weakness, dizziness, nausea with frequent urination, and eventually seizures, collapse, and unconsciousness.

Depending on desert watering holes can be a very risky business and is thoroughly not recommended in this guidebook. O.E. Meinzer, a U.S.G.S. hydrologist who studied springs in the California desert once wrote:

*"The desert has a peculiar fascination. Its solitude and silence are soothing to man...if he comes at the end of a long day, with a tired and thirsty team of horses, to an isolated watering place that has gone dry, or if he loses his bearings and the panorama assumes a strange and bewildering aspect...his feelings toward the desert will undergo a sudden change."*

Not only will your attitude toward the desert change, but without water, you will have far greater issues to worry about than attitude adjustments.

## Unfriendly Vegetation

Many desert plants, that provide important habitat for desert wildlife, while delightful to view and photograph, are unfriendly or even injurious on contact. Although there are none of the "man-eating plants" seen in many 1950's era science fictions, a 10-foot fall into an agave can be just as deadly. The cacti and yuccas are well-known hazards. The cholla, which some claim can jump at a passerby, earning the nickname "jumping cholla," has spines that break freely and defy attempts to pull them from the flesh unless tweezers or even needle-nose pliers are available. The agave has sword-like leaves that can fatally impale a falling rock climber. The catclaw can tear the shirt (and skin) right off your back. However, just because the complacent hiker may occasionally tangle with these plants, don't look harshly upon them. Desert flora are an integral part of nature's landscape.

## Desert Creatures

The desert is home to many native species of animals, birds, insects and lizards, all of which have carved out a balanced and delicate niche in this arid environment of extreme heat and cold. Many are nocturnal, protected by the shade of burrow or nest during the day, and out and about doing their business at night. It is a wonderful and fascinating world to observe from a distance. This is their home, and we are only visitors, so they deserve our respect. They also don't expect us to come crashing around the corner, so a chance encounter with a surprised creature is always a possibility. Several times, the author has heard the rattle of a snake's tail before ever seeing the snake curled up beneath the cool shade of a rocky crevice in a gully. The sound is always enough to send one flying out of harm's way.

Watch where you step and put your hands. The desert is home to scorpions, centipedes, cone-nosed bloodsuckers (aka kissing bugs), rattlesnakes, bees, wasps, hornets, tarantulas, skunks, stinkbugs, biting gnats, ticks, and non-native grazing animals like skitish and unpredictable range cattle. Add the Africanized Honey Bee to this list. This non-native insect that is virtually indistinguishable from normal honey bees, and has already been identified in several areas covered by this guide. This bee doesn't simply sting when it's disturbed. It invites thousands of its friends in on the fun, and the result can be fatal. It is virtually impossible to outrun these fellows. On my trips to the desert, I have rarely seen bees. If you do see them, be careful as it is very possible they may be the Africanized Honey Bee. Step gingerly over downed logs, as they are a favorite hive location.

One way to avoid many of the inspects and spiders described above is to shake out your shoes and clothes before putting them on. Shoes removed at night are a favorite warm spot for insects and spiders to nest. The author recalls putting on his hiking boots at camp only to feel a crunch inside his

Rattlesnake in the Silver Peak Range. Photo: Andy Zdon

shoe, the result of the squashing of a poor beetle that had taken shelter in that leather abode.

Scorpions are often found under rocks, downed wood, and in cracks and on ledges of rock piles. Two spiders to watch out for are the black widow and the brown recluse. Black widows are particularly common around old desert shacks, old cans, and wood piles. Rattlesnakes are prevalent throughout the desert southwest, and a run-in with one of these creatures can be a serious affair. Rattlesnakes will not chase anything they can't swallow and will leave you alone unless they feel threatened.

Centipedes, tarantulas, cone-nosed bloodsuckers, biting ants, wasps, and bees are common desert dwellers and can inflict a painful, but non-dangerous bite. Simply wash the bite with an alcohol pad (soap and water if in camp), treat with an antiseptic, and take an aspirin for the pain which will subside after a few hours.

Hantavirus is a concern wherever there are mice. This airborne virus, carried by the deer mouse, is present in its urine and feces. When this material is disturbed, the infected particles can become airborne and inhaled by the unsuspecting individual. To minimize the possibility of getting this frequently fatal virus, avoid contact with rodents and rodent burrows, dilapidated buildings (such as old desert shacks) that show evidence of rodent activity, don't sleep on bare ground, keep food in rodent-proof containers, use only bottled or disinfected water, and don't feed or play with mice.

After reading this section you may think, "Sounds too dangerous for me." Hiking in the desert is much safer than your daily commute to work. In all my years of desert hiking, I have only come across a few rattlesnakes. A chance encounter with some of the desert's more unsavory residents really is the rarity, but for more educated reading on the subject, pick up a copy of the excellent source book *Poisonous Dwellers of the Desert* by Trevor Hare.

## Altitude

Several of the desert ranges described in this book reach elevations of over 10,000 feet above sea level. White Mountain Peak, at 14,256 feet, is only two hundred and forty feet shorter than Mt. Whitney, the tallest peak in the contiguous United States. Living at or near-sea level, then driving straight up to the high mountains on a Friday night without the benefit of a few days to acclimatize, or to adjust to the radical change in elevation, can result in headache, and nausea, the first warning signs of mountain sickness (also known as altitude sickness). Mountain sickness does not discriminate based on age, gender or fitness level, it can strike anyone.

The best way to avoid mountain sickness is to plan your trip to allow time for a gradual ascent to altitude. On my first hike to White Mountain Peak, our small group drove from near sea level to the road-end at over 11,000 feet where we spent the night, then hiked the peak the next day. How did we feel? Nauseous, pounding headaches, and just plain awful. The next time we spent a full day at the road end, starting off with a short hike up Mount Barcroft, then climbing White Mountain Peak the second day. We felt great that day, due in part to the time spent acclimatizing.

There are some people who are just sensitive to altitude and no amount of acclimatization is going to help them. Diamox is a prescription drug that has worked for many when acclimatization did not. Prescribed by a medical doctor, Diamox is taken in gradual doses of about 125 mg (half a regular 250 mg tablet) three times a day, beginning three to four days before going to altitude. There are entire books written on the subject. The expert is Charles Houston, M.D. Considered the "Father of High Altitude Pulmonary Edema," his books *High Altitude Illness and Wellness* and *Going Higher* are recommended reading.

# Lightning

Lightning in the desert is most commonly a threat during the summer thunderstorm season. The high ranges are especially vulnerable to severe lightning storms, and it is the high desert ranges that are most likely climbed during the summer months, after the snow melts. If caught in a lightning storm, there are a few places you definitely do not want to be: under an exposed tree or worse yet, at a summit microwave or repeater installation; on any exposed high ridge; or out in the open anywhere regardless of elevation. Don't wait for the hair on your arms to start standing on end (due to the build of atmospheric charge) to minimize your exposure.

# Abandoned Mines

One of the fascinating aspects of climbing in the desert is that inevitably, old, abandoned mines, and outbuildings, that provoke curiosity and exploration, will be encountered. Investigating the areas around these mines can be as interesting as the hike. However, there are a few potential hazards associated with abandoned mines. A fall down an unmarked shaft is likely to be lethal. Miners have been known to leave behind explosives, old dynamite sticks, blasting caps and powder, most likely unstable, inside and outside mines. If you happen upon such a cache, leave them alone and report their presence to the local land management agency.

Even more hazards await the curious in tunnels and other underground workings: blind shafts hidden beneath a seemingly innocent puddle of surface water, cave-ins, and bad air (air containing poisonous gasses, or more likely, insufficient oxygen) are some of the most common. Many an old mine was abandoned because of fire. Timbers can smolder for years until the oxygen in the tunnel is gone. Poor ventilation may cause an oxygen deficient atmosphere to last for decades, and in places oxygen content in the air may be low enough to cause unconsciousness before the explorer knows what happened. Other underground hazards include cave-ins, decayed timbers that can fall on the climber, or ladders with weak rungs. The best advice is to stay out of underground mine workings.

# Confusing Landmarks

To the novice, desert mountain ranges look pretty similar. The steep barren canyons have few distinguishing characteristics for the person who is unaccustomed to them, or can't identify landmarks. All instructions for route-finding should be applied here, much more so than in alpine mountains. Before heading off into the remote desert, a knowledge of compasswork and navigation is recommended. Learn to identify landmarks on the way–an odd-shaped rock formation; a lone Joshua tree on an otherwise treeless terrain . . . these can all help locate yourself. Look behind you on your way up and pinpoint a landmark, perhaps where the car is parked so you can identify the route on the way down.

A note about following those small piles of rocks called "cairns" or "ducks." Frequently, these small piles of rock mark the route to a desert summit. Other times, they may denote the route to someone's mining claim, or may be a claim marker themselves (the standard wood posts in the desert weren't too popular in the old days considering the lack of trees). They may even have been placed by someone with the same summit goal but who was hopelessly lost and didn't realize it. Blindly following these piles of rocks puts you in the position of trusting the orienteering of others, and possibly putting your life in the hands of someone you don't know. It is best to learn to use the compass, learn to read the maps and terrain, and choose your own route.

## Unstable Terrain
Rain falls sparsely in the desert. Rocks and boulders that appear to be securely embedded in slopes often break loose and roll when touched. Smaller rocks that look stable become loose, dumping the climber to the ground (or even into a cactus). With large parties, these rolling rocks are as dangerous as the cannonading of rocks on glacial climbs. When desert granite decomposes on its surface, the resulting particles often remain in place, providing a ball-bearing effect, tripping up the unsuspecting hiker. Other rock fragments that appear to be firmly in place break loose when stepped upon, again with the same result.

## Desert Roads
Traveling along the desert back roads leading to many of the peaks described in this book can be more dangerous than the climbs themselves. Always let someone know your plans. Be sure to contact local land management agencies before your trip to check on conditions. Approach roads are often mere tracks across desert washes, perhaps a long-abandoned route to a forgotten mine site. High centers are hazardous to cars. Sand

pockets will trap the inexperienced (and often experienced) driver, and a drop of one foot into one of these sand traps may take hours of digging to escape. Memories of trying to unstick a gutless, old economy car, from the deep sand of Yuma Wash in southwestern Arizona, in the middle of the night comes to mind. Thankfully the weather was fine and the clear moonless night was pleasant, even beautiful. The same situation at a hotter time could have been a serious predicament.

If you become stuck or your car breaks down, don't attempt to walk away from your vehicle, particularly if its hot and the walk is many miles. The people who know about your trip will know where to look for you assuming no one else happens by to lend a hand. It is much easier for a search party to find a car than a solitary hiker. Once, while on a college field trip in Death Valley, our van happened to get a flat tire along a hot, dry, and seemingly unpopulated expanse of dirt road. We were dismayed to find that a lug wrench and jack-stand were not included with our van, and we had no way of changing the tire. Instead of taking on the hot afternoon sun and hiking out, the group decided to stay put. We had our camping gear, and plenty of food and water. To our surprise, within a few hours, a van load of tourists happened by and allowed us the use of their equipment. The timing of their arrival was perfect for them too. They discovered they also had a tire going flat!

Sudden flash floods can cut across these "roads." If storm clouds are present, better to let a summit go unclimbed than attempt a drive up or crossing a desert dry wash. That dry wash can become a raging torrent, rivaling a large mountain river, in a very brief period of time. If venturing more than a few miles beyond frequently traveled roads, a party should consist of not less than two cars, with much more gas and water than you expect to use. When venturing onto the desert back roads, check the condition of your vehicle first. Start with a full gas tank, check the fluid levels, tire pressure and wear, and the condition of your hoses. The Bureau of Land Management recommends that the following equipment be carried in your car: a basic tool kit with a full socket set, pliers, wrenches, screwdrivers and the like; spark plug socket; wire cutters; vice grips; channel locks; allen wrenches; hammer, knife, spare tire and jack; a tow strap; first aid kit; duct tape (one of the world's great inventions); shop manual for your car; air pressure gauge and tire inflater; shovel; fire extinguisher;

flashlight and batteries; jumper cables; and three gallons of water per person plus five gallons of water per vehicle.

Always practice minimum impact camping. The ultimate goal of everyone who makes a trip to the desert should be to come and go without leaving a trace of their visit. Stay on established roads and obey all land management agency signs concerning road access. It really is important to stay on established roads and not to cut new ones through the desert scrub. Because the desert doesn't get much rain, it can take decades for destroyed desert plants to get enough water to grow again. A sport utility vehicle (SUV) that leaves an established road just once, does devastating damage that can last for a century. During spring, native and migratory birds build their nests in desert shrubs. The author has seen nests crushed by SUV wheels that left an established road because the driver didn't know how to drive through a stretch of sand or was too lazy to get out of the vehicle and do a little road work to make the established route passable. If everyone who owned an SUV, did what the television commercials suggest (drive gonzo off established roads), the desert would be a gutted, irreparable mess. The Bureau of Land Managment has set aside desert areas specifically designated for Off-Highway Vehicle use.

A few other pointers. When hiking on established trails (or even faint climbers' paths) stay on them. Taking shortcuts, known as "cutting switchbacks" will erode the trail. Pack out what you pack in (carry out all garbage). Always dig a hole at least eight inches deep to bury your human waste. Pack out toilet paper in a ziplock bag or bury it. If you need to burn it, do it carefully, and make sure the fire is dead out! Entire forests have been burned to the ground by this practice, and a desert range fire is a difficult fire to fight. Always camp at least 100 feet from any water source be it a rare desert stream, a spring, or even the one mountain lake described in this book, Lobdell Lake in the Sweetwater Mountains. Remember: "Leave no trace."

Now that we've covered all of these potentially deadly hazards, you may ask, so why go? As Walt Wheelock once said:

*"Conducted safely, the pleasures of desert climbing, the freedoms from man's trials and tribulations, the warm dry air and peacefulness of a desert camp, when the rest of the world's mountains are snowed in, are the days that a guidebook can point toward, but are only found by climbing in these regions."*

# The Mono Peaks

This section describes the peaks in an area bounded by the Sweetwater Mountains north of Bridgeport, California; the Sierra Nevada to the west; the Nevada border to the east; and the Benton Range to the south. The mountains vary greatly in character from the lush aspen groves and pine forests of the lower ridges of the Sweetwaters to the arid, rugged volcanic Mono and Inyo Craters, which hold the distinction of being the youngest mountains in the United States.

The first Native American inhabitants of this area roamed over much of this area. They gathered the bountiful pinyon nuts for food and volcanic glass for arrowheads to trade with others. The last of these native people, the Mono Lake Paiute, used the alkali fly pupae, "Mono" in Paiute, as a dietary staple. Within their own language, they were known as the "fly-eaters." In 1833, Joseph Reddeford Walker led an expedition across the Sierra Nevada, passing through this area. In 1844, John C. Fremont passed by the Sweetwater Mountains on his route west before crossing the Sierra Nevada. His party left behind a brass cannon that was later recovered and now resides at the Nevada State Museum in Carson City. The California Geological Survey (also referred to as the Whitney Survey) explored the area during the early 1860's, and made an ascent of Crater Mountain in the Mono Craters volcanic chain. They were followed in the 1880's by the geologist Israel Russell who undertook a complete geologic reconnaissance of the Mono Basin.

Around 1860, the first miners started their diggings at nearby Bodie and Aurora. These mining districts became the most important centers of mining in the region. A stage route ran from Nevada, southward along the current route of Highways 182 (in California) and 338 (in Nevada). Sweetwater (near present day Sweetwater Summit) was an important stage stop and watering place beginning in the 1860's. Eventually a post office was built but finally closed in the 1920's. Wood and charcoal were obtained from the Mono peaks, especially at the Mono Mills (near Mono Craters) at the south end of Mono Lake.

In 1864, the Blind Spring Mining District was established south of Benton. Other mines included the Banner, Wildrose and Casa Diablo. However, by the 1880's most of the mining here had ceased. With the world wars, the demand for tungsten started a new boom. In 1953, the Black Rock Mine in the Benton Range was the second largest tungsten producer in California. 1932 saw the extension of the Los Angeles Aqueduct to Long Valley and the creation of Crowley Lake. This, with the new winter sport activity at Mammoth, brought many people into this region. Today tourists from around the world visit this desert and mountain paradise.

Supplies for hikes in the Mono Peaks area can be purchased at Bridgeport, Lee Vining, and Mammoth Lakes. These towns have grocery stores, sporting goods stores, lodging, restaurants, and gasoline stations. On the east side of the region, along Highway 6, the towns of Benton, Benton Hot Springs and Chalfant Valley have small stores that stock the very basic necessities. Gasoline is available at the one store in Chalfant Valley (Chalfant Mercantile). Information on the area can be obtained from the Mono Lake Visitor Center in Lee Vining, the Toiyabe National Forest office in Bridgeport, and the Inyo National Forest and Bureau of Land Management offices in Bishop, California.

## THE SWEETWATER MOUNTAINS

The Sweetwater Mountains, or "Wanappa" as they were called by the Northern Paiute who inhabited the area before Euro-American settlers arrived, are one of California's unknown mountain treasures. There are no wilderness areas as the range is crisscrossed with dirt roads, mostly the result of ranching and mining exploration. Don't be deceived by this though, a trip into this fine desert range will hook the prospective hiker into many return visits. The Sweetwater Mountains consist of an oval cluster of peaks at the northern end of Mono County, looming over the north end of the Bridgeport Valley and extending northeast into Nevada. This range contains some of the most forested, well-watered terrain described in this guidebook. Streams and aspen groves abound on the range's intermediate slopes, while the upper 1,000 feet of the Sweetwaters rises above the trees, presenting a stark but gentle alpine landscape.

The Sweetwaters are accessible by forest service roads on all sides, but only a few of these roads provide principal access routes to the higher peaks. The highest summit in the range, Mount Patterson (11,673 ft) provides an excellent mid to late summer hiking alternative to the nearby Sierra Nevada. In fall, the aspens change color, and the days can be warm, although an early snow is always a possibility. During early summer and late spring, several higher roads can turn into bogs, and although they may be passable, traveling on these roads during those times can result in road damage. If climbing in this range early in the season, the east side approaches are recommended. These mountains also provide outstanding midwinter ski ascents for those who are experienced in ski mountaineering.

The Sweetwater Mountains are transitional in character between the Sierra Nevada to the west, and the Basin and Range geologic provence (also known as the Great Basin) to the east. In fact, the west slopes of the range support a canopy of mountain hemlock and whitebark pine, with lodgepole pine and aspen common at lower elevations (similar to the Sierra Nevada). In contrast, the east slope of the range contains mostly limber pine, white fir and scattered aspen groves (more typical of the Basin and Range). When passing through the luxurious aspen groves that abound in the range, keep an eye out for elaborate carvings in the white bark made by the Basque shepherds that have traditionally herded their sheep through the area for the past century, and still do so today. These carvings, some more than a hundred years old, are quite detailed, and a pleasant day can be spent exploring the many aspen groves along the trails in search of them.

Camping in the Sweetwater Mountains is primitive (some of the nicest primitive sites in the region). As with all primitive campsites, there are no toilet facilities so human waste should be buried in a hole at least eight inches deep. Also, camp at least 100 feet from any streams, springs or Lobdell Lake. Plan to make your campsite bear-proof as the occasional visit by a black bear is possible. Supplies, gas, food and lodging are available in Bridgeport. For more information on the Sweetwater Mountains, contact the Bridgeport office of the Toiyabe National Forest.

### DESERT CREEK PEAK (8,969 FT; 2,734 M)

This is the northernmost peak described in this guide and its conical shape is quite distinctive when viewed from Smith Valley. Although not in Mono County (the peak is actually in Lyon County, Nevada), this is a significant Sweetwater peak, and is therefore included. Desert Creek Peak is the most "desert-like" of the Sweetwater Mountains, and a cool fall or spring day is recommended for an ascent of this peak.

*Maps:* Desert Creek Peak (CA-NV) 7.5-minute (1:24,000 scale) topographic map; Smith Valley 1:100,000 scale metric topographic map; Toiyabe National Forest-Bridgeport Ranger District map

*Best Time to Climb:* June through October

*Approach:* From the intersection of U.S. Highway 395 and Highway 182 in Bridgeport, drive north on Highway 182 (becomes Highway 338 in Nevada) over Sweetwater Summit, and down into Dalzell Canyon on the way to Wellington. Before dropping into Smith Valley, a dirt road (Forest Service Road #150) heads southwest up O'Banion Canyon. The road is approximately 1.2 miles north of the signed Sand Canyon Road. Take this dirt road to a spring at about 6,320 feet.

*Route:* From the road end, cross the creek and climb directly west to the summit, four miles round-trip, and 2,700 feet of elevation gain.

### EAST SISTER (10,402 FT; 3,171 M)

This Sweetwater peak is also in Nevada, and can be combined with the other "Sisters" for an extended outing. The "Sisters" are transitional between the more austere Desert Creek Peak and the more alpine Patterson-Wheeler sections of the range.

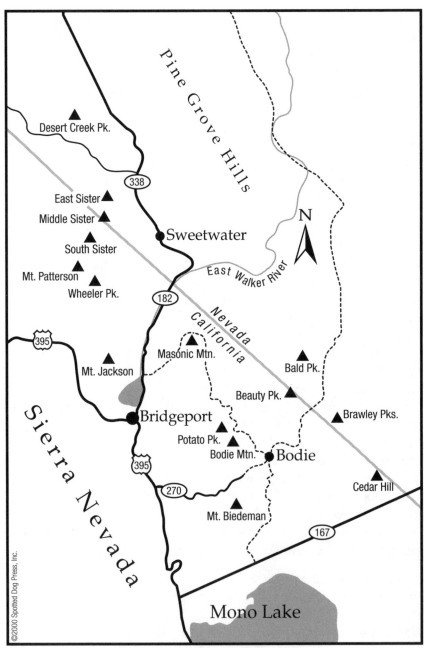

Sweetwater Mountains and the Bodie Hills

*Maps:* Desert Creek Peak (CA-NV) 7.5-minute (1:24,000 scale) topographic map; Smith Valley 1:100,000 scale metric topographic map; Toiyabe National Forest-Bridgeport Ranger District map

*Best Time to Climb:* July through October

*Approach:* From the intersection of U.S. Highway 395 and Highway 182 in Bridgeport, drive north on Highway 182 (becomes Highway 338 in Nevada) approximately 2.1 miles past Sweetwater Summit to the Risue Road (Forest Service Road #050). The road can also be accessed 2.5 miles past Sweetwater Summit. Turn west (left) on the Risue Road. After approximately 3.2 miles, turn southwest on the Rickey Mine Road. If passable, continue to an old horse corral at about 7,600 feet. If not, park here, approximately 6,400 feet.

*Route:* Follow a trail southwest to a broad saddle on East Sister's northwest ridge. Climb southeast to the main ridge, then northward to the summit. If walking from the corral, plan on a hike of seven miles round-trip with 2,800 feet of elevation gain. If walking from Risue Road, plan on a hike of ten miles round-trip with 4,000 feet of elevation gain.

### MIDDLE SISTER (10,859 FT; 3,310 M)

The northernmost peak in the California portion of the Sweetwater Mountains is of historical significance in that the Von Schmidt Line of 1873 crossed this peak west of the summit. The summit was for a time considered in Nevada!

*Maps:* Desert Creek Peak (CA-NV), and Mount Patterson (CA) 7.5-minute (1:24,000 scale) topographic maps; Smith Valley 1:100,000 scale metric topographic map; Toiyabe National Forest-Bridgeport Ranger District map

*Best Time to Climb:* July through October

*Approach:* Same as for East Sister

*Route:* Continue up the trail to the saddle then south up the peak's north ridge to the summit. Add another 900 feet of elevation gain and 1.2 miles round-trip when combined with East Sister.

### SOUTH SISTER (11,339 FT; 3,457 M)

*Maps:* Mount Patterson (CA) 7.5-minute (1:24,000 scale) topographic map; Bridgeport 1:100,000 scale metric topographic map; Toiyabe National Forest-Bridgeport Ranger District map

*Best Time to Climb:* July through October

*Approach:* From the intersection of U.S. Highway 395 and Highway 182 in Bridgeport, drive north on Highway 182 (becomes Highway 338 in Nevada) approximately 0.5 miles south of Sweetwater Summit. Turn southwest onto Forest Service Road #069, and continue up Sweetwater Canyon to Nugent Cabin (8,200 ft) or as high is practicable with your particular vehicle. With a camp at Nugent Cabin, a weekend of climbing all of the Sweetwater summits described is possible.

*Route:* From Nugent Cabin, head north up South Sister's somewhat brushy and steep south slopes. Plan on six miles round-trip with 3,300 feet of elevation gain.

*Alternate Route:* Approach the route as for Middle Sister, and climb Middle Sister. Continue south from Middle Sister along the ridge to the peak. Keep in mind that there is approximately 600 feet of elevation gain to surmount on the way back over Middle Sister. Side-hilling on the loose scree covering these peaks is not recommended. Add another four miles round-trip with 2,100 feet of elevation gain to the Middle Sister description for this ascent . . . a very long day.

### MOUNT PATTERSON (11,673 FT; 3,559 M)

The colorful highpoint of the Sweetwater Mountains, this peak is named for James H. Patterson, an early settler at Big Meadows who possibly moved to the area sometime before 1867. The summit area contains evidence of previous mining exploration. If climbing this peak in mid to late summer, or in the fall, take Route 1 for purely esthetic reasons. If climbing earlier in the season, the alternative route is recommended. Each time I have climbed this peak, the blue sky and billowing cumulus, contrasting with the calico slopes of orange, ochre, white and gray have provided outstanding photographic opportunities.

*Maps:* Mount Patterson (CA) 7.5-minute (1:24,000 scale) topographic map; Bridgeport 1:100,000 scale metric topographic map; Toiyabe National Forest-Bridgeport Ranger District map

*Best Time to Climb:* July through October

*Approach:* From the intersection of U.S. Highway 395 and Highway 182 in Bridgeport, drive about 15.5 miles north from Bridgeport on Highway 395, and turn north (right) onto the Burcham Flat Road (well-graded dirt, Forest Service Road #031). The primary destination at this point is Lobdell Lake and the route is signed. The road first doubles back about a half mile

The author en route to Mt. Patterson. Photo: Wynne Benti

then heads north 4.3 miles to a good dirt road. The route meanders through groves of aspen, whose trunks bear the hand-carvings of Basque shepherds who have herded their sheep along the same trail for more than a century. Turn east (right) onto Forest Service Road #067 and follow it to Lobdell Lake (9,100 ft). If it is early in the season, this may be as far as driving is practical. If the roads are dry enough, head around the north end of the lake, and continue northeast on Forest Service Road #115, then east for little more than two miles on a steep, poor, often boggy road. Approximately 2.5 miles up this road from Lobdell Lake, you will reach the end of the driveable road. Beautiful campsites are abundant both below and above Lobdell Lake.

*Route:* From the end of the road, hike up the old, eroded jeep road, that eventually becomes a trail passing the diggings of the Montague Mine, toward the summit. If climbing Patterson alone, one will want to linger on this summit, and enjoy the fine views of the Sierra Nevada and surrounding desert ranges. Anticipate five miles round-trip with 1,700 feet of elevation gain.

*Alternate Approach and Route:* Follow the approach described for the Nugent Cabin approach to South Sister. Hike up Sweetwater Canyon, gaining Mount Patterson's northeast ridge when practicable. Continue southwest to the summit amid colorful volcanic rock. Plan on nine miles round-trip with 2,500 feet of elevation gain.

### WHEELER PEAK (11,664 FT; 3,556 M)

The second highest peak in the range, and Mount Patterson's neighbor, this peak is one of the few features in the west named "Wheeler" that probably isn't named for Lieutenant George Wheeler, head of the famed Wheeler Survey. The peak is thought to have been named in honor of a little-known army officer of the area. The Frederick Mine reached via Alternative Route 1, is probably named for Francis Frederick, a prominent geologist in the region during the 1920's and 1930's. Frederick was part of the Bodie Volunteer Fire Department that tried to put out the great Bodie fire of 1932.
*Maps:* Mount Patterson (CA) 7.5-minute (1:24,000 scale) topographic map; Bridgeport 1:100,000 scale metric topographic map; Toiyabe National Forest-Bridgeport Ranger District map
*Best Time to Climb:* July through October
*Approach:* Same as for Mount Patterson
*Route:* The summit is a 1.5 to 2-mile up and down ramble south of Mount Patterson along the crest of the range, with about 1,200 feet of elevation gain round-trip from Mount Patterson.
*Alternate Approach and Route 1:* From Highway 338 (about one mile north of the Nevada state line), a four-wheel drive route (Forest Service Road #198) heads up the east ridge of Wheeler Peak to the Frederick Mine. The historic site of Star City is passed en route. The road follows the route of a historic stage route between Sweetwater Creek and Star City. Drive up this jeep road along Green Creek as far as practicable. Hike up to the Frederick Mine, then continue up the east slopes of the peak. With a sturdy four-wheel drive vehicle, this can be the shortest ascent route of the peak.
*Alternate Approach and Route 2:* From Bridgeport, continue 10.5 miles north on Highway 395 to the Swager Creek Road-Forest Service Road #029 (approximately two miles east of Devil's Gate). Drive up Swager Creek Road to the East Fork and park (8,200 ft). Hike up the east fork and Wheeler's southwest slopes to the summit, eight miles round-trip with 2,400 feet of elevation gain.

## MOUNT JACKSON (9,381 FT; 2,859 M)

This is a subsidiary peak on the south slope of the range overlooking Bridgeport Reservoir.

*Maps:* Mount Jackson (CA) 7.5-minute (1:24,000 scale) topographic map; Bridgeport 1:100,000 scale metric topographic map; Toiyabe National Forest-Bridgeport Ranger District map

*Best Time to Climb:* Late May through October

*Approach:* From the junction of Highways 395 and 182, drive 5.4 miles north on Highway 395 to Swager Creek Campground on the right at about 6,725 feet. Day use is permitted here.

*Route:* From the campground, climb the prominent gully east then north, reaching the ridge crest. Head northeast contouring around the north side of Peak 7,842 ft, through woods, dropping to a saddle. Continue northeast up the brushy ridge to the summit. Although not a major peak in the Sweetwater Mountains, the view directly down onto Bridgeport Reservoir with the Sierra Nevada's Sawtooth Ridge as a backdrop makes the effort worthwhile. Plan on eight miles round-trip with 3,150 feet of elevation gain.

# THE BODIE HILLS (A.K.A. BODIE MOUNTAINS)

The Bodie Hills are the high, rolling volcanic hills along the eastern end of Bridgeport Valley, and north of Mono Lake. This terrain consists of dry, sage-covered hills with isolated aspen groves near springs and streams. A few scattered groves of Jeffrey pine are found but single-leaf pinyon-western juniper-Utah juniper woodlands are more common. Limber pines are also found on some of the higher peaks, particularly the Brawley Peaks. Archeological sites abound in this range. Any trip to the peaks in the Bodie Hills should also incorporate a visit to Bodie State Historical Park, one of the best preserved ghost towns left in California, if not the entire country. The history of mining in the Bodie area is quite interesting, and the visitor will want to pick up at least one of the many historical books on the district at the state park. Gold was discovered in the Bodie Hills as early as 1859. However, the real rush to Bodie didn't occur for more than a decade. From 1872 to 1888, the town of Bodie was in its heyday. The great Bodie fire that decimated a large percentage of the town occurred in 1932, but by then the town was but a ghost. Mining activity in varying amounts (mostly very minor) occurred up until 1942.

The range and its trademark ghost town were named in honor of William S. Bodey, a prospector who died in the area during an 1860 snow storm. The misspelling of "Bodey" stuck, and the range has been called "Bodie" ever since. The Bodie Hills are crossed by several well-graded dirt roads, and the principal road to Bodie, State Highway 270, is paved most of the way to the state historic park. The highest summit in the range, Potato Peak (10,236 ft) provides an excellent early summer ascent from Bodie, when other nearby ranges are still snow-covered. The Bodie Hills also provide excellent cross-country skiing to Bodie and surrounding peaks during the winter.

This region is managed by both the Bureau of Land Management and the U.S. Forest Service. Only a small fraction of the range is administered by the Bodie State Historic Park or is privately owned. The state park is open year round, but is usually only accessible by car from May to October. The remaining portion of the year, the park is only accessible to cross-country skiers. In fact, nearly all the back roads of the Bodie Hills are inaccessible during the winter. There is no camping in the state park, but primitive campsites abound elsewhere. The usual restrictions regarding camping near streams apply here. For more information on the Bodie Hills, contact the Bodie State Historic Park, the Bridgeport Office of the Toiyabe National Forest, or the Bureau of Land Management office in Bishop.

### MASONIC MOUNTAIN (9,217 FT; 2,809 M)

This small peak was named for the nearby nineteenth-century mining camp founded by a group of prospectors who were masons from the nearby mining camp of Aurora. Gold was discovered near the town of Masonic during the 1860's. The boom of Masonic was from about 1902 to 1910, and some of the old cabins are still standing in a pleasant canyon at the base of the mountain. Sage-covered Masonic Mountain is the home of an antenna installation on its east summit (the highpoint).

*Maps:* Bridgeport (CA) 7.5-minute (1:24,000 scale) topographic map; Bridgeport 1:100,000 scale metric topographic map; Toiyabe National Forest-Bridgeport Ranger District map; Automobile Club of Southern California (AAA) Eastern Sierra map

*Best Time to Climb:* Late May through October.

*Approach:* From Bridgeport, take Highway 182 north 3.7 miles to the

View of the Sierra Nevada from Bodie Mountain.  Photo: Wynne Benti

Masonic Road-Forest Service Road #046 (dirt).  This road is also 1.2 miles south of the Bridgeport Reservoir dam.  Follow the road east approximately 6.3 miles to Lakeview Spring (about 8,400 ft).

*Route:* From Lakeview Spring, the peak is approximately 1.5 to two miles southeast with about 800 feet of elevation gain.  For those wanting an even easier way up this peak, a road leads to the summit area from the south.  The west summit contains better views, so after visiting the true summit, have your lunch on the west summit, and take in the beautiful views of Bridgeport Valley, and the glistening snowfields of the Sawtooth Ridge of the Sierra Nevada.

### POTATO PEAK (10,236 FT; 3,120 M), BODIE MOUNTAIN (10,195 FT; 3,107 M)

These peaks, the highpoints of the range, provide spectacular views across Bridgeport Valley, to the Sawtooth Ridge of the Sierra Nevada.  Some maps show Bodie Mountain as higher than Potato Peak.  However, this is an obvious error once the hiker reaches the summit of either of these peaks.  An early U.S. Geological Survey map in a report by Israel Russell, identified Bodie Peak as Mount Biedeman (and spelling it "Biderman").  That name, along with a change in its spelling, has been moved to a summit further south. When we hiked these peaks, in one meadow we observed a coyote, deer, and several pronghorn antelope, all watching us and each other. *Maps:* Bodie (CA) 7.5-minute (1:24,000 scale) topographic map; Bridgeport 1:100,000 scale metric topographic map; Toiyabe National Forest -Bridgeport Ranger District map; Automobile Club of Southern California (AAA) Eastern Sierra map

*Best Time to Climb:* Late May through October

*Approach:* These peaks can be reached from the parking area at Bodie State Historic Park or from the many access roads that wind up along Rough Creek. The road to the peaks from Bodie is sometimes open making the hike even easier.

*Route:* These gentle sloped peaks can be easily ascended from any side. From the parking lot at Bodie State Historic Park, the hike to Bodie Mountain is approximately eight miles round-trip with 1,900 feet of elevation gain. Add another two miles and 700 feet of elevation gain round-trip to include Potato Peak.

### MOUNT BIEDEMAN (8,981 FT; 2,737 M)

This peak is an easy ascent, and provides an outstanding viewpoint of Mono Lake. When the author hiked up this peak during the spring, the brush was full of white, angular, silky webs. These webs are the home of the tent caterpillar, and a look inside one will reveal scores of squirmy little beings. These caterpillars will eventually metamorphose into plain-looking brown moths. Keep an eye out for these interesting features. Mount Biedeman is named in honor of John W. Biedeman, a principal owner of the Homestake Mining Company that built a mill in the Bodie Mining District during the 1860's.

*Maps:* Bodie (CA) 7.5-minute (1:24,000 scale) topographic map; Bridgeport 1:100,000 scale metric topographic map; Toiyabe National Forest-Bridgeport Ranger District map

*Best Time to Climb:* May through October

*Approach:* From Highway 395, follow the Bodie Road (Highway 270) approximately 7.3 miles east to a broad, sage-covered highland. The paved road takes a rather sharp turn to the north. A dirt road heads south from this turn to a saddle on Mount Biedeman's west flank. Mount Biedeman's three summit cairns are visible from here. One can reach the saddle in a vehicle with good clearance.

View of Mono Lake from Mt. Biedeman.  Photo: Andy Zdon

*Route:* The peak is a short but steep scramble to the east through high rabbitbrush and sage. Plan on about one mile round-trip with a few hundred feet of elevation gain from the saddle.

### BEAUTY PEAK (9,018 FT; 2,749 M), BALD PEAK (8,821 FT; 2,689 M)

These volcanic cones reside atop a basalt plateau that issued forth from these mountains, and both summits are of easy ascent amid stark desert surroundings.  The California-Nevada state line passes over the summit of Beauty Peak.

*Maps:* Aurora (NV-CA), and Kirkwood Spring (CA-NV) 7.5-minute (1:24,000 scale) topographic maps; Excelsior Mountains 1:100,000 scale metric topographic map; Toiyabe National Forest-Bridgeport Ranger District map

*Best Time to Climb:* May through October

*Approach and Route:* From Bodie State Historic Park, drive 5.5 miles north along Bodie Creek to a dirt road that heads west.  Follow this dirt road (four-wheel drive) as it climbs 1.5 miles up a rocky route to the top of the plateau, where the route to each summit becomes obvious. Though the roads fan out across the plateau and become more rough, park here as a walk across the plateau is wonderful.  Even with a two-wheel drive vehicle and parking along Bodie Creek, both peaks can be climbed in one day.

## Brawley Peaks (9,545 ft; 2,909 m)

The California-Nevada state line passes through Brawley Peaks which were named in honor of James Brawley, an 1860's-era prospector who lived in the area. James Brawley has also been known as James Braley, so the correct name for these peaks may be Braley Peaks. Braley is the name given to them by the California Geological Survey under Josiah Dwight Whitney. Later, Israel Russell used the name Braley in his report on the Mono Basin. For those wishing to "bag" Beauty Peak and Bald Peak, two rounded summits to the north, this roadhead provides access.

*Maps:* Aurora (NV-CA), and Kirkwood Spring (CA-NV) 7.5-minute (1:24,000 scale) topographic maps; Excelsior Mountains 1:100,000 scale metric topographic map; Toiyabe National Forest-Bridgeport Ranger District map

*Best Time to Climb:* May through October

*Approach:* From Bodie State Historic Park, drive 6.1 miles north along Bodie Creek to a pullout on the right at about 7,700 feet. A faint track is visible heading up a hill to the east.

*Route:* Hop across Bodie Creek and follow the faint road as it climbs and winds into a drainage with a small grove of aspens. The shade of the aspens can provide some welcome relief on a hot day. Continue along the road as it heads up into a valley, dotted by aspen groves along its perimeter. Don't be surprised to see cows in this area. Their droppings are everywhere! The peak is straight ahead. A small valley can either be descended and reascended or contoured around to the east. Anticipate eight miles round-trip with 2,000 feet of elevation gain.

*Alternate Routes:* From the road end described above, the peak is visible to the northeast. Head directly toward it. More brush will be encountered on this route. Another alternate is to continue on the Bodie Creek Road to the Nevada-California border. The peak lies about 2.5 miles to the southeast. From near the ghost town (site) of Aurora, mining roads work their way up to the saddle north of Brawley Peaks. The summit is an easy ascent from there.

## Cedar Hill (8,437 ft; 2,572 m)

*Maps:* Kirkwood Spring, and Cedar Hill (CA-NV) 7.5-minute (1:24,000 scale) topographic maps; Excelsior Mountains 1:100,000 scale metric topographic map; Toiyabe National Forest-Bridgeport Ranger District map

*Best Time to Climb:* May through October

*Approach:* From Lee Vining, drive 7.3 miles north on Highway 395 to Pole Line Road (Highway 167). Drive east to a point approximately 0.2 miles east of the Nevada State Line. Take a dirt track north toward Cedar Hill, parking where appropriate for your vehicle (about 7,100 ft). Various other dirt roads west of the state line head off toward the peak and make for reasonable road-ends. One route for those whose vehicles prohibit much in the way of dirt road driving is to drive 20.4 miles east of Highway 395 on Highway 167 to a dirt track that heads north just before reaching the Toiyabe National Forest boundary. One can park a short distance up this road.

*Route:* From either of the parking areas described above, hike a little over a mile across the flats to the base of the peak, then scramble through pinyon and juniper to the summit. The pinyon and juniper woodlands will provide welcome shade on a warm day. For planning purposes, anticipate five miles round-trip with 1,400 feet of elevation gain.

## MONO CRATERS, BENTON RANGE & ENVIRONS

Many outstanding features of these peaks are quite recent in origin. The Mono Craters, included within the Mono Basin National Forest Scenic Area, are a string of some twenty volcanic domes, and are clearly visible from U.S. Highway 395. Fragments of pumice, obsidian, and lapilli cover much of the surrounding country. The centers of many of these cones have been invaded by plugs of viscous (obsidian) lava. Such plugs are quite distinct in Crater Mountain, where one such plug forms the highpoint of the peak. On the other hand, wind-drifted pumice covers Peak 9,138 ft (South Crater). The Mono Craters formed along a major north-south geologic structure. Crater Mountain and South Crater are probably 6,000 to 6,500 years old. However, diminutive Panum Crater may be as young as a mere 600 to 700 years.

The remaining volcanic peaks of the Benton Range such as Glass Mountain, are similarly composed of tuff, pumice and obsidian. That these mountains are of quite recent origin is shown by their pumice fields covering glacial moraines. There are numerous archaeological sites in this area as this was an important source area for fine quality obsidian for the earliest human inhabitants. The eastern portions of the Benton Range are characterized by classic Basin and Range style north-south trending ridges consisting of both granitic and volcanic rocks. The Benton Range, like the

The Mono Craters from Highway 120. Crater Peak (left) and South Crater (right). Photo: Andy Zdon

Sweetwater Mountains, is not "desert-like" in that most of the peaks are covered by Jeffrey pine, pinyon and junipers. Glass Mountain, the commanding summit of the range, is the only peak that rises above the tree line.

Within the Mono Craters-Benton Range area, primitive camping is the order of the day, and fine campsites are available most everywhere in the area. A free fire permit is required for all fires including stoves and charcoal grills. Fire restrictions may be in effect, and a phone call ahead of time to the Inyo National Forest and Bureau of Land Management offices in Bishop is recommended. Bring your own water, and since there are no toilets (except at Sawmill Meadow), plan on burying waste in a hole at least eight inches deep.

### PANUM CRATER (7,032 FT; 2,144 M)

The northernmost of the Mono Craters, this little nubbin overlooks Mono Lake and is a classic cone with a resurgent dome. Panum Crater is one of the easiest to climb in this guide, but is also one of the most interesting, geologically. It also provides a fine view of Mono Lake for those without the time to climb Crater Mountain.

*Maps:* Lee Vining (CA) 7.5-minute (1:24,000 scale) topographic map; Yosemite Valley 1:100,000 scale metric topographic map; Inyo National Forest Map; Automobile Club of Southern California (AAA) Eastern Sierra map

*Best Time to Climb:* All year; there may be snow during winter

*Approach:* From Highway 395, take Highway 120 approximately three miles east to a signed (Panum Crater) washboard dirt road that heads north toward the crater. Take this road about one mile to a parking area and interpretive sign at the base of the crater (6,850 ft).

*Route:* Follow the use-trail to the crest of the pumice-covered rim, then scramble over unstable blocky talus to the highpoint on the north side of the rim. Plan on one mile round-trip with 250 feet of elevation gain. Be careful crossing the loose blocks near the summit.

### CRATER MOUNTAIN (9,172 FT; 2,796 M)

The highest of the Mono Craters is south of Highway 120. All approach roads lead over pumice flats, and care must be taken in crossing these. This peak consists of a broken volcanic rim with several knobs. The highpoint is on the westerly edge and must be climbed over unstable volcanic talus blocks. The views of the Mono Basin and Sierra Nevada are worth the effort (although you might want to curse the author's name during the slog up the peak).

*Maps:* Lee Vining, Mono Mills, June Lake, and Crestview (CA) 7.5-minute (1:24,000 scale) topographic maps; Benton Range and Yosemite Valley 1:100,000 scale metric topographic maps; Inyo National Forest Map; Automobile Club of Southern California (AAA) Eastern Sierra map

*Best Time to Climb:* May through October

*Approach:* From U.S. 395, drive approximately eight miles east on Highway 120, to a dirt road (about one mile west of Mono Mills) leading south. Forest Service Roads 1S94 and 1N24 are both satisfactory. Follow this dirt road approximately three miles. A former jeep trail leads west to a shallow draw between Crater Mountain and South Crater (8,000+ ft).

*Route:* Climb up the draw to near the saddle, then head right (north) toward the summit basin. The highpoint lies across the crater and is marked with a pole (two miles one way with about 1,200 feet of elevation gain).

*Alternate Approach and Route:* A mining road (Road 1N11) leads south along the west base of the crater slopes and the peak may be climbed by keeping to the north of the mountain to a high saddle (starting point about 7,000 feet, about six miles round-trip with 2,200 feet of elevation gain).

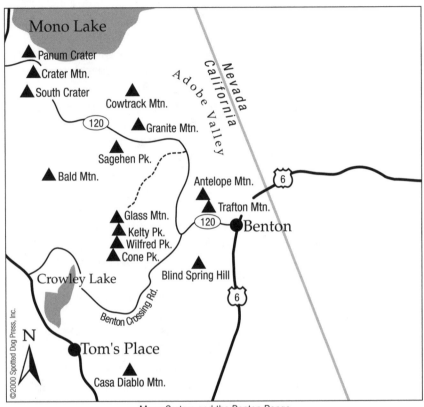

Mono Craters and the Benton Range

### "SOUTH CRATER" (9,138 FT; 2,785 M)

The second highest crater lies directly to the south of Crater Mountain. When Walt Wheelock climbed this peak in 1959, he found no signs of a previous ascent. The peak is unnamed on the topographic map.

*Maps:* Lee Vining, Mono Mills, June Lake, and Crestview (CA) 7.5-minute (1:24,000 scale) topographic maps; Benton Range and Yosemite Valley 1:100,000 scale metric topographic maps; Inyo National Forest Map; Automobile Club of Southern California (AAA) Eastern Sierra map

*Best Time to Climb:* May through October

*Route:* From the saddle between Crater Mountain and South Crater, follow a pumice scree slope to the pumice-filled crater. The highpoint is to the southwest. Add another mile and 500 feet of elevation gain round-trip when combined with the principal route for Crater Mountain.

### COWTRACK MOUNTAIN (8,874 FT; 2,705 M)

The summit of Cowtrack Mountain is actually the highpoint of a long ridge extending north from near Sagehen Summit on Highway 120. The high-point of Cowtrack Mountain, also known as Horse Point, provides a wonderful view of Mono Lake.

*Maps:* Cowtrack Mountain (CA) 7.5-minute (1:24,000 scale) topographic map; Benton Range 1:100,000 scale metric topographic map; Inyo National Forest Map

*Best Time to Visit:* May through October

*Approach:* From Highway 6 in Benton, drive about 7 miles west on Highway 120 to the Benton Crossing Road. Continue west on Highway 120 another 19.7 miles to dirt Road 1N06 on the north side of the road. The turnoff is in the middle of a hairpin curve so the road is easy to miss. Road 1N06 is sandy in places, so four-wheel drive is recommended. From Highway 120, follow 1N06, staying right at 0.7 miles. At 3.2 miles from the highway, a water tank is reached, and the road curves northwest up a shallow draw. At 4.4 miles from the highway stay, right. A fabulous view opens up of the Sierra Crest, Bodie Hills and the distant Sweetwater Mountains. During early summer, the wildflowers are spectacular. At 5.5 miles from the highway continue straight. The brush growing in the middle of the two-track dirt road will provide an undercarriage cleaning for your car. At 6.3 miles from the highway, a rough spot in the road makes for a good parking spot.

*Route:* The summit is a short walk to the northeast.

### GRANITE MOUNTAIN (8,921 FT; 2,720 M)

This isolated granitic peak, south and east of Mono Lake, provides fine views of the Sierra Nevada, Benton Range and Adobe Valley from the surprisingly small summit. For those rock climbers that might be interested, the Granite Basin area provides excellent opportunities for uncrowded rock climbing.

*Maps:* Cowtrack Mountain (CA) 7.5-minute (1:24,000 scale) topographic map; Benton Range 1:100,000 scale metric topographic map; Inyo National Forest Map

*Best Time to Climb:* May through October

*Approach:* From Highway 395, take Highway 120 east 22.4 miles. If traveling west on Highway 120, this road is 22.1 miles west of Highway 6. Granite Mountain looms to the north. Take an obvious dirt road that heads

Granite Mountain from alternate route.  Photo: Andy Zdon

north toward the saddle west of the peak, continuing as far as practicable with your vehicle.

*Route:* From the road end, gain the saddle to the north, contour a short distance northward along the west slope of the peak, then steeply up a shallow draw between the two prominent summit outcrops. The summit rocks are an easy scramble. Plan on four miles round-trip with 1,000 feet of elevation gain depending on your starting point.

*Alternate Approach and Route:*  This alternate route makes for a very pleasant day hike and is well worth the effort. From Highway 120, take either of the dirt roads that head northward across Granite Basin. Both roads lead to a canyon on the north side of the basin.  Continue up the road to the 7,680-foot contour, the road forks, park here (in the draw heading off to the northeast). Follow the faint path generally eastward through open, brushy terrain about one to 1.5 miles as it disappears and reappears, to the mine shown on the map.  Gain the northwest ridge of Granite Mountain and follow the ridge amid pinyons to the summit area. Early on, staying a little left of the crest of the ridge makes for less brushy walking.  Upon reaching the main summit mass, head toward the west slope of the peak, gaining the shallow draw described for Route 1. Anticipate seven miles round-trip with 1,600 feet of elevation gain.

## SAGEHEN PEAK (9,191 FT; 2,802 M)

This small peak makes for a fine outing when combined with Cowtrack Mountain, especially for the rewards of a pleasant, easy day. The assortment of vegetation zones one encounters on the approach to the summit, makes for varied and inspiring views.

*Maps:* Dexter Canyon (CA) 7.5-minute (1:24,000 scale) topographic map; Benton Range 1:100,000 scale metric topographic map; Inyo National Forest Map

*Best Time to Climb:* May through October

*Approach:* From Benton on Highway 6, drive seven miles west on Highway 120 to the Benton Crossing Road, then another 21.3 miles west on Highway 120 to the turnoff for Forest Road 1N02 (graded dirt) on the south side of the road. The turnoff is near the crest of Sagehen Summit. Follow 1N02 through an open ponderosa pine forest, staying left at 1.4 miles from the highway to another fork at Sagehen Meadows, two miles from the highway. Stay left at the fork, and continue up through aspens to a divide 3.7 miles from the highway. Continue another 0.1 miles and turn sharp left (east) through aspens, and up the dirt track 0.4 miles to a parking spot. Those without four-wheel drive will want to park at the aforementioned divide.

*Route:* The summit is a rock outcrop near the parking area. Those who want a little more adventure will want to climb the subsidiary, but more interesting, summit to the east. To reach it, head east to the saddle between the peaks. The summit block of the subsidiary peak can be climbed by any number of short Class 2 or 3 routes.

## BALD MOUNTAIN (9,045 FT; 2,758 M)

This high, rounded mountain is the highest point between U.S. Highway 395 and Glass Mountain. Bald Mountain provides an excellent view of this backcountry. During the winter, the peak is a popular ski tour.

*Maps:* Crestview (CA) 7.5-minute (1:24,000 scale) topographic map; Benton Range 1:100,000 scale metric topographic map; Inyo National Forest Map; Automobile Club of Southern California (AAA) Eastern Sierra map

*Best Time to Visit:* May through October

*Approach:* From Highway 395, turn east on Logging Camp Road (Forest Service Road 1S05). This road is just north of Deadman's Summit. Follow signs 12 miles to Shaft No. 1. This junction is directly above the Mono Craters Tunnel that transfers water from the Mono Basin to the Owens

River Basin. From here, turn right staying on Road 1S05. The road is signed to Bald Mountain Lookout, an additional seven miles, and is well-graded (beware of pumice). You will reach a locked gate and will likely need to walk the road the final half mile to the summit lookout.

*Alternate:* This area of the Benton Range is crisscrossed with numerous scenic and signed dirt roads. Any one of a number of access possibilities exist for this peak, and the reader may refer to the Inyo National Forest map for the route of their preference.

### GLASS MOUNTAIN (11,140+ FT; 3,396+ M)

This fine peak dominates the entire Upper Owens River Basin. If it were not for the much higher Sierra Nevada rising a few miles west of here, this would be an outstanding peak. It is a true volcanic peak, with obsidian

outcroppings and rhyolite slopes. Several streams flow from it and provide good campsites amid lodgepole pines and aspen groves. Glass Mountain is frequently considered the highpoint of the Benton Range. However, its location makes it distinct from the narrow, non-volcanic portion of the Benton Range to the east across Adobe Valley. Summit views include the Sierra Nevada from the Palisades northward to Mount Conness, Mono Lake, the White Mountains and the Sweetwaters. Keep and eye out for deer as they are plentiful in the area.

*Maps:* Glass Mountain (CA) 7.5-minute (1:24,000 scale) topographic map; Benton Range 1:100,000 scale metric topographic map; Inyo National Forest Map

*Best Time to Climb:* June through October

*Approach:* From Highway 6 in Benton, California, take Highway 120 approximately 16.8 miles west to Adobe Meadows, and a well-graded dirt road (McGee Creek Road) heading southwest toward lodgepole pine and aspen-ringed Sawmill Meadow. Follow the road to Sawmill Meadow (9,200 ft). This approach takes you on better quality roads than the signed Black

Above: View west from Glass Mountain looking across the Long Valley Caldera to the Sierra Nevada. Photo: Andy Zdon

Canyon/Sawmill Meadow Road.

*Route:* From Sawmill Meadow, the peak is a short, but steep climb on loose scree to the west. The pines are left behind about half way up, and the views become increasing expansive as the summit is reached. A few bristlecone and limber pines are found on the highest slopes of the peak. The true highpoint is the rocky ridge to the south. The north summit is also worthwhile to visit for its superior views to the north. Anticipate three miles round-trip with 2,000 feet of elevation gain.

### "Cone Peak" (10,152 ft; 3,905 m), "Wilfred Peak" (10,030 ft; 3,057 m), "Kelty Peak" (10,617 ft; 3,236 m)

These frequently overlooked but high peaks (unnamed on the topographic maps) along the ridge extending south from Glass Mountain, provide enjoyable scrambles amid pines and open pumice slopes. These peaks are named on Roy Bailey's geologic map of the Long Valley Caldera produced by the U.S. Geological Survey. This map is usually available from the Mono Lake Visitor Center in Lee Vining, and the Booky Joint in Mammoth Lakes. The views of Long Valley and the Sierra Nevada are worth the price of the map and a whole lot more!

*Maps:* Banner Ridge, Watterson Canyon, and Glass Mountain (CA) 7.5-

minute (1:24,000 scale) topographic maps; Benton Range 1:100,000 scale metric topographic map; Inyo National Forest Map

*Best Time to Climb:* June through October

*Approach:* Access to these peaks is easiest from the Benton Crossing Road that runs from Highway 395 in the Crowley Lake area to Highway 120 just west of Benton Hot Springs. From the Highway 120-Benton Crossing Road junction (seven miles west of Highway 6 on Highway 120), drive approximately 13 miles south on Benton Crossing Road until reaching a power line and adjacent dirt road. Follow the power line road west across the flat and up into a narrow, pinyon-covered canyon. As the road begins to climb out of the canyon (after 2.8 miles) look for a dirt track heading north. This track is a bit rocky at first, but improves in quality farther up, only to become rocky again as it climbs Cone Peak. Four-wheel drive is recommended. Cone Peak comes into view and it is a "follow-your-nose" drive via a wet meadow called "Clover Patch" and up the southeast ridge of the peak. During the spring, large snow drifts frequently block this road. When dry, the road can be followed to within a few hundred feet of Cone Peak's summit. The road to the Clover Patch is also accessible via the Watterson Troughs Road heading east from the Benton Crossing Road east of Crowley Lake.

*Route:* From the road end, Cone Peak is an easy scramble to the west. To climb Wilfred Peak, follow the road to the north a short distance past Cone Peak, to where the slope drops off to the north and park. Wilfred and its neighbor Kelty Peak can be seen to the west and northwest, respectively. From the road, head northwest, dropping down approximately 150 feet to a saddle. From the saddle, hike west through open forest along the ridge toward Wilfred Peak. The hiking is quite enjoyable and the scenery superb. To reach Kelty, drop down the north ridge of Wilfred, then up the steep, loose slopes of Kelty's south ridge. When returning, one can sidehill below Wilfred back to the car, avoiding additional elevation gain. For Wilfred and Kelty anticipate approximately eight miles of off-trail hiking with 2,000 feet of elevation gain round-trip depending on the route back. When planning your time anticipate taking a little longer than you would expect as the loose pumice makes for some tiring walking, particularly up Kelty. For Wilfred alone, plan on a short two miles round-trip with a maximum elevation gain of 1,000 feet.

The author along the Wilfred Peak crest. Photo: Wynne Benti

## ANTELOPE MOUNTAIN (7,617 FT; 2,322 M)

On the east side of Adobe Valley is a spur of the Benton Range, on which Antelope Mountain is a principal summit. Several roads leading to the mountain, and shown on the map are impassable with a passenger car.

*Maps:* Benton Hot Springs, and River Spring (CA) 7.5-minute (1:24,000 scale) topographic maps; Benton Range 1:100,000 scale metric topographic map; Inyo National Forest Map

*Best Time to Climb:* April through November

*Approach:* Some 37 miles east of U.S. 395 on Highway 120, is a small brackish sink called Black Lake. Follow the road along the side of this toward Antelope Lake (6,500+ ft).

*Route:* An easy ridge leads under a power line and then directly to the summit (a little more than two miles round-trip with 1,100 feet of elevation gain).

*Alternate Approach and Route:* From Benton Valley, a jeep trail leads to the summit. To gain this road, from Benton, California drive two miles west on Highway 120 to the Foothill Road and turn north. Continue another two miles to a dirt road that heads northwest toward Antelope Mountain. Turn onto this dirt road, and drive 2.3 miles to a pumice prospect at about 5,830 feet. The road becomes washed out beyond here. From the parking area, either head northwest up the easy slopes to regain the old road, or follow the old road directly to the summit of the peak. Anticipate about five to seven miles round-trip (depending on the route) and 1,800 feet of elevation gain.

### TRAFTON MOUNTAIN (7,825 FT; 2,386 M)

*Maps:* Benton Hot Springs (CA) 7.5-minute (1:24,000 scale) topographic map; Benton Range 1:100,000 scale metric topographic map; Inyo National Forest Map

*Best Time to Climb:* April through November

*Approach:* From Benton, California, drive two miles west on Highway 120

View across Adobe Valley from Antelope Mountain.
Photo: Andy Zdon

to the Foothill Road heading north. Immediately after turning onto the Foothill Road, turn west on a dirt road heading toward the mountains. Follow this dirt road 2.3 miles to a power line road and turn north. Continue on the power line road 1.4 miles to a saddle at about 6,850 feet and park. *Route:* From the saddle, head generally west over rolling terrain dotted with pinyon pine and passing through granitic outcrops to a broad saddle on the crest of the main ridge. Follow the ridge north, amid pinyon and varied volcanic rock outcrops, and with ever-increasing views of the White Mountains, and down toward Black Lake to the southwest. A survey point is eventually reached on a false summit. The true summit is a short distance north. The open flat slabs of the summit make for a fine place to while away the hours and have lunch. Anticipate five miles round-trip with 1,000 feet of elevation gain.

*Alternate Approach and Route:* Same as for alternate approach route for Antelope Mountain. From the pumice quarry, follow the washed out jeep track approximately 0.7 miles southeast to the 6,400-foot contour, then continue west to the north ridge of the peak, and south to the summit, or continue directly southwest to the summit.

## BLIND SPRING HILL (7,239 FT; 2,207 M)

This peak was the site of an extensive mining district (1864-1881) that produced more than $4,000,000 in gold. Additional mining activity occurred during the 1920's. Ruins are still present, and provide interesting places to inspect along the way to the summit. The summit provides a fine viewpoint of the Montgomery Peak-Mount Dubois portion of the White Mountains. Although one may climb this peak round-trip in half a day, wandering about the historic mining camps on the mountain should inspire anyone to take their time, and imagine when this lonely hill was bustling with activity.

*Maps:* Benton Hot Springs, and Benton (CA) 7.5-minute (1:24,000 scale) topographic maps; Benton Range 1:100,000 scale metric topographic map; Inyo National Forest Map; Automobile Club of Southern California (AAA) Eastern Sierra map

*Best Time to Climb:* April through November

*Approach:* From Highway 120 at Benton Hot Springs (approximately 3.9 miles west of U.S. Highway 6), turn south on Yellow Jacket Road and drive 1.6 miles, then left to the base of the mountain. The road is washed out beyond here.

*Route:* Follow what is left of the road, to the remains of the Comanche Mines, and onto the north ridge of the mountain in approximately 1.5 miles. Turn south, and continue another 0.5 miles to the summit area. Anticipate six miles round-trip with 1,400 feet of elevation gain.

## CASA DIABLO MOUNTAIN (7,912 FT; 2,412 M)

Casa Diablo ("house of the devil") is a prominent outcrop of sandy-colored boulders that is visible for many miles. It takes its name from the Casa Diablo Mine along the northwest base of the mountain. The jumble of granitic rocks along the summit ridge makes the ascent a classic problem of route-finding, involving Class 3 scrambling. The summit boulders of Casa Diablo Mountain provide a fine perch from which to view the axis of the Owens Valley to the south, and the seemingly converging walls of the magnificent White-Inyo Range to the east and the Sierra Nevada on the west. There is a summit register on the north summit.

*Maps:* Casa Diablo Mountain (CA) 7.5-minute (1:24,000 scale) topographic map; Benton Range 1:100,000 scale metric topographic map; Inyo National Forest Map; Automobile Club of Southern California (AAA)

Eastern Sierra map
*Best Time to Climb:* April through November
*Approach:* From the junction of Highways 395 and 6 at the north end of Bishop, follow Highway 6 approximately 1.5 miles north to Five Bridges Road. Head north on Five Bridges Road, continuing 2.4 miles (past a gravel mining operation and a wetland area created by the mine as part of their reclamation program) to a junction with the Chalk Bluff Road (to the left) and Fish Slough Road (to the right). Continue straight ahead on Road 4S04 (graded dirt with washboards and some sandy spots) 14.5 miles to a two-track road heading east toward the peak. Turn east and drive a short distance to a likely parking spot (7,350 ft).
*Route:* The summit boulders are about a half mile to the east. As half the fun of climbing this peak is the route-finding through the house-sized boulders, a detailed description of the route is not provided. However, hiking up a shallow drainage, and approaching the summit block from the north works well. The hike is short, a mere two miles round-trip with about 600 feet of elevation gain but will take a couple of hours due to the route finding.

# The White, Inyo, Coso and Argus Ranges

The White Mountains and the Inyo Mountains, collectively known as the White-Inyo Range are separated by a low saddle known as Westgard Pass. In 1903, Geologist Josiah Spurr, who performed a number of early geologic investigations in the region, referred to the entire range as the White Mountains, while Adolph Knopf, in 1918, referred to the entire range as the Inyos. Current practice is to use the name "White Mountains" for that part of the range north of Westgard Pass, and "Inyo Mountains" for the mountains south of the pass.

The rocks in these mountains are primarily of sedimentary origin. Next to Reed Flat, the rocks are Precambrian in age, with their dolomite being the oldest rocks in the entire area. Within the Inyo Mountains, the Cambrian-age rocks, known as the Waucoban Series, provide one of the best records of early Cambrian sedimentation and faunal assemblages. The region is considered the type locality for this age of rocks. Coincidentally, the planet's oldest known plant life, the bristlecone pines, are found on the slopes of these peaks. The adjoining shales, sandstones, and limestones are of slightly younger age. As we go further south, near Andrews Mountain, and south to Cerro Gordo, the rocks become progressively younger. Because of the exquisite beauty and quality of the marble, the marble facings of Mills Tower in San Francisco were quarried at the foot of the Inyo Mountains near the nineteenth century Owens Lake port town of Swansea. Volcanic rocks are found at the extreme southern end of the range. The large basaltic sheets that cover Malpais Mesa, the "bad country," are quite visible from the Owens Valley floor, south of Lone Pine.

Prospectors first entered the White Mountains in significant numbers during the 1860's. During the latter half of the nineteenth century and the first half of the twentieth century, scattered mining and grazing occurred in the range, but generally cultural activity was minimal. Then in 1949, the United States Navy constructed an equipment test site along Crooked Creek. In 1978, the Navy turned over ownership of their lab, along with the Barcroft Laboratory, to the University of California who had been operating the labs for the Navy. The Barcroft Laboratory was built in 1950, and continues (along with the Crooked Creek Laboratory) as a place of significant high altitude research for biologists, astronomers and others.

Much of the Coso and Argus Ranges are blocked from casual climbing by security measures imposed by the China Lake Naval Air Weapons Station. All of the peaks located in restricted territory are not included in this guide as the possibility of obtaining permission to climb them is slim to none unless you happen to work at the base or know somebody that does. Without permission, climbing to the summits of the peaks is prohibited. This is unfortunate, because the finest peaks in these ranges (Maturango and Argus) are within these restricted grounds. However, some wonderful peaks are accessible in the surrounding open territory.

The Coso and Argus Ranges were among the first to be explored of all of the desert ranges. In 1849, William Lewis Manly, along with other Death Valley parties crossed the Argus Range. Manly, and a group called the Jayhawkers, crossed the range probably by way of Wilson Canyon, south of Argus Peak. Others crossed near Darwin Canyon, but missed the water at Darwin Falls. In March 1860, Dr. Darwin French penetrated these mountains as far as Darwin Canyon, discovered Darwin Falls, and collected rock specimens. By the middle of that summer, quite a mining boom was going on in the Coso area. When a bill was passed creating a county east of the Sierra Nevada in 1864, it was named Coso County, but the name was changed to Inyo County the following year.

While these ranges are primarily composed of sedimentary rock, granite and various volcanic rocks are prominent. Until the closing of the center of this region by the Naval Air Weapons Station, the hot springs at Coso were a popular tourist attraction. The geothermal resource is currently tapped to produce electricity.

## THE WHITE MOUNTAINS

Despite their prominence as the fourth highest mountain range in the contiguous 48 states, the White Mountains are relatively forgotten. They rise northward from Westgard Pass to the range's culminating point of White Mountain Peak (14,246 ft). North of White Mountain Peak, the crest of the range stretches another forty miles above 10,000 feet, usually above 12,000 feet above sea level. Despite their height, the White Mountains had significantly less glaciation compared to the Sierra Nevada to the west. Although today there are a few permanent snow fields that linger east of the crest, no glaciers remain.

Many wonder how a range called "White" with a highpoint named "White" could receive such a title when White Mountain Peak is mostly brown, red and black, and is only white during the winter when it is blanketed by snow. Some say it was named White Mountain Peak because of the snow cap it frequently has when the rest of the snows in the range have melted off. A more likely story goes like this. Originally, White Mountain Peak was the name for the peak now known as Montgomery Peak. What we call White Mountain Peak today was known to early settlers as Mount Olmsted. When a mine named the Montgomery Mine opened on the north slope of what is now Montgomery Peak, the name was transferred to the peak, and the name "White Mountain Peak" was moved to the highpoint of the range, replacing the name Olmsted. This seems the more likely story given the white color of Montgomery Peak's granitic rock. Erwin Gudde reports that the U.S. Geological Survey transferred the names in 1917.

When one travels into the White Mountains, they are struck by the difference in vegetation from the west to the east sides of the range. The west side is more desert-like with dry, sage scrub-covered slopes leading to an intermediate, sparse pinyon-juniper woodland, containing groves of Jeffrey pine along some of the drainages. As the upper limit of this pinyon-juniper woodland is reached, the trees become stunted and weather-beaten, making for some striking photographic opportunities. Some of the pinyon pines reach 400 years in age, impressive, but not when compared to the bristlecone pine. A lower tree line is reached at about 9,000 feet, which is followed by another upper, sparsely forested band consisting of limber pine and bristlecone pine between 10,000 and about 11,500 feet. The east slope is much more watered, with larger streams that include Cottonwood Creek, Crooked Creek, and Trail Creek, among others, that contain trout. Aspen groves are common on the east side along the streams and on sheltered north-facing slopes. Wildlife in the White Mountains includes bighorn sheep, deer, mountain lion, a few black bears, coyotes, bobcats, and a host of other smaller mammals, birds and other smaller creatures.

The best season for climbing in the White Mountains is from June (for the lower peaks) or July through the first significant snow during autumn, usually in October. During the winter, access roads remain unplowed, and access gates locked. Camping in the White Mountains is generally primitive with the exception of the free Grandview Campground located along the White Mountain Road north of Westgard Pass. The Grandview Campground provides the only allowed camping within the boundary of the Ancient Bristlecone Pine Forest Natural Area. Campfires and stove use within the Ancient Bristlecone Pine Forest boundary are prohibited. Elsewhere in the White Mountains, campfires are permitted provided a free fire permit is issued by a field forest ranger or issued at the White Mountain Ranger Station in Bishop. Food, lodging, and any supplies are available in the Owens Valley towns of Big Pine and Bishop. On the east side of the White Mountains, limited groceries are available in the Fish Lake Valley at Dyer. If coming in from Nevada, gas up in Tonopah. Always obey the road access signs to minimize disturbance to this dreamlike, but fragile terrain. All natural features including rocks, plants, and downed wood are protected in the Ancient Bristlecone Pine Forest.

The Ancient Bristlecone Pine Forest Natural Area was established in 1958 to be managed for scientific study and public recreation. Visit the wonderful visitor center at the Schulman Grove along the White Mountain Road when passing through this region. Taking one of the nature trails from the Visitor Center can also help in providing some modest exercise at altitude prior to a climb.

For the non-botanist or plant enthusiast, telling the difference between a limber pine and a bristlecone (particularly a young bristlecone) can be difficult at first. If you are unsure, you might try looking down at the ground. If you are standing on light colored limestone or dolomite rock or soil, you're probably looking at a bristlecone. Otherwise, you probably

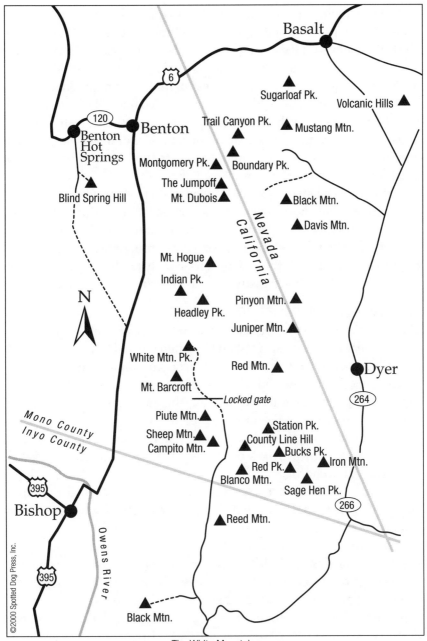

Basalt

6

120

Benton
Hot
Springs

Benton

Blind Spring Hill

Sugarloaf Pk.

Volcanic Hills

Trail Canyon Pk.

Mustang Mtn.

Montgomery Pk.

Boundary Pk.

The Jumpoff

Mt. Dubois

Black Mtn.

Davis Mtn.

Nevada
California

Mt. Hogue

Indian Pk.

Pinyon Mtn.

Headley Pk.

Juniper Mtn.

N

White Mtn. Pk.

Red Mtn.

Dyer

Mt. Barcroft

264

Locked gate

Mono County
Inyo County

Piute Mtn.

Sheep Mtn.

Campito Mtn.

Station Pk.

County Line Hill

Bucks Pk.

Iron Mtn.

Red Pk.

Blanco Mtn.

Sage Hen Pk.

395

266

Bishop

Reed Mtn.

Owens River

395

Black Mtn.

The White Mountains

are looking at a limber pine. This is far from a rule of thumb, but the bristle-cone tends to grow on the light-colored limestone soils. This may be due to the coolness of those soils, allowing the bristlecone seeds to survive.

A recent addition to the White Mountains is the Boundary Peak Wilderness. At the time of this writing, a wilderness permit is not required for travel in this area. However, the wilderness was included under the Inyo National Forest Order #04-97-1 that prohibits possessing or storing any food or refuse unless it is stored in a bear-proof container or in another manner designed to keep bears from gaining access to the food or refuse. Do not consider your vehicle a bear-proof container.

The following list of peaks is arranged north to south, from Nevada to just north of White Mountain Peak, followed by those along the White Mountain Road from Westgard Pass toward White Mountain Peak. Finally at the end, a few named peaks are added, which are impressive when viewed from Fish Lake Valley to the east, but are actually just bumps at the end of the long ridges that stretch eastward from the White Mountain crest.

### Sugarloaf Peak (9,195 ft; 2,803 m)
This beautiful, varicolored peak is visible for some time while approaching Montgomery Pass from the west on U.S. Highway 6. Only the bulldozed tracks from past mining exploration detract from its appearance. The peak provides excellent views of the Mustang Mountain-Boundary Peak areas along with Queen and Fish Lake Valleys. There are some interesting mine workings in the area for the intrepid explorer. We climbed the peak on a cold, cloudy day and after finding a fifty-year old mining claim notice in a can, we headed down to the Montgomery Pass Casino, where we enjoyed a nice cup of hot chocolate.

*Maps:* Mount Montgomery (NV-CA) 7.5-minute (1:24,000 scale) topo-graphic map; Benton Range 1:100,000 scale metric topographic map; Inyo National Forest Map

*Best Time to Climb:* May through November

*Approach:* From Bishop, California, follow U.S. Highway 6 approximately 48 miles north to Montgomery Pass. On the east side of the casino, follow a rough but graded dirt road, continuing first south, then west to the Tip Top Mine (8,700 ft), approximately six miles from the highway. A high clearance two-wheel drive vehicle is recommended for this route, although with care most cars should be able to reach the road end.

*Route:* Follow the ridge past mine ruins to the top, or follow exploration tracks along the south base of the peak, then up the west ridge to the summit. Plan on approximately one mile round-trip with about 500 steep feet of elevation gain.

## MUSTANG MOUNTAIN (10,320+ FT; 3,146+ M)

Mustang Mountain is the most northern of the high peaks of the White Mountains. Wild burros and horses range over its gentle, wooded crown. The hike from Queen Canyon Saddle, over Kennedy Point, to Mustang Mountain makes for an enjoyable outing.

*Maps:* Mount Montgomery (NV-CA) 7.5-minute (1:24,000 scale) topographic map; Benton Range 1:100,000 scale metric topographic map; Inyo National Forest Map

*Best Time to Climb:* June through October

*Approach:* From Benton, California, continue approximately seven miles northeast on Highway 6, then right on the dirt Queen Canyon Mine Road (Forest Service Road 1N14). Follow Queen Canyon Mine Road to the mine at 8,700 feet. With four-wheel drive, and later in the season after the snow melts, one can drive all the way to Queen Canyon Saddle (9,800 ft).

*Route:* From Queen Canyon Saddle, the summit is to the northeast. One climbs over Kennedy Point (10,140 ft) along the route. Once past Kennedy Point, the going becomes easy, cross country hiking through pinyon and juniper. The summit is at an open spot on the ridge, and is marked by a cairn with a summit register. Anticipate about two miles and 850 feet of elevation gain round-trip.

*Alternate Approach:* As for Sugarloaf Peak.

*Alternate Route:* Follow jeep tracks and climb over easy slopes to the summit, about six miles round-trip with 1,800 feet of elevation gain.

## "TRAIL CANYON PEAK" (11,325 FT; 3,452 M)

This is the barren, conical summit between Boundary Peak and Mustang Mountain, and immediately north of Trail Canyon Saddle. The author has taken the liberty to name this small peak for the canyon of the same name. For those who have yet to climb the highest summit in Nevada, and are looking for a shorter hike, this peak provides a fine view of the primary route up Boundary.

*Maps:* Mount Montgomery and Boundary Peak (NV-CA) 7.5-minute

Boundary and Montgomery from Highway 6. Photo: Andy Zdon

(1:24,000 scale) topographic maps; Benton Range 1:100,000 scale metric topographic map; Inyo National Forest Map
*Best Time to Climb:* June through October
*Approach and Route:* This peak may be climbed from the Queen Mine (see Mustang Mountain) or from Trail Canyon en route to Boundary Peak. From Queen Canyon Saddle, simply hike up the ridge to the summit. Anticipate four miles round-trip with 1,550 feet of elevation gain.

### BOUNDARY PEAK (13,140 FT; 4,005 M)

This high peak near Montgomery Peak receives its fame as the highest point in Nevada. It is technically simple, but physically demanding in good weather. However, it is subject to sudden storms (as is the entire crest of the White Mountains) and may become dangerous under these conditions. On one occasion, the author reached the summit as lightning began to strike below him in Middle Creek…a hasty retreat was made. This is one of the few peaks in this guide, on which you are likely to share the summit with other climbers.
*Maps:* Boundary Peak, Mount Montgomery, Davis Mountain and East of Davis Mountain (NV-CA) 7.5-minute (1:24,000 scale) topographic maps; Benton Range 1:100,000 scale metric topographic map; Inyo National Forest Map
*Best Time to Climb:* July through October

*Approach:* From Bishop, California drive 48 miles north on Highway 6 to Montgomery Pass. From the pass, continue another 7.9 miles to Nevada Highway 264. Turn right (the only way you can turn) on Highway 264, and drive 13.1 miles south to the Trail Canyon Road (Forest Service Road 2N07) heading west. From here "The Crossing Road" heads east toward the Silver Peak Range and the Mineral Ridge Mine. Follow the Trail Canyon Road 7.1 miles west from Highway 264 to a fork. Bear right at the fork (staying on Road 2N07) and continue on the rough dirt road, bearing left onto Forest Service Road 1S61 at a fork 11.4 miles from the highway. Continue another two miles to the trailhead in Trail Canyon (9,000 ft). With care, two-wheel drive vehicles with good clearance should not encounter any problems on these roads.

*Route:* Hike west about 2.5 miles up to Trail Canyon Saddle (10,800 ft) then southward up Boundary Peak's north ridge via the sandy use trail. The going is a real slog. Anticipate eight miles round-trip with 4,200 feet of elevation gain.

*Alternate Approach and Route:* One can reach Trail Canyon Saddle from the Queen Mine by continuing up to Queen Canyon Saddle, climbing up the ridge to the southwest, then contouring to Trail Canyon Saddle. This is essentially the same route as for Trail Canyon Peak. The peak is then climbed from Trail Canyon Saddle as described for the "ruta normal." To reach Queen Canyon Saddle, drive north approximately seven miles from Benton on Highway 6 to a graded road (Forest Service Road 1N14) heading south toward the mountains. Follow this dirt road to the Queen Mine, and on up narrow switchbacks (four-wheel drive recommended) to Queen Canyon Saddle (9,800 ft). Queen Canyon is an interesting place to visit even if not climbing the peaks. Anticipate eight miles round-trip with approximately 3,500 feet of elevation gain.

### MONTGOMERY PEAK (13,440 FT; 4,097 M)
This may be the most difficult peak in the White Mountains (although not the least visited). This outstanding peak is visible for miles along U.S. Highway 6. It presents some slight scrambling difficulties and a little exposure between the summit and Boundary Peak.

*Maps:* Boundary Peak, Mount Montgomery, Davis Mountain and East of Davis Mountain (NV-CA) 7.5-minute (1:24,000 scale) topographic maps; Benton Range 1:100,000 scale metric topographic map; Inyo National

Quiet camp at Trail Canyon Saddle.  Photo: Andy Zdon

Forest Map

*Best Time to Climb:* July through October

*Approach:* Approach this peak from the summit of Boundary Peak and the same approaches and routes are taken.

*Route:* From Boundary Peak, drop 300 feet to the saddle between Boundary and Montgomery.  Detour the small crags on the ridge by passing on either side.  The 600-foot climb to the summit pinnacle is made along the ridge, passing to the left to miss the steeper rocks.  This ridge can be icy in early season, and if so, a rope may be helpful.  Allow two hours for the round-trip from Boundary Peak, and add 900 feet of elevation gain to the climbing statistics for Boundary Peak.

*Alternate Route:* In 1987, Randall Danta and Wynne Benti climbed Montgomery and Boundary via the eastern ridge of Montgomery (approximately 6,500 feet of elevation gain) from the Middle Creek drainage on the Nevada side of the range.

### THE JUMPOFF (13,484 FT; 4,110 M)

The Jumpoff is not so much a separate peak, but the most northerly point on the long ridge extending north from Mount Dubois.

*Maps:* Boundary Peak, Davis Mountain and East of Davis Mountain (NV-CA) 7.5-minute (1:24,000 scale) topographic maps; Benton Range 1:100,000 scale metric topographic map; Inyo National Forest Map

*Best Time to Climb:* July through October

*Approach:* From Bishop, California drive 48 miles north on Highway 6 to Montgomery Pass. From the pass, continue another 7.9 miles to Nevada Highway 264. Turn right on Highway 264, and drive 13.1 miles south to the Trail Canyon Road (Forest Service Road 2N07) heading west. From here "The Crossing Road" heads east toward the Silver Peak Range and the Mineral Ridge Mine. Follow the Trail Canyon Road 7.1 miles west from Highway 264 to a fork. Bear left onto Forest Service Road 1S58, and continue 3.8 miles on a poor road to the roadhead along Middle Creek (8,400 ft). Suitable for two-wheel drive vehicles with high clearance.

*Route:* Follow Middle Creek westward, taking the north fork where it branches, and heading to the saddle (12,175 ft) between The Jumpoff and Montgomery Peak. Scramble south up the remaining 1,300 feet of elevation gain. This is a long, arduous route with more than 5,000 feet of elevation gain.

*Alternate Route:* Climb the principal route for Mount Dubois until it reaches the crest of the range. Then head north to the summit across gently rolling terrain.

### MOUNT DUBOIS (13,545 FT; 4,129 M)

This massive peak, the second highest in the range, is a prominent landmark in the Owens Valley. As you view the range north of White Mountain Peak from the Owens Valley, Mount Dubois is the hulking monster appearing as a high, rounded ridge. The peak is so big, it takes on the appearance of being higher than White Mountain Peak. On top may be found remains of native habitation sites, and their have been numerous bighorn sheep sightings on Dubois' high alpine slopes.

*Maps:* Boundary Peak, Mount Montgomery, Davis Mountain and East of Davis Mountain (NV-CA) 7.5-minute (1:24,000 scale) topographic maps; Benton Range 1:100,000 scale metric topographic map; Inyo National Forest Map; Automobile Club of Southern California (AAA) Eastern Sierra map

*Best Time to Climb:* July through October

After a hailstorm at 12,000 feet near Mt. Hogue. Photo: Wynne Benti

*Approach:* From Fish Lake Valley, drive to the Middle Creek road end as described for the Jumpoff.

*Route:* From the road end, cross Middle Creek and climb southward up the slope to the top of the ridge at about 10,000 feet depending on your route. Once on the ridge, head west to the crest of the range at an elevation of about 13,400 feet. Mount Dubois is an easy walk about one mile south along the undulating ridge (nine miles and 5,300 feet of elevation gain round-trip).

*Alternate Approach:* An alternate route is a fine overnight backpack up Indian Creek to Mounts Hogue and Dubois. From Fish Lake Valley, drive up Indian Creek following Forest Service Road 1S60 as far as possible. The turnoff for Indian Creek is about two miles south of the Trail Canyon Road. Four-wheel drive is best for this route. The drainage is thick with willows and is not recommended for those who can't stand the sound of branches dragging against their vehicle's paint job.

*Alternate Route:* From Indian Creek, continue up the canyon on a trail that leads southwest to the northwest portion of Chiatovich Flats. The area of springs one mile east of Mount Hogue makes for a good campsite (approximately 11,600 ft). Camp away from the springs as they are important to the local wildlife. Mount Dubois can be climbed via a four-mile hike across the broad ridge. Mount Hogue can be easily climbed en route. All along the wide-open, spectacular ridges of the White Mountains are remnant house circles, large circles measuring eight feet and more in diameter of gathered rock, once used as summer hunting camps by Paiute-Shoshone ancestors.

*Second Alternate Route:* The peak has also been climbed by backpacking over Montgomery Peak, and camping in the saddle between The Jumpoff and Montgomery.

### MOUNT HOGUE (12,751 FT; 3,887 M)

*Maps:* White Mountain Peak (CA), Juniper Mountain (NV-CA) and Dyer (NV) 7.5-minute (1:24,000 scale) topographic maps; Bishop and Benton Range 1:100,000 scale metric topographic maps; Inyo National Forest Map; Automobile Club of Southern California (AAA) Eastern Sierra map

*Best Time to Climb:* July through October

*Approach:* From Fish Lake Valley, head up Indian Creek as for the alternate route to Mount Dubois.

*Route:* This peak can be dayhiked from Indian Creek or combined with Mount Dubois as an overnight backpack. The mileage and elevation gain will vary depending on how far you can drive up the Indian Creek drainage.

### HEADLEY PEAK (12,676 FT; 3,863 M)

*Maps:* White Mountain Peak (CA), Juniper Mountain (NV-CA) and Dyer (NV) 7.5-minute (1:24,000 scale) topographic maps; Bishop and Benton Range 1:100,000 scale metric topographic maps; Inyo National Forest Map; Automobile Club of Southern California (AAA) Eastern Sierra map

*Best Time to Climb:* July through October

*Approach:* From Fish Lake Valley, head up Indian Creek as for the alternate route to Mount Dubois.  Pack to the spring area at the northwest end of Chiatovich Flats.

*Route:* From the spring area, contour to the east or over Peak 11,784 feet, reaching a narrow saddle after 1.5 miles.  From the saddle, climb the northern slopes of the twin-summited peak.  Surprisingly, the summit of Headley Peak is the lower and more westerly summit. From the springs, anticipate seven to eight miles round-trip with 2,200 feet of elevation gain.

*Alternate:* This peak is climbed when backpacking the crest of the White Mountains from the locked gate at Mount Barcroft to Trail or Queen Canyons.

### INDIAN PEAK (11,297 FT; 3,443 M)

This seldom-visited summit located west of the White Mountain crest is probably the hardest peak to reach in the range.  The author has not climbed this peak and caution is recommended when following the routes described below.

*Maps:* White Mountain Peak (CA), Juniper Mountain (NV-CA) and Dyer (Nevada) 7.5-minute (1:24,000 scale) topographic maps; Bishop and Benton Range 1:100,000 scale metric topographic maps; Inyo National Forest Map; Automobile Club of Southern California (AAA) Eastern Sierra map

*Best Time to Climb:* July through October

*Approach:* Follow the approach and route for Headley Peak.

*Route:* From Headley Peak, descend nearly 1,900 feet down Headley's northwest ridge to a saddle at 10,800 ft. The summit of Indian Peak is a half mile to the west.  Either return by reclimbing Headley Peak, or a possible descent route could continue westward down to the slope in Section 16 where two foot trails that show up on the topographic map can be followed down to the mouth of Willow Creek in Hammil Valley. This alternate route would require a long car shuttle.  If climbing Indian Peak from a camp at the springs and returning to camp via Headley Peak, anticipate 11.5 miles round-trip with 4,600 feet of elevation gain (nearly half of which is on the return trip).

*A number of peaks in the White Mountains can be reached from the road running northward from Westgard Pass to the Bristlecone Pine Forest. These peaks are listed south to north for ease of describing the driving directions.*

## BLACK MOUNTAIN (9,083 FT; 2,769 M)

This mountain is an impressive peak when seen from Big Pine and the Westgard Pass Road. Equally impressive is the amazing view of Owens Valley and the Palisades section of the Sierra Nevada it provides. When looking at this double-summited mass, the true summit is the dark, long ridge to the west, and not the grayish, more pyramidal eastern summit. Expect to spend more time than usual on this summit; the view is exquisite.

*Maps:* Westgard Pass (CA) 7.5-minute (1:24,000 scale) topographic map; Bishop 1:100,000 scale metric topographic map; Inyo National Forest Map; Automobile Club of Southern California (AAA) Eastern Sierra map

*Best Time to Climb:* May through October

*Approach:* From Big Pine, California drive approximately 13 miles east approaching Westgard Pass, then north on the paved Bristlecone Road (Forest Service Road 4S01) about a half mile. Take a dirt road (Forest Service Road 4S01A) west about four miles to an old mine at 8,400 feet. The last mile is rough and four-wheel drive will probably be necessary. One can get close enough to the peak with a high clearance two-wheel drive vehicle to easily climb it as a day hike.

*Route:* Climb about 1.5 miles along a faint trail, occasionally obscured, passing to the north around the lower but sharper east peak to the true, flatter summit. Passing through pinyons, the hiker will be surprised to happen upon a small grove of bristlecones on the north slope of the peak. The distance and mileage will vary greatly depending on where one parks along the Black Mountain Road, but anticipate a little more than a half-day hike with somewhere between 1,000 to 2,000 feet of elevation gain.

*Alternate Route:* Campy Camphausen and Ed Zdon Sr., climbed Black Mountain from the Marble Canyon Road via the north slopes. This is a much longer climb, and the north slopes of this peak can be treacherous during the winter and spring when icy snow is present.

## "REED MOUNTAIN" (11,033 FT; 3,363 M)

Reed Mountain is located near the Schulman Grove, a stand of bristle-cone pines containing the oldest known living thing. This peak provides fine views southward across the northern Inyo Mountains and off to northern Death Valley National Park. The summit is marked by a bench-mark named "Cold."

*Maps:* Blanco Mountain (CA) 7.5-minute (1:24,000 scale) topographic map;

Author on the summit of Reed Mountain, a classic desert summit. Photo: Dave Clegg

Bishop 1:100,000 scale metric topographic map; Inyo National Forest Map; Automobile Club of Southern California (AAA) Eastern Sierra map
*Best Time to Climb:* June through October
*Approach:* From Big Pine, California drive approximately 13 miles east approaching Westgard Pass, then north on the paved Bristlecone Road (Forest Service Road 4S01). Follow the paved Bristlecone Road approximately one mile past the Schulman Grove turnoff to where the road turns to dirt and reaches a parking spot on the right side of the road (10,300 ft). This approach is accessible to all cars.
*Route:* Hike about one-half mile to the saddle south of the peak, then north up a steep slope through bristlecones another half-mile to the summit. Although the going is a steep 700 feet, the slopes are easy and short.

### BLANCO MOUNTAIN (11,278 FT; 3,438 M)
This prominent peak provides excellent views of this part of the White Mountains. Blanco is one of those peaks that pays maximum returns in the way of views and a pleasant experience, for minimum effort. An old cabin, with roof intact at the time of this writing, and mine workings are

passed along the route. This area was mined by Mexican prospectors, and local legend has it that they named many of the peaks, including Blanco, Campito, and Tres Plumas Flat. Some initials, dating back more than half a century, are carved on the cabin door and walls.

*Maps:* Blanco Mountain (CA) 7.5-minute (1:24,000 scale) topographic map; Bishop 1:100,000 scale metric topographic map; Inyo National Forest Map; Automobile Club of Southern California (AAA) Eastern Sierra map

*Best Time to Climb:* June through October

*Approach:* From Big Pine, drive approximately 13 miles east approaching Westgard Pass, then north on the paved Bristlecone Road (Forest Service Road 4S01). Follow the paved Bristlecone Road north, to the Schulman Grove. From the Schulman Grove turnoff, continue on the Bristlecone Road (which turns to well-graded dirt) 9.2 miles to the Crooked Creek Road (Forest Service Road 5S01). Turn east and drive a short distance to a small drainage (10,360 ft). This approach is accessible to all cars.

*Route:* Blanco Mountain is visible to the south. Drop down into the wash and follow the dirt track southward as it passes along the east side of County Line Hill to a meadow at about 10,500 feet. In a shaded grove of pines at the base of Blanco's slopes, is an old cabin constructed of roughly-hewn timbers. A few small tailings piles dot the nearby slopes. Work up Blanco's northwest slopes or north ridge through bristlecones to the summit. Plan on a hike of approximately 1,200 feet of elevation gain and four to five miles round-trip.

## COUNTY LINE HILL (11,229 FT; 3,423 M)

This small hill has as its distinguishing feature, the Inyo-Mono County Line passing through it. Of interest are the gnarled, dead bristlecones near the summit. These old trees, along with those on neighboring Campito Mountain are higher than the current tree line in the area. They probably represent an old grove that existed during a warmer period.

*Maps:* Blanco Mountain (CA) 7.5-minute (1:24,000 scale) topographic map; Bishop 1:100,000 scale metric topographic map; Inyo National Forest Map; Automobile Club of Southern California (AAA) Eastern Sierra map

*Best Time to Climb:* June through October

*Approach:* As for Blanco Peak.

*Route:* Scramble up the north ridge of County Line Hill. The summit is a scant 1-1/4 miles to the south with about 1,000 feet of elevation gain.

On Blanco Mountain. White Mountain Peak in distance. Photo: Wynne Benti

### STATION PEAK (10,316 FT; 3,144 M)

*Maps:* Blanco Mountain, Crooked Creek and Station Peak (CA) 7.5-minute (1:24,000 scale) topographic maps; Bishop 1:100,000 scale metric topographic map; Inyo National Forest Map; Automobile Club of Southern California (AAA) Eastern Sierra map

*Best Time to Climb:* June through October

*Approach:* From the Schulman Grove turnoff, continue on the Bristlecone Road 9.2 miles to the Crooked Creek Road (Forest Service Road 5S01). Drive east on the Crooked Creek Road, passing the Crooked Creek Laboratory after one mile. Crooked Creek crosses the road several times at varying depths below the laboratory. It is best to park along the road at a broad meadow approximately two miles below the laboratory just before a wide stream crossing (9,800 ft). Beyond this point, vehicle traffic has chewed up some boggy, but beautiful grassy meadows along the creek . . . travel by foot to minimize additional impact. Two-wheel drive vehicles with high clearance are recommended for this route.

*Route:* Wade the stream (can be dry in late season), and continue down Crooked Creek Canyon about 1-1/4 miles to a dirt track that heads north up a draw to a cattle camp. Turn north and head up past the cattle camp to the broad saddle east of Station Peak. Scramble up the talus and boulders to the summit. Anticipate approximately five to six miles with about 1,000 feet of elevation gain round-trip.

### IRON MOUNTAIN (9,530 FT; 2,905 M)

The most easterly of the main peaks of the White Mountains, the views from the summit extend from Waucoba Mountain to White Mountain Peak, and off into the wilds of Nevada.

*Maps:* Blanco Mountain and Crooked Creek (CA) 7.5-minute (1:24,000 scale) topographic maps; Bishop 1:100,000 scale metric topographic map; Inyo National Forest Map; Automobile Club of Southern California (AAA) Eastern Sierra map

*Best Time to Climb:* June through October

*Approach:* As for Station Peak.

*Route:* Hike down Crooked Creek Canyon as for Station Peak, but continue another two miles past the cattle camp turnoff to a dirt track that leaves the canyon westward to Sage Hen Flat (unnamed on the topographic map but shows up as a flat area in Sections 24 and 25). Turn left and follow the track, gaining about 300 feet to Sage Hen Flat. Iron Mountain is about one mile east across the scrub covered flat. Anticipate 8.5 miles round-trip with 1,300 feet of elevation gain.

### "SAGE HEN PEAK" (9,520+ FT; 2,902+ M)
This peak is usually combined with Iron Mountain, and provides a fine bird's-eye view of the Crooked Creek country. This peak is unnamed on the topographic map.

*Maps:* Blanco Mountain and Crooked Creek (CA) 7.5-minute (1:24,000 scale) topographic maps; Bishop 1:100,000 scale metric topographic map; Inyo National Forest Map; Automobile Club of Southern California (AAA) Eastern Sierra map

*Best Time to Climb:* June through October

*Approach:* As for Station Peak.

*Route:* As for Iron Mountain. At Sage Hen Flat, head south about 0.8 miles to the summit. Add another mile and 350 feet of elevation gain when combining this with Iron Mountain.

### BUCKS PEAK (10,858 FT; 3,310 M)
The highpoint is the southernmost of the three peaks that constitute Bucks Peak. This is a fine peak to climb in the fall when the scattered aspen groves on the north-facing slopes turn a brilliant orange.

*Maps:* Blanco Mountain (CA) 7.5-minute (1:24,000 scale) topographic map; Bishop 1:100,000 scale metric topographic map; Inyo National Forest Map; Automobile Club of Southern California (AAA) Eastern Sierra map

*Best Time to Climb:* June through October

*Approach:* As for Station Peak.

*Route:* Just before the parking area for Station, Iron and Sage Hen, a dirt track (Road 35E45) heads south over a low ridge and drops into the South Fork of Crooked Creek at some springs. From the springs, head due south up the slopes to Bucks Peak. Anticipate 3.5 miles round-trip with approximately 1,500 feet of elevation gain.

### RED PEAK (10,094 FT; 3,077 M)
*Maps:* Blanco Mountain and Crooked Creek (CA) 7.5-minute (1:24,000 scale) topographic maps; Bishop 1:100,000 scale metric topographic map; Inyo National Forest Map; Automobile Club of Southern California (AAA) Eastern Sierra map

*Best Time to Climb:* June through October

*Approach:* As for Station Peak.

*Route:* This peak is best combined with Bucks Peak. From the summit of Bucks, head due east two miles to the summit across a broad, grassy basin. Round-trip stats are 7.5 miles round-trip with 2,100 feet of elevation gain. The summit of Bucks can be bypassed to the northeast on the return.

### CAMPITO MOUNTAIN (11,543 FT; 3,518 M)

This small peak along the White Mountain crest is named for a Spanish term for "little place or little camp." It was probably named by Mexican miners known to have prospected this area, as were Blanco Mountain and Tres Plumas Flat.

*Maps:* Mount Barcroft and Blanco Mountain (CA) 7.5-minute (1:24,000 scale) topographic maps; Bishop 1:100,000 scale metric topographic map; Inyo National Forest Map; Automobile Club of Southern California (AAA) Eastern Sierra map

*Best Time to Climb:* June through October

*Approach:* This peak is easily attainable from anywhere along the Bristlecone Road between the Crooked Creek turnoff and Campito Meadow. The approach is accessible to all cars.

*Route:* Easy slopes lead to the summit from any direction. Anticipate a maximum of 1,200 feet of elevation gain and three miles round-trip depending on the chosen parking spot.

### SHEEP MOUNTAIN (12,497 FT; 3,809 M)

The brown, broad cone of Sheep Mountain, along with its neighbor Piute Mountain provides an enjoyable, high elevation hike in this part of the White Mountains, and makes for a fine altitude conditioner. Hikers climbing Sheep Mountain, and neighboring Campito Mountain, will notice two groups of bristlecones . . . a belt of live bristlecones on the lower slopes, and dead bristlecone snags higher up. The upper zone of dead trees marks an older tree line. Based on the relative ages of the live and dead trees, researchers have postulated that during the period from 7,400 to 4,500 years ago, the average temperature was on the order of three to four degrees warmer than it is today.

*Maps:* Mount Barcroft (CA) 7.5-minute (1:24,000 scale) topographic map; Bishop 1:100,000 scale metric topographic map; Inyo National Forest Map;

Automobile Club of Southern California (AAA) Eastern Sierra map
*Best Time to Climb:* June through October
*Approach:* From the Crooked Creek turnoff, continue another 2.5 miles north on the Bristlecone Road to the Patriarch Grove turnoff. Stay left and gain a saddle on Sheep's east shoulder. This approach is accessible to all cars.
*Route:* The summit is a scant 3/4 mile to the west-northwest with 900 feet of gain.
*Alternate Route:* Parking areas are available about a mile north along the road. Anticipate roughly the same elevation gain with about 2.5 miles round-trip.

### PIUTE MOUNTAIN (12,564 FT; 3,830 M)

*Maps:* Mount Barcroft (CA) 7.5-minute (1:24,000 scale) topographic map; Bishop 1:100,000 scale metric topographic map; Inyo National Forest Map; Automobile Club of Southern California (AAA) Eastern Sierra map
*Best Time to Climb:* June through October
*Approach:* From Westgard Pass, take the Bristlecone Road (turns to dirt after 10.3 miles) 26.3 miles to a locked gate at a saddle between Piute Mountain and Mount Barcroft (11,650 ft). This approach is accessible to all cars.
*Route:* From the saddle, hike up Piute Mountain's broad north ridge. Anticipate 2.5 miles with about 900 feet of elevation gain round-trip.

### MOUNT BARCROFT (13,040 FT; 3,975 M)

Named for Joseph Barcroft, a leading high altitude physiologist, the peak provides a fine view of White Mountain Peak.
*Maps:* White Mountain Peak and Mount Barcroft (CA) 7.5-minute (1:24,000 scale) topographic maps; Bishop 1:100,000 scale metric topographic map; Inyo National Forest Map; Automobile Club of Southern California (AAA) Eastern Sierra map
*Best Time to Climb:* June through October
*Approach:* As for Piute Mountain.
*Route:* From the locked gate, head north-northwest up easy slopes to the summit, 3.5 miles round-trip with approximately 1,400 feet of elevation gain.

Admiring the view from the summit of White Mountain Peak. Photo: Wynne Benti

## WHITE MOUNTAIN PEAK (14,256 FT; 4,345 M)

White Mountain Peak, the highest desert peak in the United States, is one of the two 14,000-footers in California that are not in the Sierra Nevada, the other being Mount Shasta. A popular story recalls how a research project conducting a survey of the area discovered that White Mountain Peak was actually higher than Mount Whitney. The story continues on about how governmental authorities did not want to publicize the new elevation in order to keep the visitation down. Make of this story whatever you like. As it stands now, White Mountain Peak is the third highest peak in California behind Mount Whitney and Mount Williamson in the Sierra Nevada. This peak also holds a record of sorts. A bushy-tailed packrat living in the summit hut set a record for that species living at high altitudes. Larger animals occasionally encountered on the peak include bighorn sheep, and deer. On one of our dayhikes up this peak, two Golden Eagles drifted overhead on the warm summer thermals.

*Maps:* White Mountain Peak, Mount Barcroft and Juniper Mountain (CA) 7.5-minute (1:24,000 scale) topographic maps; Bishop 1:100,000 scale metric topographic map; Inyo National Forest Map; Automobile Club of Southern California (AAA) Eastern Sierra map

*Best Time to Climb:* June through October

*Approach:* As for Piute Mountain.

*Route:* Pass the locked gate, and hike up the road about two miles to the Barcroft Laboratory at 12,400 feet. From the Barcroft Laboratory, continue to hike the road 5.5 miles to the summit. Anticipate about 15 miles and 3,000 feet of elevation gain round-trip.

*The following mountains are subsidiary peaks of the White Mountains, accessible from Fish Lake Valley. These peaks are generally formed by long ridges running east from the White Mountains, imposing from Fish Lake Valley, but insignificant when viewed from the main ridge.*

### RED MOUNTAIN (7,754 FT; 2,363 M)

*Maps:* Station Peak (CA-NV) and Dyer (NV-CA) 7.5-minute (1:24,000 scale) topographic maps; Bishop and Benton Range 1:100,000 scale metric topographic maps; Inyo National Forest Map; Automobile Club of Southern California (AAA) Eastern Sierra map

*Best Time to Climb:* June through October

*Approach:* Opposite the Double-Nine Ranch (where the Fish Lake Valley Road bends from northwest to north) in Fish Lake Valley, roads lead three miles to the ridge base (5,500+ ft). Two-wheel drive vehicles with high clearance are recommended.

*Route:* The peak lies to the west-southwest from here. The first summit is the true one. Anticipate 2,300 feet of elevation gain and four miles round-trip.

### JUNIPER MOUNTAIN (7,862 FT; 2,397 M)

*Maps:* Juniper Mountain (CA-NV) and Dyer (NV-CA) 7.5-minute (1:24,000 scale) topographic maps; Benton Range 1:100,000 scale metric topographic map; Inyo National Forest Map; Automobile Club of Southern California (AAA) Eastern Sierra map

*Best Time to Climb:* April to Mid-June, September to November

*Approach and Route:* A mile south of the Circle L Ranch, just north of Dyer, a poor dirt road winds two miles toward the base of the mountains. Four-wheel drive vehicles are recommended. From the road end (5,500+ ft) it should be possible to follow the ridge southwesterly to the summit, about 2,300 feet of elevation gain.

Nieves penitentes on the eastern slope of White Mountain Peak. Photo: Wynne Benti

### PINYON MOUNTAIN (9,000+ FT; 2,744+ M)

*Maps:* Juniper Mountain (CA-NV) and Dyer (NV-CA) 7.5-minute (1:24,000 scale) topographic maps; Benton Range 1:100,000 scale metric topographic map; Inyo National Forest Map; Automobile Club of Southern California (AAA) Eastern Sierra map

*Best Time to Climb:* May through October

*Approach:* Opposite the Circle L Ranch, just north of Dyer, a signed dirt road leads some six miles up Leidy Creek. Just after crossing the state line (7,000+ ft), a ridge runs south from a small flat. Two-wheel drive vehicles with high clearance are recommended.

*Route:* Follow the ridge up 2,000 feet of elevation gain, directly to the double summit.

### BLACK MOUNTAIN (9,704 FT; 2,958 M)

A small peak extending out into Fish Lake Valley from Mount Dubois. The summit provides an excellent view of Boundary and Montgomery Peaks.

*Maps:* Boundary Peak, Davis Mountain (NV-CA) and East of Davis Mountain (NV) 7.5-minute (1:24,000 scale) topographic maps; Benton Range 1:100,000 scale metric topographic map; Inyo National Forest Map; Automobile Club of Southern California (AAA) Eastern Sierra map

*Best Time to Climb:* May through October

*Approach:* From Bishop, drive 48 miles north on Highway 6 to Montgomery Pass. From the pass, continue another 7.9 miles to Nevada Highway 264. Turn right (the only way you can turn) on Highway 264, and drive 13.1 miles south to the Trail Canyon Road (Forest Service Road 2N07) heading west. From here "The Crossing Road" heads east toward the Silver Peak Range and the Mineral Ridge Mine. Follow the Trail Canyon Road 7.1 miles west from Highway 264 to a fork. Bear left onto Forest Service Road 1S58, and continue two miles on a poor road just past the Inyo National Forest boundary (7,200+ ft). Two-wheel drive vehicles with high clearance are recommended.

*Route:* Cross Middle Creek and mount easy benches to the ridge, then west to the second summit. Anticipate 2,500 feet of elevation gain and five miles round-trip.

## DAVIS MOUNTAIN (9,369 FT; 2,856 M)

Davis Mountain is a long flattish mountain with a good view of the Dubois ridge. The peak was named in 1894 for Lieutenant Milton F. Davis who made the first recorded ascent of the peak on August 28, 1891. Davis went on to national prominence when he became the chief of staff for the Army Air Service during World War I.

*Maps:* Davis Mountain (NV-CA) and East of Davis Mountain (NV) 7.5-minute (1:24,000 scale) topographic maps; Benton Range 1:100,000 scale metric topographic map; Inyo National Forest Map; Automobile Club of Southern California (AAA) Eastern Sierra map

*Best Time to Climb:* May through October

*Approach:* From Bishop, California drive 48 miles north on Highway 6 to Montgomery Pass. From the pass, continue another 7.9 miles to Nevada Highway 264. Turn right (the only way you can turn) on Highway 264, and drive 13.1 miles south to the Trail Canyon Road (Forest Service Road 2N07) heading west. From here "The Crossing Road" heads east toward the Silver Peak Range and the Mineral Ridge Mine. Follow the Trail Canyon Road six miles west, then follow a poor dirt road left to a campsite by Chiatovich Creek (6,500 ft). Four-wheel drive is recommended.

*Route:* Cross the stream and walk up flats to the great ridge of the peak. The first 600 feet are a rather steep climb, but from there it is a gentle slope to the summit. Anticipate 2,900 feet of elevation gain and six miles round-trip.

## THE COWHORN MOUNTAINS

The Cowhorn Mountains are a subrange of the Inyo Mountains, and consist of the hills between the Westgard Pass Road and the Death Valley Road (that heads toward Eureka Valley). Rounded hills topped by scattered pinyon and juniper woodlands define the summits, and hiking is easy in this area. Primitive camping is available in the Cowhorn Mountains and all minimum impact camping methods should be applied here.

### PEAK 8,963 FT (2,732 M) AND PEAK 8,924 FT (2,720 M)

*Maps:* Cowhorn Valley (CA) 7.5-minute (1:24,000 scale) topographic map; Bishop 1:100,000 scale metric topographic map; Inyo National Forest Map; Automobile Club of Southern California (AAA) Eastern Sierra map

*Best Time to Climb:* Late April through November

*Approach:* From Big Pine, California follow Highway 168 approximately

2.4 miles to the Death Valley Road (Forest Service Road 9S18, also known as the Waucoba-Saline Valley Road) and turn right (southeast). Follow the Death Valley Road 14.6 miles, passing through the narrows of Devil's Gate to a point approximately two miles east of the Saline Valley Junction. An indistinct turnoff leads northwest up a canyon to a valley. The road is in very bad condition, and it is best to park here (7,100 ft).

*Route:* For Peak 8,963 feet, follow the road up the canyon, over a low saddle, and down into a larger valley (slightly over a mile). The peak is to the east at the head of the valley. A ridge leads directly to the summit, but passes over several broken and loose slate outcroppings. If walking from the Waucoba Road, anticipate nine miles round-trip with 2,400 feet of elevation gain. Your hike may be considerably shorter depending on the distance you're able to drive in. For Peak 8,924 feet, one can follow ridges from Peak 8,963 feet. The peak lies three miles to the northwest and is clearly visible. A roadway leads to within a mile of the top, and an easy route may be taken to the summit assuming you can drive that far. Otherwise, anticipate a very long hike from the Waucoba Road.

## THE INYO MOUNTAINS

More rugged and desert-like than the neighboring White Mountains, the Inyo Mountains were an important area for the ancestors of the Owens Valley Paiute who gave these mountains their name, Inyo, meaning "dwelling place of the great spirit." The 9,000-foot high eastern scarp of the range as seen from Saline Valley presents one of the boldest mountain fronts in North America, with similar topographic relief to the Sierra Nevada, but in a fraction of the horizontal distance. Traveling in the canyon bottoms can be extremely rough and usually will require a degree of rock climbing experience to negotiate the many dry waterfalls. Once on the crest of the range, the landscape changes to gently rolling terrain, with the exception of the north and south ridgeline of Keynot Peak.

The lower slopes of the mountains are covered by desert scrub typical for the region. At higher elevations, the climber will encounter pinyon-juniper woodlands, and groves of limber pine. The Inyo Mountains also contain some of the largest bristlecone groves in California. Wildlife includes bighorn sheep, deer, coyote and mountain lions. A few black bears reside in the Inyo Mountains Wilderness.

Unlike the White Mountains, surface water is scarce on both sides of the range, and the optimum time to climb many of the peaks with longer routes is during late spring to early summer when scattered snow patches linger and provide a source of water. This is a very rugged region. Access in the Mount Inyo, Keynot Peak, New York Butte area is limited requiring either some very long approach hikes or axle-busting driving along rough jeep roads. In the Waucoba region, the roads are more prevalent but still require four-wheel drive in many places. Camping in the Inyos is entirely in primitive sites, and the usual minimum impact camping methods apply here. Also note that the regulations concerning bear-proofing your camp-site apply within the Inyo Mountains Wilderness. Specifically, the wilderness was included under the Inyo National Forest Order #04-97-1 that prohibits possessing or storing any food or refuse unless it is stored in a bear-proof container or in another manner designed to keep bears from gaining access to the food or refuse.

Food, lodging and supplies are available in any of the Owens Valley towns (from Lone Pine to Bishop). If visiting the east side of the Inyo Mountains from Saline Valley, be sure to gas up in either Olancha, Lone Pine or Big Pine. There are no facilities in the Saline Valley. For further information on the area, contact the Bureau of Land Management offices in Bishop or Ridgecrest, and the Inyo National Forest office in Bishop.

### CHOCOLATE MOUNTAIN (7,703 FT; 2,348 M)

Chocolate Mountain, also known as Piper Mountain, is a wonderful desert peak with some of the finest desert views in the area. Situated as a "triple divide peak" separating Deep Springs, Eureka and Fish Lake Valleys, the hiker can while away the hours gazing from the summit upon the Eureka Dunes, Sierra Nevada and Inyo Mountain crests, and off into the wilds of Nevada. The peak is the main attraction of the newly created Piper Mountain Wilderness. The area is noteworthy in that it contains the northernmost stands of Joshua trees in California. The lower sagebrush slopes of the mountain give way to scattered pinyon and juniper near the summit, providing some welcome shade on a warm day.

*Maps:* Chocolate Mountain (CA) 7.5-minute (1:24,000 scale) topographic map; Last Chance Range 1:100,000 scale metric topographic map; Automobile Club of Southern California (AAA) Death Valley National Park map

*Best Time to Climb:* September through June

*Approach:* From Big Pine, follow Highway 168 into the Inyo Mountains, crossing Westgard Pass and dropping into Deep Springs Valley. The highway straightens out across Deep Springs Valley then switchbacks up to Gilbert Pass (a little more than 30 miles from Big Pine) which separates Deep Springs Valley from Fish Lake Valley. At Gilbert Pass, follow a dirt road 0.4 miles south, staying right until a wilderness marker bars entry to a dirt track heading right toward the peak (6,400 ft). All vehicles should be able to access this road end.

*Route:* Follow the dirt track, passing between the peak and a low hill, then cross-country, eventually reaching a rocky dirt track that heads up a draw on the mountain's north slopes. The track is followed to the summit plateau, marked by a sparse juniper woodland. A foot trail leaves the track and reaches the summit. Anticipate four miles round-trip with 1,400 feet of elevation gain.

### ANDREWS MOUNTAIN (9,460 FT; 2,883 M)

This, the northernmost peak along the main axis of the Inyo Mountains, is quite easy to access and climb. Its summit is a fine place from which to take in the view of the Sierra Nevada to the west, and the northern Inyo Mountains. For those who haven't climbed Waucoba or Squaw, this is a fine roost from which to plan out routes on those two fine desert peaks.

*Maps:* Waucoba Mountain (CA) 7.5-minute (1:24,000 scale) topographic map; Bishop 1:100,000 scale metric topographic map; Inyo National Forest Map; Automobile Club of Southern California (AAA) Death Valley National Park map

*Best Time to Climb:* May through November

*Approach:* From Big Pine, follow Highway 168 approximately 2.4 miles east to the Death Valley Road (Forest Service Road 9S18), also known as the Waucoba-Saline Valley Road) and turn right (southeast). Some 11 miles east, a dirt road branches to the right. This road forks at 0.1 miles. Take the right fork known as the Hines Road (Forest Service Road 9S15). Follow this about five miles, taking a left fork near the ridge to an old mine located in a saddle at 8,800 feet. Two-wheel drive with high clearance is okay.

*Route:* The peak is an easy hike a mile to the northeast, with less than a thousand feet of elevation gain round-trip.

*Alternate:* This rounded peak is accessible from any side from other roads in the area including the Squaw Flat Road.

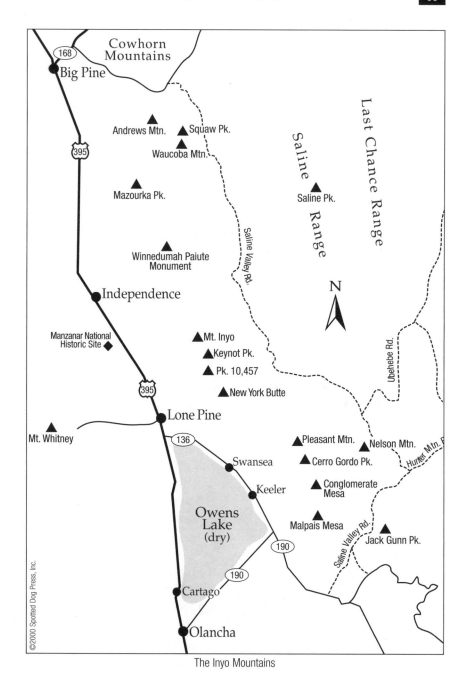

The Inyo Mountains

©2000 Spotted Dog Press, Inc.

## WAUCOBA MOUNTAIN (11,123 FT; 3,390 M)

Waucoba Mountain, the highpoint of the Inyo Mountains, is aptly named. The name "Waucoba" comes from the Paiute word meaning round, and this describes the peak perfectly. It truly is a rounded giant. The broad flat summit area provides fine views of the distant Sierra Nevada, and would make a fine spot for an overnight stay.

*Maps:* Waucoba Mountain and Waucoba Spring East (CA) 7.5-minute (1:24,000 scale) topographic maps; Bishop and Last Chance Range 1:100,000 scale metric topographic maps; Inyo National Forest Map; Automobile Club of Southern California (AAA) Death Valley National Park map

*Best Time to Climb:* May through October

*Approach:* Four-wheel drive is recommended for this route. From Big Pine, follow Highway 168 approximately 2.4 miles east to the Death Valley Road (Forest Service Road 9S18, also known as the Waucoba-Saline Valley Road) and turn right (southeast). Some 11 miles east, a dirt road branches to the right. This road forks at 0.1 miles. Take the left fork (Forest Service Road 9S14) and drive 3.4 miles on rough dirt to a saddle. Continue 0.6 miles past the saddle and bear left, then left again after another 0.2 miles onto Forest Service Road 10S07. Continue approximately 1.9 miles down the canyon to "The Narrows," 6.2 miles from the Death Valley Road. The road continues southwest 2.2 miles to a fork in Squaw Flat. Turn left here regaining Road 9S14, bearing left at a fork after 1.1 miles, and continuing another 0.8 miles to a water trough. Park here (8,000 ft). Road 10S07 may be bypassed by following Road 9S14 the entire distance to Squaw Flat.

*Route:* Head east across the sagebrush and up the draw between Points 8,829 feet and 9,143 feet. Once at the head of this draw continue southeast up the steep ridge to the summit. Once the upper slopes of Waucoba are reached, a cool breeze accompanied by pleasant pine forest will make you forget about the hot dry slopes below. Approximately six miles and 3,200 feet of elevation gain, round-trip.

*Alternate Approach and Route:* This is the better route for those who do not have four-wheel drive vehicles. From Highway 168 and the Death Valley Road, follow the Death Valley Road 13 miles to the dirt Saline Valley Road (Forest Service Road 9S01). Turn south on the Saline Valley Road and follow it 12.5 miles. Turn right (west) and follow the poor dirt road as far as practicable. From the roadend, hike southwest through pinyons

Squaw Peak (left) and Waucoba (right) from Andrews Mountain. Photo: Andy Zdon

then directly up Waucoba's northeast ridge. If you start out climbing a bare talus slope, you're on the right track. Anticipate five miles round-trip with 3,800 feet of elevation gain.

### SQUAW PEAK (10,358 FT; 3,161 M)

The more pointed, though lower neighbor of Waucoba Mountain is a prominent and desirable Inyo Mountains summit.

*Maps:* Waucoba Mountain and Waucoba Spring (CA) 7.5-minute (1:24,000 scale) topographic maps; Bishop and Last Chance Range 1:100,000 scale metric topographic maps; Inyo National Forest Map; Automobile Club of Southern California (AAA) Death Valley National Park map

*Best Time to Climb:* May through October

*Approach:* As for Waucoba Mountain.

*Route:* Squaw is usually combined with a climb of Waucoba Mountain. As described earlier climb Waucoba, then from its summit head north to a saddle, climbing Squaw's south ridge to the summit. Descend to Squaw Flat without reclimbing Waucoba. If climbing Squaw only, anticipate five miles round-trip with 2,400 feet of elevation gain. If climbing in a tandem with Waucoba, add another two to three miles and 800 feet of elevation gain to the Waucoba round-trip statistics.

## MAZOURKA PEAK (9,209 FT; 2,808 M)

Of the "drive-up" peaks listed in this guide, this peak holds probably the best views. The Sierra Nevada stands as a serrated spine on the skyline, with the broad, deep gulf of the Owens Valley below. On the summit, you are likely to find clumps of Mojave mound cactus, and dwarf plants such as globe buckwheat, mat sandwort, dwarf daisy, and a low mountain onion. I recommend this peak to those who have never climbed a desert peak. It is one of the few drive-ups that provides the kind of views and serenity that desert peaks have to offer.

*Maps:* Mazourka Peak (CA) 7.5-minute (1:24,000 scale) topographic map; Mount Whitney 1:100,000 scale metric topographic map; Inyo National Forest Map; Automobile Club of Southern California (AAA) Eastern Sierra map

*Best Time to Visit:* April through November

*Approach and Route:* From the south end of Independence, head east on the signed and paved Mazourka Road, crossing the Owens River. The road eventually turns to graded dirt (Forest Service Road 13S05), and makes a northward bend up Mazourka Canyon. The peak is visible to the north with its repeater antennae. Continue up the Mazourka Canyon road to Badger Flat, then up the rough service road (Forest Service Road 11S01) to the summit. A two-wheel drive with good clearance should be able to drive to the summit.

## WINNEDUMAH PAIUTE MONUMENT (8,369 FT; 2,552 M)

This 80-foot slender pinnacle of granite along the crest of the Inyos, is visible from near the Oak Creek-Sawmill Creek areas north of Independence in the Owens Valley. The pinnacle is the source of Native American lore. One of the tales, as described in Genny Schumacher's book *The Deepest Valley* goes like this:

*"When Digger Indians crossed the Sierra to raid the Paiute's hunting grounds, they fought a terrible battle lasting many days. Defeated, the Paiute fled—some hiding in caves at Blackrock, others escaping into the Inyos. When the exhausted Winnedumah reached the Inyo crest, he stopped to wait for his brother. While he prayed to the Great Spirit on behalf of his beaten people, the earth shook and thundered, frightening the Diggers so that they retreated from the Valley; the faithful Winnedumah was turned into a pillar of stone that still watches over his people."*

*Maps:* Bee Springs Canyon (CA) 7.5-minute (1:24,000 scale) topographic map; Mount Whitney 1:100,000 scale metric topographic map; Inyo National

Doug Bear and Randall Danta preparing to descend Winnedumah Paiute Monument.
Photo: Tina Bowman

Forest Map; Automobile Club of Southern California (AAA) Eastern Sierra map

*Best Time to Climb:* Spring and Fall

*Approach:* From the south end of Independence, head east on the signed and paved Mazourka Road, crossing the Owens River. The road eventually turns to graded dirt (Forest Service Road 13S05) and makes a northward bend up Mazourka Canyon. Park below Barrel Spring, 12 miles from Highway 395. This approach is accessible to all vehicles.

*Route:* Follow a track that heads up to the spring, then southeast about two miles. Continue another three miles east to the crest following use trails. The pinnacle will be in view during your hike. The final climb is a 70-foot mid-Class 5 rock climb. Anticipate ten miles round-trip with about 3,000 feet of elevation to reach the pinnacle.

*Directions for the remaining peaks along the south end of the Inyo Mountains are given assuming a base at Lone Pine. The hiker can also bypass Lone Pine by taking Highway 190 east from Olancha. However, it is recommended that the additional mileage to Lone Pine be undertaken to get supplies, road information, maps, see Mount Whitney, and visit the Interagency Visitor Center.*

### MOUNT INYO (10,975 FT; 3,346 M)

Mount Inyo is a classic desert peak, with no easy way up. To the west, the great gulf of the Owens Valley opens up below you, 8,000 feet below the summit. Beyond, the Sierra Nevada crest rises 10,000 feet to the summit of Mount Whitney. To the east, the salt flats of Saline Valley lie 9,000 feet below, separated from Mount Inyo's summit, by some of the most rugged canyons in the United States. For the desert explorer, this is paradise.

*Maps:* New York Butte and Union Wash (CA) 7.5-minute (1:24,000 scale) topographic maps; Mount Whitney and Saline Valley 1:100,000 scale metric topographic maps; Automobile Club of Southern California (AAA) Eastern Sierra or Death Valley National Park maps

*Best Time to Climb:* May through June, late September through November (all summer if starting from along the crest)

*Approach:* From Lone Pine on Highway 395, drive to the north end of town and turn right (east) on the paved Lone Pine Narrow Gauge Road. Follow the Lone Pine Narrow Gauge Road three miles to the well-graded Dolomite

Road. Turn north (left), and drive 4.7 miles to a very rough dirt road heading east, up Union Wash, toward the Inyo Mountains. Follow this rough dirt road 1.8 miles to a fork. Two-wheel drive vehicles bear right 0.3 miles to the end of the road (4,560 ft). Four-wheel drive vehicles can bear left and continue another mile to a road head at 5,500 feet. If you have a couple of hours to spend at the trailhead (if you reach the trailhead the day before your climb), investigate the ridge that meets Union Wash due south of the four-wheel drive trailhead. A 15-foot thick zone of Triassic-age fossiliferous gray siltstone and limestone contains fossil ammonoids called Meekoceras. An ammonoid is a creature that resembled a nautilus. With a little luck, you may find a nice specimen.

*Route:* From the four-wheel drive parking area, follow the reddish-brown ridge on the right (south) side of the wash, up steep, scree-covered slopes for more than 3,300 feet to a use trail east of Point 9,155 feet. Cross the ridge about 100 feet above Point 9,155 feet, and up a shallow draw to a saddle on the Inyo Crest at about 10,100 feet. En route, you will pass Bedsprings Camp, a good spot for a dry bivouac (unless snow is present providing a source of water). From the saddle, head north for about a mile to the summit of Inyo. From the four-wheel drive road end anticipate 5,500 feet of gain with eight miles round-trip. From the two-wheel drive road end anticipate 6,500 feet of elevation gain with ten miles round-trip.

*Alternate Route:* From the four-wheel drive road end, an old miner's trail bypasses the reddish- brown ridge, and heads up the wash about 0.5 miles to two large cairns at the base of a ridge to the right. The miner's trail then switchbacks up the steep slopes directly to Bedsprings Camp.

*Alternate Route 2:* Mount Inyo can be climbed as part of a car shuttle (four-wheel drive only) and traverse of the Southern Inyo Mountains starting at the Burgess Mine (or from a flat parking area about a mile north of Cerro Gordo along the road to the Burgess Mine) and following the crest northward, then down to a car shuttle at the normal road end. The road is narrow and hair raising in parts. Memorable are the stretches when the vehicle swings out over a several hundred foot drop on the northbound driver's side. Passengers have been known to get out of the car and walk while the driver ventures on alone.

*Alternate Route 3:* In 1987, Randall Danta and Wynne Benti climbed Mt. Inyo from the north side of Union Wash, and reported a stretch of Class 3.

Mt. Inyo (left) and Keynot Peak (right) with Union Wash in center. Photo: Andy Zdon

### KEYNOT PEAK (11,101 FT; 3,384 M)

Keynot Peak is the second highest peak in the Inyos, and has also been called Mount Monarch and Keynote Peak. All of these names were derived from mines lower on the peak. The peak is usually climbed in conjunction with it's neighbor to the north (Mount Inyo).

*Maps:* New York Butte and Union Wash (CA) 7.5-minute (1:24,000 scale) topographic maps; Mount Whitney and Saline Valley 1:100,000 scale metric topographic maps; Automobile Club of Southern California (AAA) Eastern Sierra or Death Valley National Park maps

*Best Time to Climb:* May through June, late September through November (all summer if starting from along the crest)

*Approach:* Same as for Mount Inyo.

*Route:* Climb to the Inyo Crest as described for Mount Inyo. Upon reaching the crest, head southeast up the ridge to Keynot Peak. Stay east where large blocks hinder progress, then cross-over to the west side of the crest for the finale. Keynot Peak adds another two miles and 1,000 feet of elevation gain round-trip when combined with Mount Inyo. If climbed alone from this route, the elevation gain and round-trip distance is about the same as for Mount Inyo.

*Alternate Route:* From the junction of the Lone Pine Narrow Gauge Road and Dolomite Road, drive north (left) 1.8 miles to the French Spring Road. Turn right and follow the French Spring Road 1.8 miles to roadend at 5,200 feet, or as far as practicable. An old miner's trail leads up the canyon to Forgotten Pass, south of Keynot Peak. The miner's trail continues over the crest to Saline Valley, but before doing so at the pass, it meets the faint use-trail which comes along the crest from New York Butte to the south. Turn left and head north along Keynot's south summit ridge, bypassing rocky sections along the way. Anticipate eight miles round-trip with 6,000 feet of elevation gain.

*Alternate Route 2:* Keynot Peak can be climbed as part of a Cerro Gordo to Mount Inyo traverse as described above.

### Peak 10,457 ft (3,187 m)

This peak lies between Keynot Peak and New York Butte, and is most easily climbed by ridge- running between the two peaks.

*Maps:* New York Butte (CA) 7.5-minute (1:24,000 scale) topographic map; Saline Valley 1:100,000 scale metric topographic map; Automobile Club of Southern California (AAA) Eastern Sierra or Death Valley National Park maps

*Best Time to Climb:* May through June, Late September through November (all summer if starting from along crest)

*Route:* This peak is normally climbed as part of a Cerro Gordo to Mount Inyo traverse as described above. If climbing this peak alone, follow the alternate route for Keynot Peak to Forgotten Pass, then head south along the crest to the summit.

### New York Butte (10,668 ft; 3,252 m)

New York Butte is another desert classic with fine views of Saline Valley and across the Owens Valley to the Sierra Nevada. The Burgess Mine, about a mile south of the peak, makes for a great campsite. The mine which produced silver, lead, zinc and gold operated around 1910.

*Maps:* New York Butte and Dolomite (CA) 7.5-minute (1:24,000 scale) topographic maps; Saline Valley 1:100,000 scale metric topographic map; Automobile Club of Southern California (AAA) Eastern Sierra or Death Valley National Park maps

*Best Time to Climb:* May through June, late September through November

(all summer if starting from along the crest)

*Approach:* From Lone Pine on Highway 395, drive to the north end of town and turn right (east) on the paved Lone Pine Narrow Gauge Road. Follow Lone Pine Narrow Gauge Road three miles to the well-graded Dolomite Road. Turn south (right) 0.3 miles then left onto a poor dirt road (four-wheel drive recommended) 1.8 miles into Long John Canyon (4,640 ft).

*Route:* From the road-end, head up the ridge that runs directly northeast then southeast up the mountain. Anticipate eight miles round-trip with 6,300 feet of elevation gain.

*Alternate Routes:* New York Butte can be climbed from the Burgess Mine (south of the peak) with a round-trip distance of about two miles and 1,000 feet of elevation gain. So why is this not the primary route? Getting to the Burgess Mine involves either a harrowing drive up (down is worse) the famed Swansea Grade (not recommended!) or a drive along an airy, narrow jeep trail from Cerro Gordo. Either route is for experienced four-wheel drivers only. Check with the Inyo National Forest office in Lone Pine for current conditions and directions.

### "PLEASANT MOUNTAIN" (9,690 FT; 3,178 M)

Besides having fine views in all directions, the grove of limber pines on the north side of the peak adds a nice touch to this peak. Much of the west slope of this mountain is comprised of dark gray slopes of the Mississippian-age Chainman Shale. This gives way to Tin Mountain limestone at the summit. The impressive cliffs on the east slope are dolomites of the Lost Burro Formation, more widely known in the Death Valley area. The hike from the west is up the dip slope of these formations.

*Maps:* Cerro Gordo Peak (CA) 7.5-minute (1:24,000 scale) topographic map; Saline Valley 1:100,000 scale metric topographic map; Automobile Club of Southern California (AAA) Death Valley National Park map

*Best Time to Climb:* April through November

*Approach:* From the south end of Lone Pine, take Highway 136 south 12.6 miles to Keeler. The Highway 136 turnoff is marked by the Interagency Visitor Center (well worth the stop). Just south of Keeler, a signed dirt road heads east up to the old mining town of Cerro Gordo. The road is well-graded but quite steep, and four-wheel drive, though not required, is handy for traction. The author has driven the road in a Volkswagen Bug and other two-wheel drive vehicles in low gear without any serious difficulty. The road is graded, and high clearance is usually not necessary. Follow the Cerro Gordo Road 7.5 miles to the historic town site. Just past the town, you'll reach a saddle at 8,200 feet. Park here, making sure that you heed all "No Trespassing" signs. Much of the Cerro Gordo area is private property. It is also possible to drive from Cerro Gordo an addi-

Eastern escarpment of Pleasant Mountain from Cerro Gordo Peak. Photo: Andy Zdon

tional mile or so along the "airy" road heading north to the Burgess Mine where a flat area can be used for parking.

*Route:* From the saddle, hike north to a fork in the road, and take the right branch, passing a locked gate, and continuing another 1.5 miles to the crest of the Inyos at 9,080 feet. Leave the road and hike north along the crest 1.5 miles to the summit. Anticipate six miles round-trip with 1,600 feet of elevation gain.

*Alternate Route:* If driving the road between Cerro Gordo and the Burgess Mine, the peak is an easy 700-foot scramble from the northwest. Getting

Cerro Gordo Peak and townsite. Photo: Andy Zdon

to this point along the road is the difficult part, and is more hair-raising than most of the hikes in this book.

### CERRO GORDO PEAK (9,188 FT; 2,801 M)

This is the prominent peak that provides a backdrop for the old mining camp of Cerro Gordo. The name Cerro Gordo, ("fat hill" in Spanish) was named during the 1860's by a party of Mexican prospectors who discovered the future legendary silver deposit there. Standing on the summit of this peak, one has a bird's-eye view of this formerly important California mining center. During the later part of the nineteenth century, considerable silver and lead were mined at Cerro Gordo. Later in the early twentieth century, the emphasis was on zinc. The minerals were found in limestone replaced by mineralization, and in veins adjacent to a body of granite. The summit of Cerro Gordo Peak is comprised of Mississippian-age Tin Mountain limestone, like its neighbor Pleasant.

*Maps:* Cerro Gordo Peak (CA) 7.5-minute (1:24,000 scale) topographic map; Saline Valley 1:100,000 scale metric topographic map; Automobile Club of Southern California (AAA) Death Valley National Park map

*Best Time to Climb:* All Year

*Approach:* Same as for Pleasant Mountain.

*Route:* From the saddle scramble up the peak to the southeast.

### CONGLOMERATE MESA (7,700+ FT; 2,347 M)

This rounded summit provides interesting hiking leading up to rolling slopes, dotted with Joshua trees and sagebrush.

*Maps:* Keeler, Santa Rosa Flat, Cerro Gordo Peak and Nelson Range (CA) 7.5-minute (1:24,000 scale) topographic maps; Darwin Hills and Saline Valley 1:100,000 scale metric topographic maps; Automobile Club of Southern California (AAA) Death Valley National Park map

*Best Time to Climb:* October through May

*Approach:* From the junction of Highways 395 and 190 in Olancha, drive 14.7 miles east on Highway 190 to the junction of Highways 190 and 136. Turn right (Highway 190) and continue 17 miles to the Saline Valley Road. Turn north (left) on the Saline Valley Road which is alternating paved and dirt. Be careful for washouts on this road. Drive 8.2 miles to a fork. Take the left fork (White Mountain Talc Road), and go 3.8 miles to another junction. Stay left and continue on the White Mountain Talc Road as it crosses over a pass to a dirt road on the left. Follow the dirt road, which heads directly for the mesa, about 1.5 miles and park (about 6,200 ft).

*Route:* Hike up a wash to the mesa cap, then scramble to the top of the mesa. Anticipate five miles round-trip with 1,500 feet of elevation gain.

*Alternate Approach and Route:* An interesting, though longer (depending on your starting point), approach is to drive to Keeler on the east side of Owens Lake. A little over a mile south of Keeler, a dirt track heads east toward the mountains, passing the carcass of an old wrecked car, and reaching a fork in about 2.4 miles. Take the right fork and continue as far as practicable with your vehicle. The track passes through a badlands of sorts, as it winds its way towards the mesa. The track can be followed to about 6,800 feet. From here, the summit is about two miles to the north-west and 900 feet higher.

## MALPAIS MESA (7,731 FT; 2,356 M)

This is one of the author's favorite hikes in this guide. Malpais Mesa is within the newly-created 32,000-acre Malpais Mesa Wilderness. The hike involves hiking through red and black volcanic rocks to the Joshua tree-covered mesa top with views across the Owens Valley to Mount Whitney. This hike provides an outstanding desert experience. The name "Malpais" means "badland" and refers to its rough appearance, a result of the mesa's volcanic origin, a series of stacked basalt flows. The starting point of the hike, the Santa Rosa Mine, holds a place of distinction among California mines. It was the eighth largest lead producer in the state with past produc-tion amounting to 12 million pounds of lead, 490,000 pounds of copper, 4,000 pounds of zinc and 427,000 ounces of silver. What is surprising, is that one would expect a mine capable of this production to be much larger. Today, the long-abandoned mine site provides nice flat camping locations in a wind-protected canyon.

*Maps:* Santa Rosa Flat and Keeler (CA) 7.5-minute (1:24,000 scale) topo-graphic maps; Darwin Hills 1:100,000 scale metric topographic map; Automobile Club of Southern California (AAA) Death Valley National Park map

*Best Time to Climb:* October through May

*Approach:* From Olancha, follow Highway 190 east, turning right at the T-junction with Highway 136, and continue ten miles east to a desert road (BLM Road S111) heading north. Follow this major dirt road, staying left at a fork, to the Santa Rosa Mine, about ten miles from Highway 190. Two-wheel drive vehicles with good clearance should have no problem reaching the mine. With care, most cars should be able to reach the mine (about 6,400 ft).

*Route:* From the Santa Rosa Mine, follow a bulldozed track above the mine, and then scramble up to the mesa rim. From here, it is easy walking north amid a wonderful Joshua tree forest with expansive views west to the Mount Whitney area of the Sierra Nevada. The actual summit is a pointed outcrop on the north side of the mesa. Anticipate six miles round-trip with 1,300 feet of elevation gain.

# THE NELSON RANGE

The Nelson Range is a small subsidiary range separated from the Inyo Mountains by Lee Flat. Joshua trees sporadically cover the lower slopes of the range, while higher slopes support a pinyon-juniper woodland. When winter snows cover the Lee Flat area and surrounding peaks, the place becomes a magical winter wonderland where the silhouettes of Joshua trees seem to dance against the desert's snowy backdrop. There is fine primitive camping along the Saline Valley and Lee Flat Roads. Supplies and lodging are available in Lone Pine. The range was named in honor of Edward William Nelson who explored this area with the Death Valley Expedition of 1891.

## "NELSON MOUNTAIN" (7,696 FT; 2,346 M)

There are great views from the summit of this peak. To the north, one looks out across the vast Saline Valley and the Inyos looming over it to the west. The Racetrack Playa is visible as are Telescope Peak, the Argus and Coso Ranges, and the Sierra Nevada peaking over low points along the Inyo crest. On a clear day, even Charleston Peak near Las Vegas is visible. The winter day we climbed the peak, the snow was about two-feet deep on the summit, and deep enough on the way up to make some of the talus work a little easier. Although the hike begins in Paleozoic-age Bird Spring formation limestones, the bulk of the mountain is comprised of quartz monzonite. The summit of this peak is marked with the benchmark "Galena," for the ore mineral prospected by the vanished miners whose deserted cabins and lead-silver ore workings are found along the peak's lower slopes.

*Maps:* Nelson Range (CA) 7.5-minute (1:24,000 scale) topographic map; Darwin Hills 1:100,000 scale metric topographic map; Automobile Club of Southern California (AAA) Death Valley National Park map

*Best Time to Climb:* October through May

*Approach:* From the junction of Highways 395 and 190 in Olancha, drive 14.7 miles east on Highway 190 to the junction of Highways 190 and 136. Turn right (Highway 190) and continue 17 miles to the Saline Valley Road. Turn north (left) on the Saline Valley Road which is alternating paved and dirt. Be careful for washouts on this road. Drive 8.2 miles to a fork. Take the left fork (White Mountain Talc Road), and go 3.8 miles to another junction. Turn right and follow the dirt road (four-wheel drive recommended) northward through Joshua trees 3.5 miles to another fork. Turn right and drive a half mile to an old cabin (5,500 ft).

*Route:* Climb any likely looking ridge to the east to the summit ridge amid pinyons. The open summit is to the southeast. When descending, stay on the ridges as the gullies are loose and miserable. Anticipate two miles round-trip with 2,200 feet of elevation gain.

### "JACK GUNN PEAK" (5,594 FT; 1,705 M)

Named for a former Confederate soldier and owner-operator of the Minnietta Mine in Panamint Valley, the Eastern California Museum in Independence has in its collection, a music box once owned by Gunn. This small peak is not in the Nelson Range, but in an area to the south called the Santa Rosa Hills. In fact, the peak is not noteworthy as a primary destination, but has nice views and can be combined with any of the peaks in the area. The peak is unnamed on the topographic map.

*Maps:* Lee Wash (CA) 7.5-minute (1:24,000 scale) topographic map; Darwin Hills 1:100,000 scale metric topographic map; Automobile Club of Southern California (AAA) Death Valley National Park map

*Best Time to Climb:* October through May

*Approach:* From the junction of Highways 395 and 190 in Olancha, drive 14.7 miles east on Highway 190 to the junction of Highways 190 and 136. Turn right (Highway 190) and continue 17 miles to the Saline Valley Road. Turn north (left) on the Saline Valley Road which is alternating paved and dirt. Be careful for washouts on this road. Follow that road six miles to where a dirt road turns right. Follow that rough dirt road about one mile, passing an abandoned mine (the Lee Mines), and park. Two-wheel drive vehicles with good clearance are recommended.

*Route:* The summit is about one mile to the southeast.

## THE COSO RANGE

South of Owens Lake is a group of predominantly volcanic peaks, the northwestern end of the Coso Range. In fact, the name "Coso" is from a Shoshonean dialect meaning "fire," a reference to the volcanic features in the area. It is interesting to note that the geologic derivation of these mountains was clear to the early Native American people that inhabited the region. A number of old mining roads thread their way among these mountains, but are often blocked by the Naval Air Weapons Station. Their summits provide great views of the Sierra Nevada and Owens Valley.

The Coso Range is a typical Basin and Range-style desert range. These mountains are primarily composed of Tertiary to Recent-age volcanic rocks, overlying granitic and metasedimentary rocks. When one stands on the summit of one of the peaks surrounding Joshua Flat, they will look down upon the vast expanse of the Owens Valley, but what will really catch the eye are the fabulous badlands along the Coso Range escarpment. These badlands (Vermillion Canyon has the best exposures) are comprised of a series of rocks called the Coso Mountains formation. These rocks represent a period during which deposition of inland erosional debris occurred. Within these deposits, fossils of hyenid dogs, horses, mastedons, camels, and peccaries have been found.

Ed Zdon on the way to Joshua Mountain. Photo: Andy Zdon

Most of the peaks listed here, fall within the 50,000-acre Coso Range Wilderness. At lower elevations, creosote scrub is present with Joshua trees and a few junipers the most common larger vegetation types at the higher elevations. The mountains are occasionally visited by bighorn sheep and mule deer. Additionally, wild horses and burros roam these rolling mountains. While visiting the area, a hike up Centennial Canyon is recommended to observe some of the best petroglyphs in the region. Camping in the northern Coso Range is primitive so all the minimum impact camping methods apply. Lodging and supplies are available in Lone Pine and Olancha. The area is managed by the Bureau of Land Management district offices in Ridgecrest and Riverside.

Desert Summits

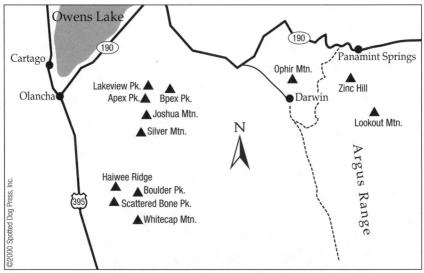

The peaks of the Coso and the northern Argus Range

## "JOSHUA MOUNTAIN" (7,122 FT; 2,171 M), "LAKEVIEW PEAK" (6,562 FT; 2,001 M), "APEX PEAK" (7,191 FT; 2,192 M), "BPEX PEAK" (7,256 FT; 2,212 M)

These peaks form the west and northern rim of Joshua Flat, one of the more scenic areas within the Coso Wilderness. None of these peaks are named on the topographic maps.

*Maps:* Centennial Canyon (CA) 7.5-minute (1:24,000 scale) topographic map; Darwin Hills 1:100,000 scale metric topographic map; Automobile Club of Southern California (AAA) Death Valley National Park map

*Best Time to Climb:* October through May

*Approach:* From Olancha, follow Highway 190 eastward to its junction with Highway 136. Turn right (south) and continue ten miles on Highway 190 to a dirt road that heads south toward the Cosos. Follow this dirt road southward 1.5 miles to a corral and take the right fork. Continue another 3.8 miles, staying right at a junction, to the road end at Lower Centennial Spring, marked by a mine shack. The Coso Wilderness boundary is within a few hundred yards. Most cars should be able to drive to within one or two miles of the mine shack, although a two-wheel drive vehicle with good clearance is all that is needed to reach the shack.

*Route:* Follow the unnamed wash west of Centennial Canyon that heads southwest. This wash is crossed just before reaching the cabin.

Follow the wash to its end where an old dirt track heads west. The dirt track is followed to Joshua Flat. From Joshua Flat, Joshua Mountain is the rounded peak to the west. Apex Peak is reached by following a track that ends at mine workings on Apex's south ridge. Apex Peak is connected to Lakeview Peak by an easy ridge. Bpex Peak is reached by following an old mining road that crosses a saddle immediately north of the peak. Peak 7,130 feet north of Bpex, is known as Cpex Peak, but it is hardly a separate peak. All of these peaks should be reachable in one very long day. Anticipate 17 to 18 miles round-trip with 3,300 feet of elevation gain round-trip. These summits all make great individual destinations if a shorter hike is desired. Hikes involving climbing these peaks individually will be on the order of 10+ miles round-trip with 2,000+ feet of elevation gain.

### SILVER MOUNTAIN (7,495 FT; 2,285 M)

This is the highest peak in the Coso Range Wilderness, and within the open portions of the range. This volcanic peak was named as a result of the mining activity in the area, although little activity occurred on the mountain itself.

*Maps:* Centennial Canyon and Upper Centennial Flat (CA) 7.5-minute (1:24,000 scale) topographic maps; Darwin Hills 1:100,000 scale metric topographic map; Automobile Club of Southern California (AAA) Death Valley National Park map

*Best Time to Climb:* October through May

*Approach:* From Olancha, drive south about two miles, then east on the Cactus Flat Road (well-graded). This is a good graded road to a triangle-junction at 7.2 miles from Highway 395 at the west end of Cactus Flat. Take the left fork. Numerous tracks wander over the flats and with four-wheel drive, one should be able to drive to the mouth of Lacey Canyon and the wilderness boundary.

*Route:* Follow the canyon east then north toward Silver Mountain. A small dry lake will be passed before reaching Silver Mountain. Anticipate nine miles round-trip with 2,800 feet of elevation gain.

*Alternate Approach and Route:* Follow the driving directions as for Joshua, Lakeview, Apex and Bpex Peaks. Hike to Joshua Flat as described above. The peak is directly southwest. Anticipate 12 miles round-trip with about 2,400 feet of elevation gain (depending on the route chosen).

## HAIWEE RIDGE (5,952 FT; 1,184 M)

This peak, also known as Jurassic Peak, lies directly east of South Haiwee Reservoir, and provides excellent views of the reservoir area, and northwest to Olancha Peak in the Sierra Nevada. Haiwee Ridge is easily combined with Scattered Bone Peak to the south. The peak is named for the area called "Haiwai" which was the meadow area inundated by Haiwee Reservoir. "Haiwai" is the Paiute word for "dove" in reference to the wild pigeons that inhabit the area. The name's spelling was changed to Haiwee in acceptance of the usage of the Whitney Survey map for the area.

*Maps:* Haiwee Reservoir (CA) 7.5-minute (1:24,000 scale) topographic map; Darwin Hills 1:100,000 scale metric topographic map; Automobile Club of Southern California (AAA) Death Valley National Park map

*Best Time to Climb:* October through May

*Approach:* From Olancha, drive south about two miles, then east on the Cactus Flat Road, paved for the first 1.5 miles, dirt after that. Follow the road to a junction 7.2 miles from Highway 395 at the west end of Cactus Flat. Take the right fork (the main road) and continue about 2.4 miles to a lesser used dirt road to the right that heads south. Turn right and continue another 2.5 miles to a dirt track heading west to a saddle at 4,993 feet. Park here and walk the pleasant track to the saddle. In spring, this track is covered with the striking red-orange desert mariposa and other beautiful native plants. Driving will crush this natural desert garden.

*Route:* Follow the dirt track as it heads northwest, on a fault block that has been down-dropped from the summit ridge of Scattered Bone Peak, to the saddle between Haiwee Ridge and Scattered Bone. The summit is about one mile north of the saddle. Class 3 bouldering will be encountered along the ridge. Anticipate four miles round-trip with approximately 1,100 feet of elevation gain.

## SCATTERED BONE PEAK (5,737 FT; 1,749 M)

This rarely ascended peak can be combined with Haiwee Ridge to the north. The author's dog "Ruby" is credited with the first recorded domestic canine ascent. Careful inspection of the summit rocks reveals the contact point between the granitic (at ground surface when the volcanics were deposited) and volcanic rocks. The view west across the two Haiwee Reservoirs to 12,000-foot Olancha Peak, and north to Owens Lake is spectacular.

*Maps:* Haiwee Reservoir (CA) 7.5-minute (1:24,000 scale) topographic map; Darwin Hills 1:100,000 scale metric topographic map; Automobile Club of Southern California (AAA) Death Valley National Park map

*Best Time to Climb:* October through May

*Approach:* Use the same approach described for Haiwee Ridge.

*Route:* Hike to the saddle between Scattered Bone Peak and Haiwee Ridge as described for Haiwee Ridge. The peak is less than one mile south. Anticipate three to four miles round-trip with about 800 feet of elevation gain.

Photographing the vivid spring color of *Opuntia basilaris* (beavertail cactus) on the way up Scattered Bone Peak. Haiwee Reservoir behind. Photo: Wynne Benti

## "BOULDER PEAK" (A.K.A. MCCLOUD PEAK) (6,085 FT; 1,855 M)

This summit of this peak is marked by a benchmark named "Boulder."

*Maps:* Haiwee Reservoir (CA) 7.5-minute (1:24,000 scale) topographic map; Darwin Hills 1:100,000 scale metric topographic map; Automobile Club of Southern California (AAA) Death Valley National Park map

*Best Time to Climb:* October through May

*Approach:* From Olancha, drive south about two miles, then east on the Cactus Flat Road (well-graded). This is a good graded road to a junction at a 7.2 miles from Highway 395 at the west end of Cactus Flat. Take the right fork (the main road) and continue about 2.4 miles to a lesser used dirt road to the right that heads south. Stay right and continue another 1.7 miles to a dirt track heading east toward a draw on the north side of the peak. Follow the road to its end.

*Route:* Climb east up the draw, then south up the north slopes of the peak. Anticipate three miles round-trip with 1,200 feet of elevation gain.

## WHITECAP MOUNTAIN (6,117 FT; 1,865 M)

*Maps:* Haiwee Reservoir (CA) 7.5-minute (1:24,000 scale)topographic map; Darwin Hills 1:100,000 scale metric topographic map; Automobile Club of Southern California (AAA) Death Valley National Park map

*Best Time to Climb:* October through May
*Approach:* Use the same approach described for Haiwee Ridge.
*Route:* Climb Boulder Peak as described above. From Boulder Peak, head south about 1.5 miles to the summit. Add three miles and another 500 feet of elevation gain to the round-trip statistics for Boulder Peak. Whitecap can also be climbed from the end of the Scattered Bone Peak road.

## ARGUS RANGE

The portions of the Argus Range covered in this guide are similar to the northern Coso Range. Unfortunately, the most outstanding peaks in the Argus Range including Maturango, French Madam, Burl Parkinson and Argus are within the boundary of the China Lake Naval Air Weapons Station and access is not permitted. The only peak described in this book that falls within the newly created Argus Range Wilderness is Zinc Hill. A small population of bighorn sheep makes the wilderness their home, so keep a watchful eye out for these denizens of the desert. Vegetation types you'll encounter consist mainly of a creosote scrub. At higher elevations a few Joshua trees and junipers have carved out their niche.

The major historical site in the area is the old mining town of Darwin. Named for E. Darwin French who led an expedition into the area during 1860, lead-silver ore was discovered at Ophir Mountain in 1874 and the rush was on. By the end of the next year 700 people lived here. The town had a violent reputation. Many shootings were the result of claim jumping which was quite common in the district. The boom busted by 1876 when word of the strikes at Bodie reached the camp and Darwin's ore began to play out. Mining did continue off and on into the twentieth century, and the district ended up producing about 5,900 ounces of gold, 7.6 million ounces of silver, 118 million pounds of lead, 52 million pounds of zinc, and 1.5 million pounds of copper.

A private campground and lodging is located at Panamint Springs Resort. Gasoline is available in Olancha and Lone Pine. For major supplies, Lone Pine is your best bet. Elsewhere, camping is primitive and all of the minimum impact camping methods apply here.

### OPHIR MOUNTAIN (6,019 FT; 1,835 M)

This peak overlooks the town of Darwin, and is considered part of the Darwin Hills despite its position as a separate mountain. The slopes of

View from Ophir Mountain into Darwin. Photo: Andy Zdon

the peak are covered with sagebrush amid a few Joshua trees. The ascent is easy and provides fine views of Darwin, and the Panamint, Argus and Coso Ranges. Based on the number of entries recorded in the summit register, the peak is not climbed all too often. Only four groups had reached the summit over a period of eight years.

*Maps:* Darwin (CA) 7.5-minute (1:24,000 scale) topographic map; Darwin Hills 1:100,000 scale metric topographic map; Automobile Club of Southern California (AAA) Death Valley National Park map

*Best Time to Climb:* October through April

*Approach:* From the junction of Highways 395 and 190 in Olancha, California, follow Highway 190 east from U.S. Highway 395, turning right at a T-junction with Highway 136, and continuing 12.8 miles on Highway 190 to the junction with the Darwin Road on the right. Head 3.6 miles south on the Darwin Road, then turn left on a rough dirt road approximately two miles to a saddle at 5,520 feet. Two-wheel drive vehicles with high clearance are recommended.

*Route:* Follow the easy ridge to the highpoint at the right. Anticipate two miles round-trip with 600 feet of elevation gain.

### ZINC HILL (5,584 FT; 1,702 M)

As one drives east on Highway 190 where the road begins to drop into Panamint Valley, a prominent summit catches the attention of the desert hiker. This peak, Zinc Hill, is the northernmost highpoint of the Argus

Range. The peak overlooks the Panamint Springs area and the northern Panamint Valley, making for a nice climb, especially when combined with a good lunch at Panamint Springs Resort. When the author climbed this peak with Campy Camphausen and Ed Zdon Sr., a winter storm was passing through, and the summit was shrouded with clouds. The only views were glimpses of some mysterious mountains, the snowy Coso Range, through a gap in the ever-changing clouds.

*Maps:* Darwin and Panamint Springs (CA) 7.5-minute (1:24,000 scale) topographic maps; Darwin Hills 1:100,000 scale metric topographic map; Automobile Club of Southern California (AAA) Death Valley National Park map

*Best Time to Climb:* October through April

*Approach:* From Highway 190 at Panamint Springs, drive one mile north to the Darwin Falls turnoff (signed Darwin Canyon Road). Follow the Darwin Canyon Road, passing the Darwin Falls trailhead, until a shallow draw on Zinc Hill's west slope is reached at approximately 3,680 feet. Most cars should have no trouble reaching this point.

*Route:* Hike up the wash about a half mile, then left on a poor mining road another half mile to a large cairn on the right-hand side of the road. A mine trail leads to a high saddle a short distance west of the summit. Anticipate 2,000 feet of elevation gain, with about five miles round-trip.

### LOOKOUT MOUNTAIN (4,100 FT; 1,250 M)

This low, flat ridge extends east from the Argus Range, and is much lower than the main crest. However, the mining town of Lookout Mountain was located on its summit, and the ruins of its once valiant stone buildings are still there. The town site provides an excellent view of the Panamint Valley. The old silver mines of Minietta and Modoc are located on the mountain's slopes.

*Maps:* Panamint Springs (CA) 7.5-minute (1:24,000 scale) topographic map; Darwin Hills 1:100,000 scale metric topographic map; Automobile Club of Southern California (AAA) Death Valley National Park map

*Best Time to Climb:* October through April

*Approach:* From Highway 190 just east of Panamint Springs, turn south on the Panamint Valley Road. At 7.4 miles, turn west on the graded dirt Minietta Road. Follow this road three miles to the dirt Nadeau Road. Lookout Mountain is the prominent ridge directly west, and jeep roads wander all over its base and slopes. A four-wheel drive may be able to reach the town site.

## THE SLATE RANGE

The Slate Range is not one of those ranges that fits among the previous trans-Sierra ranges described in this chapter. It would be more neatly listed among the Death Valley area peaks. However, the range is listed here because access to the range is from Trona, and fits nicely with hikes in the southern Argus Range accessible from the Trona area. Although mostly off-limits to travel due to the China Lake Naval Air Weapons Station, one lone peak, Searles Peak, is left open to desert summiteers.

### SEARLES PEAK (5,093 FT; 1,553 M)

The peak, and valley over which it sits, were named in honor of the Searles brothers who first discovered borax at Searles Lake in 1863, and began mining the deposit in 1873.

*Maps:* Trona East and Copper Queen Canyon (CA) 7.5-minute (1:24,000 scale) topographic maps; Ridgecrest 1:100,000 scale metric topographic map; Automobile Club of Southern California (AAA) Death Valley National Park map

*Best Time to Climb:* October through April

*Approach:* From Trona, drive approximately five miles north to Valley Wells Road. Turn east on Valley Wells Road, and continue 2.3 miles to a fork. Bear right, and continue a quarter mile to another fork. Turn left and continue 2.6 miles to a fork, then right. Continue another mile, passing through a mine gate and park (3,000 ft). Two-wheel drive vehicles with good clearance are recommended.

*Route:* From the parking area, ascend a ridge to the east attaining the crest of the range. Head south to the summit, passing benchmark Slate en route. Anticipate eight miles round-trip with 2,600 feet of elevation gain.

# The Death Valley Country

To the geographer, Death Valley is the deep valley lying just west of the California-Nevada border; to the early miners, prospectors and other inhabitants of this region, any place in this area was always called "Death Valley." From the time the desert wanderer left Mojave, heading east or northeast, until he reached Las Vegas or Tonopah, he was in Death Valley.

Many of these peaks were first climbed during the nineteenth century. It was in 1849 that an unfortunate cluster of argonaut parties left Salt Lake City to reach California, guided by a rumor and a rough sketch map. It was late in the year and the tragedy of the Donner Party was still fresh in their minds. The old Spanish Trail route, via Las Vegas Springs and Los Angeles seemed to them too far south. So when an allegedly fast and safe shortcut was offered, they jumped at the opportunity. After a short time, most turned back to the established route, but several parties continued on the fanciful shortcut. William Lewis Manly, a young man, evolved as the trail guide and later was to be the rescuer of the party stranded in Death Valley. Manly seemed filled with energy and often ran up minor desert peaks to scout out possible routes. The following are typical quotations from his account of that fateful journey in the Valley of Death:

*"I went to the top of a high butte and scanned the country very carefully, especially to the west and north, and found it very barren. There were no trees, no fertile valleys, nor anything green. Away to the west some mountains stood out clear and plain, their summits covered with snow. This I decided was our objective…"* Later:

*"Our line soon brought us in sight of a high butte which stood apparently about twenty miles south of our route and I determined to visit and climb it to get a better view of things ahea…"*

In 1860, a party under Dr. Sidney G. George, explored this region and one member, W.T. Henderson, climbed the highpoint of the Panamint Range, saying he had never seen so far without using a telescope. His observations resulted in the mountain being named Telescope Peak.

The next to climb any of these peaks were members of Lt. George Wheeler's Army Survey of 1871, who were commissioned to make a survey of the southwest, including eastern California and Nevada. In all, 22,250 miles were covered, though at times, their surveying was a bit off-schedule, they covered Death Valley in August and the Sierra Nevada in October.

Mining activity brought many more into Death Valley, especially after the bloom faded from the Gold Rush in the Mother Lode country. Camps were established at Panamint City, Goler, Atolia, Rhyolite, Goldfield, Tonopah and Silver City. Many peaks described in this chapter lie near these old mining towns or their ruins. Borax and soda-ash deposits also brought workers into the Valley, with the Harmony Borax Works at Death Valley bringing attention to this spot with its famous 20-mule teams. In 1933, Death Valley was set aside as a national monument by presidential proclamation and since then has been under the supervision of the National Park Service. In more recent times the Bureau of Land Management has administered much of the remaining public lands, except those taken over by various military bases. In 1995, Death Valley National Monument was expanded to include much of the Panamint and Saline Valley areas, becoming Death Valley National Park. Additionally, areas of several regional desert mountain ranges were designated as wilderness.

Geologically, these peaks (with the exception of those peaks in the Front Tier) lie within the Basin and Range geologic provence, often called the Great Basin. The Basin and Range provence is characterized by a conspicuous series of nearly north-south trending fault-block mountain ranges separated by desert valleys that are closed basins. No surface drainage from the Great Basin ever reaches the sea (except that portion along the Virgin River in southern Nevada that drains into the Colorado River and toward the Gulf of California). Rainfall is sparse and the weathered rock surfaces are often sharp and rough; foliage is similarly sparse and often sharp. The southern limit of the El Paso Mountains marks the location of the Garlock Fault, a major fault that runs generally east-west

View northwest from the summit of Corkscrew Peak.  Photo: Andy Zdon

across eastern California. This fault has also been used as marker between the Basin and Range to the north, and the Mojave Desert to the south. The most conspicuous fault in the Death Valley region is the Death Valley-Furnace Creek Fault Zone. This fault zone which has offset rocks on either side of the fault more than 50 miles, extends from the Amargosa River Valley, through Furnace Creek, north through Death Valley toward distant Fish Lake Valley. A classic location to observe evidence of this fault is at Shoreline Butte in the Confidence Hills where clearly-defined fault scarps are evident. For a bird's eye view, climb Ashford or Desert Hound Peaks.

The oldest rocks consisting of Precambrian-age schists and gneisses are exposed in the Black Mountains, forming the escarpment of that range above Death Valley. Younger Precambrian rocks consisting of sandstone, shale and conglomerate, are exposed in the Funeral Range and southern Panamint Range. These younger Precambrian rocks are represented by the Crystal Spring conglomerate, Beck Spring dolomite, and Kingston Peak sandstone, collectively called the "Pahrump Group." The Pahrump Group rocks were probably deposited in a shoreline environment, although some of the sandstones may be glacial/marine deposits. The transitional Precambrian/Cambrian to Cambrian-age sedimentary rocks make up a large percentage of the "rock pile" in Death Valley. With a thickness of more than 17,000 feet, their areal extent is correspondingly great. It is the earliest Cambrian-age rocks in which we see the evidence of the first multicellular organisms. These Precambrian/Cambrian formations include the Noonday, Johnnie, Stirling and the Wood Canyon formations. Some researchers consider the Wood Canyon formation the oldest true Cambrian formation in the region. Others consider the Wood Canyon to be Precambrian. Younger Paleozoic-age rocks can be found in the Cottonwood Mountains, among other places. The fossiliferous Devonian-age Lost Burro formation is particularly conspicuous. Mesozoic-age sedimentary and volcanic rocks are found in the Greenwater, Black, Last Chance and Panamint Ranges. Tertiary sedimentary formations are conspicuous in the Furnace Creek area. Late Tertiary volcanic rocks are prominent in the Black and Greenwater Mountains. For a brief geologic description of the Mojave Desert ranges, read the section on the Mojave National Preserve area.

The ranges described may be more than a hundred miles in length, such as the Amargosa Range, or may be reduced to isolated points, such as Mount Jackson, Eagle Mountain, or Lane Mountain. At first glance, the proliferation of names seems endless. Counting only the major ranges, this chapter includes: Avawatz Mountains, Black Mountains, Clark Mountains, Cottonwood Mountains, El Paso Mountains, Funeral Mountains, Grapevine Mountains, Greenwater Range, Kingston Range, Last Chance Range, Montezuma Range, Nopah Range, Panamint Range, Resting Spring Range, Saline Range, Excelsior Mountains, and the Silver Peak Range.

The area covered in this chapter is bounded on the south by California State Highway 58 and Interstate 15, on the east by the California-Nevada border, on the north by Highway 6, and on the west by the Panamint and Saline Valleys. Because of the large area involved, the Death Valley Country peaks have been split between those along and south of the Garlock Fault (called the Front Tier); those within the Basin and Range portion of the area in California (Death Valley National Park Area) and those peaks east of Death Valley in Nevada (Tonopah to Beatty).

## THE FRONT TIER

In the original *Desert Peaks Guide* series, Walt Wheelock described the following portion of the California desert as the "Front Tier." According to *Desert Peaks Guide 1* and 2 author, Walt Wheelock:

*"Those of you who are used to the great cordilleras of our land such as the Rocky Mountains, the Appalachians, the Cascades, or the Sierra Nevada will have trouble relating to these ranges of the Great Basin and the Death Valley Country. True, the Panamints and the Black-Funeral-Grapevine axis do extend many miles, but many of these so-called ranges are loaf-shaped mountain masses, often only ten miles long and a mile or two wide, possibly even smaller. Viewed from the air, or looking at a small scale topographic map, this entire region appears to be a flat land, accented by many north-northwest to south-southeast trending ridges, each of which bears the noble title of "range."*

*"Likewise, when attempting to catalog neatly or describe these peaks, we are frustrated in trying to find suitable groupings. However, due partially to the geography and largely to the military verbotens, we are channeled into a couple of major west side roads (U.S. 395 and California State Highway 14), or Interstate 15. As you drive along, you will surely view the ends of many of these mini-ranges, each of which stands out as an interesting desert peak. Therefore, we have dubbed these, the mountains of the "Front Tier," and to the miners and prospectors of the Randsburg, Calico, and Death Valley periods, these truly did form the frontier to this land. "*

The Front Tier group of peaks is largely located on lands administered by the Bureau of Land Management. Information regarding current access in these areas can be obtained by contacting the Ridgecrest or Riverside offices of that agency. Most of the Front Tier peaks can be easily reached from the desert towns extending from Mojave on the west to Baker on the east. Food, gas and lodging are easily obtained in any of these towns. Additionally, Ridgecrest, north of the El Paso Mountains, has just about anything the hiker would need, including a nice little backpacking/climbing shop.

Beginning at Mojave and working east, we first find a small group of peaks just east of that town. These peaks are best climbed during the spring when desert wildflowers put on their annual pageant.

### DESERT BUTTE (2,851 FT; 869 M)

This small volcanic plug consisting of a volcanic rock called dacite (part of the group of local rocks called the Tropico Group) provides a pleasant view of the California City area.

*Maps:* California City South (CA) 7.5-minute (1:24,000 scale) topographic map; Cuddeback Lake 1:100,000 scale metric topographic map; Automobile Club of Southern California (AAA) Kern County map

*Best Time to Climb:* November through April

*Approach:* From Mojave, California drive 14.6 miles east on Highway 58, then left on California City Boulevard 5.2 miles. A dirt road leads west passing Twin Buttes of which Desert Butte is the higher butte. There are many sandy real estate streets cutting up the desert, so choose ones that bring you to the south base of the peak (about 2,400 ft). This approach is driveable by all vehicles.

*Route:* The southwest slope is a short scramble, a few hundred yards at the most. Anticipate less than one mile round-trip with 450 feet of elevation gain.

### CASTLE BUTTE (3,145 FT; 959 M)

Another small volcanic plug, similar to its neighbor Desert Butte, this little peak is composed of volcanic tuff of the Tropico Group. It can easily be combined with Desert Butte for a short outing.

*Maps:* California City South and North Edwards (CA) 7.5-minute (1:24,000 scale) topographic maps; Cuddeback Lake 1:100,000 scale metric topographic map; Automobile Club of Southern California (AAA) Kern County map

*Best Time to Climb:* November through April

*Approach:* From the California City Boulevard turnoff along Highway 58 for Desert Butte, drive seven miles north on California City Boulevard to a dirt road leading east. This road follows a pole line. Three miles along this pole line road will bring you to a desert road leading through a pass crossing the western part of the cluster of buttes. Park at the pass (2,775 ft). This approach is driveable to all vehicles.

*Route:* Scramble along a ridge to the top. Anticipate one mile round-trip with 400 feet of elevation gain.

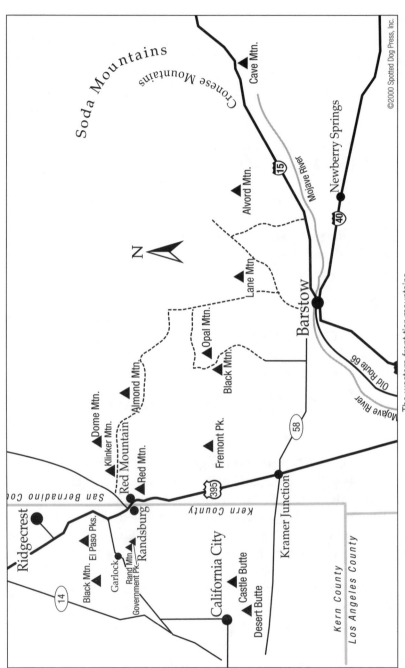

The western front tier mountains

Main Street in Randsburg, home to the last great nineteenth century soda fountain in the Mojave Desert. Photo: Wynne Benti

## RAND MOUNTAINS

In terms of historical interest, when Mojave desert mining camps are discussed, the cluster of Randsburg, Johannesburg, and Red Mountain will always rank near the top. Small ranges with short hikes, and one drive-up, surround this century-old mining center which is well worth visiting if even just to drink a malt, Green River, or to have a hot fudge sundae with pink peppermint ice cream at the Randsburg General Store's soda fountain. This fountain, one of the few remaining original soda fountains in the United States, came by boat from Europe, around Cape Horn to Los Angeles. It was then hauled by wagon across Cajon Pass to the Mojave Desert and Randsburg, where it has been in the same building ever since. As you sit at the fountain, you will be joining the company of some of the west's most legendary characters.

The Rand Mountains are a northeast trending mountain range southeast of the Garlock Fault, and lying in the heart of this historic territory. Consisting primarily of a metamorphic rock called the Rand schist, it is thought to be correlative to the Pelona schist in the San Gabriel Mountains of Southern California, and the Orocopia schist in the Orocopia Mountains south of Joshua Tree National Park. Bodies of quartz monzonite and volcanic rocks are also present in the area.

These peaks are reached by driving north from Kramer Junction (the junction of U.S. Highway 395 and California State Highway 58), or east from the junction of California State Highway 14 and the Randsburg Cutoff Road just south of Red Rock Canyon State Park. If you are looking for pristine wilderness, these peaks are definitely not for you. Much of the range is crisscrossed by motorcycle tracks, and is in an area designated by the Bureau of Land Management for motorcycle riding. Despite the heavy use this area receives, it is also within the habitat of the desert tortoise, a threatened species. However, the peaks do provide fine views of the surrounding desert, and a glimpse into the mining past of the region. If a desert tortoise is observed, please leave it alone.

If camping in the Rand Mountains, there are five areas open to camping which are marked by white signs and camping allowed emblems. If an area is unmarked, no camping is allowed. All camping is primitive. Rand Mountain Management Area trail maps produced by the Bureau of Land Management showing the campsites can be obtained from the Bureau of Land Management office in Ridgecrest, the Jawbone Canyon Visitor Center along Highway 14, or at kiosks scattered throughout the area. The closest available and reliable sources of gasoline are in Ridgecrest, and Kramer Junction. Groceries can also be obtained at these locations (Ridgecrest has the best variety). Plan on staying in Ridgecrest if you're a member of the motel set.

### GOVERNMENT PEAK (4,755 FT; 1,450 M)
It was on the north side of this peak that the famed Yellow Aster Mine was located. The views from the summit (and from its neighbor Rand Mountain) across the wide gulf of open desert toward the El Paso Mountains are worth the trip. There is an installation on the summit, and access to the summit may be closed at any time.

*Maps:* Johannesburg (CA) 7.5-minute (1:24,000 scale) topographic map; Cuddeback Lake 1:100,000 scale metric topographic map; Automobile Club of Southern California (AAA) Kern County map

*Best Time to Climb:* November through April

*Approach:* From the Highway 395-Trona Road junction north of Red Mountain, drive south 1.4 miles on Highway 395 through Red Mountain to a graded dirt road (Osdick Road–named in honor of the Osdick brothers who founded the town of Osdick that later became Red Mountain) heading west. Follow this dirt road 0.6 miles, then straight another 0.3 miles to a fork. Take the right fork (Rand-Mojave Road) 1.2 miles, then make another right onto BLM Road R20. After one mile on R20, turn right and continue 1.9 miles to a T-intersection. For Government Peak turn right and drive as far as practicable with your vehicle.

*Route:* Walk up the dirt road to the summit microwave station, less than a mile away. The elevation gain will be less than 1,000 feet.

### "RAND MOUNTAIN" (4,740 FT; 1,445 M)

*Maps:* Johannesburg (CA) 7.5-minute (1:24,000 scale) topographic map; Cuddeback Lake 1:100,000 scale metric topographic map; Automobile Club of Southern California (AAA) Kern County map

*Best Time to Visit:* November through April

*Approach:* Drive to the T-intersection described in the approach for Government Peak. Turn left and drive a dirt road southwest 0.8 miles to just below the highpoint of the ridge, then walk 200 yards east to the flat-topped summit and its microwave facility. The road is driveable to most vehicles. Wandering around the summit area, the desert explorer will find much of interest to observe (such as the distant desert views, and old mining operations).

## EL PASO MOUNTAINS

Looming over the windswept site of the now-abandoned mining camp of Garlock, the El Paso Mountains mark the southern boundary of the Basin and Range geologic provence. The El Pasos consist of two distinct areas. The Black Mountain area consists of stacked lava flows that issued from Black Mountain forming a high desert mesa. Black Mountain still retains a summit crater as any respectable volcano should. The entire range is bounded on the south by the Garlock Fault, considered by geologists to be the dividing line between the Basin and Range to the north and the east and the Mojave Desert to the south. To the east, the El Pasos consist of rolling, granitic terrain.

Within the Black Mountain area of the El Paso Mountains, the 24,000-acre El Paso Mountains Wilderness was formed as part of the California Desert Protection Act. The area is home to a variety of species including desert tortoise, coyotes, various small mammals, and hawks with the occasional Golden Eagle, along with a list of other birds, mammals, and reptiles. Generally, camping in the area is primitive and all minimum impact hiking and camping methods should be used here. The exception is at Red Rock Canyon State Park at the west end of the range, where a campground with restrooms, and a visitor center are located.

Besides this interesting natural area, some of the finest early cultural sites to be found in this part of California can be found in the southern part of the wilderness. The Last Chance Archaeological District within the wilderness is listed on the National Register of Historic Places. The area is managed by the Bureau of Land Management offices in Ridgecrest and Riverside.

## EL PASO PEAKS (4,578 FT; 1,396 M)

This small peak provides great views that include the southern end of Searles Lake, Owens Peak, the Coso Range, the Tehachapis and a particularly interesting view of the Rand Mountains. If you are lucky, you will reach the microwave station at the parking area when there are workmen present. When I reached the road end, an AT&T employee was doing some work and allowed me to take a look inside the installation, all batteries, transformers, and dials.

*Maps:* El Paso Peaks (CA) 7.5-minute (1:24,000 scale) topographic map; Cuddeback Lake 1:100,000 scale metric topographic map; Automobile Club of Southern California (AAA) Kern County map

*Best Time to Climb:* November through April

*Approach:* About seven miles north of Johannesburg on U.S. Highway 395, opposite the Searles turnoff, an oiled road (Searles Station Cutoff) runs west to two microwave installations. Follow the oiled road west about 3.2 miles, passing the first microwave station, to the second installation at 4,391 feet.

*Route:* The summit lies about a mile to the west over an easy rolling ridge.

## PEAK 4,888 FT (4,888 FT; 1,490 M)

This, the second highest peak in the El Pasos, is an unnamed butte looming above the ghost town of Garlock. The summit area consists of Permian-age shale and chert.

*Maps:* Garlock (CA) 7.5-minute (1:24,000 scale) topographic map; Cuddeback Lake 1:100,000 scale metric topographic map; Automobile Club of Southern California (AAA) Kern County map

*Best Time to Climb:* November through April

*Approach:* Drive 11 miles east of Highway 14 along the Randsburg cutoff road (just north of Cantil), to the Mesquite Canyon Road (BLM Road

EP100). Follow this fair desert road four miles north up the canyon to a saddle, then right on a very poor dirt road two miles to a microwave complex at 4,450 feet. The last half mile to the microwave complex is very steep and this entire road suffers from flash flooding. If in doubt, park at 1.5 miles from the saddle (4,250 ft) where a steep jeep track climbs a draw to this saddle. This alternative trades a half mile of very rough driving for an easy 650-foot climb.

*Route:* Walk around the fenced area to a shallow saddle; cross to the false peak, then south to the true summit.

### BLACK MOUNTAIN (5,244 FT; 1,599 M)

This large lava mountain is famous for its Indian house rings near the top. It is also the highest peak in the range, and is the only significant peak within the El Paso Mountains Wilderness Area. The age of the volcanic activity of Black Mountain has been dated as between 14.6 and 19.5 million years. We climbed this peak on a cold, cloudy day, the dark weather adding a touch of mystery to this desert summit occupied by native people many centuries ago.

Route up open ridge to Black Mountain summit.
Photo: Wynne Benti

*Maps:* Garlock (CA) 7.5-minute (1:24,000 scale) topographic map; Cuddeback Lake 1:100,000 scale metric topographic map; Automobile Club of Southern California (AAA) Kern County map

*Best Time to Climb:* November through April

*Approach:* Drive 11 miles east of Highway 14 along the Randsburg Cutoff Road (just north of Cantil), to the Mesquite Canyon Road (BLM Road EP100). Follow this fair desert road up the canyon four miles to a saddle, continuing straight and downhill where the road swings to the west and a fork. Stay left at the fork, then a take a quick right onto BLM Road EP26. Continue another mile to where a jeep road forks to the left and park (3,920 ft).  Four wheel drive vehicles are recommended.

*Route:* Hike northwest up the former jeep road past a wildlife guzzler, and continue up Black Mountain's sagebrush-covered, southeast ridge.  The summit crater is bypassed to the west.  Anticipate five miles round-trip with 1,400 feet of elevation gain.

## LAVA MOUNTAINS

East of U.S. Highway 395 at Red Mountain are several peaks of interest. First is Red Mountain, then the main portion of the Lava Mountains.  Much of the Lava Mountains is included within the 38,000-acre Golden Valley Wilderness, another wilderness area that was created as part of the California Desert Protection Act.  This is prime desert tortoise country with one area containing 20 to 50 desert tortoises per square mile. The Red Mountain/El Paso Mountains area is also one of the densest known raptor breeding areas in the California desert with both Golden Eagle and Prairie Falcon eyries present.  Bedrock Springs, Steam Well, Old Wells and all of Golden Valley have been nominated for the National Register of Historic Places.

The Lava Mountains are also very dry, and while the hiker will note the presence of many wells on the maps, these wells are largely dry and/or have fallen into disuse.  They should not be relied upon as a source of water, so carry all water .  Camping in the area is primitive.  However, at some of the more popular locations, heavy use along with private target practice, has left the campsites littered with broken glass and shotgun shells. Camping in the El Paso Mountains or the designated sites in the Rand Mountains is recommended as an alternative to camping in this area.  The closest supplies, food, gas and lodging are in Ridgecrest about ten miles away. The area is administered by the Bureau of Land Management district offices in Ridgecrest and Riverside.

### RED MOUNTAIN (5,261 FT; 1,604 M)

This great red dome looms above the town of the same name.  The inscriptions of many turn of the century geologists are carved into some of the summit rocks.

*Maps:* Red Mountain (CA) 7.5-minute (1:24,000 scale) topographic map; Cuddeback Lake 1:100,000 scale metric topographic map; Automobile Club of Southern California (AAA) San Bernardino County map

Inscriptions on the summit of Red Mountain, a classic desert peak summit. Photo: Andy Zdon

*Best Time to Climb:* November through April

*Approach:* Drive north on Highway 395 to the northern limits of Red Mountain, then right on Trona Road. Turn right on the Trona Road, and just past the intersection, a dirt road turns toward the peak and ends (3,700 ft).

*Route:* Scramble up the ridge to the east, bypassing the first obvious false summit, then south to the true summit. A return can be made down scree slopes. Anticipate about five miles round-trip with 1,600 feet of elevation gain.

**KLINKER MOUNTAIN (4,562 FT; 1,391 M), DOME MOUNTAIN (4,974 FT; 1,516 M)**
Skillim Well, the starting point for the climb of Klinker, is yet another misspelled official version of an original place name. The site was originally named Skillings Well for Eben M. Skillings who developed the Skillings Water Company. From a well at this site, Skillings would deliver water via a horse-drawn 100-gallon tank to Randsburg. The cost–one dollar per fifty gallons. In 1898, the Yellow Aster Mine purchased the spring and installed a five-inch pipeline to Randsburg along with a pumping plant. The remains of this pipeline can be seen to this day. One can imagine the bustle that the operations created at one time. Now only the buzz of an insect or the din of a desert breeze are heard. After Klinker and Dome, one could continue eastward on Road RM1444 past the Lava Mountains to an isolated butte, Almond Mountain, due north of Cuddeback Dry Lake. Almond Mountain could then be climbed via its south slopes.

*Maps:* Klinker Mountain (CA) 7.5-minute (1:24,000 scale) topographic map; Cuddeback Lake 1:100,000 scale metric topographic map; Automobile Club of Southern California (AAA) San Bernardino County map

*Best Time to Climb:* November through April

*Approach:* From Highway 395, between the towns of Red Mountain and Johannesburg, drive north on the Red Mountain-Trona Road 1.3 miles, then east on Steam Wells Road (BLM Road RM1444) 1.7 miles to a fork. Those with two-wheel drive may want to park here, but with four-wheel drive, turn left (north) and continue another half mile to the abandoned site of Skillim Well (3,400 ft).

*Route:* From Skillim Well, hike up the road a short distance to a saddle. From the saddle, follow a cross-country route along a sawtooth ridge to the high mesa, on which Klinker is the highpoint. You will pass at least four false summits. Anticipate five miles round-trip with 1,400 feet of elevation gain from Skillim Well. To climb Dome Mountain, from the summit of Klinker, a huge, often flower-covered mesa extends over seemingly level land to Dome. It looks to be a short distance away but is a 3.5-mile up-and-down walk from Klinker. To climb both peaks anticipate 12 miles round-trip with 2,500 feet of elevation gain.

*The following group of peaks is scattered in a generally east-west trend across the Mojave Desert.*

### FREMONT PEAK (4,584 FT; 1,398 M)

Despite it having been given his name, it is unlikely that Lieutenant John C. Fremont ever noticed this beautiful little cone as he passed 25 miles to the southeast in 1844. This isolated peak forms a small range of its own, and is not considered part of any other desert range. It looks particularly interesting when viewed from near Red Mountain along Highway 395. Its slopes, along with the surrounding area, are covered by desert shrubs, primarily creosote. Old mine workings dot the lower slopes of the peak, and it is from one of these diggings that our ascent begins.

*Maps:* Boron NE and Fremont Peak (CA) 7.5-minute (1:24,000 scale) topographic maps; Cuddeback Lake 1:100,000 scale metric topographic map; Automobile Club of Southern California (AAA) San Bernardino County map

*Best Time to Climb:* November through April

*Approach:* Drive 12.9 miles north on Highway 395 from its junction with

State Highway 58 (Kramer Junction). A dirt road (BLM Road EF411) appears to run straight toward the peak to the east. It is a good desert road and ends at the old Monarch-Rand Mine site (at 4,000 ft) after about seven miles. Most vehicles should be able to reach the mine site.

*Route:* Either scramble the ridge, or swing to the right for an easier route.

### LANE MOUNTAIN (4,522 FT; 1,379 M)

*Maps:* Barstow, Nebo, and Lane Mountain (CA) 7.5-minute (1:24,000 scale) topographic maps; Victorville, Newberry Springs, and Soda Mountains 1:100,000 scale metric topographic maps; Automobile Club of Southern California (AAA) San Bernardino County map

*Best Time to Climb:* November through April

*Approach and Route:* From the junction of I-15 and Highway 58 east of Barstow, California, drive two miles west on Highway 58 to Fort Irwin Road. Drive north on Fort Irwin Road 6.2 miles to the graded dirt Copper City Road that angles off to the north. Follow the Copper City Road north 5.6 miles. The mountain and its summit installation, now looms against the eastern skyline, and a narrow bladed road wanders over to it and climbs to within 100 yards of the top. Because of the facilities on this mountain, access to the mountain may be closed at any time.

### OPAL MOUNTAIN (3,950 FT; 1,204 M)

*Maps:* Hinkley, Water Valley and Opal Mountain (CA) 7.5-minute (1:24,000 scale) topographic maps; Victorville and Cuddeback Lake 1:100,000 scale metric topographic maps; Automobile Club of Southern California (AAA) San Bernardino County map

*Best Time to Climb:* November through April

*Approach:* From the junction of Highways 395 and 58 at Kramer Junction, drive about 21 miles east to Hinkley Road. If driving from the east, Hinkley Road is about 12 miles west of Interstate 15. Drive 7.4 miles north through Hinkley on Hinkley Road, then northeast another four miles and finally northwest on the Opal Mountain Road (BLM Road C297) 7.5 miles to a campsite often filled with eager rockhounds.

*Route:* The hill may be climbed directly from the campsite, or one may drive to a saddle at 3,350 feet, found between Opal and Black Mountains. Anticipate one mile round-trip with less than 1,000 feet of elevation gain regardless of the route chosen.

## Black Mountain (3,941 ft; 1,202 m)

This mountain is the highpoint of the newly created, 14,000-acre Black Mountain Wilderness. Black Mountain is a broad basalt mesa rising more than 2,000 feet above the surrounding valley floors, and is frequently graced by a fine spring wildflower display. The dominant vegetation type is creosote bush although a few Joshua trees are found in the area. Golden Eagles and Prairie Falcons frequent the area. Supplies, food and lodging are available in Barstow, California. Gasoline is available in Barstow and at Kramer Junction (along with a couple of restaurants). The area is managed by the Bureau of Land Management offices in Barstow and Riverside.

*Maps:* Hinkley, Water Valley and Opal Mountain (CA) 7.5-minute (1:24,000 scale) topographic maps; Victorville and Cuddeback Lake 1:100,000 scale metric topographic maps; Automobile Club of Southern California (AAA) San Bernardino County map

*Best Time to Climb:* November through April

*Approach:* While one could climb this long basaltic mountain from the above saddle near Opal Mountain, it would be a long walk over basalt. Instead, drive 9.4 miles north from Hinkley to Fossil Bed Road (BLM Road EF401), then left 3.5 miles passing through Water Valley to Black Canyon Road (BLM Road EF373). Follow Black Canyon Road north up the canyon four miles, choosing a likely looking departure spot (around 2,800 ft) to climb the cliffs to the east. There is loose sand in the canyon; stay in the track or if you do not mind a long day hike, walk the four miles up the canyon. Four-wheel drive is recommended on the Black Canyon Road due to sand.

*Route:* Scramble over an easy basalt formation to reach the summit mesa, then cross-country to the highpoint, about three miles round-trip depending on your departure point. If walking from the junction of Fossil Bed Road and Black Canyon Road, anticipate 11 miles round-trip with about 1,200 feet of elevation gain.

## Calico Peak (4,542 ft; 1,385 m)

This peak, the highpoint of the Calico Mountains presents to the hiker, stark mottled earth tones against the blue winter sky. A geologist once wrote:

*"The colors are a kaleidoscope mixture of light and dark–the light shades are yellowish white to buff, and dark shades of dull pink to red. Such assemblages*

*of particolored Tertiary volcanic rocks are called calico by the prospectors throughout the desert region and the hills formed from them are called calico hills, the Calico Peaks being themselves and example of this usage."*

Access to Calico Peak is from a locked gate at the head of Odessa Canyon, and several dirt roads can be followed to reach this gate. The route described below is that chosen by the author, and was found to be a scenic although at times rough route.

*Maps:* Yermo (CA) 7.5-minute (1:24,000 scale) topographic map; Newberry Springs 1:100,000 scale metric topographic map; Automobile Club of Southern California (AAA) San Bernardino County map

*Best Time to Climb:* November through April

*Approach:* From Interstate 15, take the Yermo offramp (ten miles east of Barstow), and drive 0.8 miles north on Calico Road to the Mule Canyon Road. Drive up this road through colorful hills 1.5 miles to a fork. Stay right and continue two miles through badland hills, crossing a divide and dropping to another junction. Turn left, and continue 3.6 miles west, climbing a rough, loose grade where four-wheel drive is recommended, to another junction. Turn north (right) and continue 0.4 miles to the locked gate at 3,200 feet. Most of the route is driveable to all vehicles. However, the steep hill will stop many two-wheel drive vehicles. One could easily walk the extra couple of miles to the locked gate from here though.

*Route:* Walk past the locked gate, and follow the steep road to the microwave station on the summit. Anticipate six miles round-trip with 1,400 feet of elevation gain from the locked gate. Hiking from the steep grade will add some significant mileage and elevation gain, but will still make for a fine, winter dayhike.

### ALVORD MOUNTAIN (3,456 FT; 1,054 M)

When climbing this peak, watch under your feet and you may find a bit of rare blue chalcedony float. Also watch your route as much of the country looks the same as you retrace your steps.

*Maps:* Alvord Mountain West and Alvord Mountain East (CA) 7.5-minute (1:24,000 scale) topographic maps; Soda Mountains 1:100,000 scale topographic map; Automobile Club of Southern California (AAA) San Bernardino County map

*Best Time to Climb:* November through April

*Approach:* There is an overpass on I-15 at Manix, but no connection with I-15 at that point. So, take the Harvard offramp, the second east of Yermo, and drive the old road back to Manix. Cross over the freeway, and follow a dirt road directly to the Alvord Well at 5.7 miles. Park here (approximately 2,060 ft). Two wheel drive with high clearance recommended, although four-wheel drive is helpful due to some sandy spots.

*Route:* Enter the wash near Alvord Well, and walk the remaining 1.3 miles to the Alvord Mine at 2,200 feet, staying right at a fork in the wash. From the Alvord Mine, follow the canyon east to its end. Turn left onto the mesa and the peak may be seen in the far distance to the northeast. Anticipate eight miles round-trip with roughly 1,500 feet of elevation gain.

### CAVE MOUNTAIN (3,585 FT; 1,093 M)

This nice-looking granite peak is the looming mountain just south of Interstate 15 between Yermo and Baker. The peak is a major landmark in the Mojave Desert, and its summit yields far-ranging views of the entire "Front Tier" along with a large portion of the Mojave National Preserve.

*Maps:* Cave Mountain (CA) 7.5-minute (1:24,000 scale) topographic map; Soda Mountains 1:100,000 scale topographic map; Automobile Club of Southern California (AAA) San Bernardino County map

*Best Time to Climb:* November through April

Cave Mountain from Basin Road. Photo: Andy Zdon

*Approach:* From Interstate 15, exit on Basin Road (24 miles north of the Manix turnoff or 15.3 miles south of Baker). Drive south on Basin Road approximately two miles to a fork. Take the right fork, and continue 1.7 miles to a parking area at a locked gate.

*Route:* From the parking area, head north eventually gaining Cave Mountain's southwest ridge at any likely looking spot. Follow the ridge to the summit area. This route is steep but the constant far-ranging views across the wide-expanse of desert makes for an enjoyable climb. Anticipate five mile round-trip with about 2,300 feet of elevation gain.

Summit of Cave Mountain looking down on I-15, Soda Mountains in background. Photo: Andy Zdon

# TURQUOISE HILLS

Between Los Angeles and Las Vegas, east of Baker and north of Interstate 15 is a small grouping of rolling desert hills scattered with stately Joshua trees. There are no jagged peaks, or even rugged peaks. This small range, known as the Turquoise Hills, offers a pleasant diversion to the long interstate drive, though most desert hikers will not make a separate trip to climb them for these peaks are not typical of mountaineering objectives. They are simply easy peaks alongside old turquoise mine workings just waiting to be explored, a great diversion if you only have an hour to spare, or even an entire weekend! Despite their gentle appearance, these peaks have commanding views of this portion of the Mojave Desert. The Turquoise Hills also offer fine but primitive camping (though you may be invaded by the occasional herd of range cattle). The closest town is Baker, California with service stations, motels, restaurants, and a store. For further information, contact the Bureau of Land Management offices in Barstow and Riverside.

### TURQUOISE MOUNTAIN (4,400 FT; 1,341 M)

*Maps:* Turquoise Mountain (CA) 7.5-minute (1:24,000 scale) topographic map; Ivanpah 1:100,000 scale metric topographic map; Automobile Club of Southern California (AAA) San Bernardino County map
*Best Time to Climb:* November through April
*Approach:* From the Halloran Springs offramp, 13 miles east of Baker, follow an alternating blacktop and graded dirt road seven miles north to a locked gate at the microwave station (visible from Interstate 15). Note the many turquoise diggings along the road; there are more farther west. The road is passable to all cars.
*Route:* Scramble 100 yards east to the highpoint. The views of Telescope Peak, Charleston Peak, and much of the Mojave National Preserve during the late afternoon on a winter day are enough to make one forget about the installation on the summit of the peak.

### SQUAW MOUNTAIN (4,880 FT; 1,487 M)

*Maps:* Turquoise Mountain and Solomons Knob (CA) 7.5-minute (1:24,000 scale) topographic maps; Ivanpah 1:100,000 scale metric topographic map; Automobile Club of Southern California (AAA) San Bernardino County map

*Best Time to Climb:* November through April

*Approach:* From Interstate 15 east of Baker, California, exit at Halloran Springs. From the cattle guard on the north side of the road, drive 5.9 miles north on the Turquoise Mountain Road to a turnoff on the right. Take the rough dirt road four miles east, passing through a fine Joshua tree grove and parking at a fork in the road. The road is accessible to high clearance two-wheel drive vehicles.

*Route:* The peak is an easy climb to the northwest. Anticipate three miles round-trip with 500 feet of elevation gain.

### SOLOMON'S KNOB (4,474 FT; 1,364 M)

*Maps:* Turquoise Mountain and Solomons Knob (CA) 7.5-minute (1:24,000 scale) topographic maps; Ivanpah 1:100,000 scale metric topographic map; Automobile Club of Southern California (AAA) San Bernardino County map

*Best Time to Climb:* November through April

*Approach:* From Interstate 15 east of Baker, California, exit at Halloran Springs. From the cattle guard on the north side of the road, drive 2.8 miles north, then right up Bull Spring Wash 3.1 miles on a graded dirt road, passing mine workings on the left, to a fork. Turn left and park at the small talc mine (two-wheel drive should be able to reach the mine). The peak is the volcanic knob ahead of you. Here one of the small mining pits contains standing water during the spring when the local water table is high enough to intersect the ground surface, and the area is rich with the sound of chirping birds. One could also drive around to the west or south sides of the peak and climb from there (visiting the Great Wannamingo Mine).

*Route:* From the mine, follow the ridge, avoiding the occasional cholla, and delighting in the sound of the breeze through the Joshua trees, southeast to a point just west of the small cliff band. The breaks in the cliff band provide easy but loose scrambling to the summit area. Views from the summit include Telescope Peak and Charleston Peak. Anticipate two miles round-trip with 800 feet of elevation gain.

### SHADOW MOUNTAIN (4,197 FT; 1,279.2 M)

This isolated peak serves as a fine viewpoint. The peak is comprised of Precambrian-age metamorphic rocks. However, looking down to the west and northwest base of the peak, the hiker will note the presence of some

Solomon's Knob. Photo: Andy Zdon

clay beds. A thrust fault has placed the older crystalline rocks on top of the much younger clays.

*Maps:* East of Kingston Spring (CA) 7.5-minute (1:24,000 scale) topographic map; Mesquite Lake 1:100,000 scale metric topographic map; Automobile Club of Southern California (AAA) San Bernardino County map

*Best Time to Climb:* November through April

*Approach:* From Baker, California, drive approximately 26 miles northeast on Interstate 15 to Cima Road. Take the alternately paved Cima Road north (also known as the Excelsior Mine Road) a little more than eight miles to a powerline road and turn west. Follow the powerline road three miles to a road that heads north toward Shadow Mountain. Turn right and drive 1.7 miles to a prospect or as far as practicable with your vehicle.

*Route:* The peak is a scant mile to the northwest, with about 700 feet of elevation gain.

## AVAWATZ MOUNTAINS

Standing above the Mojave desert plain north of the town of Baker, California is one of the author's favorite desert ranges. Although not as high as the nearby Kingston and Clark Ranges, and not as rugged as the New York or Providence Mountains, the Avawatz Mountains still hold a special charm all its own. Perhaps it is the feeling of remoteness that one gets, of leaving civilization behind, when in the Avawatz Mountains that is the attraction. It is highly unlikely that you will encounter any fellow desert travelers when driving into these mountains. According to Erwin Gudde, the name Avawatz is derived from "na-hu-watz "meaning mountain sheep. The replacement of ivah (meaning white) for "na" would mean white sheep or White Sheep Range. Local settlers starting calling the peak Avawatz and the U.S.G.S. named the peak based on the phonetic spelling of the locals' pronunciation of the peak's name. The Avawatz Mountain bighorn sheep herd resides here, as there are several good sources of water (springs) in the area.

The Avawatz Mountains are composed of Precambrian, Paleozoic and Mesozoic-age sedimentary and igneous rocks with some Tertiary-age sediments. This range lies near the junction of the Garlock Fault running east-west, and the Death Valley-Furnace Creek Fault Zone running north-south. The area has been much studied as the Garlock Fault is one of the major faults in California, and seems to disappear after its junction with the Death Valley-Furnace Creek Fault Zone. The reason for this is a topic of much interest and research by geologists. Unfortunately, a clear answer for this occurrence has not been determined.

Camping in the area is primitive so all minimum impact camping methods should be applied here. Supplies, gas, food and lodging area available in Baker. For further information, contact the Bureau of Land Management offices in Barstow, Needles or Riverside.

### "AVAWATZ PEAK" (6,154 FT; 1,876 M)

The fine hike to this peak, the range highpoint, passes through creosote and sage scrub with a few scrawny Joshua trees. The dawn light on the surrounding ridges is one of the more pleasing sites that one will find in the desert. The peak is unnamed on the topographic map.

*Maps:* Sheep Creek Spring and Red Pass Lake NE (CA) 7.5-minute (1:24,000 scale) topographic maps; Owlshead Mountains and Soda Mountains

En route to Avawatz. Photo: Wynne Benti

1:100,000 scale metric topographic maps; Automobile Club of Southern California (AAA) San Bernardino County map

*Best Time to Climb:* October through May

*Approach:* From Baker, California, drive 19.1 miles north on California State Highway 127 and turn left on a faint dirt road. Sometimes finding the road is difficult due to grading of the highway shoulder. The road first heads south then west toward the Avawatz Mountains. At 4.5 miles, stay left at the Old Mormon Springs Road, and head up a canyon 1.9 miles on a rough four-wheel drive road to a junction. Turn right and continue up a hill about one mile to another junction. Turn left and after another 0.2 miles you will reach a saddle. Contour along the hillside another 0.6 miles to a parking area at about 4,500 feet. This road is subject to washouts and in the past has been extremely tough to drive. However, the road is occasionally graded for access to a repeater on a nearby ridge. Four-wheel drive is required.

*Route:* Hike the road about 500 feet and turn left climbing 200 feet up to a ridge. After dropping down to a saddle, continue generally in a northwest direction, eventually picking up a use trail, to the summit. Anticipate about six miles round-trip with 2,400 feet of elevation gain.

# KINGSTON RANGE

One of the outstanding desert ranges, the Kingston Range is within the 210,000-acre Kingston Range Wilderness. The range looms high above three low desert valleys, Mesquite, Shadow and Silurian. This isolated position makes the Kingston Range a key desert landmark. The rock types comprising the range include granitic rocks in the central portion of the range, with limestone and dolomite occurring along the range's margins. The Kingston Range is one of the most botanically diverse (with more than 500 plant species) desert ranges and is home to a relict stand of white firs covering about 150 acres on the north slope of the range. The area also includes a stand of nolina (yucca-like) plants of great size, more than 15 feet high and 10 feet in girth. There are also dense stands of Joshua trees in the area. The range's wildlife is also diverse with bighorn sheep, deer, coyotes, kit foxes, ringtails and various raptors. The banded Gila monster has also been confirmed to be present in this range. The range is named in honor of an early local character named Kingston who was once a mail carrier between Salt Lake City and San Bernardino.

Camping in the area is primitive so all minimum impact camping methods apply here. The closest gasoline, food, lodging and supplies are found in Baker, California, nearly 50 miles away. For further information, contact the Bureau of Land Management offices in Barstow, Needles and Riverside.

## KINGSTON PEAK (7,323 FT; 2,235 M)

This peak is one of the classic desert peaks in this region. Kingston Peak is the highpoint of the range, offering outstanding views of the surrounding valleys. Washes below the peak are favorite gemstone hunting areas with occasional finds of amethysts. When climbing this peak, keep an eye out for ticks. After hiking the first two miles, the author noticed that his legs were crawling with ticks. Amazingly, none decided to bite, and all were brushed off harmlessly.

*Maps:* Horsethief Springs and Kingston Peak (CA) 7.5-minute (1:24,000 scale) topographic maps; Mesquite Lake 1:100,000 scale metric topographic map; Automobile Club of Southern California (AAA) San Bernardino County map

*Best Time to Climb:* November through May

*Approach:* From Baker, California, drive northeast on Interstate 15 about 26

miles to Cima Road. Take the alternately paved and dirt Cima Road north (also known as the Excelsior Mine Road) about 28 miles to a large turnoff and parking area on the right (5,080 ft). Two-wheel drive vehicles will have no problem reaching this point. With a four-wheel drive, cut off another 0.7 miles by taking a dirt road south from the parking area as far as practicable. *Route:* From the end of the four-wheel drive road described above, drop into the wash heading south about two miles to a saddle at about 6,660 feet. Turn right (west) at the saddle and head up the ridge to another saddle at 6,920 feet. Head southwest up the ridge from here with some ups and downs to the summit. Anticipate nine miles round-trip and 3,800 feet of elevation gain.

## MESQUITE MOUNTAINS

These forgotten mountains are surrounded by more "glamorous" desert ranges, but on their own, the Mesquite Mountains are a fine desert range. The gradual west slope provides a deceiving face to the hiker reaching the Mesquite Mountains from that direction. Upon reaching the crest, the east slope is found to be much steeper and rougher terrain. The mountain slopes are covered by extensive stands of Joshua trees, yuccas, cactus and the ubiquitous creosote.

The highpoint of the range, Mesquite Mountain, is within the newly-created 47,000-acre Mesquite Mountains Wilderness. Camping in the area is primitive. The nearest supplies, gasoline, food, and lodging are in Baker, California, about 50 miles away. For further information, contact the Bureau of Land Management offices in Needles and Riverside.

### "MESQUITE MOUNTAIN" (5,151 FT; 1,570 M)

*Maps:* Mesquite Mountains (CA) 7.5-minute (1:24,000 scale) topographic map; Mesquite Lake 1:100,000 scale metric topographic map; Automobile Club of Southern California (AAA) San Bernardino County map
*Best Time to Climb:* November through April
*Approach:* From Baker, California, drive east on Interstate 15 to the Cima Road offramp. Drive north on Cima Road (also known as Excelsior Mine Road) 12 miles to a fork. Stay right, and continue 3.4 miles and park. Two-wheel drive vehicles should have no problem reaching this point.
*Route:* Walk east to the base of the mountain, then follow Mesquite's west ridge to the summit. Anticipate nine miles round-trip with 1,800 feet of elevation gain.

# CLARK MOUNTAINS

The Clark Mountains are the highest mountains within the newly established Mojave National Preserve. One of the most biologically diverse ranges in the California desert, the vegetation of the Clark Range is similar to that of the nearby Kingston Range. On the north slope of the Clark Mountains is a relic stand of white firs (about 1,000 trees). On the lower slopes of the range, in between the pinyon-juniper woodlands, are beautiful stands of Joshua trees, among the finest in the Mojave Desert. Wildlife is abundant in the area including bighorn sheep, mule deer, mountain lions, bobcats, desert tortoise, and Golden Eagles. Numerous uncommon or rare birds visit this area making it a bird watcher's paradise.

Camping in the area is primitive so all minimum impact camping methods apply here. Gas, food and lodging are available in Baker to the west, or at State Line (Primm), Nevada to the northeast along Interstate 15. For more information, contact the Mojave National Preserve office in Barstow, or the Visitor Centers in Baker and Needles.

## CLARK MOUNTAIN (7,929 FT; 2,410 M)

Massive limestone cliffs, caves, and spectacular dry waterfalls make this, the highpoint of the Clark Mountains, a particularly interesting climb. This is the only peak listed in this chapter that falls within the newly created Mojave National Preserve, and is the highest peak within the preserve. The views from the summit are breathtaking. The mountain is named in honor of William A. Clark, the copper king, railroad tycoon and Senator from Montana who built the San Pedro, Los Angeles & Salt Lake Railroad into the Las Vegas area.

*Maps:* Clark Mountain (CA) 7.5-minute (1:24,000 scale) topographic map; Mesquite Lake 1:100,000 scale metric topographic map; Automobile Club of Southern California (AAA) San Bernardino County map

*Best Time to Climb:* October through May

*Approach:* From Mountain Pass on Interstate 15, drive north several hundred yards, turning left and continuing about one mile, passing the Caltrans station, then another 0.4 miles of dirt road to a junction. Turn right and continue 0.6 miles, then left and follow a power line road about 1.8 miles to a fork. Turn left, and immediately turn left again. The road switchbacks then heads up the canyon to the end at a picnic area at about 6,000 feet. Two-wheel drive vehicles with good clearance are recommended.

The Class 3 section on Clark. Photo: Wynne Benti

*Route:* Walk up the small canyon behind the picnic area until a dry waterfall is reached. Climb a slope to the right bypassing the waterfall and reaching a saddle. From the saddle, drop down into a wash heading up toward the peak. Follow the wash as far as desired until the brush becomes tiresome, then bear left and climb scree to the base of a limestone cliff. Continue up along the base of the cliff to the east-west ridge. Climb a 20-foot, steep and loose Class 3 section (some may want a belay here) that gives access to the ridge. Ascend the ridge to the left and onto the summit. Anticipate 2.5 miles round trip with 1,900 feet of elevation gain.

*Alternate:* In 1980, the author, with Phil Gonzalez and Dave Clegg, drove to the Copper World Mine on Clark Mountain's southwest flank, and climbed a beautiful canyon behind the mine. The hiking was up a limestone wash, and through a delightful pinyon-juniper woodland to a false summit at the end of Clark's southwest ridge (approximately a half mile south of Clark's summit-marked with a small antenna). Although we did not walk over to the true summit that day, the connecting ridge appeared to be a relatively easy affair. This route is much longer than the primary route listed above.

## DEATH VALLEY NATIONAL PARK & ENVIRONS

Two series of desert ranges border Death Valley, the lowest depression in the western hemisphere: the Panamint-Cottonwood-Last Chance complex to the west and the Black-Funeral-Grapevine complex to the east. While there are some roads and trails reaching into these mountains from the floor of Death Valley, these mountains are more easily reached via side roads from the Panamint and Saline Valleys to the west, or from the Greenwater Valley and U.S. Highway 95 from the east.

In 1994, the California Desert Protection Act greatly enlarged the former Death Valley National Monument to include much of the country surrounding Panamint Valley and that part of Saline Valley east of the Saline Valley Road. Additionally, the park's status was upgraded from monument to national park. Therefore, the peaks in this section are described in the following order: western peaks from north to south starting with the Saline Range and the Last Chance Range at Last Chance Mountain southward to the south end of the Panamint Range, followed by the eastern ranges from the Grapevine Mountains on the north to the peaks around Shoshone, California including the Resting Spring and Nopah Ranges.

## Saline Range

This brooding, volcanic range at the north end of Saline Valley, has all the true characteristics of a desert range. The Salines have dry slopes that at a distance appear devoid of life. Like most desert ranges, this is only a facade. Besides providing a choice habitat for Golden Eagles and Prairie Falcons, the range includes more than 180 square miles of desert bighorn habitat, about 90 percent of the area traveled by the Last Chance herd. A visit to the Saline Range is a visit to one of California's truly lonely regions. A broken ankle in the Saline Range, by a solo hiker who has neglected to inform anyone of his whereabouts, may become a fatal injury. Saline Peak is little visited, and waiting for someone to come along to help could be a wait of several months. Usually, a National Park Service ranger can be found in the Warm Springs vicinity, and it will be rare when vacationers will not be present at the springs. Otherwise, the closest areas for help are the towns of Big Pine and Lone Pine in the Owens Valley. Likewise, these towns also provide the closest supplies and gasoline for your car so be sure to fill up before entering this wild desert landscape. For further information contact the Death Valley National Park Visitor Center.

### Saline Peak (7,045 ft; 2,047 m)

*Maps:* Saline Peak (CA) 7.5-minute (1:24,000 scale) topographic map; Saline Valley 1:100,000 scale metric topographic map; Automobile Club of Southern California (AAA) Death Valley National Park map

*Best Time to Climb:* October through April

*Approach:* From the junction of Highways 395 and 190 in Olancha, California drive 14.7 miles east on Highway 190 to the junction of Highways 136 and 190. Turn right onto Highway 190 and continue 17 miles to the Saline Valley Road. Turn left on this about 15.5 miles to Grapevine Canyon, where the Saline Valley Road stays left. The Grapevine Canyon Road (right) heads up to the Hunter Mountain country. Stay left on the Saline Valley Road and continue another thirty miles to the Warm Springs Road on the right. Take the Warm Springs Road about seven miles to the springs (four-wheel drive is recommended but high clearance two-wheel drive vehicles have been known to make it his far). This is where the crazed, serious summiteer is separated from the normal, sane person. Do you stop here and relax in a nice warm hot spring, or continue across rough tracks and dry landscapes to a desert summit. Assuming you're a crazed summiteer, continue another 11 miles on rough four-wheel drive roads to a point east of a basalt outcrop near Point 3,275 feet on the topographic map and park. *Route:* Head west, passing along the wash just south of the basalt outcrop, then up the ridge heading northwest to the summit. Anticipate eight miles round-trip with 3,900 feet of elevation gain.

## THE LAST CHANCE RANGE

The lengthy Last Chance Range includes those peaks between Last Chance Mountain on the north and Ubehebe Peak to the south. Deep canyons and colorful rock formations found within the range provide fine photographic opportunities. The highpoint of the range, Dry Mountain, lies in the central portion of the range, looming more than 7,000 feet above Saline Valley. In the Last Chance Mountain/Sandy Peak area, most routes follow the range crest which is more friendly to the typical hiker. The flanks of the range are much more imposing. The highest elevations of the range support fine pinyon-juniper woodlands (near Last Chance Mountain). Additionally, the Last Chance herd of bighorn sheep resides here seasonally, although their numbers appear to be dwindling since the 1970's.

The name Last Chance probably comes from a Lieutenant Lyle who visited the area as part of the Wheeler Survey. As described in W.A. Chalfant's book *Death Valley-The Facts,* and discussed in T.S. Palmer's *Place Names of the Death Valley Region*:

*"Lyle and 33 men left Camp Independence . . . They had much trouble crossing the mountains, trying one box canyon after another, and were in a desperate plight. When at the end of the second day after Hahn's departure they reached a place they named Last Chance Spring."*

Camping in the Last Chance Range is primitive so all the minimum impact camping methods apply. There is a developed campground at Mesquite Spring in the northern end of Death Valley. Lodging and supplies (food, gas, etc.) are available in Big Pine (if hiking in the northern end of the range), or to the south in Death Valley. Other than those places, there are no opportunities for communication with the outside world, other than the occasional fellow desert traveler, so come to this area prepared.

## LAST CHANCE MOUNTAIN (8,496 FT; 2,578 M)

Last Chance Mountain stands as the northern sentinel of the Last Chance Range, and tends to be snow covered during a normal winter. When the author climbed this peak during March 1990, the route was about 50 percent covered with snow. The Crater Mine near the road end was discovered in 1915, and during a 30-year period produced 62,000 tons of sulfur. The deposit consists of large zones of sulfur-rich hot springs deposits that have replaced Carrara limestone and Bonanza King dolomite. *Maps:* Last Chance Mountain (CA-NV) 7.5-minute (1:24,000 scale) topographic map; Last Chance Range 1:100,000 scale metric topographic map; Automobile Club of Southern California (AAA) Death Valley National Park map

*Best Time to Climb:* Fall and Spring

*Approach:* From Big Pine, California, take Highway 168 east 2.4 miles to the Death Valley Road (Forest Service Road 9S18, also known as the Waucoba-Saline Valley Road) and turn southeast (right). Follow this paved (at first) and well-graded dirt (from Eureka Valley onward) road as it crosses the Inyo Mountains and drops into Eureka Valley before climbing up into the Last Chance Range. Approximately 43 miles east of Big Pine, a large open pit of the former Crater Mine is reached, and a dirt road heads north along the west edge of the mine. Take this road north, which becomes rough, 2.5 miles to a shallow canyon leading up to a ridge to the west and park (6,200 ft). Two-wheel drive vehicles with high clearance are recommended.

*Route:* Hike up the canyon gaining the main north-south crest. Follow the ridge north over many ups and downs, passing a false summit and continuing to the true summit, about four miles from the car. This route has constant far-ranging views, and the pinyons along the crest afford some pleasant shade en route. A faint use trail will be followed for much of the distance along the crest. Anticipate seven miles round-trip with 2,300 feet of elevation gain.

*Alternate Approach and Route:* From the sulphur mine, continue east on the main road over the crest of the Last Chance Range, and drop into northern Death Valley to Crankshaft Junction. Turn north (left) at Crankshaft Junction onto a dirt road (high-clearance recommended) and continue 0.8 miles. Bear left on another dirt road (four-wheel drive vehicles recommended) 1.7 miles and bear right at another fork, following the track one mile to an old miner's cabin at Last Chance Spring (5,700 ft). Hike a

Heading along the ridge to Sandy with Sierra Nevada in view. Photo: Andy Zdon

faint road west of the cabin to Last Chance Spring. Follow the wash a short distance then exit south out of the wash to the ridge line. The ridge is then followed generally westward to the summit. Anticipate five miles round-trip with 3,000 feet of elevation gain.

### "SANDY PEAK" (7,062 FT; 2,153 M)

The summit of this peak is marked by a benchmark named "Sandy."

*Maps:* Sand Spring (CA-NV) and Hanging Rock Canyon (CA) 7.5-minute (1:24,000 scale) topographic maps; Last Chance Range 1:100,000 scale metric topographic map; Automobile Club of Southern California (AAA) Death Valley National Park map

*Approach:* Drive to the pass at the crest of the Last Chance Range as described for Last Chance Mountain's alternate route, parking at a pullout near the pass. If unsure of the precise point, continue to Crankshaft Junction, and backtrack three miles to the pullout (4,900 ft). This graded dirt road is driveable to all cars.

*Best Time to Climb:* November through April

*Route:* Hike across open sagebrush about one mile to the southeast, then eastward up a shallow canyon about 0.8 miles to a flat area just south-east of Point 5,829 feet. Gain a ridge to the southeast, then head south-ward along the crest to the summit. Some climbers consider this ridge boring, but opening oneself up to the tremendous views in every direc-tion, particularly when the Inyos and Sierra Nevada are draped in snow makes this ridge anything but boring. Just pleasant hill-walking in great desert surroundings. The dirt roads are well-graded and accessible to all cars. Anticipate 11 miles round-trip with 2,700 feet of elevation gain.

### DRY MOUNTAIN (8,674 FT; 2,645 M)

A secondary front ridge masks this, the highpoint of the Last Chance Range, when parked at the road end.

*Maps:* Dry Mountain (CA) 7.5-minute (1:24,000 scale) topographic map; Saline Valley 1:100,000 scale metric topographic map; Automobile Club of Southern California (AAA) Death Valley National Park map

*Best Time to Climb:* November through April

*Approach:* Drive north up Death Valley to the Grapevine Ranger Station, then west 5.2 miles to Ubehebe Crater, once described by Walt Wheelock as *"a recent blowout worthy of inspection."* The dirt road leading south to the Racetrack has caused blowouts of its own but not of the volcanic kind. On a trip to Racetrack Valley, the author was in a van that had two flat tires. While repairing the second flat, someone passed by and offered help, only to discover that they had flat tire as well. From Ubehebe Crater in northern Death Valley, drive south on the Racetrack Road about eight miles, just north of the low summit (Tin Pass) on the road at about 4,800 feet. Two-wheel drive vehicles with high clearance should be able to reach this point. Driving or parking off the road can result in a federal parking ticket.

*Route:* Hike west across the broad alluvial fan and climb to a low point on the ridge at about 7,900 feet. A slightly lower, wide valley must then be crossed to reach the summit, over a mile to the west. Anticipate 12 miles round-trip with 5,900 feet of elevation gain. This a long route!

### UBEHEBE PEAK (5,678 FT; 1,731 M)

This fine desert peak provides a bird's-eye view of the Racetrack and Saline Valley. The Racetrack is a dry lake, noted for its mysterious sliding rocks. After climbing this peak, spend some time out on the dry lake to inspect these mobile rocks, and their resulting "tracks."

*Maps:* Ubehebe Peak (CA) 7.5-minute (1:24,000 scale) topographic map; Saline Valley 1:100,000 scale metric topographic map; Automobile Club of Southern California (AAA) Death Valley National Park map

*Best Time to Climb:* November through April

*Approach:* From Ubehebe Crater, drive the Racetrack Road 19.7 miles south to Teakettle Junction, and another six miles to the Racetrack, a desert playa

Ubehebe Peak (on left) from the Racetrack Road. Photo: Andy Zdon

with a rock outcrop known as the Grandstand. Park at the Grandstand parking area (3,710 ft). This road is recommended for four-wheel drive, though high clearance two-wheel drives have made it.

*Route:* The peak, a broken mass of rock, lies a short distance west. A trail leads steeply up to the summit from the Grandstand parking area. Anticipate six miles round-trip with 2,000 feet of elevation gain.

## COTTONWOOD MOUNTAINS

For the purposes of this guide, the Cottonwood Mountains are considered as that section of the Panamint Range extending northward from Towne Pass on Highway 190 to Tin Mountain. The Cottonwood Mountains are second only to the Panamint Range as the highest mountains within the Death Valley National Park. Their slopes are covered with creosote at lower elevations, sagebrush at intermediate elevations, and sparse pinyon and juniper at the highest elevations. Supplies, gas, food and lodging are available at Stovepipe Wells and in Furnace Creek, inside the park. Gasoline may be available at Scotty's Castle. For further information, contact the Death Valley National Park Visitor Center in Furnace Creek.

## TIN MOUNTAIN (8,953 FT; 2,730 M)

This rugged limestone peak east of Dry Mountain is the highpoint of the Cottonwood Mountains.

*Maps:* Dry Mountain and Tin Mountain (CA) 7.5-minute (1:24,000 scale) topographic maps; Saline Valley 1:100,000 scale metric topographic map; Automobile Club of Southern California (AAA) Death Valley National Park map

*Best Time to Climb:* November through April

*Approach:* Follow the driving instructions for Dry Mountain. However, continue south to a point where the road enters some narrow washes, and park at a wide spot in the road some 10.5 miles from the end of the pavement (4,800 ft).

*Route:* The peak is adjacent to the road to the east and can be climbed by any of several washes and/or ridges to the east. A somewhat crooked-appearing ridge in the middle of the face may be followed all the way to the summit ridge. The summit is then a half-mile to the northeast. This route involves some loose gravel and easy rock-scrambling. Anticipate seven miles round-trip with 4,200 feet of elevation gain.

## WHITE TOP MOUNTAIN (7,607 FT; 2,319 M)

*Maps:* White Top Mountain (CA) 7.5-minute (1:24,000 scale) topographic map; Saline Valley 1:100,000 scale metric topographic map; Automobile Club of Southern California (AAA) Death Valley National Park map

*Best Time to Climb:* November through April

*Approach:* From Ubehebe Crater, follow the Racetrack Road 19.7 miles south to Teakettle Junction. Turn east, and head toward Hidden Valley, passing through Lost Burro Gap, and following the dirt road to another junction 3.2 miles from the Racetrack Road. Turn left, and continue another ten miles, to where the road exits a narrow canyon and park (6,600 ft). Four-wheel drive is recommended for this route.

*Route:* The peak is a relatively easy affair to the southeast. Anticipate two miles round-trip with 1,000 feet of elevation gain.

## HUNTER MOUNTAIN (7,455 FT; 2,272 M)

This large, flattish mountain has long been the cattle range for the pioneer Hunter family of the Owens Valley. Hunter Mountain is a large granitic massif that encompasses several highpoints. The true summit is marked

*"It was already ninety degrees at 6am when we started across the alluvial fan with that huge monster of vertical limestone, my first desert peak, bearing down upon us.*

*We hiked up crumbly limestone ledges and eroded staircases to higher ridges, where the pungent odor of junipers permeated the heat-weighted air. Not far below Tin's summit, we heard crying. Our eyes followed the mournful sound until we saw a young bighorn sheep, alone and precarious, stashed safely by its mother perhaps, on an unreachable limestone shelf.*

*By late afternoon, the talus in the descent gully was so hot, that the soles of my boots began to stick slightly to the rocks. How I wanted to sit down just for a moment, but the talus burned my skin. Stretched before me was the gully's broken rock, pouring out onto the white heat alluvial fan. Everyone was already out of sight. I was alone.*

Across the quintessential desert alluvial fan to Tin Mountain. Photo: Wynne Benti

*Through the waves of heat rising from the ground, I finally saw the cars. A climber sat in his lawn chair, boots off and legs outstretched, watching me come in like a small plane about to land for the first time on an unfamiliar runway. As I stumbled in, tee-shirt stained white from perspiration, hair bedraggled, someone handed me a cold 7-UP. With only hot water to drink, there was nothing to match the taste of the sugary soda and the cold can pressed upon my lips, then my cheeks. I climbed into the back of a friend's pickup and went to sleep.*

*While I slept, our group moved to Mesquite Springs, where a tub fire now cast its light upon the triple-digit June night. Sitting back about twenty feet on all sides from the blaze, where firelight meets the outer darkness of night, were the other climbers. Quiet and accomplished, they stared peacefully into the fire. I pulled up a lawn chair and joined them."*

–TIN MOUNTAIN ON JUNE 30TH, WYNNE BENTI

Fred Camphausen hiking to Canyon Point via Cottonwood Spring. Photo: Andy Zdon

by the benchmark "Jackass." Keep an eye out while hiking in the area for mule deer and bighorn sheep. The Hunter Mountain area is one of the most sensitive Native American regions of the California desert, and it includes areas of ritual use, pinyon collection areas, and sites of seasonally occupied villages and camps of the Owens Valley Paiute.

*Maps:* Jackass Canyon (CA) 7.5-minute (1:24,000 scale) topographic map; Saline Valley 1:100,000 scale metric topographic map; Automobile Club of Southern California (AAA) Death Valley National Park map

*Best Time to Climb:* October through April (can be inaccessible due to snow in winter)

*Approach:* From the junction of Highways 395 and 190 in Olancha, California drive 14.7 miles east on Highway 190 to the junction of Highways 136 and 190. Turn right onto Highway 190 and continue 17 miles to the Saline Valley Road. Turn north on this road and continue 15.5 miles to Grapevine Canyon, where the main road turns left toward Saline Valley. Keep right and drive about 2.8 miles to the flattish top (7,100 ft). Four-wheel drive vehicles are recommended.

*Route:* Stroll west to the summit. Anticipate two miles round-trip with 400 feet of elevation gain. If only a two-wheel drive vehicle is available, one can park at the intersection of the Saline Valley Road and the Hunter

Mountain Road (6,002 ft) and walk from there. Anticipate eight miles round-trip with 1,500 feet of elevation gain.

### "CANYON POINT" (5,890 FT; 1,795 M)

This peak is unnamed on the topographic maps, but is marked by a bench-mark named Canyon. This is a pleasant hike by either route.

*Maps:* Harris Hill and Cottonwood Canyon (CA) 7.5-minute (1:24,000 scale) topographic maps; Saline Valley 1:100,000 scale metric topographic map; Automobile Club of Southern California (AAA) Death Valley National Park map

*Best Time to Climb:* November through April

*Approach:* From Stovepipe Wells head west on the Cottonwood-Marble Canyon Road 8.3 miles to the mouth of a large canyon. Continue another 1.4 miles up the canyon to a fork and turn left up Cottonwood Canyon. Drive another 0.8 miles to a fork and stay left. Continue 8.2 miles south to the end of the road at a turnaround near a grove of cottonwood trees (2,900 ft). Four-wheel drive vehicles with high clearance are required.

*Route:* From the end of the road, climb west up a steep loose chute about 50 feet to a wash heading west toward the peak. Hike up the wash to the 3,800-foot level, then climb to the left up a slope to an east-west ridge. Follow the ridge west to a saddle at 5,280 feet, then head north-northwest a half mile to the summit. For a quick return, the sand slope to the east can be used to return to the wash. Anticipate six miles round-trip with 3,000 feet of elevation gain.

*Alternate Route:* Using the same approach route, a fine route for this peak is to hike up tree-lined Cottonwood Canyon to Cottonwood Spring. From here the peak is an easy ramble to the north. Anticipate 12.5 miles round-trip with 3,200 feet of elevation gain.

### PANAMINT BUTTE (6,584 FT; 2,007 M)

When viewed from across Panamint Valley at Crowley Overlook along Highway 190, the stripes on this massive-looking desert peak are actually wildly folded layers of limestone. Upon reaching the summit of this peak, one enters a gentle land with a volcanic past. The entire summit plateau is capped with a 3.5 to 5.0 million year old basalt flow. This basalt flow is probably the same flow that occurs in the Argus Range west of Panamint Valley but which has been separated due to the faulting and spreading apart of Panamint Valley.

*Maps:* The Dunes, Panamint Butte, and Lemoigne Canyon (CA) 7.5-minute (1:24,000 scale) topographic maps; Saline Valley and Darwin Hills 1:100,000 scale metric topographic maps; Automobile Club of Southern California (AAA) Death Valley National Park map

*Best Time to Climb:* November through April

*Approach:* Although this is the only route on the mountain requiring a four-wheel drive approach route, this route is so pleasant that the author has brashly taken the liberty of recommending this as the primary route to the mountain. The road is, in fact, one of the roughest four-wheel drive routes in the national park. From Stovepipe Wells, drive six miles west on Highway 190 to the Lemoigne Canyon Road on the right. If driving in from the west, the road is 3.1 miles east of Wildrose Station on Highway 190. Follow the extremely rough route about five miles to the marked road end (about 2,400 ft). Four-wheel drive may not be enough for this route – make sure your vehicle has high approach and exit clearance as the road drops in and out of several washes suddenly, and hanging up on your bumper or undercarriage could be a very real problem. The author has a Toyota four-wheel drive pickup and has driven the road twice without incident.

*Route:* From the road end, hike up Lemoigne Canyon to a broad valley east of Panamint Butte. This valley is dotted with Joshua trees, and in the past, before the National Park Service began to remove them from within park boundaries, wild horses could be seen on distant slopes. The peak is visible to the west as the highest, rounded summit on the skyline. Head directly to the peak. The broad valley makes for pleasant, but dry, overnight camping if Panamint Butte is climbed as an overnighter. Anticipate 18 miles round-trip with 4,300 feet of elevation gain.

*Alternate Approach and Route:* From Highway 190 in Panamint Valley, follow the graded road branching north from Highway 190, two miles east of the junction with the Panamint Valley Road. Follow this road 5.7 miles to where it curves northeast toward the mountains. Park here (1,560 ft) if you have a two-wheel drive vehicle, or with four-wheel drive vehicles, continue up the road another 0.8 miles or farther to the Big Four Mine (2,460 ft). A route from here is up the ridge to the left, but it is a long 4,000-foot climb. This is the route most frequently climbed on this peak but

Up the north fork of Lemoigne Canyon to Panamint Butte.  Photo: Andy Zdon

Panamint Butte from the west looking across Panamint Dry Lake after a winter storm. Photo: Andy Zdon

the Lemoigne Canyon route is much more pleasant. Anticipate eight miles round-trip with 5,000 feet of elevation gain if you have a two-wheel drive vehicle.

*Second Alternate:* On climbing Towne Peak, continue over three summits to reach the Butte. Anticipate 16 miles round-trip with 5,000 feet of elevation gain. Much of the elevation gain will be on the return trip.

*"Rock, sand, cactus, and creosote. The walk up the north fork of Lemoigne Canyon is quiet and gentle, through a sandy desert wash walled in on either side by steep slabs of limestone, polished smooth by centuries of flash floods. By early afternoon, we reach our overnight camp spot in the warm soft sand at the shallow head of the wash. Early winter shadows have embraced the distant ridges and canyons. Joshua trees, seemingly out of place in the harsh country of Death Valley, speckle the horizon.*

*The next morning, we follow a pair of wild horses to the summit of Panamint Butte, a massive striped limestone buttress in the Cottonwood mountains. Towering steeply above Panamint Dry Lake on the west while on the east, broad canyons and ridges spread gently across the desert to Stovepipe Wells and the sand dunes just beyond."*

PANAMINT BUTTE FROM LEMOIGNE CANYON, WYNNE BENTI

## "TOWNE PEAK" (7,287 FT; 2,221 M)

This peak is a great conditioner and a fine desert peak. The views of Telescope Peak, Panamint Valley and in the distance Mount Whitney, White Mountain Peak and Charleston Peak, all snow clad in winter, are spectacular. The peak is unnamed on the topographic map.

*Maps:* Panamint Butte (CA) 7.5-minute (1:24,000 scale) topographic map; Darwin Hills 1:100,000 scale metric topographic map; Automobile Club of Southern California (AAA) Death Valley National Park map

*Best Time to Climb:* November through April

*Approach:* From Death Valley drive west (or east if coming from Panamint Valley) on State Highway 190 to the summit of Towne Pass and a large parking area (4,926 ft). The paved highway is driveable to all cars.

*Route:* Climb the rubbly slope to the north, then follow a fairly easy ridge that may be traversed cross-country as it winds to the summit. Anticipate seven miles round-trip with 3,300 feet of elevation gain.

## THE PANAMINT RANGE

Standing more than 11,000 feet above the floor of Death Valley, the Panamint Range presents one of the tallest up-sweeps of vertical relief in

LeRoy Johnson describes the characteristics of a prehistoric trail north of Tucki Mountain.
Photo: Wynne Benti

North America. As if this were not enough, the range towers 10,000 feet over the Panamint Valley on the west. During a warm spring day, the snow-capped ridge of 11,049-foot Telescope Peak is reflected in the tepid ponds of Badwater at 282 feet below sea level. The terrain is extremely variable, from the wide, creosote-lined washes emptying into the valley floors, to the limber and bristlecone pine-dotted slopes of the highest peaks. The range contains numerous historic and prehistoric cultural sites, as the Panamints have traditionally been an important part of the local native culture. The Shoshone name "Panamint" was probably applied by the Darwin French Party that explored the area in 1860.

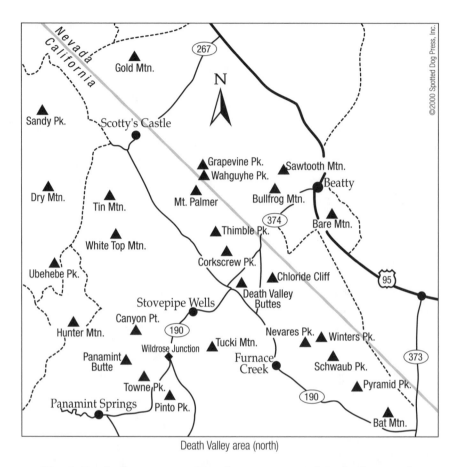

Death Valley area (north)

Vegetation in the area consists of a creosote scrub in the lowest elevations. Sagebrush scrub becomes prominent with increasing elevation, and eventually pinyons and junipers dot the hillsides from about 5,000 feet upward. The pinyon-juniper woodlands become dominant above 7,000 feet, and bristlecone and limber pine are found along the crest of Telescope Peak. Animals in the area include bighorn sheep, mule deer, coyote, and foxes. Wild burros and horses can be observed on occasion, though this will end by about 2005 as the National Park Service plans to remove the non-native grazers from within the park boundaries.

Surface water is virtually nonexistent with the exception of the many springs that are found throughout the range. Unlike the other mountains around Death Valley, late spring and summer are fine times to climb Telescope Peak. During early spring, the ridge to the summit can be snow-covered, even corniced. Many access routes require four-wheel drive.

Only a few peaks (from Bald Peak south to Telescope) may be accessed with a standard sedan. Camping in the Panamints is typically primitive although nice campgrounds are available along the Wildrose Road to Mahogany Flat. Thorndyke camp is the former site of a tourist camp operated by Thorndyke and his wife. They had originally wished to build their camp on the summit of Telescope Peak, but found the shady hollow below Mahogany Flat more agreeable. Food, lodging and supplies are available in Stovepipe Wells in Death Valley, or in Ridgecrest. Additionally, gas, a restaurant, private campground and lodging are available at Panamint Springs Resort along Highway 190 on the west end of Panamint Valley. For further information on the area, contact the National Park Visitor Center in Furnace Creek.

### PINTO PEAK (7,508 FT; 2,288 M)

This peak is south of Towne Pass along Highway 190. Although the only route described is from Emigrant Pass, other routes are possible from Towne Pass. The routes from Towne Pass are over considerably rougher terrain, and although shorter, these routes may not save much in the way of time. The route from Emigrant Pass is the same route that was used by Edna Brush Perkins on her ascent of this peak in 1921, possibly the first recorded ascent of a desert peak for the pure fun of it.

The basalt present on top of Panamint Butte is also present here on Pinto Peak. However, here, the basalt lies on top of sediments of the Nova formation (which one passes through on his drive along west side of Towne Pass on Highway 190). The summit area of Pinto Peak, is composed of a conglomerate that rests atop the basalt, and is also part of the Nova. The story here is that the massive basalt flow occurred during the period in which the Nova sediments were being deposited.

Oddly, the naming of this peak does not have a significance to the coloration or appearance of this summit, or even the naming of someone named "Pinto." The name Pinto was purely a mistake. In a great piece of topographic detective work, historians LeRoy and Jean Johnson uncovered a bit of mapping smoke and mirrors. The name Pinto is the name provided by the Wheeler Survey on their maps, except that their Pinto Peak was today's Towne Peak. Upon looking at the actual field maps in Washington D.C., the Johnsons discovered that Wheeler didn't actually name Towne Peak "Pinto," he named the Cottonwood Mountains the

Returning from the summit of Tucki. Photo: Wynne Benti

Pinto Mountains. The transcription on the map placed the name Pinto Mountain by chance next to the point of today's Towne Peak, so the naming of Pinto (today's Towne) was also an accident. To make matters worse, in 1908, the U.S.G.S. published a topographic map with the name "Pinto" moved to its present location. Thankfully, it has managed to stay in one place for nearly a hundred years. May it stay there in perpetuity.

*Maps:* Emigrant Pass and Emigrant Canyon (CA) 7.5-minute (1:24,000 scale) topographic maps; Darwin Hills 1:100,000 scale metric topographic map; Automobile Club of Southern California (AAA) Death Valley National Park map

*Best Time to Climb:* November through April

*Approach:* From Wildrose Station on Highway 190, drive the Emigrant Canyon/Wildrose Road 13.5 miles south to Emigrant Pass (5,318 ft). The road is paved.

*Route:* From the pass, hike the northernmost of the two trails that take off on the north side of the road. The trail steadily climbs up Pinto's southeast slopes, eventually reaching the summit. Anticipate 13 miles round-trip with 4,000 feet of elevation gain.

## TUCKI MOUNTAIN (6,726 FT; 2,050 M)

Tucki Mountain is the northern sentinel of the Panamint Range and is an enormous massif covering an area of about 140 square miles. A glance at the map suggests the peak is an easy day but this is not the case! This is one peak where having a four-wheel drive vehicle results in a hike that makes for a pleasant day's outing. A hike from the two-wheel drive parking area is something of an epic. The views of the north end of Death Valley are breathtaking.

This peak is the supposed location of the fabled Lost Gunsight Lode, and has been one of the key areas of interest in the region for treasure hunters. In 1849, Jim Martin, an emigrant with a party called the Georgians, stumbled upon some fabulously rich silver ore on the slopes of this mountain. Planning on heading to southern California, Martin and his friends intended to return. They were in desperate straights, and were forced to leave their animals and head out on foot. In order to pare down their loads, they also buried a stash of gold coins under a bush. The site of this treasure, and the Lost Gunsight Lode has never been found.

*Maps:* Stovepipe Wells, Emigrant Canyon, Grotto Canyon, and Tucki Wash (CA) 7.5-minute (1:24,000 scale) topographic maps; Saline Valley and Darwin Hills 1:100,000 scale metric topographic maps; Automobile Club of Southern California (AAA) Death Valley National Park map

*Best Time to Climb:* November through April

*Approach:* From Wildrose Station on Highway 190, follow the Emigrant Canyon/Wildrose Road south about 1.5 miles to where the Tucki Mine Road (rough dirt) heads off on the left. When approaching the road, drive slow as the turnoff is easy to miss. Drop into the wash, then back up the other side. The road follows the base of the mountains for a while then heads up Telephone Canyon. Four-wheel drive is recommended, although two-wheel drive vehicles with high clearance may be able to negotiate the road. Follow the road up the canyon about 9.3 miles just crossing a saddle to where a side canyon heads off north to another saddle. Park here (4,880 ft). If you reach the Tucki Mine Cabin, you've gone a bit too far.

*Route:* From the road end, head north up the side canyon to a saddle. Head northwest from the saddle dropping into a broad valley, then continue northwest climbing over Point 5,730 feet, then dropping to yet another saddle at 5,480 feet. Continue northwest up Tucki's south ridge, crossing

The Wildrose Charcoal Kilns:  Wynne Benti

several false summits en route. Anticipate seven miles round-trip with 3,300 feet of elevation gain.

*Alternate Route and Approach:*  This is the route for those without four-wheel drive. From the junction of Highway 190 and the Emigrant Canyon/Wildrose Road, drive 9.5 miles south on the Emigrant Canyon/Wildrose Road to the Skidoo Road. Turn east (left) and drive 6.3 miles of well-graded dirt road to a faint dirt road heading north. Park here at about 5,660 feet. Walk north along the dirt road about 0.2 miles to a saddle. Continue to another saddle east of Point 5,820 feet, then drop down into Telephone Canyon to the dirt road described for Route 1. Follow the road east (right) about 1.2 miles. From here, follow the principal route to the summit. Anticipate 14 miles round-trip with 4,300 feet of elevation gain.

## BALD PEAK (7,764 FT; 2,366 M)

This peak, which has also been called Baldy, is apparently the peak that the National Park Service wanted to name Manly Peak in 1936. Thankfully, they reserved the name for a more substantial peak to the south. The peak has also been referred to as Manly Dome.

*Maps:* Emigrant Pass and Wildrose Peak (CA) 7.5-minute (1:24,000 scale) topographic maps; Darwin Hills 1:100,000 scale metric topographic map; Automobile Club of Southern California (AAA) Death Valley National Park map

*Best Time to Climb:* Fall and Spring

*Approach:* From Emigrant Pass on the Emigrant Canyon/Wildrose Road, drive about 1.8 miles south to an old dirt road that heads east up a broad canyon. Park along the road here (5,380 ft). The road is paved and driveable to all cars.

*Route:* Follow the track as it heads east up the canyon to a saddle and a fork. The right-hand trail drops down to Nemo Canyon. Take the trail continuing east to a mine, then gain the ridge to the south. This ridge is then followed east, passing Point 7,391 feet to Bald's north ridge. The summit is a short distance to the south. Anticipate 8.5 miles round-trip with 2,850 feet of elevation gain.

## WILDROSE PEAK (9,064 FT; 2,763 M)

Overshadowed by its more famous and higher neighbor to the south, this peak is surprisingly seldom climbed despite the good trail that leads to the summit. The views from the top are outstanding, and provide a fine place for an extended stay.

*Maps:* Wildrose Peak (CA) 7.5-minute (1:24,000 scale) topographic map; Darwin Hills 1:100,000 scale metric topographic map; Automobile Club of Southern California (AAA) Death Valley National Park map

*Best Time to Climb:* Spring through Fall

*Approach:* Drive the Emigrant Pass Road to Wildrose Canyon, 45 miles out of Trona. Turn east up a well-graded dirt road seven miles to the Charcoal Kilns. The giant beehive-shaped kilns are worth the drive alone. The dirt road (washboard surface) is driveable to all vehicles.

*Route:* Follow the well-graded trail that starts behind the Charcoal Kilns, and winds its way through pinyon and juniper to the summit. The round-trip distance is 8.4 miles with 2,200 feet of elevation gain.

**BENNETT PEAK (9,980 FT; 3,042 M), ROGERS PEAK (9,994 FT; 3,036+ M)**
While these peaks may be climbed directly via a closed jeep road from
from Mahogany Flat to the repeater on Rogers, they are usually climbed
as a side excursion while returning from Telescope Peak. Bennett Peak
is named in honor of Asabel Bennett, a member of the '49ers party that
crossed Death Valley in 1849. Rogers Peak is named in honor of John
Rogers, who with Manly traversed the region to get help for the '49ers.
*Maps:* Telescope Peak (CA) 7.5-minute (1:24,000 scale) topographic
map; Darwin Hills 1:100,000 scale metric topographic map; Automobile
Club of Southern California (AAA) Death Valley National Park map
*Best Time to Climb:* Late April through November
*Approach:* Drive the Emigrant Pass Road to Wildrose Canyon, 45 miles
out of Trona. Turn east up a well-graded dirt road seven miles to the
Charcoal Kilns. The dirt road (rough) is driveable to all vehicles. Continue
up the road to Mahogany Flat (8,100 ft) where a few nice campsites are
located. Between the Charcoal Kilns and Mahogany Flat, the dirt road
becomes rougher and steep, and some two-wheel drive vehicles may have
difficulty reaching the Flat. At times, the road becomes rough enough for
four-wheel drive vehicles to be recommended.
*Route:* From Mahogany Flat, the peaks can be reached by following the
Telescope Peak trail to Arcane Meadow, the broad saddle between Bennett
and Rogers, or by hiking up the closed jeep road that leads to the antenna
on Rogers Peak. However, these peaks are usually ascended along with
Telescope and the following route is recommended.
*Route from Telescope Peak:* Climb Telescope Peak as described below.
Leaving Telescope Peak, drop to a saddle (9,600 ft) between Telescope and
Bennett. An easy stroll takes you to the top of Bennett. Now head north
to Arcane Meadow at about 9,600 feet and then climb another 400 feet to
Rogers. Now it is all downhill along the trail or down the dirt road back
to Mahogany Flat. Climbing the two peaks in combination with Telescope
Peak adds less than a mile and about 500 or 600 feet of elevation gain to
the climb of Telescope.

**TELESCOPE PEAK (11,049 FT; 3,367 M)**
Telescope Peak is the highest point in Death Valley National Park. This
peak receives much snow in winter and fierce winds soon form a dangerous
crust. There have been several fatal accidents here. During November of

En route to Telescope Peak. Photo: Andy Zdon

1960, a 17-year old reached the summit as he was beset by an early season snowstorm. He became lost in a white-out during his descent, and plunged head first down a gully to his death. Six years later, two young climbers attempted Telescope in December. The south ridge was covered with icy snow. They had taken a basic mountaineering course and were carrying ice axes. As they descended the east slope into Hanaupah Canyon, one of the climbers slipped, and was unable to arrest his fall with his ice axe. He fell over a thousand feet to his death. An ice-axe and crampons (and knowing how to use them) should be carried on a climb of this desert peak in winter. After the snow melts, it is a pleasant trail-walk amid the dolomite and associated rocks of the Johnnie formation. When the author and a friend climbed this peak during the late winter of 1981, the hard snow and corniced ridge made us glad to have carried our snow gear. As a side note, if taking a rest along the ridge between Bennett and Telescope, watch where you sit. The author once managed to sit on a low, matted cactus and ended up spending over an hour pulling cactus spines from his pants.

*Maps:* Telescope Peak (CA) 7.5-minute (1:24,000 scale) topographic map; Darwin Hills 1:100,000 scale metric topographic map; Automobile

View across Sentinel, Porter, and the southern portion of the Panamint Range from Telescope Peak.
Photo: Andy Zdon

Club of Southern California (AAA) Death Valley National Park map
*Best Time to Climb:* Late April through November
*Approach:* Follow the approach route description for Bennett and Rodgers as described earlier.
*Route:* An excellent trail with ever-expanding views toward the salt flats of Death Valley, 11,000 feet below, leads to the summit. The trail winds gently around Rogers and Bennett Peaks, then switchbacks up to the pointed summit. The views from the summit are among the finest of any desert peak. On a clear day, the views include San Gabriel and San Bernardino Mountains to the south near Los Angeles, the Sierra Nevada to the west, the White Mountains to the north, and Charleston Peak to the southwest. Anticipate 14 miles round-trip with 3,200 feet of elevation gain.

## SENTINEL PEAK (9,634 FT; 2,936 M)

When you follow Surprise Canyon to the top of Sentinel Peak, you are following a historic route that once played an important role in the region's history. During the period from 1873 to 1876, Panamint City, in upper Surprise Canyon was a bustling mining town, with a population that exceeded 1,500 people. Security problems were ever-present, as bandits frequently robbed the silver shipments heading down the old wagon road in Surprise Canyon. With a rather ingenious idea for outwitting the bandits, the mining operations began to process the silver into 500-pound cannon-balls, making a quick get away with any silver nearly impossible. Eventually, word got around, and guards were no longer needed on the bullion shipments. In 1876, as the ore in the mines began to pan out, a cloudburst over Surprise Canyon resulted in a flash flood that virtually swept away the entire town. In the early 1980's, new mining operations were set up, only to be swept away once again in a flash flood. Standing on end near the mouth of the canyon, are the victims of this later flood, the rusted hulls of vehicles that tried to beat the flood waters, but didn't make it. They are a vivid reminder of a flash flood's potential for destruction.

*Maps:* Telescope Peak (CA) 7.5-minute (1:24,000 scale) topographic map; Darwin Hills 1:100,000 scale metric topographic map; Automobile Club of Southern California (AAA) Death Valley National Park map

*Best Time to Climb:* April through November

*Approach:* From Trona, California, drive 23 miles north on the Trona-Emigrant Canyon/Wildrose Road crossing a divide between Searles and Panamint Valleys, to the Ballarat Road. Turn east (right) and follow this 3.6 miles to the town of Ballarat (no fishing allowed in the lake–contact the Ballarat yacht club)! At Ballarat, you'll reach a junction with the Wingate Road. Turn north (left) and drive 1.9 miles to the Surprise Canyon Road. Turn northeast (right) and drive 3.4 miles to the end of the road at Novak's Camp (referred to as Chris Wicht's in earlier guides). Park here at 2,800 feet. Two-wheel drive vehicles with good clearance are recommended.

*Route:* From the camp, cross a small gully and enter the rocky mouth of Surprise Canyon. Hike east up the Canyon about five miles to the site of Panamint City, where a dirt track is followed behind the old smokestack and up Sentinel's northwest ridge. Anticipate 16 miles round-trip with 7,000 feet of elevation gain. This is usually done as an overnight backpack with a camp made at Panamint City. Several years ago, Wynne Benti found several boxes of old dynamite and blasting caps in the mine magazine. The Inyo County Sheriff was notified (Panamint City was outside the park boundary at that time), so hopefully the explosives were removed. Wynne also reported getting some gnarly insect bites while sleeping near the abandoned buildings, so bug repellent is recommended.

*Alternate Approach and Route:* Climb Porter Peak from Pleasant Canyon as described below. From Porter Peak, follow the ridge north to the summit of Sentinel. Add eight miles round-trip and 2,900 feet of elevation gain to your climb of Porter.

*Alternate Approach and Route 2:* From the junction of Highways 178 and 127 north of Shoshone, drive 29.1 miles west on Highway 178 to the West Side Road. Turn left and follow the West Side Road 15 miles to a poor dirt road (four-wheel drive vehicles recommended) leading west toward Johnson Canyon. After entering the canyon, a fork will be reached in a couple of miles. Bear right, driving another mile to a spring. Hike west up the canyon two miles to the ruins of Hungry Bill's Ranch. Continue on a faint use trail three miles to Panamint Pass. Turn southwest and Sentinel is reached after a mile's scramble. Anticipate 12 miles round-trip with 5,700 feet of elevation gain.

## PORTER PEAK (9,101 FT; 2,774 M)

This fine viewpoint on the crest of the Panamint Range, is named for the Porter brothers who operated the mercantile store in Ballarat during the boom years.
*Maps:* Telescope Peak (CA) 7.5-minute (1:24,000 scale) topographic map; Darwin Hills 1:100,000 scale metric topographic map; Automobile Club of Southern California (AAA) Death Valley National Park map
*Best Time to Climb:* All Year
*Approach:* From Trona, California, drive 23 miles north on the Trona-Emigrant Canyon/Wildrose Road crossing a divide between Searles and Panamint Valleys, to the Ballarat Road. Turn east (right) and follow this 3.6 miles to the town of Ballarat. At Ballarat, you'll reach a junction with the Wingate Road. Continue northeast past this junction a half mile to a fork. Go right, and follow the road up Pleasant Canyon 5.5 miles to a gate at Clair Camp. Four-wheel drive may be required along sections of this road. The gate across the road should be open. Continue another 2.5 miles to a corral. If driving a two-wheel drive vehicle, park here (5,960 ft). With

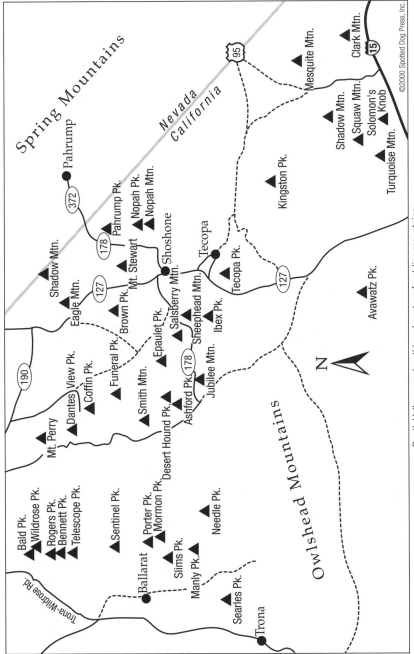

Death Valley area (south) and eastern front tier mountains

a four-wheel drive vehicle, bear left and continue another 1.5 miles to below the Cooper Mine (6,880 ft).

*Route:* From below the Cooper Mine, scramble northeast to a saddle, then follow the ridge east to Porter Peak. Anticipate four miles round-trip with 2,300 feet of elevation gain (from the four-wheel drive vehicle road end) or seven miles round-trip with 3,150 feet of elevation gain from the two-wheel drive vehicle parking area.

*Alternate Approach and Route:* With a four-wheel drive vehicle, bear right at the stone corral, and drive 1.3 miles to a fork. Bear left, and drive one mile to the 7,000 foot level. Hike north up easy slopes to the summit or the ridge line to the northeast toward the summit. Anticipate 2.5 miles round-trip with 2,100 feet of elevation gain.

### "MORMON PEAK" (8,270 FT; 2,774 M)

On the map, this peak shows up as a benchmark name on the summit, not as an officially named peak. It was probably named in reference to its close proximity to Mormon Gulch at the head of Pleasant Canyon. Mormon settlers conducted some prospecting in the area during the nineteenth century and a party of Mormons, led by Charles Alvord, passed through here between 1868 and 1869.

*Maps:* Panamint (CA) 7.5-minute (1:24,000 scale) topographic map; Darwin Hills 1:100,000 scale metric topographic map; Automobile Club of Southern California (AAA) Death Valley National Park map

*Best Time to Climb:* Fall and Spring

*Approach:* From Trona, California, drive 23 miles north on the Trona-Emigrant Canyon/Wildrose Road crossing a divide between Searles and Panamint Valleys, to the Ballarat Road. Turn east (right) and follow this 3.6 miles to the town of Ballarat. At Ballarat, you'll reach a junction with the Wingate Road. Continue northeast past this junction a half mile to a fork. Go right, and follow the road up Pleasant Canyon 5.5 miles to a gate at Clair Camp. Four-wheel drive may be required along sections of this road. The gate across the road should be open. Continue another 2.5 miles to a corral and a fork. The left fork heads up to the Cooper Mine. The right fork heads up to a saddle south of Mormon Peak. Drive up the right fork as far as practicable.

*Route:* From your parking spot, hike up the road to the saddle, then north to the summit. If parked at the corral, anticipate approximately eight miles round-trip with 2,400 feet of elevation gain.

### SLIM'S PEAK (7,115 FT; 2,169 M)

This peak which is named in honor of prospector Charles Ferge, also known as Seldom Seen Slim, overlooks Slim's home, the Panamint Valley. Slim passed away in Trona during 1968. He was known as "the last of the single blanket and jack ass prospectors."

*Maps:* Panamint (CA) 7.5-minute (1:24,000 scale) topographic map; Darwin Hills 1:100,000 scale metric topographic map; Automobile Club of Southern California (AAA) Death Valley National Park map

*Best Time to Climb:* November through April

*Approach:* From Trona, California, drive 23 miles north on the Trona-Emigrant Canyon/Wildrose Road crossing a divide between Searles and Panamint Valleys, to the Ballarat Road. Turn east (right) and follow this 3.6 miles to the town of Ballarat. At Ballarat, you'll reach a junction with the Wingate Road. Continue northeast past this junction a half mile to a fork. Go right, and follow the road up Pleasant Canyon 5.5 miles to a gate at Clair Camp. Four-wheel drive vehicles may be required along sections of this road. The gate across the road should be open. Continue another 0.9 miles up the canyon until a dirt road heading off to the right toward the World Beater Mine is reached. Park here (5,160 ft).

*Route:* Hike up the road to the World Beater Mine. This was one of the more important mines in the area during the early 1900's, and a 10-stamp mill stood here until it was burned by vandals during the early 1980's. From the mill site, either climb up the draw to the southwest, or climb the ridge to the west of the draw. Once the crest of the ridge is reached, climb south until an east-west ridge is reached. Once on the east-west ridge, drop to the west toward Slim's Peak. Anticipate four miles round-trip with 2,800 feet of elevation gain.

### MANLY PEAK (7,194 FT; 2,193.3 M)

Covered by sparse desert vegetation with some pinyons and junipers on its higher slopes, this peak is named in honor of William Lewis Manly. Some believe that Manly climbed at least part way up the peak in 1849 while trying to find a route out of Death Valley in an effort to rescue a party of emigrants he had been traveling with. The peak was originally named Needle Peak by the Wheeler Survey, but another peak nearby was

On the main route up Manly Peak looking north across the Panamints.  Photo: Wynne Benti

christened "Needle," when Manly was honored by having a mountain named after him. Anvil Spring, at Russell Camp, is also of historical significance. Sergeant Neal of the Bendire Expedition of 1867 found an anvil, wagon rims and some old iron scrap at the spring. These artifacts may have been part of the blacksmith's equipment brought to Death Valley by Asabel Bennett in 1849.

*Maps:* Manly Peak (CA) 7.5-minute (1:24,000 scale) topographic map; Ridgecrest 1:100,000 scale metric topographic map; Automobile Club of Southern California (AAA) Death Valley National Park map

*Best Time to Climb:* November through April

*Approach:* From Trona, California, drive 23 miles north on the Trona-Emigrant Canyon/Wildrose Road crossing a divide between Searles and Panamint Valleys, to the Ballarat Road. Turn east (right) and follow this 3.6 miles to the town of Ballarat. At Ballarat, you'll reach a junction with the Wingate Road. Head south on the well-graded Wingate Road about 15 miles until you reach the Goler Wash Road that takes off to the east toward the Panamint Range. Follow the Goler Wash Road about nine miles to Mengel Pass. The Goler Wash Road is definitely for four-wheel drive vehicles only. Before you reach Mengel Pass, you'll drive near an abandoned stone building known as the Barker Ranch, where the members of the Inyo County Sheriff's Department and the California Highway Patrol found infamous gang leader, Charles Manson, hiding out in the bathroom cabinet. When the author visited the Barker Ranch, someone had removed the famous cabinet, but its outline was still visible on the wall. Poking around surrounding washes, we located some of the gang's sentry stations at rock outcroppings and an old truck imbedded in wash sands, with the words "Helter Skelter" spray-painted on its cab. Bullet holes riddled the truck and given the amount of rust that had formed over the words painted in white, it is probable that the "Helter Skelter" was from Manson's era. Up the road is Meyers Ranch (inhabited), also one of the gang's haunts.

From Mengel Pass, drop into Butte Valley, and continue another 1.3 miles to a road that forks left. Turn left continue a few hundred feet then turn left again. Another half mile of driving brings you to Russell Camp (4,430 ft). If approaching Butte Valley from the Death Valley side, take the west side road on the south end of Death Valley where it leaves Highway 178 (29 miles west of the Highway 178-127 junction north of Shoshone).

The "Helter Skelter" truck. Photo: Wynne Benti

Follow the West Side Road 2.8 miles north to the Warm Springs Canyon Road heading west toward Butte Valley. Turn left here and follow the Warm Springs Canyon Road 21.9 miles to the Russell Camp fork in Butte Valley. The condition of the Warm Springs Road can change significantly depending on recent flash floods. The first time the author drove this road, a hair-raising crux move over a bedrock outcrop in the wash was needed near the Warm Springs Mine. The second time, after some flash flooding, the move was hardly noticeable as sediment had apparently been deposited around the outcrop. Regardless, four-wheel drive was required. Check with the Park Visitor Center before driving the Warm Springs Road.

*Route:* From Russell Camp, hike southwest to the obvious saddle, then northwest up the ridge to a small peak about one-half mile northeast of Manly Peak. Along this ridge, you will have fine views of the Manly Peak summit block. Now follow the ridge southwest to the Manly Peak

Striped Butte as seen from route up Manly.  Photo: Wynne Benti

summit block.  The summit register is just below the summit block.  To climb the summit block, climb the third class friction slab.  The author avoided the slab on the way down by working his way down the boulders directly to the summit register and found descending the block easier then ascending, a rarity. Anticipate six miles round-trip with 2,800 feet of elevation gain.

### STRIPED BUTTE (4,773 FT; 1,455 M)
This is probably one of the most photographed points in Death Valley National Park. The peak was previously named Curious Butte.  Manly passed by this butte after ascending Redlands Canyon on his way back to Death Valley.
*Maps:* Manly Peak (CA) 7.5-minute (1:24,000 scale) topographic map; Ridgecrest 1:100,000 scale metric topographic map; Automobile Club of Southern California (AAA) Death Valley National Park map
*Best Time to Climb:* November through April

Breccia knobs on the main route up Needle.  Photo: Wynne Benti

*Approach:* To reach Striped Butte, drive to Butte Valley as described for Manly Peak. Drive to a point level with the west side of the butte (4,000 ft).
*Route:* It is an easy climb from the west. Anticipate two miles round-trip with 800 feet of elevation gain. It is not until actually on the Butte, that one realizes how rugged the east slopes of this small peak actually are.

### NEEDLE PEAK (5,803 FT; 1,768.8 M)

*Maps:* Manly Peak (CA) 7.5-minute (1:24,000 scale) topographic map; Ridgecrest 1:100,000 scale metric topographic map; Automobile Club of Southern California (AAA) Death Valley National Park map
*Best Time to Climb:* November through April
*Approach:* Drive to Mengel Pass as described for Manly Peak. Follow the road 1.8 miles into Butte Valley to a fork near the Geologist's Cabin (stone). Turn right and go 0.2 miles, then right again and about two miles to Willow Spring (about 3,540 ft).
*Route:* Hike south about a half-mile, then head east-southeast about 0.8 miles, crossing a broad saddle and contouring from the saddle to a large canyon between Points 1,489 and 1,525 meters. Several small drainages are traversed en route. Head south up the canyon, taking the middle fork at a three-way fork, and finally gain Needle's west ridge at the head of the canyon. The summit is less than a mile to the east but a steep scramble. Anticipate six miles round-trip with 2,500 feet of elevation gain round-trip.

## GRAPEVINE MOUNTAINS

Rising 7,000 feet above the northern end of Death Valley, the Grapevine Mountains form an imposing barrier on the east side of the valley floor. The west side of the Grapevine Mountains is extremely rugged, with deeply incised canyons that are frequently blocked by dry waterfalls. Presented from the east they take on a more gentle and approachable appearance. The vegetation contrasts from the west to east sides of the range are striking. On the west side, the mountains appear dry, almost barren of life. But creosote scrub cling to these slopes, and at the higher elevations sagebrush is found. Meanwhile, on the east side, sagebrush gives way to a pinyon-juniper woodland much further downslope. The crest of the range on Grapevine and Wahguyhe Peaks is dotted with limber pine.

Food, gasoline, lodging and supplies are available in Beatty, Nevada or in Stovepipe Wells. Camping in the range is primitive and all minimum impact camping methods should be applied here.  For climbs of Thimble, Corkscrew, or the Death Valley Buttes, a campsite in one of the several Death Valley campgrounds such as at Stovepipe Wells, Furnace Creek, or Texas Spring will be practical.  For further information on the Grapevine Mountains, contact the National Park Visitor Center at Furnace Creek.

### GRAPEVINE PEAK (8,738 FT; 2,663 M)

This peak, the highpoint of the Grapevine Mountains, provides a fine view of the northern end of Death Valley.  The hiker will notice that over the last several hundred feet to the summit, the pinyon pines of the lower slopes give way to limber pines.

*Maps:* Grapevine Peak and Wahguyhe Peak (NV-CA) 7.5-minute (1:24,000 scale) topographic maps; Saline Valley 1:100,000 scale metric topographic map; Automobile Club of Southern California (AAA) Death Valley National Park map

*Best Time to Climb:* Fall and Spring

*Approach:* From Beatty, Nevada, drive north on Highway 95 about 13.7 miles to the Phinney Canyon Road, a dirt road heading west (0.6 miles north of highway post 71).  Passing through a gate (close it after you pass through), continue west 12.3 miles (staying straight at road forks) to a fork.  Bear right, and drive another 4.9 miles to where the road drops into a wash.  Continue up the road about 3.8 miles to where the road becomes four-wheel drive condition and park.  Four-wheel drive vehicles may be able to continue on to the saddle at 7,520 feet.

*Route:* From the 7,520-foot saddle, head north then northwest along the ridge line to the summit.  Anticipate six miles round-trip with 2,500 feet of elevation gain (for most cars).

### WAHGUYHE PEAK (8,628 FT; 2,630 M)

Southern sentinel of the Phinney Canyon area, Wahguyhe is easily recognized by its nicely-sculpted conical shape.  As with Grapevine Mountain, the hiker will notice the shift from pinyon pine to limber pine as the summit is reached.

*Maps:* Wahguyhe Peak (NV-CA) 7.5-minute (1:24,000 scale) topographic map; Saline Valley 1:100,000 scale metric topographic map; Automobile Club of Southern California (AAA) Death Valley National Park map

*Best Time to Climb:* Fall and Spring

Corkscrew
Thimble

Telescope

View of main ridge route to Palmer from Grapevine. Photo: Wynne Benti

*Approach:* Same as for Grapevine Peak.

*Route:* From the 6,800-foot contour in Phinney Canyon, proceed southwest up a draw to a saddle northwest of the peak. Steep talus is then climbed to the summit. Round-trip distance is four miles with approximately 1,850 feet of elevation gain.

## MOUNT PALMER (7,958 FT; 2,426 M)

*Maps:* Grapevine Peak and Wahguyhe Peak (NV-CA) 7.5-minute (1:24,000 scale) topographic maps; Saline Valley 1:100,000 scale metric topographic map; Automobile Club of Southern California (AAA) Death Valley National Park map

*Best Time to Climb:* Fall and Spring

*Approach:* Same as for Grapevine Peak.

*Route:* From the 6,800-foot contour in Phinney Canyon, hike the road to the saddle at 7,520 feet, then contour southwest to another saddle east of Peak 7,780 feet. Follow this ridge southwest over that peak and over the next low peak to a saddle, then south-southwest along a fairly narrow ridge at about 7,240 feet to Point 7,720+ feet. Proceed southeast along the ridge, contouring left on occasion to a 100-foot third class pitch which will bring you to the summit. Anticipate 11 miles round-trip with 3,100 feet of elevation gain, and a 10-hour day.

*Alternate Route:* The third class pitch can be bypassed from the last saddle by climbing toward the cliff ahead and picking up a faint ducked trail heading toward the right (south). The trail traverses a chute and drops to a notch. Proceed to the next chute and climb up about 50 feet to exit right on easy slopes leading to the summit. Anticipate 11 miles round-trip with 3,100 feet of elevation gain and a ten-hour day.

### THIMBLE PEAK (6,381 FT; 1,945 M)

This is the impressive, sharp peak to the east when viewed from near Stovepipe Wells in Death Valley. The summit views down the sheer limestone cliffs to Titanothere Canyon, and out to Death Valley are breathtaking. The peak

was named in reference to its shape and was known as "Squaw Teat" to Death Valley old-timers.

*Maps:* Thimble Peak (CA) 7.5-minute (1:24,000 scale) topographic map; Saline Valley 1:100,000 scale metric topographic map; Automobile Club of Southern California (AAA) Death Valley National Park map

*Best Time to Climb:* November through April

*Approach:* This peak is reached from the Titus Canyon Road that turns north off the Daylight Pass road seven miles east of the pass (between the pass and Beatty, Nevada). The Titus Canyon Road is a one-way road with steep grades and is often closed due to summer washouts. Check at the Death Valley National Park Visitor Center for current road conditions. Follow the

Russ White and Dave Clegg along the route to Thimble Peak, which swings to the right out of the picture, reaching the summit from behind.
Photo: Andy Zdon

Titus Canyon Road about 12 miles to Red Pass (5,250 ft) and park.

*Route:* An obvious ridge leads south three miles to the peak. The summit has steep east and south faces, so contour around the face and climb to the summit from the northwest. Anticipate six miles round-trip with 1,800 feet of elevation gain.

Wynne Benti backpacking to Corkscrew from Titus Canyon, Thimble in background. Photo: Randall Danta

## CORKSCREW PEAK (5,804 FT; 1,769 M)

This beautiful peak with its "Corkscrew" banding is a prominent peak as seen from Death Valley. The peak was described by Edna Brush Perkins in her Death Valley classic, *White Heart of Mojave* as a:

"... *symmetrical mass, striking both on account of its red color like crumbling bricks and for the perpendicular cliff which spirals around it like a corkscrew. Through the field-glass the cliff was a dark violet and might be a hundred or more feet high. Corkscrew Mountain stands out boldly from its fellows, nor while we were in the valley did we ever lose sight of its sun-bright bulk. It became our landmark in the north.*"

The interesting, swirling bands are the result of a "recumbent fold." A recumbent fold is a fold in the rock layers that is so distorted that it over-turns on itself. In the case of Corkscrew Peak, the folded rocks consist of Cambrian limestones of the Carrara formation (as seen on the crest) and the Wood Canyon formation (lower down from the summit).

*Maps:* Thimble Peak, Daylight Pass and Chloride City (CA) 7.5-minute (1:24,000 scale) topographic maps; Saline Valley and Beatty 1:100,000 scale metric topographic maps; Automobile Club of Southern California (AAA) Death Valley National Park map

*Best Time to Climb:* November through April

*Approach:* From Furnace Creek, drive 11.8 miles north along Highway 190 to the Beatty Junction, then right to a second junction after another ten miles. Keep right about two miles to the Corkscrew Peak sign (2,600 ft). The roads are paved and accessible to all vehicles.

*Route:* The peak can be seen to the northwest. Hike over gently sloping terrain about two miles toward the base of the peak. A narrows in the wash will be reached containing two dry waterfalls that can be climbed third class or bypassed on the left. Just above the second waterfall, take a wash that forks right and continues to another wash fork at about 4,100 feet. Stay left and hike toward the notch to the left of a prominent pinnacle on the skyline. Head up and through this notch to a saddle at about 5,080 feet. Turn west-northwest and follow the use trail 0.4 miles to the break in the cliffs on the north side of the peak, and onto the summit. Anticipate seven miles round-trip with about 3,300 feet of elevation gain.

### DEATH VALLEY BUTTES (3,017 FT; 920 M)

These buttes provide a fine perch from which to take in the panorama of Death Valley. The west butte is the highest, although when the author hiked up here, a summit register was also present on the lower east butte. Death Valley Buttes have also been referred to as Breyfogle Buttes, named for Jacob Breyfogle who discovered the Breyfogle Mine. According to Dane Coolidge in his book Death Valley Prospectors, *"Breyfogle traveled east up Boundary Canyon past two or three black buttes named Death Valley Buttes, but more often called Breyfogle Buttes."*

*Maps:* Chloride City (CA) 7.5-minute (1:24,000 scale) topographic map; Beatty 1:100,000 scale metric topographic map; Automobile Club of Southern California (AAA) Death Valley National Park map

*Best Time to Climb:* November through April

*Approach:* From Furnace Creek, drive 11.8 miles north along Highway 190 to the Beatty Junction, then right to a second junction after another 10 miles. Turn left (south) about a half mile until due east of the Buttes and park (2,040 ft). The road is paved and driveable to all cars.

*Route:* From the parking spot, climb the east butte directly to the northwest, then follow the rough and narrow ridge west to the true summit marked by the benchmark "Red Top." Anticipate three miles round-trip with 1,700 feet of elevation gain.

## FUNERAL MOUNTAINS

This stark range, bordered on the east by Death Valley, and on the west by the Amargosa Valley, was originally named the Amargosa Range by the Boundary Commission of 1861. Five years later, the name was changed by the Blasdell Expedition to its current name. "Amargosa Range" was then used to identify the Grapevine Mountains, Funeral Mountains, and the Black Mountains that extend as a single, north-south mountain chain.

Sparse vegetation is typical of the range, with creosote being the most abundant vegetation type. Scrawny pinyons and junipers are found atop the high ridges. The Pyramid Peak area is home to a herd of bighorn sheep, though their numbers are reported to be in decline.

Another peak not listed below but worthy of attention to the desert mountaineer is Bat Mountain (4,950 ft). This rugged, limestone peak is the highpoint of the 28,000-acre Funeral Mountains Wilderness and is the southernmost peak in the range. Climbs of this peak begin along Highway 190 south of the Pyramid Peak parking spot. The peak is on the East of Ryan and Death Valley Junction 7.5-minute topographic maps.

The nearest supplies, gasoline, food and lodging are at Furnace Creek. Developed campgrounds are also available in Furnace Creek. There are also numerous opportunities for primitive camping in the area. For further information, contact the National Park Visitor Center at Furnace Creek, or for the Funeral Mountains Wilderness Area (Bat Mountain), contact the Bureau of Land Management offices in Barstow and Riverside.

### CHLORIDE CLIFF (5,279 FT; 1,609 M)

Chloride Cliff, with its magnificent views of Death Valley, is the easiest of the east-side peaks assuming one has a four-wheel drive vehicle. A high clearance vehicle with two-wheel drive should be able to make it to the town site, but four-wheel drive is definitely recommended. While in the area, take some time to explore the old site of Chloride City. Here, gold-bearing quartz and barite veins in metamorphic rocks were mined from 1900 to 1916.

*Maps:* Chloride City (CA) 7.5-minute (1:24,000 scale) topographic map;

Beatty 1:100,000 scale metric topographic map; Automobile Club of Southern California (AAA) Death Valley National Park map
*Best Time to Climb:* November through April
*Approach:* From Furnace Creek, drive north on Highway 190 to the Daylight Pass Road. Follow the Daylight Pass Cutoff Road northeast, passing to the south of the Death Valley Buttes, to a junction with the Daylight Pass Road at Hell's Gate. Drive east on the Daylight Pass Road 3.4 miles to a dirt road heading off to the right. Follow the dirt road eight miles south to the site of Chloride City.
*Route:* With steady nerves, one can drive nearly to the top, or better yet, park at the town site, and walk the short distance to the peak.

### WINTERS PEAK (ALSO KNOWN AS ECHO MOUNTAIN) (5,033 FT; 1,534 M)
*Maps:* Nevares Peak (CA) 7.5-minute (1:24,000 scale) topographic map; Beatty 1:100,000 scale metric topographic map; Automobile Club of Southern California (AAA) Death Valley National Park map
*Best Time to Climb:* November through April
*Approach:* From the Furnace Creek Inn, drive two miles east on Highway 190 to the Echo Canyon dirt road on the left. Follow the Echo Canyon Road east (four-wheel drive) as it passes the Eye of the Needle (a natural arch) at 4.8 miles, and then enters an open valley in another half mile. A fork is reached at 7.2 miles from Highway 190. Stay left and follow the road close to the saddle east of the peak.
*Route:* Hike to the saddle east of Winters Peaks. From the saddle, head west to Point 4,260 feet, then west and southwest following the ridge to the summit. Anticipate seven miles round-trip with 2,000 feet of elevation gain.

### SCHWAUB PEAK (6,440+ FT; 1,963+ M)
This peak, at the head of Echo Canyon, is named in honor of Charles M. Schwab (but is officially misspelled), who made his fortune in the steel business, and later became involved with numerous mining ventures in Death Valley, including the Greenwater boom. The town site of Schwab is about a mile away from the Inyo Mine. The town was unique in that it was established by women, Gertrude Fesler, Mrs. F.W. Dunn and Mrs. Dunn's daughter. They decided after much thought to run gamblers out of town and banned "sporting women." This tent town soon disappeared. The Inyo Mine deposit was discovered in 1905 by two prospectors, and operated for

the next seven years after producing over a half million dollars in gold. The mine enjoyed a brief revival from 1935 to 1941, but has been closed since.
*Maps:* Echo Canyon (CA) 7.5-minute (1:24,000 scale) topographic map; Death Valley Junction 1:100,000 scale metric topographic map; Automobile Club of Southern California (AAA) Death Valley National Park map
*Best Time to Climb:* November through April
*Approach:* From the Furnace Creek Inn, drive two miles east on Highway 190 to the Echo Canyon dirt road on the left. Follow the Echo Canyon Road east (four-wheel drive) as it passes the Eye of the Needle (a natural arch) at 4.8 miles, and then enters an open valley in another half mile. A fork is reached at 7.2 miles from Highway 190. Stay right and continue another 1.7 miles to the Inyo Mine (3,760 ft).
*Route:* From the Inyo Mine, hike up Echo Canyon along the old railroad grade until the canyon opens up and the peak is visible two miles to the southeast. Follow a ridge-route to the summit. Anticipate ten miles round-trip with 3,000 feet of elevation gain.

## NEVARES PEAK (2,859 FT; 871 M)

This small peak stands as a prominent eminence along the west slope of the Funeral Mountains. The peak is named in honor of Adolphe Joseph Nevares, an early Death Valley character, whose cabin is still standing near Nevares Spring.
*Maps:* Nevares Peak (CA) 7.5-minute (1:24,000 scale) topographic map; Beatty 1:100,000 scale metric topographic map; Automobile Club of Southern California (AAA) Death Valley National Park map
*Best Time to Climb:* November through April
*Approach:* Old versions of Walt Wheelock's *Desert Peaks Guides* recommended driving through the Cow Creek residential area to reach this peak. This is now prohibited. The new route starts along Highway 190 about 1.7 miles north of the Cow Creek Road (north of Furnace Creek) at an elevation of about 220 feet below sea level.
*Route:* From Highway 190, walk due east up the wash through the hills. Follow the wash generally eastward, then start heading for a wash along the north base of Nevares Peak. Follow the wash past the peak, eventually reaching a saddle southeast of the peak, then hike northwest along the ridge to the summit. Anticipate 13 miles round-trip with 3,600 feet of elevation gain.

PYRAMID PEAK (6,703 FT; 2,043 M)

This spectacular peak is a Death Valley favorite. It is a landmark that can be seen for many miles, and is the highpoint of the Funeral Mountains.

*Maps:* East of Echo Canyon and East of Ryan (CA) 7.5-minute (1:24,000 scale) topographic maps; Death Valley Junction 1:100,000 scale metric topographic map; Automobile Club of Southern California (AAA) Death Valley National Park map

*Best Time to Climb:* November through April

*Approach:* From Death Valley Junction, drive 11.5 miles west on Highway 190 to a faint track heading north (0.2 miles east of highway marker 129) toward the peak. From the west, this track is about 17.5 miles east of the Furnace Creek Inn. With a good pair of eyes, a rock cairn is visible a couple of hundred yards off the road. Park on the shoulder of the highway at about 3,025 feet. The approach is driveable to all cars.

*Route:* Hike north-northeast up the dry wash to an obvious low saddle. From here, head up the southeast ridge to the summit. Anticipate 11 miles round-trip with 3,700 feet of elevation gain.

## BLACK MOUNTAINS

Standing in Badwater, one can't help but be awed by the snow-capped Panamint Range across the valley, an impressive 10,000-foot wall rising up from near sea-level. Turning to the east, a myriad of steep cliffs, gullies, and seemingly unreachable country presents yet another magnificent desert vista. This is the escarpment of the Black Mountains, the impressive, seemingly untouchable east wall of Death Valley.

A herd of bighorn sheep roam between the creosote and sage of the Black Mountains, and the neighboring Greenwater and Funeral Ranges. There are coyotes, and the occasional Golden Eagle or Prairie Falcon sweeping across the sky overhead.

This is wild country. Water in the Black Mountains is exceedingly scarce. The lack of water was the key factor in why so many of the early mining operations in the area failed. The ore was there, but there was no water for the most basic of needs. The cost of transporting water to the area was far more expensive than the minerals were worth.

Food, gasoline, lodging and supplies are available in Furnace Creek and Stovepipe Wells. At the southern end of the range, the small town of Shoshone contains a motel, restaurant and gas station. Developed

Ed M. Zdon on the trail to Dante's View Peak. Photo: Andy Zdon

campgrounds in the area are available in Death Valley. However, primitive camping opportunities abound. For further information on the Black Mountains, contact the National Park Service Visitor Center in Furnace Creek.

### MOUNT PERRY (5,716 FT; 1,742 M)
This peak, the northernmost named mountain in the range, is named in honor of John S. Perry, the first foreman of the Harmony Borax Works in Death Valley. Perry also designed the freight wagons used by the mule teams to carry the borax to market.

*Maps:* Dantes View and Ryan (CA) 7.5-minute (1:24,000 scale) topographic maps; Death Valley Junction 1:100,000 scale metric topographic map; Automobile Club of Southern California (AAA) Death Valley National Park map

*Best Time to Climb:* November through April

*Approach:* From Furnace Creek, follow the paved and signed road to Dante's View (paved, passable to all vehicles).

*Route:* From Dante's View, the ridge can be followed past Dante's View Peak to the summit. Anticipate eight miles and 3,300 feet of elevation gain round-trip. Although the peak isn't that much higher than Dante's View, there are considerable "ups and downs" along the ridge.

## "Dante's View Peak" (5,704 ft; 1,739 m)

Although this peak is only a short walk from the parking area, the views are far superior to those at the viewpoint. Badwater lies nearly 6,000 feet below, where its white salt pan and ponds of surface water reflect the heat and sun. Across Death Valley is Telescope Peak, highpoint of the Panamints, and to the east is Charleston Peak in the Spring Mountains of Nevada. My brother and I walked this trail one crisp, clear winter day, when the slopes of the peak were dashed with snow. Although the peak is only a short hike from the parking lot, the noise of the cars and people were quickly left behind. *Dante's Inferno* was the inspiration behind the naming of the peak and viewpoint. This is a gentle mountain, and unlike Dante's mountain ascent, there will be no need for the assistance of a "Virgil."

*Maps:* Dantes View (CA) 7.5-minute (1:24,000 scale) topographic map; Death Valley Junction 1:100,000 scale metric topographic map; Automobile Club of Southern California (AAA) Death Valley National Park map

*Best Time to Visit:* November through April

*Approach:* From Furnace Creek, follow the paved and signed road to Dante's View at 5,475 feet (paved, passable to all vehicles).

*Route:* The peak is a short trail walk northward from the Dante's View parking area. Anticipate less than one mile round-trip with 230 feet of elevation gain.

## Coffin Peak (5,490 ft; 1,674 m)

This easy ridge ramble makes for a colorful late afternoon hike when the sun turns the surrounding mountain slopes brilliant orange and brown. The name "Coffin" was first applied to the entire range by William Lewis Manly in his book *Death Valley in '49*. According to Manly:

*"The range next east of us across the low valley was barren to look upon as naked single rock... I believe this range is known as the Coffin's Mountains. It would be difficult to find earth enough in the whole of it to cover a coffin."*

*Maps:* Dante's View (CA) 7.5-minute (1:24,000 scale) topographic map; Death Valley Junction 1:100,000 scale metric topographic map; Automobile Club of Southern California (AAA) Death Valley National Park map

*Best Time to Climb:* November through April

*Approach:* From Furnace Creek, follow the paved and signed road toward Dante's View (passable to all vehicles). The road climbs the gradual east slope of the Black Mountains in generally a southwest direction. A large pullout on the south side of the road just before the road makes a 90-degree turn northwest, is the road-end for this peak (5,150 ft).

*Route:* From the parking area, follow the rolling ridge first east, then south, then east again to the summit. Anticipate 2.5 miles round-trip with about 950 feet of elevation gain.

### FUNERAL PEAK (6,384 FT; 1,946 M)

Funeral Peak, the highpoint of the Black Mountains, was formerly named Mount LeConte in honor of the famed nineteenth century geologist Joseph LeConte by J.J. McGillivray, a mineral surveyor who visited the area in 1891.

*Maps:* Funeral Peak (CA) 7.5-minute (1:24,000 scale) topographic map; Death Valley Junction 1:100,000 scale metric topographic map; Automobile Club of Southern California (AAA) Death Valley National Park map

*Best Time to Climb:* November through April

*Approach:* From Furnace Creek, follow the paved and signed road toward Dante's View to the dirt Greenwater Valley Road. Proceed southeastward along the Greenwater Valley Road about ten miles to a point east-northeast of the peak. Two-wheel drive vehicles with good clearance recommended.

*Route:* Hike across open desert, then up the gradual east slope of the peak. Anticipate eight miles round-trip with 2,400 feet of elevation gain.

### SMITH MOUNTAIN (5,913 FT; 1,802 M)

Another peak named by J.J. McGillivray (see Funeral Peak), this peak was named in honor of Frances Marion Smith, better known as "Borax" Smith.

*Maps:* Gold Valley (CA) 7.5-minute (1:24,000 scale) topographic map; Death Valley Junction 1:100,000 scale metric topographic map; Automobile Club of Southern California (AAA) Death Valley National Park map

*Best Time to Climb:* November through April

*Approach:* From the junction of Highways 127 and 178 north of Shoshone, drive 5.7 miles west on 178 to the dirt Greenwater Valley Road. Head north on the Greenwater Valley Road 10.5 miles to the Gold Valley Road junction. Turn left, and drive 4.9 miles to a fork at the head of Gold Valley. Turn right, dropping into Gold Valley and drive 3.5 miles to another junction. Turn left (southeast) and drive another 1.5 miles and park (3,800 ft). Four-wheel drive vehicles are required for this approach.

*Route:* Head west a mile to the mouth of a prominent canyon, then up the canyon a half mile. From here, climb a loose chute and upon reaching the

Smith Mountain, looking west to the Panamint Range. Photo: Andy Zdon

top of the chute, head toward a hill to the west. Pass the hill on its left side and Smith Mountain will come into view. Continue west-southwest, over a false summit and up to the highpoint. Anticipate 5.5 miles round-trip with 2,300 feet of elevation gain.

### DESERT HOUND PEAK (4,471 FT; 1,363 M)
*Maps:* Shoreline Butte and Epaulet Peak (CA) 7.5-minute (1:24,000 scale) topographic maps; Owlshead Mountains 1:100,000 scale metric topographic map; Automobile Club of Southern California (AAA) Death Valley National Park map
*Best Time to Climb:* November through April
*Approach:* Drive the Badwater Road either south from Badwater, or north from Ashford Junction to the remains of the Ashford Mill on the west side of the road. Across from the mill site, a dirt road heads up the alluvial fan of the Black Mountains to Ashford Canyon. Follow this road, as far as practicable with your vehicle, staying left at a fork after 0.7 miles, to the canyon mouth and park (1,100 ft). Two-wheel drive vehicles with high clearance should be able to reach this point.
*Route:* Cross the wash, and follow the remains of the old Ashford Mine Road as it heads up the canyon. Following the wash instead of the old

road will lead to some dry waterfalls that require roped climbing. Continue up the canyon about two miles to the old Ashford Mine. From the Ashford Mine, head north up a drainage, or on a ridge next to the drainage, up to the ridge crest east of Point 1,032 meters. Then follow the ridge east, then south to the summit, passing the Desert Hound Mine en route. Anticipate eight miles round-trip with 4,300 feet of elevation gain.

### Ashford Peak (3,546 ft; 1,081 m)

This front-range peak provides excellent views of the Amargosa River Valley, and the faulted scarps of the Confidence Hills. The peak is situated along the axis of a geologic structure called the Desert Hound anticline. An anticline is an upward-pointed fold in the rocks, and can be identified by the opposing tilt of the rocks in the area. The peak itself is composed of Precambrian-age gneiss and schist.

*Maps:* Shoreline Butte and Epaulet Peak (CA) 7.5-minute (1:24,000 scale) topographic maps; Owlshead Mountains 1:100,000 scale metric topographic map; Automobile Club of Southern California (AAA) Death Valley National Park map

*Best Time to Climb:* November through April

*Approach:* Drive to Ashford Canyon, same as Desert Hound Peak.

*Route:* Hike to the Ashford Mine as described in the route for Desert Hound Peak. From the mine, follow the canyon east a short distance to a steep side canyon heading south. Climb this side canyon to a saddle northeast of the peak, then climb southwest to the summit. Anticipate five miles round-trip with 2,550 feet of elevation gain.

### Epaulet Peak (4,765 ft; 1,452.7 m)

This peak looms over Bradbury Well, but is most easily reached via Greenwater Valley. It is named for the dark volcanic caprock resembling the epaulet on a military uniform's shoulder.

*Maps:* Epaulet Peak, Deadman Pass and Funeral Peak (CA) 7.5-minute (1:24,000 scale) topographic maps; Owlshead Mountains and Death Valley Junction 1:100,000 scale metric topographic maps; Automobile Club of Southern California (AAA) Death Valley National Park map

*Best Time to Climb:* November through April

*Approach:* From the junction of Highways 127 and 178 north of Shoshone, drive 5.7 miles west on Highway 178 to the dirt Greenwater Valley

Ed M. Zdon on Jubilee Mountain. Photo: Andy Zdon

Road. Follow the Greenwater Valley Road north 6.3 miles, then west on a very rough mining road two miles to a fork (3,400 ft). By this time the road may be washed out and the hike will begin from here. When the author drove this road with a high clearance two-wheel drive, he decided to stop by this point. If the road is in decent shape, and you have a four-wheel drive, you can turn left and drive closer to the peak.

*Route:* The peak is an easy slope to the southwest. If starting from the point two miles west of the Greenwater Valley Road, anticipate seven miles round-trip with 1,850 feet of elevation gain.

### Salsberry Peak (4,254 ft; 1,297 m)

This handsome peak lies just north of Salsberry Pass, and is named for Jack Salsberry, promoter of the ill-fated camps of Leadfield, Greenwater and Ubehebe.

*Maps:* Salsberry Peak (CA) 7.5-minute (1:24,000 scale) topographic map; Owlshead Mountains 1:100,000 scale metric topographic map; Automobile Club of Southern California (AAA) Death Valley National Park map

*Best Time to Climb:* November through April

*Approach:* Although this peak lies just north of Salsberry Pass, that route is broken and rough. A better route is to park about three miles west of the Greenwater Valley Road on the Salsberry Pass Road (Highway 178). The terrain is gentle to begin with and the peak is clearly visible to the west. The road is paved and passable to all cars.

*Route:* Head west toward Montgomery Spring, tucked away under a rocky ledge in a small ravine. Climb to the saddle north of the peak and then follow the loose ridge to the top. Anticipate five miles round-trip with 1,600 feet of elevation gain.

### JUBILEE MOUNTAIN (2,527 FT; 770+ M)

The infrequently climbed summit of this minor peak provides some of the finest views to be had of the southern end of Death Valley and toward the Kingston and Avawatz Ranges. One does not have to wait until reaching the summit to enjoy the views. The entire hike up the narrow ridge composed of Precambrian-age gneiss is packed with fine desert vistas.

*Maps:* Epaulet Peak (CA) 7.5-minute (1:24,000 scale) topographic map; Owlshead Mountains 1:100,000 scale metric topographic map; Automobile Club of Southern California (AAA) Death Valley National Park map

*Best Time to Climb:* November through April

*Approach:* Drive 21.6 miles west of Highway 127 on the Salsberry Pass Road (Highway 178) to Jubilee Pass (1,320 ft). The road is paved and passable to all cars.

*Route:* From Jubilee Pass, the narrow north ridge leads directly to the top. Anticipate two miles and 1,200 feet of elevation gain round-trip.

## GREENWATER RANGE

The Greenwater Range varies considerably from rolling hills to jagged peaks. Creosote is the most common vegetation in the area although desert holly, sagebrush, prickly pear, cholla and grasses are also present. These mountains serve as a corridor for bighorn sheep to move back and forth between the Funeral and Black Mountains. The nearest lodging, restaurant and gasoline is at Shoshone, California to the west. For general supplies, one will have to drive in to Pahrump, Nevada, or to the Furnace Creek area, either one a considerable drive, so come prepared. For further information on the Greenwater Range, contact the National Park Service Visitor Center in Furnace Creek.

### BROWN PEAK (4,947 FT; 1,508 M)

*Maps:* Deadman Pass and East of Deadman Pass (CA) 7.5-minute (1:24,000 scale) topographic maps; Death Valley Junction 1:100,000 scale metric topographic map; Automobile Club of Southern California (AAA) Death Valley National Park map

*Best Time to Climb:* November through April

*Approach:* From the junction of Highways 127 and 178 north of Shoshone, drive 5.7 miles west on Highway 178 to the dirt Greenwater Valley Road. Turn north, following this road ten miles to the turnoff (east) for Deadman Pass. The poor dirt road to Deadman Pass is best driven with a four-wheel drive vehicle. Drive over the pass, 6.5 miles from the Greenwater Valley Road and park at the large parking area (3,000 ft).

*Route:* To the east-southeast, a small hill juts out from the base of Brown Peak. Hike across the alluvial fan to the saddle separating the small hill from the rest of Brown Peak. From the saddle, head northeast, dropping into a wash and over a ridge to a major wash that heads directly toward Brown Peak. At a fork in the wash below the east slopes of Brown Peak, bear north, and follow the drainage to a saddle at about 3,640 feet. From here climb Brown's northwest ridge directly to the summit. Anticipate seven miles round-trip with 2,000 feet of elevation gain.

*Alternate Approach:* This route is for those with vehicles that are "low-slung beasts" and who may otherwise have trouble with poor dirt roads. From Shoshone, drive north on Highway 127, and park along the highway about a quarter mile past Milepost 25.

*Alternate Route:* From the parking spot, head due west up the alluvial fans to the mouth of the canyon directly below Brown Peak. Follow the wash past some dry waterfalls, and up some steep talus to a saddle on Brown Peak's southeast shoulder. From here, head northwest to the summit. Anticipate ten miles round-trip with about 3,200 feet of elevation gain.

## IBEX HILLS

South of Highway 178, the Ibex Hills rise as rather small, dispersed, and rugged desert range. Early morning and late afternoon photographic opportunities in the area abound as the colorful volcanic and metamorphic rocks provide a fine backdrop. The Black Mountain herd of desert bighorn sheep uses this area from time to time, although the usage appears to be declining. As with most of the desert ranges in this area, creosote is the dominant plant present. The summits of Ibex Peak and Sheephead Mountain lie on the western boundary of the newly created, 26,000-acre Ibex Hills Wilderness. The Ibex Hills Wilderness also includes portions of the Dublin Hills and the Black Mountains. The nearest lodging, restaurant and gasoline is at Shoshone, California to the west. For general supplies, one will have to drive in to Pahrump, Nevada, or Furnace Creek, either way a considerable drive, so come prepared. The area is managed by the Bureau of Land Management offices in Barstow and Riverside.

### IBEX PEAK (4,752 FT; 1,448 M)

This peak is the highpoint of the Ibex Hills Wilderness. Bighorn sheep are sometimes spotted, particularly at nearby Sheephead and Salsberry Springs.
*Maps:* Salsberry Peak (CA) 7.5-minute (1:24,000 scale) topographic map; Owlshead Mountains 1:100,000 scale metric topographic map; Automobile Club of Southern California (AAA) Death Valley National Park map
*Best Time to Climb:* November through April
*Approach:* From Salsberry Pass on Highway 178, drive 1.3 miles west to a dirt track on the south side of the road that roughly parallels the highway. Follow this track 0.4 miles to a dirt road heading south toward the peak. Turn south, and follow the dirt road 0.7 miles to a fork. Stay left, and follow the road 1.8 miles to a saddle at about 3,940 feet. Four-wheel drive is needed for this last bit of driving, and even with four-wheel drive, it may be necessary to stop before reaching the saddle.
*Route:* From the saddle, follow the ridge east then south to the summit. Anticipate two miles round-trip with 1,000 feet of elevation gain. If hiking in from the junction of the road paralleling the highway with the road to the peak, anticipate seven miles round-trip with 3,000 feet of elevation gain.

### SHEEPHEAD MOUNTAIN (4,274 FT; 1,303 M)

This peak lies south of Salsberry Pass. Its bands of buff, pink, red and black tuff, rhyolite and basalt provide interesting and easy climbing.
*Maps:* Salsberry Peak (CA) 7.5-minute (1:24,000 scale) topographic map; Owlshead Mountains 1:100,000 scale metric topographic map; Automobile Club of Southern California (AAA) Death Valley National Park map
*Best Time to Climb:* November through April
*Approach:* Park on the south side of Highway 178 just west of Salsberry Pass (3,288 ft). The road is paved and passable to all cars.
*Route:* Climb toward the peak, contouring below the ridge, then up to a notch just north of the top. A bit of easy broken rock leads to the apex. Anticipate 2.5 miles round-trip with 1,200 feet of elevation gain.

# RESTING SPRING RANGE

A compact grouping of mountains, the Resting Spring Range is surrounded by the Amargosa River, Stewart, and Chicago Valleys. Situated within the 79,000-acre Resting Spring Range Wilderness, Mount Stewart (the range highpoint) provides a pleasant desert ascent amid colorful rock formations. This is fine country to observe wildlife including desert bighorn sheep, wild horses, burros, and the occasional Golden Eagle. Although the route is not described here, a climb of Shadow Mountain at the north end of the range is feasible from the Stewart Valley Road northeast of the peak. The range is named for Resting Springs, a noted watering place in the region. According to Erwin Gudde, author of *California Place Names*:

*"In 1844, Fremont had named the springs Agua de Hernandez, in honor of the sole survivor of an Indian attack. In the 1850's, the springs assumed the present name because Mormon travelers bound for San Bernardino stopped here to rest and recuperate their livestock."*

Camping is available in the county park at Tecopa Hot Springs. Otherwise, camping in the area is primitive, and all minimum impact camping methods should be applied here. The nearest supplies, gas, food and lodging are in Shoshone, California, or for a little more diversity, Pahrump, Nevada. For further information, contact the Bureau of Land Management offices in Barstow and Riverside.

### "MOUNT STEWART" (5,265 FT; 1,604+ M)

Mount Stewart provides an enjoyable desert scramble amid fine limestone terrain. The rocks that are climbed consist of east-dipping limestones and dolomites of the Cambrian-age Bonanza King formation. The summit supposedly provides a rather fine view. However, on our ascent of this peak, the summit was shrouded in clouds after a winter storm, and only glimpses of the Nopah Range to the east were available.

*Maps:* Stewart Valley (CA) 7.5-minute (1: 24,000 scale) topographic map; Death Valley Junction 1:100,000 scale metric topographic map; Automobile Club of Southern California (AAA) San Bernardino County map (Las Vegas area inset)

*Best Time to Climb:* November through April

*Approach:* From the junction of Highways 127 and 178 at Shoshone, California, drive 15.5 miles east then north on Highway 178 to a turnout one mile past the highpoint of the road, and next to Milepost 58.50. Park here (2,650 ft). The road is paved and passable to all cars.

*Route:* Head west to a shallow saddle at 3,215 feet along the base of the mountains. Drop down into the main wash and follow it northwest, taking a right just after a black rock outcrop. A ten-foot Class 3 dry waterfall is easily surmounted. Scramble out of the wash a short distance to avoid some more difficult dry waterfalls, then drop back down into the wash. At a major fork (3,790 ft), continue up the ridge that bisects these drainages, eventually reaching the summit. Plan on 6.5 miles round-trip with about 2,600 feet of elevation gain.

### TECOPA PEAK (2,688 FT; 819+ M)

This peak, part of the Sperry Hills, overlooks the town of Tecopa, formerly an old mining camp, to the north. The peak is named after Paiute Chief Tecopa. According to Gudde:

*"Tecopa was a very fine Indian, who saved the people of Pahrump Valley from being killed by Indians… the name is derived from the Paiute word 'tecopet' for wild cat."*

*Maps:* Ibex Pass (CA) 7.5-minute (1:24,000 scale) topographic map; Owlshead Mountains 1:100,000 scale metric topographic map; Automobile Club of Southern California (AAA) San Bernardino County map

*Best Time to Climb:* November through April

*Approach:* From Shoshone, California, drive about 11 miles south on Highway 127 to a point about due west of the peak and park at about 1,900 feet.

*Route:* Hike east across the desert, crossing several washes. Climb via any feasible-looking route to Tecopa's south ridge, then north to the summit. Anticipate five to six miles round-trip with 1,200 feet of elevation gain.

## NOPAH RANGE

The Nopah Range is among the author's favorite desert ranges. Technically easy but interesting route-finding in narrow desert canyons and along rocky ridges is only part of the payoff for climbing these mountains. The Nopah Range was among those areas protected by the Desert Protection Act through the creation of the 11,000-acre Nopah Range Wilderness. As one drives through Chicago Valley and gazes at this range, their eyes will be drawn to the distinct banding of the rocks along the escarpment. These rocks are primarily limestone and dolomite and consist of a lower band of Bonanza King formation (the same unit seen to the west in the Resting Spring Range), and the Nopah formation

Wynne Benti heads up Pahrump Peak as the first winter snow begins to fall. Photo: Asher Waxman

which can be identified by the broad striped appearance (five dark and light gray bands). These formations are traversed on our ascents of Pahrump Peak and the Nopah peaks.

The landscape is truly desert-like and appears barren, although creosote, grasses, and sparse junipers at the highest elevations are all present. As with other craggy ranges in the area, this is fine desert bighorn habitat. Prairie Falcon and Golden Eagle eyries have been noted in the area. "Nopah" is probably a term that surveyors used for these mountains, "pah" being the word for water in Shoshonean, therefore the name "no water range." Camping in the area is primitive, so all minimum impact camping methods apply here. The exception is at Tecopa Hot Springs where a fee campground is located. The nearest supplies, gas, food and lodging are in Shoshone, California, and Pahrump, Nevada. For further information, contact the Bureau of Land Management offices in Barstow and Riverside.

### "PAHRUMP PEAK" (5,740 FT; 1,749.6 M)
The summit is marked by a benchmark named "Pahrump."
*Maps:* Twelvemile Spring (CA) 7.5-minute (1:24,000 scale) topographic map; Death Valley Junction 1:100,000 scale metric topographic map;

Automobile Club of Southern California (AAA) San Bernardino County map (Las Vegas area inset)

*Best Time to Climb:* November through April

*Approach:* From the junction of Highways 127 and 178 at Shoshone, California, drive 10.5 miles east then north on Highway 178 to a faint road that heads northeast toward the Nopah Range. A wilderness boundary sign is found shortly off the highway. Park here at about 2,400 feet. This approach is passable to all cars.

*Route:* Walk two miles up the alluvial fan on the dirt road to the mouth of a canyon. Continue up the canyon following it through three 90-degree turns to a fork at 3,770 feet. We encountered a rattlesnake in the wash here, so when hopping from a boulder, keep an eye out. A climbers' use trail can be followed occasionally up the canyon. Take the left fork and continue up the canyon to another fork at 4,120 feet. Turn right until you approach a short, dry waterfall. Climb up a scree slope to the right, eventually reaching a saddle (you will likely see the use trail at this point) at about 5,100 feet. From here on, one can follow the faint path heading up the peak. Head up the ridge through a couple of notches. Then follow an obvious chute gaining the summit ridge. Once the summit ridge is reached, head north to the delightfully narrow summit. Eight miles round-trip with about 3,350 feet of elevation gain.

## "NOPAH MOUNTAIN" (6,394 FT; 1,949.9 M), NOPAH PEAK (6,383 FT; 1,946 M)

The ascent of these peaks involves pleasant walking up limestone dip slopes. A few scattered, small junipers are encountered near the crest, but for the most part, sparse desert scrub typical of the area covers the route. The fine views include all of the Chicago and Pahrump Valleys, along the crest of the Nopah Range, and the entire Spring Mountain Range. Nopah Mountain is unnamed on the topographic map, but its summit is marked by a benchmark named "Nopah."

*Maps:* Nopah Peak, North of Tecopa Pass, Resting Spring, and Twelvemile Spring (CA) 7.5-minute (1:24,000 scale) topographic maps; Death Valley Junction and Owlshead Mountains 1:100,000 scale metric topographic maps; Automobile Club of Southern California (AAA) San Bernardino County map (Las Vegas area inset)

*Best Time to Climb:* November through April

*Approach:* From the junction of Highways 127 and 178 at Shoshone,

Author heading up the canyon to Pahrump on an old miner's trail. Photo: Wynne Benti

California, drive 5.3 miles east and north on Highway 178 to a signed dirt road ("Chicago Valley") heading east. Turn right, and follow this road 0.6 miles to where the road turns right. Continue straight on a poor dirt road to a junction after 1.3 miles. Turn right, and drive another 1.3 miles to Twelvemile Spring. Do not drive this road when wet. High clearance two-wheel drive vehicles are recommended.

*Route:* From Twelvemile Spring, hike east-southeast across the flats to a canyon that separates the two peaks. Ascend the first minor gully south of the canyon mouth, heading southeast to a ridge at 3,940 feet. Turn northeast, and follow the ridge as it curves toward the summit of Nopah Mountain. This is a very long hike of 10 miles round-trip with 4,200 feet of elevation gain over rough terrain. Nopah Peak is another 1.5 miles north along the circuitous crest with another 800 feet of gain round-trip returning over Nopah Mountain. Given the already long hike, Nopah Peak is either for extremely strong hikers, or for the overnighter who may wish to spend the night (dry camp) at the canyon mouth, three miles from Twelvemile Spring or bivouac higher on the mountain.

EAGLE MOUNTAIN (3,806 FT; 1,160 M)
This small but sharp peak is the author's favorite in this area. The peak stands as a separate eminence above the Amargosa River and is a fine perch to survey the surrounding country. A dispatch from the 1861 Boundary Commission Survey described the peak as being *"so conspicuous from its isolation, is a single rocky peak rising about sixteen hundred feet above the plain, its dark bare mass, treeless and herbless, giving a most sullen aspect, and making it a fitting outpost to the desolate plain which stretches north from its base some sixty miles."* The views include much of the eastern Death Valley region. The peak was originally named Amargosa Butte by the Boundary Commission of 1861. In 1866, one of the tragedies of the desert occurred near the usual starting point for the peak's climb. A member of the 1866 Boundary Commission Party, G. Gillis, headed toward Eagle Mountain to find some water along the Amargosa River. He never returned, and when the party searched for him, they found his desiccated body, dead from dehydration, along the river bed four miles from the mountain. They buried him on the spot, and upon starting to dig his grave, they encountered water a mere two feet below the surface.

*Maps:* Eagle Mountain and West of Eagle Mountain (CA) 7.5-minute

dry waterfall

Eagle Mountain route. Photo: Wynne Benti

(1:24,000 scale) topographic maps; Death Valley Junction 1:100,000 scale metric topographic map; Automobile Club of Southern California (AAA) Death Valley National Park map

*Best Time to Climb:* November through April

*Approach:* From Shoshone, drive north on Highway 127 about 17 miles to where the highway begins to head west. A quarter mile past highway marker 33.5, a good dirt road heads off to the right. Follow this 0.1 miles to a fork, and bear left to a second fork in about 50 yards. Turn right and drive about 500 feet to a parking spot along the Amargosa River at about 2,000 feet. This approach is passable to all cars.

*Route:* Looking across the river, three chutes in a large gully head up from the base of the mountain. Hike across the old railroad grade, the ephemeral Amargosa River, and about one mile up the alluvial fan to the northern-most (far left) chute in the large gully, of sharp limestone and loose ball-bearing style gravel. Stay as far left as possible, bypassing a dry waterfall. Continue up the left chute until naturally forced right at a white band of rocks. The sheer rocky headwall of the crest comes into view above you. Pass under this by moving to the right, in a southerly direction, then upward to the crest, passing behind boulders, to the east side, then moving back out onto the west side, reaching an open slope. Follow a faint use-trail across the open slope. The rocky fin-shaped crest is now on your left (east),

View north down along Eagle's third class fin-shaped ridge. The use-trail bypasses the fin shown above, to the west, and ends at the base of the third class summit block. Photo: Wynne Benti

while the west side of the plateau drops off into a sheer canyon. Follow the plateau as it narrows to a wide ledge, passing in between Point 3680 feet on the left (east) and the sheer canyon that drops off on the right (west).

At Point 3,680 feet on your left, you may notice ducks (piles of rocks used to denote trails) leading back up to the fin-shaped ridge. This marks the exposed 3rd class alternate route which follows the northern fin of the crest to Eagle's summit. Ignore the ducks on your left, and continue on the easy walking use-trail along the wide ledge which passes below the fin-shaped crest, then turns slightly east, climbing up a few ledges, to the base of Eagle's third class summit block. Climb up about fifteen feet of exposed third class rock, with solid hand and foot holds (those with little rock experience may want a roped belay here). Then walk south about twenty feet to the register, passing two benchmarks on the way.

*Alternate Route:* The alternate route essentially follows the entire fin-shaped ridge from Point 3,680 feet and is exposed third class. From the use-trail at Point 3,680 feet climb up reddish-orange ledges to a small, one-person u-notch on the crest. Pass through this small u-notch to the east side of the fin and immediately downclimb about a five foot section to a ledge, where a use-trail is followed south to a much larger notch, the "second notch." Some may want to leave their packs here to be retrieved on the return, however don't leave your pack if you plan to hike back from the summit block via the easy use-trail, that passes way under this second notch depositing you back at the base of Point 3,680 feet (which means you have to backtrack to get your pack). The most difficult climbing on the fin occurs past the second notch, but before the summit block section of third class. The limestone is firm and the handholds good, but the route is steep and exposed in places as it winds its way back and forth along the fin to the base of Eagle's summit block. The alternate route takes twice as long as walking the use-trail. Anticipate three miles round-trip with 1,800 feet of elevation gain. Consider wearing leather bicycle gloves on the sharp limestone.

## TONOPAH TO BEATTY

North and east of Death Valley lies a high, sparsely populated and watered region known for its mining strikes. These gold and silver strikes of Rhyolite-Bullfrog, Goldfield and Tonopah were found around the turn of the century. Less well known were the strikes of Montezuma in 1867, and Silver Peak in 1864. Other mines were in the Palmetto, Sylvania and other local ranges. In fact, it might be said that about every one of the Basin ranges in this area was the site of a mining strike at one time or another. In keeping with our assigned territorial limits, we will treat those peaks lying west of U.S. Highway 95 starting from the north at the Excelsior Mountains.

## EXCELSIOR MOUNTAINS

This east-west trending range is little known to hikers, but provides a glimpse into the region's mining past, along with providing some of the finest views of any of the Tonopah to Beatty ranges. Of particular interest to the hiker, will be the fantastic view of Teel's Marsh and Marietta. The history of Marietta is key to the Death Valley country in that it is here that Borax Smith initiated the mining of borax deposits that would even-tually lead to Smith's legendary stature among historic characters of Death Valley. Today, only a few people live in Marietta, but the remains of the stone buildings along Main Street stand as mute testimony to the area's bustling past.

The Excelsior Mountains are within the Bureau of Land Management's Marietta Wild Horse and Burro Range, set aside twenty years after Congress passed the Wild Free Roaming Horse and Burro Act:

*"...wild free-roaming horses and burros are living symbols of the historic and pioneer spirit of the West... they contribute to the diversity of life forms within the nation and enrich the lives of the American people."*

Of interest is that these wild horses and burros coexist with one of the most vibrant bighorn sheep herds in the region. It is common to see the wild horses and burros around the old townsite of Marietta, and in the mountains. Horses and burros are protected at Marietta. Outside the range, however, herds of these animals have been illegally killed or wounded for no reason. This federal crime made national headlines when two men, responsible for shooting a herd of wild horses just for sport were caught. Many times the perpetrators are never caught.

The Excelsior Mountains are remote, and food, gas, supplies and lodging are largely unavailable anywhere near these mountains. There is a restaurant and lodging at Montgomery Pass, gasoline lodging and supplies in Hawthorne, Tonopah or Bishop (all long distances away) with possible gasoline in the small town of Mina. Camping in the area is primitive, so apply all minimum impact camping methods here. For further information contact the Bureau of Land Management offices in Las Vegas or Tonopah.

### EXCELSIOR MOUNTAIN (8,671 FT; 2,643 M)

*Maps:* Rattlesnake Flat (NV) 7.5-minute (1:24,000 scale) metric topographic map; Excelsior Mountains 1:100,000 scale metric topographic map
*Best Time to Climb:* Fall and Spring
*Approach:* From Mina, Nevada along Highway 95, drive west on the Garfield Flat Road, passing through Douglas Canyon to a fork about eight

miles from the highway. The right fork heads northwest through the Garfield Hills toward Hawthorne. Follow the left fork generally west, passing the Garfield Mill after about three miles, and continuing along the north slope of the Excelsior Mountains to Rattlesnake Well and a junction. Take Forest Road 200 south a little over three miles to Summit Spring and a junction. Turn east (left) and follow the road as it

Wild horses in the Marietta Wild Horse and Burro Range, Excelsior Mountains. Photo: Wynne Benti

winds along the ridge to the peak, driving as far as practicable with your vehicle. Four-wheel drive is recommended.
*Route:* From the crest road, hike eastward to the summit. If hiking from Summit Spring anticipate 12 miles round-trip with about 2,500 feet of elevation gain. With a four-wheel drive, your hike should be considerably shorter than this.

## MOHO MOUNTAIN (8,805 FT; 2,684 M)

This is the highpoint of the range, and provides fantastic views of the surrounding pinyon-covered slopes and the classic topography of the basin and range. Once, we encountered two wild horses near the summit. They wandered ahead, curious about us but keeping their distance. They strolled over the summit, then disappeared on Moho's north slopes.

*Maps:* Moho Mountain and Teel's Marsh (NV) 7.5-minute (1:24,000 scale) topographic maps; Excelsior Mountains 1:100,000 scale metric topographic map

*Best Time to Climb:* Fall and Spring

*Approach:* From Benton, California, follow Highway 6 north, then east over Montgomery Pass to its junction with Highway 360 in Nevada. Drive 18 miles north on Highway 360 to a graded dirt road heading west, and

signed, "Marietta Wild Burro Range." Follow this road 3.2 miles west to a dirt road heading north toward the Moho Mine. Four-wheel drive is recommended from this point on. Drive 2.2 miles north up the road through scattered pinyon and juniper, passing an open gate and continuing up to the base of the peak. Mining roads switchback up the south slope of the mountain, but by following the main track, one should be able to reach an elevation of about 7,500 feet.

*Route:* Follow the mining tracks as they continue up the mountain to the ruins of the Moho Mine.

Moho Mountain. Photo: Andy Zdon

A dirt track heads up a hill to the right of the workings to a shoulder with an abandoned cabin. Follow a steep track northward up the peak (loose-ball bearing like surface) to the crest, then follow the summit ridge northwest, then northeast to the summit. Anticipate four miles round-trip with 1,400 feet of elevation gain.

Miller Mountain. Photo: Andy Zdon

## ISOLATED PEAKS NORTH OF TONOPAH

The isolated peaks north of Tonopah generally receive greater amounts of precipitation throughout the year than their southern counterparts. As a result, forests of pinyon and juniper can be found at their higher elevations, while the vast rolling lowlands leading up to higher ridges are covered with sagebrush.

### MILLER MOUNTAIN (8,729 FT; 2,661 M)

This peak, which is prominently displayed in the east after crossing eastward over Montgomery Pass, stands as an isolated summit, covered by pinyon and juniper woodlands amid stark surroundings. Although a separate peak, a case could be made that this mountain is actually part of the Candelaria Hills.

*Maps:* Miller Mountain and Basalt (NV) 7.5-minute (1:24,000 scale) topographic maps; Excelsior Mountains 1:100,000 scale metric topographic map

*Best Time to Climb*: Fall and Spring

*Approach:* From Benton, California, follow Highway 6 north, then east over Montgomery Pass to its junction with Highway 360 in Nevada. Continue another two miles on Highway 6 to a dirt road that heads north along the west base of Miller Mountain. Head north on this dirt road about 1.4 miles to a junction. Stay left, and continue another mile where the road ends at a wash at about 6,400 feet. Two-wheel drives with high clearance should be able to reach this point.

*Route:* From the road end, hike north to a larger wash marked by some stately pinyons. From here two options are available. One can follow the wash eastward toward the peak, gaining its southwest slopes, or scramble west directly to the peak's west ridge amid pinyons and junipers. Either route can then be followed to the top. Anticipate ten miles round-trip with 2,500 feet of elevation gain. Other routes up this peak are plentiful.

### VOLCANIC HILLS (7,398 FT; 2,255 M)

Rising over 3,000 feet above the flats of Columbus Salt Marsh, this small group of mountains is situated between Miller Mountain and the northern end of Fish Lake Valley. This mini-range provides a colorful backdrop to the valley in contrast to the surrounding White Mountains and Silver Peak Range. Although small, the Volcanic Hills will provide an interesting and view-packed hiking experience. The Volcanic Hills consist of eleven million year old volcanic rocks derived from explosive eruptions that resulted in the ash flow deposits we see today. Some interlayered sedimentary units can also be found. Much of the range is capped by basalt flows, and a small package of Paleozoic-age sedimentary rocks, similar to those in the Inyo Mountains, are present along the eastern margin of the range.

*Maps:* Volcanic Hills West and Volcanic Hills East (NV) 7.5-minute (1:24,000 scale) topographic maps; Benton Range 1:100,000 scale metric topographic map

*Best Time to Climb:* November through April

*Approach:* From Bishop, California drive 48 miles north on Highway 6 to Montgomery Pass. From the pass, continue another 7.9 miles to Nevada Highway 264. Turn right (the only way you can turn) on Highway 264, and drive 13.1 miles south on Highway 264 to the junction with Highway 773. Head east on Highway 773 about 1.3 miles to a large clearing on the north side of the road where piles of asphalt are sometimes stored for highway work. Pass through the highway storage area, and follow a poor dirt road (high-clearance two-wheel drive should be sufficient) 1.3 miles to its end at the southern base of the mountains.

*Route:* Follow a wash, then ridges northwest to the summit. Anticipate four miles round-trip with about 1,700 feet of elevation gain. Mileage and elevation gain will differ somewhat based on how far up the road you get, and your chosen route.

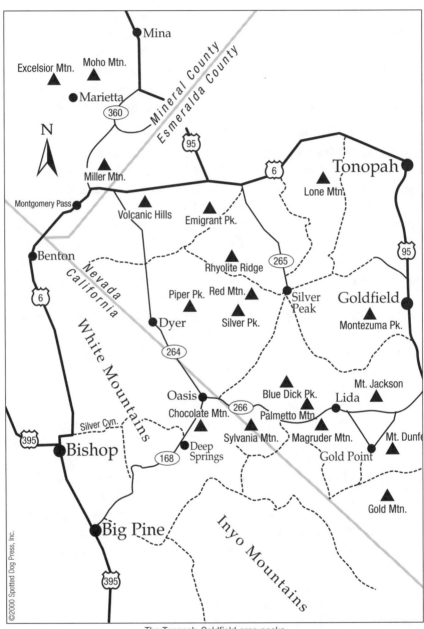

The Tonopah-Goldfield area peaks

©2000 Spotted Dog Press, Inc.

Lone Mountain. Photo: Andy Zdon

## LONE MOUNTAIN (9,108 FT; 2,776 M)

Vertical, granitic ramparts guard this prominent desert mountain as it rises more than 4,000 feet above the south end of the Big Smoky Valley. However, the south side of the mountain affords the desert-peaker a non-technical route starting from a pleasant desert canyon. Bighorn sheep roam across the peak's steep slopes. The summit is capped by a small island of Precambrian-age siltstone of the Wyman formation. The rocks of the Wyman formation are the oldest found in the region. Here, the granitic rocks were emplaced at depth beneath the Wyman. The whole package was then uplifted as a result of faulting, and the rocks overlying the granite were eroded away, only leaving a small remnant of the Wyman formation.

*Maps:* Lone Mountain (NV) 7.5-minute (1:24,000 scale) topographic map; Tonopah 1:100,000 scale metric topographic map

*Best Time to Climb:* Fall and Spring

*Approach:* From Miller's Rest Area, 11 miles west of Tonopah on Highway 6, go east 1.3 miles on Highway 6, then turn southwest on a dirt road. Stay on the main desert road, crossing the old T&G Railroad grade at 0.8 miles. Turn left, going southward over a series of hills, then follow an alluvial fan climbing to a small mining camp, 6.6 miles from the highway. Our road goes east, through the camp, then turns south around a rocky point. Two miles from the camp, take the right fork at a crossroads into Springdale Canyon, and a campsite at a spring at about 6,800 feet. Four-wheel drive vehicles are recommended.

*Route:* There is no trail to the summit; simply scramble up the canyon and follow ridges to the summit. Anticipate five miles round-trip with about 2,400 feet of elevation gain.

## SILVER PEAK RANGE

If not for the presence of the tallest desert range in North America being located directly to the west across Fish Lake Valley, the Silver Peak Range would likely be far more recognized as a fine desert range worthy of exploration. However, the White Mountains are there, and the Silver Peak Range remains a little visited mountain range. For those of us who have discovered the joys of hiking in these mountains though, the lack of visitation just adds to the charm of each visit. The variability of its peaks, from the rugged rhyolite tuff of Rhyolite Ridge, to the high plateau of Piper Peak, to the perfect cone of Red Mountain lends something of appeal to most any hiker. The range is typical for mountains in the region. Sagebrush and shadscale scrub give way to pinyon-juniper woodlands, and montane shrubs on the highest peaks. A small grove of bristlecones also can be found here.

According Alvin R. McLane, the Silver Peak Range was named for the town of Silver Peak along the east base of the range. It is also noted that there is an actual peak called Silver just southwest of Red Mountain. Whether the range is named for the peak or the town will probably never be answered. The Wheeler Survey passed through here in 1871, crossing the range near Red Mountain (which they ascended along with Silver Peak).

Camping in the area is primitive so all minimum impact camping methods should be applied here. The nearest source of gasoline, supplies and food are either Tonopah or Bishop. However, a small market can be found in Dyer, within Fish Lake Valley. For further information, contact the Bureau of Land Management office in Las Vegas.

### EMIGRANT PEAK (6,790 FT; 2,070 M)

This volcanic peak is at the far northern end of the ridge that extends northward from the Silver Peak Range. Emigrant Peak is comprised of Tertiary-age volcanic rocks, although the first half of the hike from Emigrant Pass is on claystones of the Cambrian-age Emigrant formation.

*Maps:* Rhyolite Ridge NW and Rhyolite Ridge NE (NV) 7.5-minute (1:24,000 scale) topographic maps; Goldfield 1:100,000 scale metric topographic map

Rhyolite Ridge. Photo: Andy Zdon

*Best Time to Climb:* November through April

*Approach:* The goal for the approach is to reach Emigrant Pass on the northern end of the Silver Peak Range. From Benton, California follow Highway 6 to its junction with Highway 95 at Coaldale Junction in Nevada. From Coaldale Junction, stay right (east) and continue about six miles to Blair Junction. Turn south on Highway 265 (the road to Silver Peak) and continue about one mile to a good dirt road that heads southwest. Follow the dirt road about two miles to Emigrant Pass and park. The road is generally passable to all cars.

*Route:* From Emigrant Pass (6,064 ft), climb northward along a rolling ridge. In a good spring, you will be in fields of wildflowers, making it an idyllic stroll. Anticipate nine miles round-trip with 2,000 feet of elevation gain.

### RHYOLITE RIDGE (8,550 FT; 2,606 M)

This impressive peak when viewed from east, is comprised of six-million year old rhyolite.

*Maps:* Rhyolite Ridge (NV) 7.5-minute (1:24,000 scale) topographic map; Goldfield 1:100,000 scale metric topographic map

*Best Time to Climb:* November through April

*Approach:* Follow the directions to Red Mountain Pass as described for Red Mountain. About a mile below the pass, a road takes off to the north, heading directly for a rim rock break at the northern end of Rhyolite Ridge. This is an extremely rough road, and four-wheel drive is required. It may be necessary to park along the Red Mountain Pass Road. Continue on this rough road as far as practicable with your vehicle and park.

*Route:* Continue hiking on the road until near 7,000 feet, then scramble through the gap and stroll along the flat top to a cairn at the highpoint. Anticipate nine miles round-trip with 2,000 feet of elevation gain.

### RED MOUNTAIN (8,957 FT; 2,730 M)

Red Mountain's summit cone of Tertiary-age rhyolite is one of the most distinctive peaks in the region. The view east toward Clayton Valley is particularly interesting.

*Maps:* Rhyolite Ridge and Silver Peak (NV) 7.5-minute (1:24,000 scale) topographic maps; Goldfield 1:100,000 scale metric topographic map. Note: if using the Benton 1:100,000 scale map on the approach drive, note that Nevada Highway 264 does not pass in an east-west direction south of the Volcanic Hills. Highway 264 runs south from U.S. Highway 6, down the length of Fish Lake Valley.

*Best Time to Climb:* Fall and Spring

*Approach:* The goal for the approach is to reach Red Mountain Pass in the northern Silver Peak Range. For a west side approach from Benton, California on U.S. Highway 6, continue east on Highway 6 about 22.7 miles

to Nevada Highway 264 heading south for Fish Lake Valley. Take Highway 264 south 13.7 miles to "The Crossing" road, a well-graded dirt road heading east. Turn east and follow the main road, passing Hot Ditch Picnic Area at 6.7 miles, staying right at a junction with the road to Emigrant Pass, and bearing left at a fork

Red Mountain. Photo: Andy Zdon

8.3 miles from the highway. From the fork continue another 14.2 miles to Red Mountain Pass (do not turn left at the Mineral Ridge Mine Road just before the pass). A two-track dirt road leads south from the pass onto a flat parking area at 7,280 feet. Red Mountain looms as a red pyramid to the south. If approaching Red Mountain Pass from the east side (from Tonopah) drive west/north on Highways 6/95 to Blair Junction and a signed route (Nevada Highway 265) to Silver Peak, Nevada. Just to the south of town, take a sharp right onto the Coyote Spring Road. It is a moderately steep pull 5.6 miles to the spring, but climbs very steeply from there to Red Mountain Pass, 7.7 miles from Silver Peak. Most cars should be able to drive the approach from Fish Lake Valley.

*Route:* From the parking area, drop into a shallow saddle, then climb the connecting ridge through pinyon and over broken ledges to a ridge crest. Turn left (southwest) and follow the ridge as it curves south toward the peak. The final 500 feet of elevation gain to the summit are over steep, loose scree.

## SILVER PEAK (9,376 FT; 2,858 M)

*Maps:* Rhyolite Ridge and Silver Peak (NV) 7.5-minute (1:24,000 scale) topographic maps; Goldfield 1:100,000 scale metric topographic map
*Best Time to Climb:* Fall and Spring
*Approach:* As for Red Mountain.
*Route:* Climb Red Mountain. From the summit of Red Mountain, drop southwest on loose slopes to a saddle, then follow the ridge southwest to the open summit. Add another seven miles and 1,300 feet of elevation gain round-trip to the ascent of Red Mountain assuming one skirts Red Mountain on the way back, and does not reclimb the peak.
*Alternate Approaches and Routes:* Numerous dirt roads approach Silver Peak from the south. If climbing Silver Peak alone, climbing the peak from the Nivloc Mine or Company Spring can save a lot of distance, although on rougher terrain.

## PIPER PEAK (9,450 FT; 2,880 M)

This peak, the highpoint of the Silver Peak Range, makes for a fine point from which to view the White Mountains, with the gulf of Fish Lake Valley far below. The peak was named for a rancher, N.T. Piper who owned the Oasis Ranch in Fish Lake Valley. The summit rocks consist of four to six million year old basalt.

*Maps:* Piper Peak (NV) 7.5-minute (1:24,000 scale) topographic map; Goldfield and Benton Range 1:100,000 scale metric topographic maps
*Best Time to Climb:* April to December
*Approach:* From Nevada Highway 264 in Fish Lake Valley, turn east on any of a number of farm roads to the base of the mountain road that runs along the base of the Silver Peak Range on the east side of Fish Lake Valley. A gravel road heads east up McAfee Canyon to a saddle (7,520 ft).

A cloudy day on Piper Peak's summit. Photo: Wynne Benti

Park here. If conditions are good, most cars should be able to reach this parking spot.

*Route:* Hike along a mining road that generally heads north, then winds northwesterly to a ridge. Continue cross-country skirting to the left of the rocky ledges to the summit. When the peak is snow-covered, the high sagebrush combined with deep snow can result in some tedious hiking, but the snow-covered panorama from the summit is worth the effort. Anticipate about seven miles round-trip with 2,000 feet of elevation gain.

### "BLUE DICK PEAK" (9,286 FT; 2,830 M)

Blue Dick Peak, along with Palmetto Mountain are within a subrange of the Silver Peak Range called the Palmetto Mountains. Located between the main mass of the Silver Peak Range and Magruder Mountain, these mountains are largely covered by a pinyon-juniper woodland that gives way to a grassy montane zone with scattered sagebrush.

This peak was unofficially named for a miner, Blue Dick Hartman, whose face had been blasted with black powder in an explosion, giving it a blue cast. Blue Dick one time faked his own death as a con to collect contributions for his funeral, which would then be split with his co-conspirators. At a bar in Pickhandle Gulch in the Candelaria Hills, he was laid out in state beneath a sheet (boots sticking out) on a billiard table, while mourners contributed fond reminiscences and cash to the event. Finally, one fellow proceeded to insult his memory. To everyone's horror, the "corpse" sprang up, guns drawn, and chased the fellow out of town. Upon returning to the saloon, the remaining money was used by mourners and corpse (Blue Dick) alike at the bar.

On another occasion, Blue Dick was sent out to look for a missing resident of Lida. Dick found his body (it is not clear how the chap died) near Mount Jackson, but unfortunately the body was not in the best of condition having been exposed to the desert environment. Dick slung the body over the back of his horse and headed back into Lida. It was not until reaching the small hamlet, that it was pointed out that somewhere along the route, the poor fellow's head had fallen off. The townspeople refused to pay Dick for his services until he retrieved the missing appendage, which he accomplished shortly thereafter.

The author (right) and his father on Blue Dick Peak.

*Maps:* Lida Wash and Magruder Mountain (NV) 7.5-minute (1:24,000 scale) topographic maps; Goldfield and Last Chance Range 1:100,000 scale metric topographic maps; Automobile Club of Southern California (AAA) Death Valley National Park map

*Best Time to Climb:* Fall and Spring

*Approach:* From the junction of Highways 95 and Highway 266, drive about 25 miles west on Highway 266 to Lida Summit at (7,409 ft). Lida Summit is also reached by driving east on Highway 266 from Fish Lake Valley. Five miles west of Lida Summit (15 miles east of the junction of Highways 168 and 266 in Fish Lake Valley) are the ruins of the Pigeon Spring Stamp Mill. A fair dirt road runs north from across the highway, passing several side roads leading to cattle ranches. Keep to the roadway that follows the main wash, heading for the Palmetto-Blue Dick saddle at 8,000 feet. The dirt road drops in quality to a jeep trail after six miles but may be washed out before you get that far.

*Route:* Either head up the canyon to the saddle, then follow the easy rolling ridge north to the summit, or follow any of the other plentiful routes that lead to this gentle but high desert summit. For planning purposes, expect roughly five miles round-trip with 1,500 to 2,000 feet of elevation gain, depending on the route chosen.

### PALMETTO MOUNTAIN (8,945 FT; 2,726 M)

The name "Palmetto" was derived from the resemblance of the scrubby Joshua trees to the palmetto palms that early southeastern travelers through the area were used to seeing back home. This peak is comprised of Ordovician-aged shale, limestone and quartzite of the Palmetto formation. The summit is marked by a small relay station.

*Maps:* Magruder Mountain (NV) 7.5-minute (1:24,000 scale) topographic map; Last Chance Range 1:100,000 scale metric topographic map; Automobile Club of Southern California (AAA) Death Valley National Park map

*Best Time to Climb:* Fall and Spring

*Approach:* From the junction of Highways 95 and 266, drive about 25 miles west on Highway 266 to Lida Summit (7,409 ft). Lida Summit is also reached by driving east on Highway 266 from Fish Lake Valley.

*Route:* From the pass, head north following abandoned mining roads at first, then trails until you reach the first ridge. Follow the ridge across a dip to the top, marked with a radar or microwave installation. On my hike up this peak, a strange incident occurred. Shortly after reaching the summit, a military aircraft flew towards the peak from the south. The jet seemed to hang around, flying in the vicinity of the peak until I left, at which time, it headed south and wasn't seen again. Curious...I wonder what that summit installation is?

### MAGRUDER MOUNTAIN (9,046 FT; 2,757 M)

Although this peak is part of the large Silver Peak Range, Magruder Mountain can almost be considered a small range itself, separated from the mountains to the north by Lida Summit. The mountain rises 3,800 feet above Lida Valley on the east, and to the west lie the Sylvania Mountains. The lower slopes of the mountain are covered by a generous pinyon-juniper woodland with scattered mountain mahogany that gives way to the open, grassy summit. The peak was named in honor of J. Bankhead Magruder, a confederate army officer. The mountain was also referred

Broad summit plateau of Magruder Mountain, looking south into Death Valley. Photo: Wynne Benti

to as Lookout Mountain in an 1866 journal. When the author first hiked up this peak, it was on a brilliant but cold (about ten degrees Fahrenheit) new year's day. The hike involved trudging through two to three feet of snow to the summit, which was spectacular with all of the surrounding desert terrain blanketed in white.

*Maps:* Magruder Mountain (NV) 7.5-minute (1:24,000 scale) topographic map; Last Chance Range 1:100,000 scale metric topographic map; Automobile Club of Southern California (AAA) Death Valley National Park map

*Best Time to Climb:* Fall and Spring

*Approach:* From the junction of Highways 95 and 266, drive about 25 miles west on Highway 266 to Lida Summit (7,409 ft). Lida Summit is also reached by driving east on Highway 266 from Fish Lake Valley.

*Route:* Magruder Mountain lies southeast of Lida Summit. From the highway, follow a dirt road down into the drainage and then up to the base of the mountain. Climb south, edging east through pinyons until you reach the open summit ridge. Follow the summit ridge east to the high-point along a use-trail. Anticipate six miles round-trip with 1,700 feet of elevation gain.

# MONTEZUMA RANGE

The Montezuma Range is a small group of mountains west of Goldfield. The range supports a hardy pinyon-juniper woodland, with the highest summits rising above the "first tree-line" typical in this part of the Basin and Range, and providing unobstructed views. The approach route to Montezuma Peak passes by the old mining camp of Montezuma. The camp's old lime kilns are passed on the way to the peak. The Montezuma District operated from 1867 to 1907 during which small booms and periods of ceased activity were the order of the day. However, during that period, the district produced about $500,000, primarily in silver.

Gasoline, food, supplies and lodging are available in Tonopah. A restaurant and limited groceries are also available in Goldfield. Plan on primitive camping, so all minimum impact camping methods should be applied here. For further information, contact the Bureau of Land Management offices in Tonopah or Las Vegas.

### MONTEZUMA PEAK (8,376 FT; 2,553 M)

This peak, the highpoint of the Montezuma Range, is one of the author's favorites, having climbed it several times because of the fine views from the summit. Eight different dry lakes are visible including Alkali Lake, Mud Lake, two in Stonewall Flat, Clayton Valley, and the southernmost end of Big Smoky Valley. The peak is comprised of Miocene-age ash flow deposits.

*Maps:* Split Mountain and Montezuma Peak (NV) 7.5-minute (1:24,000 scale) topographic maps; Goldfield 1:100,000 scale metric topographic map
*Best Time to Climb:* October through May
*Approach:* Three miles north of Goldfield, turn right on the Silver Peak road, passing Alkali Spring at 7.4 miles. The road reaches a low pass at 13.2 miles. An AT&T road to a microwave station cuts sharply back to the left. Turn left, and after seven miles a junction is reached where a poor side road turns left and deadends almost immediately at the site of the gold camp of Montezuma (7,170 ft). Stay right and follow an old road around the ruins, then left to a low saddle west of the peak. Park here. The road is passable to two-wheel drive vehicles with good clearance.
*Route:* Climb east-southeast up the barren ridge to the isolated summit. Anticipate three miles round-trip with 1,200 feet of elevation gain.

Mt. Jackson. Photo: Andy Zdon

## SYLVANIA MOUNTAINS

From the Lida Road, the Sylvania Mountains appear as rolling, pinyon-covered hills; but viewed from northern Death Valley, the true mountainous aspect of the range becomes clear. Deer are common and the Last Chance herd of bighorn sheep occasionally roams through these mountains. The range was originally named "Green Mountain." Later, the name was changed to Sylvania in honor of the mineral "sylvanite," a silver telluride mineral found in the area. The range furnished the name for the Sylvania Mining District that was located on its slopes. Camping in the area is primitive so all minimum impact camping methods should be applied here. Supplies, gas, food and lodging are available in Tonopah along Highway 95, or in Big Pine, California, a distant drive to the west.

### "SYLVANIA MOUNTAIN" (8,160 FT; 2,487 M)

The range highpoint, this summit is unnamed on the topographic map.
*Maps:* Sylvania Mountains (NV) 7.5-minute (1:24,000 scale) topographic map; Last Chance Range 1:100,000 scale metric topographic map
*Best Time to Climb:* October through May
*Approach:* From the junction of Highways 168 and 266 in Fish Lake Valley, drive east on Highway 266 about 13 miles, and take a dirt road heading

south. There are many dirt roads crisscrossing the area, but the most heavily traveled track (generally staying left) traverses the range. At three miles from Highway 266, you will reach the ruins of the Sylvania Mine and after another mile, reach a low saddle where the road crosses from the north to the south slope. Park here at 7,600 feet.

*Route:* An easy pinyon-covered ridge runs south from here. Stroll through the trees south then southwest three miles to the summit. It is not visible en route, but keep to the ridge and you will finally make it.

## GOLD POINT AREA

Fifty miles north of Beatty on Highway 95 (15 miles north of Scotty's Junction and south of Goldfield), Highway 266 turns west toward Fish Lake Valley. This road will take you by many old mining camps and into some timbered country standing high above the barren uplands of Esmeralda County. Among the old mining towns is Gold Point which is still occupied by a few old-timers and weekenders. Camping in the area is primitive so all minimum impact camping methods should be applied here. Supplies, gas, food and lodging are available in Tonopah along Highway 95, or in Big Pine, California, a distant drive to the west.

### MOUNT JACKSON (6,412 FT; 1,954 M)

This peak resembles a layer cake. The layers consist of volcanic rocks units with a summit icing of rhyolite. Mount Jackson provides a very enjoyable scramble.

*Maps:* Lida and Mount Jackson (NV) 7.5-minute (1:24,000 scale) topographic maps; Last Chance Range 1:100,000 scale metric topographic map; Automobile Club of Southern California (AAA) Death Valley National Park map

*Best Time to Climb:* November through April

*Approach:* From Highway 95, drive 14.5 miles west on Highway 266 to a well-graded dirt road that heads north. At 2.2 miles, take a right fork and continue to what seems a likely takeoff point at about 5,250 feet. All cars should be able to reach, or nearly reach, the road end.

*Route:* Climb east up over easy ledges to the mesa, then north to a cairn marking the summit. There is much chalcedony float on the ledges and summit plateau. Anticipate three miles round trip with about 1,200 feet of elevation gain.

## MOUNT DUNFEE (7,024 FT; 2,141 M)

Mount Dunfee is the highpoint of a minor Nevada Range called Slate Ridge. The peak is named in honor of J. William Dunfee, superintendent of the Orleans Mine at the mining camp of Hornsilver (later to become Gold Point). Slate Ridge trends generally east-west, similar to Magruder Mountain to the northwest. Joshua trees dot the mountain's slopes.

*Maps:* Gold Point (NV) 7.5-minute (1:24,000 scale) topographic map; Last Chance Range 1:100,000 scale metric topographic map; Automobile Club of Southern California (AAA) Death Valley National Park map

*Best Time to Climb:* November through April

*Approach:* From Highway 95, drive 7.2 miles west on Highway 266, and turn southwest on the road to Gold Point. Gold Point is reached in 7.6 miles. The peak lies to the east. Of the cluster of roads leaving "downtown" Gold Point, take a left one that passes to the south of the peak. Choose a likely takeoff point after about three miles (6,000 ft).

*Route:* An obvious ridge leads up easy slopes to the summit, and its fine views including the Sierra Nevada from Mount Langley to Mount Tom. There are also interesting views of White Mountain Peak, the Silver Peak Range and Mount Jackson, and a bird's-eye view of Gold Point. Anticipate four miles round-trip with 1,200 feet of elevation gain.

## GOLD MOUNTAIN (8,152 FT; 2,485 M)

This peak is not easy to find as it is not visible from Gold Point and there are many roads in the area to add a bit of confusion.

*Maps:* Gold Mountain and Gold Point (NV) 7.5-minute (1:24,000 scale) topographic maps; Last Chance Range 1:100,000 scale metric topographic map; Automobile Club of Southern California (AAA) Death Valley National Park map

*Best Time to Climb:* October through May

*Approach:* On the south edge of Gold Point, a cluster of roads head off in different directions. Take the best graded road in the center of the group about seven miles to Oriental wash then east about two miles. Bear right to a small canyon and follow this to a saddle at 7,400 feet, northeast of the peak.

*Route:* From the saddle, an easy hike leads southwest to the summit.

# Bullfrog Hills

In 1904, Shorty Harris and Ed Cross struck it rich at Bullfrog, and for a few years Bullfrog and Rhyolite were booming mining towns. Now there are a few tourist activities and not many visitors. However, the area is interesting to explore, but watch for open mine shafts. The Bullfrog Hills consist almost entirely of volcanic rocks. The slopes of the range are covered with shadscale and Mojavean scrub including creosote, and a smattering of sagebrush.

The aptly named ghost town of Rhyolite is reached by a side road off the Daylight Pass Road from Death Valley, about four miles west of Beatty, Nevada. Supplies, gas, food and lodging are available in Beatty. Management of the range is split between the National Park Service and the Bureau of Land Management. Bullfrog Mountain lies within the Death Valley National Park, while Sawtooth is on lands administered by the Bureau of Land Management in Las Vegas. For further information on these mountains, contact those agencies.

### SAWTOOTH MOUNTAIN (6,002 FT; 1,829 M)

Sawtooth Mountain is the most impressive peak in the Bullfrog Hills and is also the highest. The summit area has a microwave tower.

*Maps:* Beatty (NV) 7.5-minute (1:24,000 scale) topographic map; Beatty 1:100,000 scale metric topographic map; Automobile Club of Southern California (AAA) Death Valley National Park map

*Best Time to Climb:* November through April

*Approach:* A service road for the microwave installation near its summit leads to the base of the peak. To reach this road from Beatty, drive west on the Daylight Pass Road (Highway 374) to the Rhyolite Road. Turn north (right) on the Rhyolite Road, and continue about a mile to a fork. The right fork heads toward Rhyolite. Stay left, and continue about 1.5 miles to a dirt road that heads north toward the saddle between Bullfrog Mountain and Sawtooth Mountain. From near the saddle the service road heads northeast.

*Route:* From the base of the peak, a bulldozed track, which is too steep to drive, leads to the installation near the summit. A rocky ridge leads directly to the highpoint, but it is much easier to contour right, following easy ledges to the summit.

## BULLFROG MOUNTAIN (4,959 FT; 1,511 M)

This strangely named hill was named in honor of Shorty Harris' Bullfrog Mine. The name is derived from the green color of the ore.

*Maps:* Beatty and Bullfrog Mountain (NV) 7.5-minute (1:24,000 scale) topographic maps; Beatty 1:100,000 scale metric topographic map; Automobile Club of Southern California (AAA) Death Valley National Park map

*Best Time to Climb:* November through April

*Approach:* From Beatty, drive west on the Daylight Pass Road (Highway 374) to the Rhyolite Road. Turn right on the Rhyolite Road, and continue about a mile to a fork. The right fork heads toward Rhyolite. Stay left, and continue about 1.5 miles to a dirt road that heads north toward the saddle between Bullfrog Mountain and Sawtooth Mountain. Drive to the saddle and park (4,400 ft).

*Route:* Walk up an easy slope to the summit. Anticipate three miles round-trip with 600 feet of elevation gain.

## BARE MOUNTAIN AREA

Bare Mountain is the name given to that long, rugged ridge that extends southward from Beatty, and east of Highway 95. This limestone mountain rises 3,500 feet above the Amargosa Desert and presents an imposing facade when viewed from that dry valley. Directions for the highpoint are provided below. Other peaks on the Bare Mountain massif include Wildcat Peak (5,047 ft), Meiklejohn Peak (5,940 ft) and Beatty Mountain (4,282 ft). These peaks are accessed from the Secret Pass/Steve's Pass Road which is reached from Highway 95 south of the Carrara turnoff, or east of Beatty.

Camping in the area is primitive so all minimum impact camping methods should be used here. Unfortunately, these methods have not been applied by many thoughtless campers here. Supplies, gas, food and lodging are available in Beatty, a short drive to the north.

## BARE MOUNTAIN (6,317 FT; 1,925 M)

Carrara, the site of the beginning of our climb, is the type location for the regionally important geologic unit called the Carrara formation. The townsite of Carrara, formed as a result of marble quarries on Bare Mountain, and was dedicated during 1913. This now bleak place, had a celebration that included a band from Goldfield, baseball game, and other festivities. A railroad was completed to Carrara in 1914, but the town slowly declined

Bare Mountain from the ruins of Carrera. Photo: Wynne Benti

over the next ten years. The concrete buildings that we see today are the leftovers of a 1930's era Filipino-owned cement company that attempted to operate here for a while. The impressive west face of Bare Mountain owes much of its beauty to the bedding of the Carrara and other formations that have been folded and pushed to a near vertical orientation. Covering these interesting rocks are scattered creosote and blackbrush. A wide variety of reptiles make Bare Mountain their home including horned lizards, Panamint rattlesnakes, desert iguanas, chuckwallas, whipsnakes, collard lizards and leopard lizards.

*Maps:* Carrara Canyon (NV) 7.5-minute (1:24,000 scale) topographic map; Beatty 1:100,000 scale metric topographic map; Automobile Club of Southern California (AAA) Death Valley National Park map

*Best Time to Climb:* November through April

*Approach:* From Beatty, Nevada drive about seven miles south on Highway 95 to a dirt road heading east toward Bare Mountain. The stone ruins of Carrara are visible from the highway. Drive about two miles up this dirt road to the mountain front where an old jeep track heads northwest. Park here (3,920 ft).

*Route:* Hike up the old jeep track to a flat spot on the ridge, then drop about 100 feet into the next drainage. Contour around the next ridge to a larger canyon that heads toward the peak. At a fork, climb the ridge that winds between the two drainages to the summit. Anticipate four miles round trip with 2,600 feet of elevation gain.

# Southern Nevada

*"...We reached the cold, windy summit in just under three hours. The north-facing slopes were completely covered in snow, while only a few patches were all that remained near the top. From our vantage point on the summit, we could see the white crown of San Gorgonio in the San Bernardino Mountains near Los Angeles, the snowy peaks of Death Valley's Panamint Range, and the Pine Valley Mountains in Utah to the east. Just off the summit, in the cool winter shade of pinyons and junipers, we discovered a perfectly formed nautilus-shaped ammonite, perhaps two inches in diameter, embedded in a block of steel-grey colored limestone.*

*On the return, the wind ceased its relentless gale and the afternoon became quite warm. The mountain shadows cast long upon the desert, and through the quiet of the winter day, all that could be heard was the sound of our boots crunching gravel against rock and the occasional gust of wind blowing hollow in the pinyons."*
POTOSI MOUNTAIN, WYNNE BENTI

When I look over the list of the desert peaks of southern Nevada, each one jumps out at me as a favorite for one reason or another. Even Frenchman Mountain, which has the development of Las Vegas lapping up against its stark slopes, provides fond memories of a pleasant day's ascent. Part of the fondness for these peaks comes from a combination of the scenery, pleasant company on a trip, or the resulting funny comment written in my journal by one of my hiking companions. But another very important part, is the interesting history of this region, the historical significance of these mountains. In the following paragraphs, I hope to give the reader a glimpse into this region's history.

Of course the native inhabitants of the region lived here for thousands of years before the first Europeans set foot in the area. The Colorado River,

Las Vegas Springs, and springs in the nearby mountains provided water in this otherwise harsh environment. Then in 1776, while some colonists back east were declaring their independence, a Spanish explorer, Francisco Garces, passed through the region, on the Arizona side of the Colorado. The first party of American explorers to pass through southern Nevada were led by the noted trapper Jedediah Smith who was on his way to California. Tying together the routes of Garces, and another noteworthy Spanish explorer named Escalante, the Spanish Trail route to California was born. Variations on the route were to occur over the ensuing years, but this route became the principal route to southern California from parts east. It was such a significant route, that much of today's Interstate 15 either follows or parallels this trail.

During the 1840's and 1850's, Mormon traffic along the route to southern California resulted in the establishment of a fort at Las Vegas. During the late 1850's the Mormons, searching for a source of lead for bullets, happened upon the lead deposits on Potosi Mountain. The lead was unsatisfactory for making bullets and the mining ceased. Mormon settlement of the Las Vegas Valley was left behind. However, in 1860 a prospecting party discovered the reason for Potosi's poor quality lead, it was contaminated with silver! A mining boom ensued on the west side of the mountain, and the mine operated sporadically for many years. During the later part of the nineteenth century, area pioneers whose names grace many of the area's peaks such as Gass and Bonelli, moved into the area and started ranches and farms. During the 1890's the mining districts of El Dorado and Searchlight were being discovered.

During the 1920's, mining at the above-mentioned districts along with Goodsprings, made Las Vegas a principal stopping place for the railroad. The growth of the region proved slow and fitful, but by the 1930's, with water issues rising throughout the southwestern U.S., a dam was proposed on the Colorado River. Hoover Dam was constructed, forming Lake Mead, creating jobs, and leading to economic growth and a corresponding growth in population. The railroad had moved into the area during the early 1900's and provided a means for getting goods into the region. The small town of Las Vegas, became known as one of the last places with legal gambling, and with the birth of the resort and gaming industry, the future of one of the nation's fastest growing cities was defined.

## THE SPRING MOUNTAINS

The tallest and most extensive of southern Nevada's ranges, the oft snow-capped Spring Mountains offer a year-round alpine alternative to the warm, dry Las Vegas Valley. During the summer, these cool summits are a tantalizing oasis in the hot Nevada desert, providing pleasant, cool climbing while other southern Nevada ranges, lower in elevation, bake beneath the hot, summer sun. This is no reason to become complacent though. Once, the author hiked up to Griffith Peak via the Griffith Peak trail route, starting out on a fine summer day, with only a few scattered clouds adorning the morning sky. By mid-afternoon, on the way down from the summit, the author and friends were pelted with hail while thunder crashed and bolts of lightning illuminated the dark, foreboding sky. These are classic summer thunderstorm conditions in the Spring Mountains, and if thunderstorms are in the weather report, a predawn start may be needed to reach the summit before the conditions on the higher exposed ridges become too dangerous.

Intriguing in their ever-changing character, the northernmost end of the Spring Mountains, from Mount Stirling to McFarland Peak is typical of the many single-ridged, north-south trending ranges so common in the Great Basin. To the south, is the Charleston Peak-Mummy Mountain portion of the range, having greater mass than the northern end of the range, and typical of a more extensive mountain range. In the shadow of the Charleston-Mummy massif is the La Madre Mountain-Sandstone Bluffs portion of the range that resembles a cross between a desert version of the Dolomites and the great sandstone cliffs of Zion National Park in Utah. To the south, across Mountain Springs Summit, Potosi Mountain rises as a great calcareous dome, known more for being the mountain on which Carol Lombard's plane crashed than as a fine desert peak worthy of ascent. This is the last mountain in the range with forested slopes. South of Potosi, the range again becomes linear and dry, more characteristic of a classic Mojave Desert-style range.

The most striking geologic features in the Spring Mountains are the thrust faults. Oriented at low angles, thrust faults occur where the land has been squeezed together, forcing one group of rocks to ride atop another. These phenomena result in older rocks lying on top of younger rocks, just the opposite of what would be the logical progression. The most striking

View from the Trail Canyon Trail in the Spring Mountains. Photo: Andy Zdon

of the thrust faults in the area is the Keystone thrust which places much older, Cambrian-age Bonzana King formation limestones on top of the striking white and red Aztec sandstone that inspired the naming of Red Rock National Conservation Area. When climbing the peaks of the Sandstone Bluffs (Bridge, Rainbow, Wilson) or Turtlehead Peak, the climber will pass over the trace of this fantastic structure.

Current estimates suggest that there are more than 1,000 species of plants that occur within this single range. Charleston Peak is topped by an alpine zone that is only sparsely vegetated by scattered dwarf plants. Below this, and found on many of the higher ridges, bristlecone pines and limber pines provide fine photographic opportunities. The south ridge of Charleston contains some especially photogenic trees. Below the bristlecones, a mixed forest of aspen, white fir, and ponderosa pine are found. These trees are common in the Charleston-Mummy region. However, a few pines and firs can also be found on the slopes of Potosi and La Madre Mountain. Beneath this pine-fir-aspen forest, the pinyon-juniper woodlands become prominent, giving way to sagebrush scrub with scattered Joshua trees and yuccas on the lower slopes. In the lower mountains south of Potosi (below about 4,000 feet) creosote becomes dominant.

Among the animals known to occur within the Spring Mountains are coyote, elk, porcupine, bobcat, mule deer, bighorn sheep, badger, gray fox and a host of smaller mammals. The reptiles are also very diverse here: desert iguanas, geckos, whiptails, collard, horned, fence, and leopard lizards just to name a few. The Mojave Desert sidewinder, Panamint rattlesnake, desert glossy snake, Mojave shovel-nosed snake, king snakes, night snakes, and gopher snakes are just a few of the many snakes that have carved out their niche in the Spring Mountains. Keep an eye out for these mountain inhabitants during your excursions.

Camping is available in several campgrounds throughout the range. Supplies, gas, food and lodging are available in Las Vegas. Fine lodging and dining are also available at the Mt. Charleston Hotel in Kyle Canyon. For further information on the portion of the Spring Mountains from Mount Stirling to Harris Mountain, contact the Toiyabe National Forest-Spring Mountain National Recreation Area office in Las Vegas. For information on the La Madre Mountain/Sandstone Bluffs area, contact the Red Rock National Conservation Area. Information for the area south of Mountain Springs Summit, can be obtained from the Bureau of Land Management office in Las Vegas.

## MOUNT STIRLING (8,218 FT; 2,505 M)

This pinyon-covered peak marks the north end of the Spring Mountains. Numerous petroglyphs are found on the slabs along the ridge east of the summit. Their meaning has been lost to the ages. Maybe they just describe the exhilaration of standing atop a fine desert summit, taking in the sun, and gazing out in wonder across the vast desert landscape.

*Maps:* Mount Stirling (NV) 7.5-minute (1:24,000 scale) topographic map; Las Vegas 1:100,000 scale metric topographic map; Automobile Club of Southern California (AAA) San Bernardino County map (Las Vegas area inset)

*Best Time to Climb:* October through May

*Approach:* From Indian Springs along Highway 95 north of Las Vegas, continue 11.2 miles northwest to a dirt road heading south toward the mountains. Follow this dirt road about nine miles to a junction and park. In all cases follow the main route. Some landmarks along the way include a power line that is passed 0.9 miles from Highway 95, and a wash six miles from Highway 95 that is driven in for about 200 yards and exited on the right. Four-wheel drive is helpful on these roads, although a two-wheel drive vehicle with high clearance should be able to reach the road end.

*Route:* The summit is not visible from the road end, and when combined with the thick pinyon forest, the route provides an excellent opportunity to brush up on compass skills. From the road end, head up the left fork of the road about 0.8 miles, then southwest up a forested ridge to the north ridge of Stirling. The north ridge is then followed to the top. Anticipate five miles round-trip with 2,200 feet of elevation gain.

## WILLOW PEAK (9,977 FT; 3,038 M)

*Maps:* Willow Peak (NV) 7.5-minute (1:24,000 scale) topographic map; Las Vegas 1:100,000 scale metric topographic map; Toiyabe National Forest-Las Vegas Ranger District map; Automobile Club of Southern California (AAA) San Bernardino County map (Las Vegas area inset)

*Best Time to Climb:* May through November

*Approach:* From the intersection of Interstate 15 and Highway 95 in Las Vegas, drive 36 miles north on U.S. Highway 95 to the Cold Creek Road heading west. The turnoff is unmistakable given the presence of the So. Desert Correctional Center at the turnoff. Follow the Cold Creek Road 13.1 miles to a gravel road on the right. Take this gravel road as it passes Willow Creek Campground, and eventually reaches Wheeler Pass

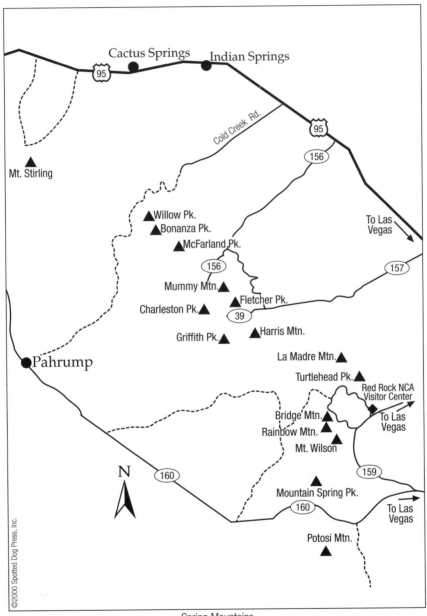

Cactus Springs

Indian Springs

95

Cold Creek Rd.

95

156

To Las Vegas

157

Mt. Stirling

Willow Pk.

Bonanza Pk.

McFarland Pk.

156

Mummy Mtn.

Fletcher Pk.

Charleston Pk.

39

Griffith Pk.

Harris Mtn.

La Madre Mtn.

Pahrump

Turtlehead Pk.

Red Rock NCA Visitor Center

Bridge Mtn.

To Las Vegas

Rainbow Mtn.

Mt. Wilson

N

159

160

Mountain Spring Pk.

160

To Las Vegas

Potosi Mtn.

Spring Mountains

(7,680 ft), about 7.5 miles from the pavement. Two wheel drive vehicles with good clearance are recommended.

*Route:* From Wheeler Pass, climb Willow Peak's steep west ridge to the summit. Anticipate three miles round-trip with 2,300 feet of elevation gain. *Alternate Route:* A possible alternate would be to follow the Bonanza Trail from Camp Bonanza (see Bonanza Peak approach) to the ridge crest, then follow a cross-country route along Willow Peak's undulating southeast ridge to the summit. This trip would involve about ten miles and 4,200 feet of elevation gain round-trip. All vehicles will be able to reach this road end.

### BONANZA PEAK (10,397 FT; 3,169 M)

This peak does not see the same amount of traffic as its more popular neighbors to the south, but with its open, bristlecone sprinkled northwest ridge, is still a fine peak.

*Maps:* Cold Creek and Charleston Peak (NV) 7.5-minute (1:24,000 scale) topographic maps; Las Vegas 1:100,000 scale metric topographic map; Toiyabe National Forest-Las Vegas Ranger District map; Automobile Club of Southern California (AAA) San Bernardino County map (Las Vegas area inset)

*Best Time to Climb:* Summer through Fall

*Approach:* From the intersection of Interstate 15 and Highway 95 in Las Vegas, drive 36 miles north on U.S. Highway 95 to the Cold Creek Road heading west. The turnoff is unmistakable given the presence of the So. Desert Correctional Center at the turnoff. Continue on the Cold Creek Road 13.1 miles to a gravel road on the right. Stay left, and continue on the road, which turns to dirt 3.1 miles to the Bonanza Trailhead (7,540 ft). All vehicles should be able to reach the trailhead.

*Route:* Follow the Bonanza Trail about 4.2 miles to the northwest side of Bonanza Peak. Scramble the remaining 200 feet to the summit. Anticipate nine miles with 2,900 feet of elevation gain round-trip.

### MCFARLAND PEAK (10,772 FT; 3,275 M)

Rising in castellated grandeur, McFarland Peak is the most imposing and difficult of the high peaks of the Spring Mountains. Its summit sees few visitors compared to other summits in the range. This peak is only recommended for experienced desert climbers with excellent route-finding skills.

*Maps:* Charleston Peak (NV) 7.5-minute (1:24,000 scale) topographic map; Las Vegas 1:100,000 scale metric topographic map; Toiyabe National Forest-Las Vegas Ranger District map; Automobile Club of Southern California (AAA) San Bernardino County map (Las Vegas area inset)

*Best Time to Climb:* Summer through Fall

*Approach:* From the intersection of Interstate 15 and Highway 95 in Las Vegas, drive 30 miles north on U.S. Highway 95 to the Lee Canyon Road (State Route 156). Head west on the Lee Canyon Road to the end of the road at the Lee Canyon Ski Area and the Bristlecone Trailhead (8,660 ft). The road is paved and all vehicles will be able to reach the trailhead.

*Route:* From the northwest corner of the parking lot, head up the forested Bristlecone Trail about 2.3 miles to its junction with the Bonanza Trail. Gaining the ridge crest on the Bonanza Trail continue about three miles north from the Bristlecone Trail to a point where the trail drops off of the southwest ridge of McFarland. After descending from the ridge, a peculiar outcrop is reached where the trail is left behind, and a northwesterly traverse on loose scree is followed to a steep gully that ascends the steep southwest face. Loose, Class 3 scrambling is negotiated up the gully to the summit area. Reportedly, staying left in the gully when difficulties are encountered works well. Anticipate 12 miles round-trip with 4,200 feet of elevation gain.

### CHARLESTON PEAK (11,915 FT; 3,631.8 M)

When it comes to southern Nevada peaks, Charleston Peak, the highpoint of the range, is usually first on the list of goals for the desert mountaineer. Charleston is frequently referred to as the third highest peak in Nevada, but this is not the case. The Spring Mountains are the fourth highest mountain range in Nevada. The White Mountains (rising to over 13,000 feet at Boundary Peak), Snake Range (rising to over 13,000 feet at Wheeler Peak with several other peaks higher than Charleston), and the Toquima Range (rising to 11,943 ft at Mount Jefferson) all rise above Charleston Peak.

Charleston Peak was known as "Noovu'uhunt" meaning "has snow" by the Southern Paiutes, and is an important place in the lore of both the Southern Paiutes and the Chemehuevi Indians. It is not surprising since its snow-capped summit is visible from highpoints throughout the Mojave, southern Nevada and Death Valley regions. According to Southern Paiute lore, there was a great flood that killed everyone. The only survivors were

Charleston Peak from the South Loop Trail. Photo: Andy Zdon

people who were transformed into the large wood ants found in these mountains. They survived by waiting out the flood on Charleston Peak. Legend has it that these ants were once people, so it is bad luck to kill them.
*Maps:* Charleston Peak and Griffith Peak (NV) 7.5-minute (1:24,000 scale) topographic maps; Las Vegas 1:100,000 scale metric topographic map; Toiyabe National Forest-Las Vegas Ranger District map; Automobile Club of Southern California (AAA) San Bernardino County map (Las Vegas area inset)
*Best Time to Climb:* Summer through Fall
*Approach:* From the intersection of Interstate 15 and Highway 95 in Las Vegas, drive 16.5 miles north on U.S. Highway 95 to the Highway 157-Kyle Canyon turnoff. Drive 20.4 miles west on Highway 157 to the intersection with Echo Road at a sharp curve. Stay left and drive on to the trailhead (signed). Some of the parking areas require a fee, so be sure to be prepared. All roads are paved.
*Route:* Follow the South Loop Trail as it climbs the forested slopes east of Cathedral Rock, to the saddle between Harris Mountain and Griffith Peak. Continue on the trail, contouring around Griffith Peak, through some of the most photogenic bristlecone pines covered in this book, and on up to the barren summit. Anticipate a long day of 18 miles round-trip with 4,300 feet of elevation gain assuming the ascent and descent routes are the same.

*Alternate Approach:* Drive to the Highway 157-Echo Road junction described above. Turn right onto Echo Road, and continue about a half mile to the trailhead (7,750 ft).

*Alternate Route:* Follow the Trail Canyon Trail (Trail No. 147) northward through the aspens and pines of Trail Canyon to a junction at a saddle (9,330 ft). Here the Trail Canyon Trail meets the North Loop Trail coming up from Highway 158. Head about a mile northwest (left) on the North Loop Trail to a spring at a shelter cave. From here, continue on the North Loop Trail to the summit. Anticipate a long day of 18 miles round-trip with 4,300 feet of elevation gain assuming the ascent and descent routes are the same.

*Second Alternate:* One can climb Charleston Peak as a loop trip by hiking up the South Loop Trail and descending via the North Loop and Trail Canyon Trails to Echo Road. This will require a walk along the road in Kyle Canyon 1.2 miles for the connection between trail heads or a car shuttle.

## MUMMY MOUNTAIN (11,528 FT; 3,513.7 M)

Although not as high as Charleston Peak, Mummy Mountain is a more interesting peak to climb. Mummy Mountain is named for its similarity in profile to an Egyptian mummy when viewed from the northeast.

*Maps:* Charleston Peak (NV) 7.5-minute (1:24,000 scale) topographic map; Las Vegas 1:100,000 scale metric topographic map; Toiyabe National Forest-Las Vegas Ranger District map; Automobile Club of Southern California (AAA) San Bernardino County map (Las Vegas area inset)

*Best Time to Climb:* Summer through Fall

*Approach:* Drive to the Trail Canyon Trail trailhead on Echo Road as described for Charleston Peak's alternate route.

*Route:* Follow the Trail Canyon Trail northward through the aspens and pines of Trail Canyon to a junction at a saddle ( 9,330 ft). Head northwest (left) about 1.8 miles passing a spring en route. Just past the last switch-back on an open slope (about a mile past the spring), slog up the scree slope to the north, finally reaching a saddle. After catching your breath, head east amid bristlecones, to the cliff band that guards the Mummy's summit. At the base of the cliff, turn left (north) and contour along the base of the cliffs to a narrow, scree-filled chute that heads up to the summit plateau. On ascending and descending this route, one person at a time should head up this chute due to rockfall hazard. If the chute is icy, and the climber is

Walter Hines heads down the scree-filled chute from Mummy Mountain's summit. Photo: Andy Zdon

adept at difficult scrambling, upon reaching the base of the cliff band, one can turn right and scramble up a 15-foot Class 3-4 cliff band. Once surmounted, the walk to the summit is an easy stroll. Beware, while climbing this cliff band is not all that difficult to the experienced scrambler, adding a bit of spice to the ascent, the top of the band slopes toward the cliff with some loose scree on top. Descending this section is much more difficult than ascending and the hiker may want to descend by the normal route, assuming it is ice-free, or descend the short difficult section with a belay. Anticipate ten miles round-trip with 3,750 feet of elevation gain.

### FLETCHER PEAK (10,319 FT; 3,120 M)

*Maps:* Charleston Peak and Angel Peak (NV) 7.5-minute (1:24,000 scale) topographic maps; Las Vegas 1:100,000 scale metric topographic map; Toiyabe National Forest-Las Vegas Ranger District map; Automobile Club of Southern California (AAA) San Bernardino County map (Las Vegas area inset)

*Best Time to Climb:* Summer through Fall

*Approach:* From the intersection of Interstate 15 and Highway 95 in Las Vegas, drive 16.5 miles north on U.S. Highway 95 to the Highway 157-Kyle Canyon turnoff. Drive 17.5 miles west on Highway 157 to the intersection with Highway 158 heading over to Lee Canyon. Follow Route 158 north 4.8 miles to the North Loop Trailhead (8,400 ft). The roads are paved and accessible to all vehicles.

*Route:* Follow the North Loop Trail (also known as the Mummy Spring Trail here) about three miles to a small saddle between Point 3,075 meters and Point 3,060 meters on the metric topographic map. The trail is left behind, and the route drops about 150 feet to a saddle northwest of the peak, then climbs Fletcher Peak's northwest ridge to the summit. Anticipate about seven miles and 2,400 feet of elevation gain round-trip.

### GRIFFITH PEAK (11,072 FT; 3,370.8 M)

Another fine Spring Mountain summit with great views of the head of Kyle Canyon and south to Potosi Mountain and beyond. The peak was named in honor of Senator E.W. Griffith who developed the Charleston Peak Resort in Kyle Canyon.

*Maps:* Charleston Peak, Griffith Peak and La Madre Spring (NV) 7.5-minute (1:24,000 scale) topographic maps; Las Vegas 1:100,000 scale metric topographic map; Toiyabe National Forest-Las Vegas Ranger District map; Automobile Club of Southern California (AAA) San Bernardino County map (Las Vegas area inset)

*Best Time to Climb:* Summer through Fall

*Approach:* See Charleston Peak-South Loop Trailhead.

*Route:* This peak is easily reached by a short hike from the Charleston Peak-South Loop Trail via Griffith's southeast or northwest slope. Add one mile round-trip with 600 feet of elevation gain round-trip when combined with Charleston Peak. If only climbing Griffith Peak, anticipate 9.2 miles and 3,650 feet of elevation gain round-trip from the South Loop Trailhead (8,350 ft).

*Alternate Approach:* From the intersection of Interstate 15 and Highway 95 in Las Vegas, drive 16.5 miles north on U.S. Highway 95 to the Highway 157-Kyle Canyon turnoff. Drive west on Highway 157 about 12.6 miles to the north end of the dirt Harris Springs Road. Turn left and follow the Harris Springs Road about 2.3 miles to a fork. Stay right and continue another six miles (becomes rough; two-wheel drive with high clearance is okay) to a trailhead with parking for about ten cars.

*Alternate Route:* From the end of the Harris Springs Road (8,360 ft), follow a good trail contouring along Harris Mountain's slopes, and reaching the Griffith-Harris saddle. Switchback up through a notch in the limestone cliffs, and then up forested terrain until a grassy slope is reached on Griffith's east ridge. Follow this slope to the summit. Anticipate nine miles round-trip with 2,900 feet of elevation gain.

### HARRIS MOUNTAIN (10,018 FT; 3,052.3 M)

*Maps:* Charleston Peak, Griffith Peak and La Madre Spring (NV) 7.5-minute (1:24,000 scale) topographic maps; Las Vegas 1:100,000 scale metric topographic map; Toiyabe National Forest-Las Vegas Ranger District map; Automobile Club of Southern California (AAA) San Bernardino County map (Las Vegas area inset)

*Best Time to Climb:* Summer through Fall

*Approach:* See alternate route for Griffith Peak.

*Route:* From the end of the Harris Spring Road (8,360 ft), follow a good trail contouring along Harris Mountain's slopes, reaching the Griffith-Harris saddle. From the saddle, scramble directly up Harris' west ridge. Anticipate 7.5 miles and 1,700 feet of elevation gain round-trip.

## La Madre Mountain (8,154 ft; 2,485 m)

This limestone peak is very imposing when viewed from Red Rock Canyon National Conservation Area, and provides a fine view of the Red Rock backcountry.

*Maps:* La Madre Mountain (NV) 7.5-minute (1:24,000 scale) topographic map; Las Vegas 1:100,000 scale metric topographic map; Automobile Club of Southern California (AAA) San Bernardino County map (Las Vegas area inset)

*Best Time to Climb:* Fall and Spring

*Approach:* From the intersection of Interstate 15 and Highway 95 in Las Vegas, drive 16.5 miles north on U.S. Highway 95 to the Highway 157-Kyle Canyon turnoff. Drive west on Highway 157 about 8.4 miles to the south end of the dirt Harris Springs Road. Follow the Harris Springs Road about 2.9 miles to a rough dirt road that heads south toward the peak. Follow this dirt road 2.4 miles or as far as practicable and park.

*Route:* From the road end, cross the wash to the east, and follow the steep, loose ridge as it winds its way past Point 7,044 feet to the summit. Anticipate 4.5 miles round-trip and 2,400 feet of elevation gain if you have a four-wheel drive vehicle. Otherwise, about nine miles round-trip with about 3,000 feet of elevation gain. The route is Class 2 to 3.

## Turtlehead Peak (6,323 ft; 1,927 m)

This delightful peak provides maximum views for the effort and is popular with local hikers. The views of the "Sandstone Bluffs" and Las Vegas are great, and distant views include the Virgin Mountains and the Hualapai Mountains in Arizona. As the climber progresses from the sandstone slick-rock onto the upper mountain consisting of limestone, he takes a giant leap back in time, hundreds of millions of years in fact. The contact marks the trace of the Keystone Thrust, a fault that places much older limestone on top of the younger sandstone. The peak is named for its surprisingly similar profile to that of the head of a desert tortoise. Unfortunately, a fine route from Brownstone Canyon that the author used to climb the peak, has recently been closed, as a developer has closed access to the canyon.

*Maps:* La Madre Mountain (NV) 7.5-minute (1:24,000 scale) topographic map; Las Vegas 1:100,000 scale metric topographic map; Automobile Club of Southern California (AAA) San Bernardino County map (Las Vegas area inset)

Blue Diamond Mesa from the summit of Turtlehead Peak.  Photo: Andy Zdon

*Best Time to Climb:* October through May

*Approach:* From Interstate 15 in Las Vegas, take the Charleston Boulevard exit.  Follow Charleston Boulevard about 15 miles east to the Red Rock Canyon National Conservation Area Visitor Center.  Spend some time in the visitor center to view their many interesting displays, and visit their bookstore. From the visitor center, follow the Scenic Loop Drive 2.8 miles, then right into the Sandstone Quarry Parking Area.  This approach is accessible to all vehicles. The sandstone quarry operated from 1905 to 1912, and supplied fine, hard, decorative rock for buildings in Las Vegas and southern California.

*Route:* From the road end, hike up the wash about a half mile to where the impressive south face of Turtlehead comes into view.  Leave the wash, and head northeast to the first major gully west of the face, leading up to the summit area.  Scramble up the Class 2 gully to the crest of the ridge, then southeast to the summit. Anticipate five miles round-trip with about 1,900 feet of elevation gain.

## BRIDGE MOUNTAIN (6,824 FT; 2,080+ M)

This peak, with a virtual obstacle course for a route, is both challenging in terms of the climb itself, along with the route-finding. Bridge Mountain is for experienced desert mountaineers only, and should not be climbed alone. There is quite a bit of Class 3 climbing on this route, and it should not be attempted by those suffering from a fear of heights.

*Maps:* La Madre Spring (NV) 7.5-minute (1:24,000 scale) topographic map; Las Vegas 1:100,000 scale metric topographic map; Automobile Club of Southern California (AAA) San Bernardino County map (Las Vegas area inset)

*Best Time to Climb:* Fall and Spring

*Approach:* From Interstate 15 in Las Vegas, exit on Blue Diamond Road (Highway 160), and follow Highway 160 to the Red Rock Road (Highway 159). Follow Highway 159 to the Red Rock National Conservation Area Visitor Center (paying the entrance fee), and continue on the Scenic Drive Road 7.5 miles to the White Rock Picnic Area turnoff. Turn northwest, and follow the poor dirt road (four-wheel drive definitely required) five miles to Red Rock Summit (6,430 ft). The visitor center can also be reached by following Charleston Blvd. west out of Las Vegas about 15 miles from I-15.

*Route:* From Red Rock Summit, follow a trail east about one mile to the crest of the Red Rock Ridge. Hike south about a half mile to where the trail begins to descend to the east. Stay on the crest to a highpoint, then descend a gully to a cliff overlooking Pine Creek. Continue east along the sandstone ridge as it extends across an area of domes. In this area you should observe route marks such as painted lines, arrows or rock ducks. A Class 3 descent leads to the base of Bridge Mountain's natural bridge. The route continues northeast across the bridge, and up a 100-foot tall Class 3 crack that is exited to the left on a wide ledge. From the ledge, walk up to yet another natural bridge, passing through the arch, and up another 50-foot Class 3 slab with a fallen tree leaning against it. Walk to the south of the grove of pine trees encountered above the slab, and climb on exposed sandstone slabs northeast toward the summit. Anticipate six miles round-trip with 3,400 feet of elevation gain. The climb will take a full day.

## MOUNT WILSON (7,070 FT; 2,155 M)

*Maps:* Mountain Springs and Blue Diamond (NV) 7.5-minute (1:24,000 scale) topographic maps; Las Vegas 1:100,000 scale metric topographic

Mt. Wilson from the east. Traditional route is on the west side. Photo: Andy Zdon

map; Automobile Club of Southern California (AAA) San Bernardino County map (Las Vegas area inset)

*Best Time to Climb:* Fall and Spring

*Approach:* From Interstate 15 in Las Vegas, exit on Blue Diamond Road (Highway 160), and follow Highway 160 over Mountain Springs Summit about 3.5 miles to the Lovell Canyon Road heading north. Follow the Lovell Canyon Road north three miles to a dirt road (two-wheel drive with high clearance recommended) that heads northeast. Follow this dirt road 2.6 miles to a campsite and park (about 5,800 ft).

*Route:* Follow the wash about a half mile to a fork, then stay right (northeast) and follow the wash until a northeast-trending ridge is reached and climbed to the crest. Climb Point 6,968 feet, then drop down north of Point 6,968 feet over loose rubble and possibly over some Class 3 ledges (belay probably required, should be able to avoid the ledges though), to a saddle that separates Mount Wilson from the main crest, then continue east to the summit. The final sandstone slickrock approach to the summit is Class 2, and the immensity of the view against the stark sandstone escarpment will provide inspiration for all. Anticipate six miles round-trip with 2,600 feet of elevation gain.

## RAINBOW MOUNTAIN (6,800+ FT; 2,073 M)

*Maps:* Mountain Springs and Blue Diamond (NV) 7.5-minute (1:24,000 scale) topographic maps; Las Vegas 1:100,000 scale metric topographic map; Automobile Club of Southern California (AAA) San Bernardino County map (Las Vegas area inset)

*Best Time to Climb:* Fall and Spring

*Approach:* Same as for Mount Wilson.

*Route:* Follow the wash about 0.7 miles, staying north at a fork, then following a north-trending ridge, that eventually leads northeast toward the main crest. Upon reaching the crest, head north, passing over Peak 7,211 feet, and when due west of Rainbow Mountain and having passed another bump on the ridge, drop down to a deep saddle (Class 3-4, belay probably required for this section), then follow the ridge toward the peak. Difficulties can generally be bypassed on the north side of the ridge, and additional Class 3 scrambling will be encountered en route. Anticipate about ten miles and 4,500 feet of elevation gain round-trip.

## "MOUNTAIN SPRING PEAK" (6,641 FT; 2,024 M)

This seldom-climbed peak, that shows up on the topographic map as benchmark Mountain Spring, provides expansive views of the Red Rock backcountry, Charleston Peak, and Potosi Mountain.

*Maps:* Mountain Springs and Blue Diamond (NV) 7.5-minute (1:24,000 scale) topographic maps; Las Vegas 1:100,000 scale metric topographic map; Automobile Club of Southern California (AAA) San Bernardino County map (Las Vegas area inset)

*Best Time to Climb:* October through May

*Approach:* From Interstate 15 in Las Vegas, exit on Blue Diamond Road (Highway 160), and follow Highway 160 east over Mountain Springs Summit continuing about 0.6 miles to a minor road that accesses some residences. Please respect all private property in this area. Drive this road north about 300 yards to a dirt track that veers to the left, and follow that track 0.2 miles to a fork. Turn right, and continue another 0.3 miles to the north side of a spring field (5,540 ft). Sturdy four-wheel drive vehicles may drive farther up the track, but is much better style to park here. This is Mountain Springs, a major watering place for early travelers in the area. John C. Fremont camped here during the 1840's. Please respect the spring area, and camp elsewhere. It is an important watering place for wildlife.

*Route:* Hike northeast up the old four-wheel drive track, then east as the track drops to a saddle. From the saddle, leave the road and climb the ridge east until the crest is reached at Point 6,440+ feet. The peak is about a half mile north along the view-packed ridge. Anticipate four miles round-trip with 1,450 feet of elevation gain.

## POTOSI MOUNTAIN (8,514 FT; 2,595.1 M)

When viewed from Las Vegas, this fine peak stands as a rounded sentinel at the southern end of the Spring Mountains. When climbing this peak, keep an eye out for the many fossils to be found in Potosi's limestone. Early names for this peak were Olcott Peak, Silver Buttes and Double-Up Mountain. Thankfully these lackluster names didn't stick. Legend has it that an early miner named the mountain, along with the mining district, Potosi, after the Potosi lead-zinc district in Wisconsin, which was named for the centuries-old mining district in Mexico.

*Maps:* Potosi and Cottonwood Pass (Nevada) 7.5-minute (1:24,000 scale) topographic maps; Mesquite Lake 1:100,000 scale metric topographic map; Automobile Club of Southern California (AAA) San Bernardino County map (Las Vegas area inset)

*Best Time to Climb:* October through May

*Approach:* This route is not as popular as the alternate route and four-wheel drive is recommended. However, the route up Potosi on this approach takes the hiker past a beautifully water-sculptured and fossiliferous limestone wash, and through more pleasing terrain than the route from the site of Potosi. To reach this road end from the south end of Las Vegas, take State Highway 160 (Blue Diamond Road) 18.5 miles west from Interstate 15 to the Potosi Mountain Road (graded dirt). Follow the dirt road 4.2 miles south to the Potosi Spring area. This road gets rough in places toward the spring and four-wheel drive is recommended. Bear right, and continue 0.9 miles to a fork. Take the left fork to Goodsprings, and continue 1.2 miles, going up a steepish hill to another fork. Turn left and drive a quarter-mile and bear left. Another 1.4 miles take you to an old, deserted cabin. Park here at 5,850 feet.

*Route:* Hike up the wash about a quarter-mile, observing the many fossils in the limestone wash, to a dry waterfall that can be bypassed on the left. After passing this little obstacle, continue another quarter mile to where the wash forks. Leave the wash, and follow the ridge between the washes. Head northeast up this pleasant ridge to Potosi's west ridge, and proceed to the obvious summit, near an antenna installation. Anticipate five miles round-trip with 2,900 feet of elevation gain.

*Alternate Approach and Route:* Drive to Potosi Spring as for Route 1. At the spring drive up the hill a quarter mile to the Potosi Mine Ruins. Some recent private property issues have cropped up, so heed all no trespassing signs. From the mine and mill site, hike up the road about a half mile then turn left up the ridge to a flat area north of the mine. The ridge can be followed northeast, then east to the summit from here. Anticipate six miles round-trip with 2,900 feet of elevation gain.

### SHENANDOAH PEAK (5,864 FT; 1,787 M)

After the Civil War, may Civil War veterans moved west to try their hand at prospecting. The metals deposits at Goodsprings were founded by soldiers turned prospectors in 1868. Along the way, they left many references to that war in the form of geographic names. Shenandoah Peak is named for the Shenandoah Valley of Virginia, the scene of several Confederate victories. The entire hike will be over limestone, shales, and sandstone of the Pennsylvanian-age Bird Spring formation. Keep an eye out for fossils en route.

*Maps:* Shenandoah Peak (NV-CA) and Goodsprings (NV) 7.5-minute (1:24,000 scale) topographic maps; Mesquite Lake 1:100,000 scale metric topographic map; Automobile Club of Southern California (AAA) San Bernardino County map (Las Vegas area inset)

*Best Time to Climb:* October through May

*Approach:* From Las Vegas, drive south on Interstate 15 to Jean (home to casinos, a prison and a bucket factory), then follow State Route 160 west 6.2 miles to a fork. Stay right and continue 0.5 miles to Goodsprings. Pass the road to the Rainbow Quarry on the right, then immediately after the Rainbow Quarry Road, stay right on the well-graded Wilson Pass road. Follow this road to Wilson Pass (5,023 ft) and park. All vehicles should be able to reach Wilson Pass.

*Route:* Follow the easy ridge south to the peak. Anticipate six miles round-trip with 1,400 feet of elevation gain.

### Table Mountain (5,152 ft; 1,570 m)

The cap rock of this undulating mesa is of volcanic origin. The summit plateau provides an interesting view toward Mesquite Valley.

*Maps:* Goodsprings (NV) 7.5-minute (1:24,000 scale) topographic map; Mesquite Lake 1:100,000 scale metric topographic map; Automobile Club of Southern California (AAA) San Bernardino County map (Las Vegas area inset)

*Best Time to Climb:* November through April

*Approach:* From Las Vegas, drive south on Interstate 15 to Jean, then follow State Route 160 west 6.2 miles to a fork. Stay left, and drive 3.5 miles to Columbia Pass (4,400 ft). The road is paved and passable to all cars.

*Route:* Follow the ridge south to the flat summit. Anticipate three miles round-trip with about 800 feet of elevation gain.

### Little Devil Peak (5,597 ft; 1,706 m)

This peak is comprised of fossiliferous limestone formations. Although the hike is relatively short (depending on where you start), one may want to take some additional time to search for fossils.

*Maps:* State Line Pass (NV-CA) 7.5-minute (1:24,000 scale) topographic map; Mesquite Lake 1:100,000 scale metric topographic map; Automobile Club of Southern California (AAA) San Bernardino County map

*Best Time to Climb:* November through April

*Approach:* From Las Vegas, drive south to Jean. Once in Jean, follow a paved frontage road on the east side of the interstate, heading south five miles to where it turns west under the interstate. The road turns to dirt and in 0.4 miles a fork is reached. Follow the right fork seven miles (or as far as practicable with your car) to the Christmas Mine. The road may be washed out considerably before reaching the mine. If the road is not passable in the first few miles, you may try taking the Devil Peak road to near the top of the alluvial fan where a cross road runs north and enters Devil Canyon. Four-wheel drive vehicles are recommended.

*Route:* The peak is about two miles west of the Christmas Mine. Anticipate four miles round-trip with 1,300 feet of elevation gain.

## DEVIL PEAK (5,881 FT; 1,793 M)

This rarely-visited desert peak, formerly known as Diablo Grande Peak, is a prominent landmark above Ivanpah Valley. When the author climbed this peak in 1990, it had been six years since someone had signed the summit register. Devil Peak is of volcanic origin and is best described as a rhyolite plug. This plug was a volcanic center that was the source of the volcanic flows and tuff deposits in the surrounding area.

*Maps:* State Line Pass (NV-CA) 7.5-minute (1:24,000 scale) topographic map; Mesquite Lake 1:100,000 scale metric topographic map; Automobile Club of Southern California (AAA) San Bernardino County map

*Best Time to Climb:* November through April

*Approach:* From Las Vegas, drive south to Jean. Once in Jean, follow a paved frontage road on the east side of the interstate, heading south five miles to where it turns west under the interstate. The road turns to dirt and in 0.4 miles a fork is reached. Take the left fork, the dirt road runs straight toward the peak, and enters a small canyon after 4.5 miles (about 3,500 ft). We had to stop a little short of the canyon due to a road wash out. Four-wheel drive vehicles are recommended.

*Route:* Hike up to a saddle (4,400 ft) at the head of the canyon, then climb northward up the south ridge on loose talus and scree to the top. The summit provides fine views of the New York Mountains, Clark Mountains, Kingston Range and Mesquite Valley. The Charleston Peak and Potosi Mountain areas are also clearly visible. Anticipate three miles round-trip with 2,300 feet of elevation gain.

## THE SHEEP RANGE

Named for the Nelson bighorn sheep that roam across its slopes, this beautiful desert range is situated within the Desert National Wildlife Range which shares its northwest boundary with Nellis Air Force Base. Not too long ago, the lights of Las Vegas were miles away leaving the Sheep Range and the Desert National Wildlife Range remote and practically untouched, but today, as Las Vegas grows, its city limits are literally pushing against this unique and very special desert place.

Hidden forests of fir, aspen, limber pine, bristlecone pine, and small fragile springs are home to many desert species, including bighorn sheep, mule deer, coyotes, badgers, bobcats, foxes, mountain lions, numerous birds, and insects. The lowest slopes of the range are speckled with Joshua trees, and with every step up a mountain ridge, one is drawn closer to the welcome shade of pinyon and juniper woodlands. Summit panoramas rival those found on any other desert range.

The Desert National Wildlife Range, one of the country's oldest wildlife refuges, was established in 1936 to protect the bighorn sheep that reside here. Camping is permitted within 100 feet of any road (without driving off-road) in the refuge. Additionally backcountry camping is permitted at the cabin in Hidden Canyon. Do not camp within a quarter mile of any spring. Not only is it against refuge regulations, but human activity disrupts the wildlife that make these mountains their home. Portions of the refuge are not open due to their inclusion in Nellis. Lodging, food and supplies are available in Las Vegas. Further information on the Sheep Range can be obtained by contacting the Desert Wildlife Refuge.

### HAYFORD PEAK (9,912 FT; 3,021 M)

The gem of this peak's route is Wiregrass Spring, a quiet place beneath tall ponderosa pines and white firs. Sit awhile at the picnic table and listen to the sound of wind through the trees, water trickling from the spring, the songs of several species of birds, and the buzzing of a few insects. Up the canyon from the spring, the trees change; ponderosas become bristlecone pines. From Hayford's summit, a vast desert panorama of bristlecone-covered ridges and distant desert ranges awaits those who reach the top. *Maps:* Hayford Peak and Sheep Peak (NV) 7.5-minute (1:24,000 scale) topographic maps; Indian Springs 1:100,000 scale metric topographic map;

Wiregrass Spring.  Photo: Wynne Benti

Automobile Club of Southern California (AAA) San Bernardino County map (Las Vegas area inset)

*Best Time to Climb:* Spring and Fall (the beginning of the hike can be very warm in summer)

*Approach:* Two-wheel drive vehicles should have no problem reaching the trailhead for this fine desert peak. From Las Vegas, take Highway 95 north about 23 miles to the signed exit "Desert National Wildlife Refuge" at Corn Creek Station Road. Turn east (right) and follow a well-graded dirt road 4.1 miles to the signed Alamo/Mormon Well Road junction just past the Corn Creek Ranger Station (stop to visit their excellent interpretive display). Turn left and head 8.8 miles north to the signed Cow Camp Road. Stay left, and continue another 6.2 miles to the Hidden Forest Road. Turn east (right) and drive 3.6 miles to the road end at a locked gate, the mouth of Deadman Canyon. Two-wheel drive vehicles with good clearance are recommended.

*Route:* Hike up Deadman Canyon five miles to the Hidden Forest Cabin near Wiregrass Spring. From the cabin, one can either follow the canyon 1.8 miles to a saddle, then up the southwest ridge to the summit, or one can follow the ridge immediately east of the canyon and up Hayford's south ridge. Anticipate 16 miles round trip with 4,100 feet of elevation gain.

### SHEEP PEAK (9,750 FT; 2,972 M)

*Maps:* Sheep Peak (NV) 7.5-minute (1:24,000 scale) topographic map; Indian Springs 1:100,000 scale metric topographic map; Automobile Club of Southern California (AAA) San Bernardino County map (Las Vegas area inset)

*Best Time to Climb:* Spring and Fall (the beginning of the hike can be very warm in summer)

*Approach:* As for Hayford Peak

*Route:* Hike up Deadman Canyon five miles to the Hidden Forest Cabin near Wiregrass Spring. One will probably want to set up an overnight camp near here. From the cabin, follow a wash east that heads up to the crest, then follow the crest south to the summit. Anticipate eight miles round trip with 2,500 feet of elevation gain round trip from the Hidden Forest Cabin.

*Alternate Approach and Route:* The peak has also been climbed from Pine Nut Camp on the east side of the peak. This route will provide a much

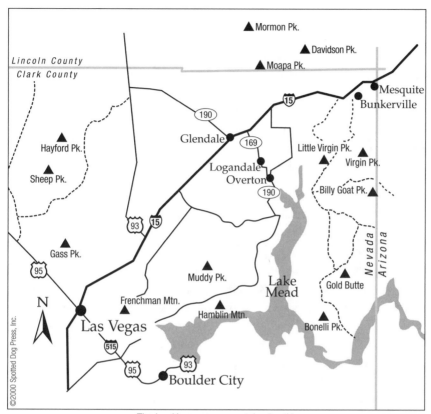

The Las Vegas area mountains (north)

shorter ascent of this peak. Anticipate about six miles round trip with 2,500 feet of elevation gain.

## LAS VEGAS RANGE

The Las Vegas Range is not a typical mountain mass, but a mixture of various ridges and buttes that have been lumped together under the term "range." At the south end of the range, the Las Vegas Range merges with the south end of the Sheep Range at Gass Peak. The highpoint, Quartzite Peak (7,133 ft), stands more than 4,000 feet above the surrounding valleys. Because of the fine views to be had from Gass Peak, its route is described here, though ambitious hikers may want to include a hike up Quartzite Peak on their agenda. Primitive camping is available in the area. Lodging, food and supplies can be obtained in Las Vegas. For further information, contact the Bureau of Land Management office in Las Vegas.

## GASS PEAK (6,943 FT; 2,116 M)

Named in honor of the early Las Vegas ranger Octavio Gass, Gass Peak is the northern sentinel of the Las Vegas Valley, visible from the glitzy Las Vegas Strip. Travel out to the peak and the hustle and bustle is quickly left behind, replaced by open desert and its solitude.

*Maps:* Gass Peak (NV) 7.5-minute (1:24,000 scale) topographic map; Las Vegas 1:100,000 scale metric topographic map; Automobile Club of Southern California (AAA) San Bernardino County map (Las Vegas area inset)

*Best Time to Climb:* November through April

*Approach:* From Las Vegas, follow Highway 95 north about 23 miles to the signed exit "Desert National Wildlife Refuge" at Corn Creek Station Road. Turn east (right) and follow a well-graded dirt road 4.1 miles to the signed Alamo/Mormon Well Road junction just past the Corn Creek Ranger Station (stop to visit their excellent interpretive display). Stay right and continue another four miles to a fork. The main road (Mormon Well Road) stays left. Follow the right fork (Gass Peak Road) as it first heads southeast, then northeast up a broad canyon to a saddle at about 5,000 feet and park. Two-wheel drive with high clearance or four-wheel drive vehicles are recommended.

*Route:* From the saddle, climb southwest to the summit. Anticipate five miles round trip with about 2,000 feet of elevation gain.

## THE MORMON MOUNTAINS

Rising more than 5,000 feet above Meadow Valley Wash, the Mormon Mountains are a complicated mountain mass bounded on the west by Meadow Valley Wash, the Muddy River to the south, and the Virgin River Valley on the east. These mountains, along with their sub-range, the East Mormon Mountains (topped by Davidson Peak) are a diverse, desert range mostly cloaked in creosote, blackbrush, and Joshua trees. Higher ridges are covered by pinyon-juniper woodlands. A few ponderosa pine occur in the uppermost portions of the range. The area provides excellent opportunities for primitive camping, and all minimum impact camping methods should be applied here. Food, gas and lodging are available in Las Vegas or Mesquite, Nevada. For further information, contact the Bureau of Land Management office in Las Vegas.

## "Mormon Peak" (7,414 ft; 2,260 m)

*Maps:* Rox NE (NV) 7.5-minute (1:24,000 scale) topographic map; Overton 1:100,000 scale metric topographic map; Automobile Club of Southern California (AAA) San Bernardino County map (Las Vegas area inset–for primary approach route only)

*Best Time to Climb:* Fall and Spring

*Approach:* From Las Vegas, drive north on Interstate 15, and take the Glendale Exit (Exit 90). Drive 2.8 miles west on State Route 168 to a dirt road heading north generally following Meadow Valley Wash. Follow the Meadow Valley Wash Road as it crosses and recrosses the railroad tracks 19 miles to a fork a little past Hoya Siding. Take the right fork about two hundred yards to a faint track heading up a wash. Follow this faint track about a mile to a fork. Bear left and drive another 0.2 miles to yet another fork. Bear left again, and continue 1.9 miles to where the road leaves the wash for the alluvial terrace. Continue another four miles to the road end at about 4,000 feet. Four-wheel drive will be needed. This route is definitely not recommended during periods of rain, particularly during the summer thunderstorm season. Meadow Valley Wash drains a huge area of southern Nevada, and although the weather may appear fine near Mormon Peak, storms far to the north may cause the area to flood.

*Route:* From the road end, head south-southeast up a gully, eventually reaching Point 4,738 feet. From here, follow the ridge west avoiding excessive ups and downs by passing south of Point 5,245 feet, north of Point 6,190 feet, and south of Point 6,271 feet, eventually reaching the summit. Anticipate nine miles round trip with about 4,200 feet of elevation gain round trip. The going is rough but Class 2.

*Alternate Approach and Route:* Drive to the Meadow Valley Wash Road as described above. Follow the Meadow Valley Wash Road as it crosses and recrosses the railroad tracks 16 miles to another fork. Stay right, passing through a gate, and continuing a quarter mile to a fork. Stay right and continue about 8.5 miles, staying straight at junctions, to a campsite at roughly 4,200 feet. Four-wheel drive is required for this approach. Do not drive if thunderstorms are occurring in the region. From the campsite, hike up the road to a large canyon heading north. Follow this canyon about 0.8 miles to a fork. Take the right fork and continue to a saddle at 5,680 feet. From the saddle, head northeast up the ridge, then east to the summit. Plan on about eight miles round trip with 3,200 feet of elevation gain.

Dan Richter on Moapa's Class 3 summit ridge following a December snow.  Photo: Wynne Benti

## Moapa Peak (6,471 ft; 1,972 m)

When viewed from the Moapa Valley and Interstate 15, this magnificent peak is a prominent presence at the southern end of the Mormon Mountains. Helen Carlson wrote that the name "Moapa" is derived from "Moapariats" meaning "mosquito creek people" referring to the Southern Paiutes living in Moapa Valley. John Wesley Powell referred to the people as "Mo-a-pats" or the people living on the Muddy River.

*Maps:* Moapa Peak (NV) 7.5-minute (1:24,000 scale) topographic map; Overton 1:100,000 scale metric topographic map; Automobile Club of Southern California (AAA) San Bernardino County map (Las Vegas area inset)

*Best Time to Climb:* November through April

*Approach:* From Las Vegas, drive 60 miles north on Interstate 15, and leave the interstate at Exit 100 for Carp and Elgin.  After exiting at the truck parking area, follow the frontage road back along the interstate to where it crosses under the highway. Follow the road under the highway, then right on the frontage road about 100 yards to a junction with a dirt road heading north. Follow the dirt road north 8.7 miles, passing a corral and power lines to a good parking area. The parking area is behind a low ridge, and is a fine place to camp out of eye-or-ear-shot of the interstate.

*Route:* Head northwest a quarter mile to "Jack's Pockets," and continue northwest to a large wash that is followed north around the east side of Point 4,542 feet at about 3,900 feet. While hiking along the wash keep a lookout for fine specimens of fossil coral in the limestone float. Leave the wash, and head west up a slope to the saddle located immediately west of Point 4,542 feet. Climb northwest to a headwall, and climb a 100-foot section of ducked cracks and ledges (Class 3). Above the Class 3 section, head northeast, following a ramp to easy slopes that lead to the base of the cliffs on Moapa's southwest face. Continue northeast, contouring along the base of the cliffs about a half mile and then climb to the summit ridge between the peak and Point 6,091 feet. Follow the summit ridge southwest to the summit. An airy knife-edge Class 3 ridge is traversed en route. Some climbers may want the security of a rope along the ridge.

### DAVIDSON PEAK (5,324 FT; 1,623 M)

This prominent, wedge-shaped mountain, is the highpoint of the East Mormon Mountains, and is clearly visible from Interstate 15 when driving across Mormon Mesa between Las Vegas and Mesquite. Upon closer inspection, the cliffs contain large, but mostly inaccessible alcoves and caves.

*Maps:* Davidson Peak (NV) 7.5-minute (1:24,000 scale) topographic map; Overton 1:100,000 scale metric topographic map

*Best Time to Climb:* November through April

*Approach:* From Las Vegas, drive north on Interstate 15 and take the Carp-Elgin turnoff (Exit 100). After exiting at the truck parking area, follow the frontage road back along the freeway to where it crosses under the interstate. Head north on the frontage road on the north side of Interstate 15 (Old Spanish Trail). At 3.5 miles, turn left onto a well-graded gravel road following it 3.3 miles to a power line road. Head 5.1 miles northeast on the power line road to a fork and stay left. Continue another 2.8 miles to another fork and stay right. Continue two miles to another fork, passing under the power line en route. Stay left and continue another 1.1

Davidson Peak. The east ridge is on the right-hand skyline. Photo: Andy Zdon

miles to a campsite. There are many roads in the area and it is easy to get off-route. If you start driving up a steep grade to a saddle, you're off-route. The campsite is located between Davidson Peak and a sub-peak with a radio antenna on its summit.

*Route:* From the campsite, gain Davidson's east ridge which is then followed to the summit. Anticipate four miles round-trip with about 1,800 feet of elevation gain.

## THE VIRGIN MOUNTAINS

When driving Interstate 15 along the Virgin River between Las Vegas and St. George, Utah, the desert climber's eyes will be drawn to a fine desert range to the east, that is usually snow-capped during winter and early spring. Being the most northeasterly range described in this book, the Virgin Mountains provide the best views eastward toward the Arizona Strip country and off to the Pine Valley Mountains, a fine desert range in southwestern Utah. The Virgin Mountains are thought to have been named for an early Spanish name for the Virgin River, either "Rio Virgin" or "Rio de la Virgin," River of the Virgin. Others believe that the Virgin River and Mountains were named for an early settler named Thomas Virgin who was part of Jedediah Smith's party that passed through the Virgin River Valley on their way to California in 1827.

The Virgin Mountains are quite diverse with respect to vegetation types and the animals that live there. Among the highest peaks are stands of white fir and Rocky Mountain Douglas-fir. Gambel's oak and canyon maple occur on many of the upper slopes of the range. Below these trees, a pinyon-juniper-oak woodland appears, with the oaks generally relegated to the drainages. Below the pinyon-juniper zone, Joshua trees are found dotting hillsides along with yucca.

Although not listed here, the desert mountaineer will likely want to climb Mount Bangs, at the north end of the range over the border in Arizona. There are outstanding opportunities for primitive camping in the Gold Butte area. All minimum impact camping methods should be applied here. Gas, food and lodging are available in Mesquite, Nevada to the north. For further information, contact the Bureau of Land Management office in Las Vegas.

### Virgin Peak (8,071 ft; 2,460 m)

This peak, the highpoint of the range, has over 5,000 feet of relief above its north base overlooking the Virgin River Valley. The views from its summit of the Virgin River Valley and south to the Lake Mead Country are outstanding.

*Maps:* Virgin Peak (NV-AZ) 7.5-minute (1:24,000 scale) topographic map; Overton 1:100,000 scale metric topographic map; Automobile Club of Southern California (AAA) San Bernardino County map (Las Vegas area inset)

*Best Time to Climb:* Fall and Spring

*Approach:* From Las Vegas, drive 68 miles north on Interstate 15, and exit at the Riverside/Bunkerville off ramp (Exit 112). Drive three miles, passing Riverside and crossing the Virgin River to the Gold Butte Road. Turn south on the Gold Butte Road, and drive twenty miles to a fork at some fine Aztec sandstone outcroppings marking Whitney Pockets. Initially you'll pass several ranches including an ostrich farm! Stay left at the fork, and drive 2.4 miles east on a well-graded dirt road to a junction with a rough road that heads north (left). Turn left and drive 0.9 miles to a corral at about 4,200 feet. This is a good place for those with two-wheel drive vehicles to park. Two-wheel drive vehicles with high clearance should be able to drive farther, but with a four-wheel drive vehicle one can easily continue three miles north (stay right at a fork shortly after the corral) and park (5,840 ft). Some remains of an old mining venture are found here.

*Route:* From the four-wheel drive parking area, climb the minor ridge to the west up to the crest of Virgin Peak's southeast ridge. Follow the ridge

Virgin Peak. Photo: Andy Zdon

northwest to the summit. A use-trail will make the route through the brush easier to follow. For those with two-wheel drive, anticipate ten miles round trip with 3,900 feet of elevation gain. Those with four-wheel drive can plan on four miles round trip with 2,250 feet of elevation gain.

### LITTLE VIRGIN PEAK (3,514 FT; 1,017 M)

This peak, an easy scramble from the Gold Butte Road, provides fine views of the lower Virgin River Valley and the Overton Arm of Lake Mead.

*Maps:* Whitney Pocket (NV) 7.5-minute (1:24,000 scale) topographic map; Lake Mead 1:100,000 scale metric topographic map; Automobile Club of Southern California (AAA) San Bernardino County map (Las Vegas area inset)

*Best Time to Climb:* November through April

*Approach:* From Las Vegas, drive 68 miles north on Interstate 15, and exit at the Riverside/Bunkerville offramp (Exit 112). Drive three miles, passing Riverside and crossing the Virgin River to the Gold Butte Road. Turn south on the Gold Butte Road, and drive about 12.5 miles to the north side of Little Virgin Peak and park.

*Route:* The peak is an easy scramble to the south amid creosote-dotted slopes. Plan on two miles round trip with about 500 feet of elevation gain.

## BILLY GOAT PEAK (5,735 FT; 1,748 M)

This fine, rugged desert peak overlooks the Grand Wash and Gold Butte country. The author only partially scouted this peak, and is not aware of any prior write-ups or trip reports. Climbing Billy Goat Peak will lead the hiker to some rarely visited desert country.

*Maps:* Virgin Peak and St. Thomas Gap (NV-AZ) 7.5-minute (1:24,000 scale) topographic maps; Overton and Lake Mead 1:100,000 scale metric topographic maps; Automobile Club of Southern California (AAA) San Bernardino County map (Las Vegas area inset)

*Best Time to Climb:* November through April

*Approach:* From Las Vegas, drive 68 miles north on Interstate 15, and exit at the Riverside/Bunkerville offramp (Exit 112). Drive three miles, passing Riverside and crossing the Virgin River to the Gold Butte Road. Turn south on the Gold Butte Road, and drive twenty miles to a fork at the Aztec sandstone outcroppings marking Whitney Pockets. Stay left and continue another 4.1 miles to Whitney Pass. About 0.2 miles past Whitney Pass, a rough dirt track on the right heads steeply up a draw about a quarter-mile. Park here. Two-wheel drive vehicles may want to park down at the main road.

*Route:* Follow Billy Goat's north ridge, which is at first somewhat cholla infested, but soon gives way to pinyon, juniper and scattered mountain mahogany. Follow the ridge south, dropping to a saddle, then passing east below the prominent cliffs to steep talus leading to the summit area. Some Class 3 scrambling may be encountered en route. Anticipate four miles round trip with about 1,000 feet of elevation gain.

## GOLD BUTTE (5,049 FT; 1,539 M)

This peak was named in honor of the surrounding mining district where gold was discovered in 1905.

*Maps:* Gold Butte (NV) 7.5-minute (1:24,000 scale) topographic map; Lake Mead 1:100,000 scale metric topographic map; Automobile Club of Southern California (AAA) San Bernardino County map (Las Vegas area inset)

*Best Time to Climb:* November through April

*Approach:* This peak can be climbed from most any side. Therefore, directions are provided to the site of Gold Butte. From there, the hiker can find their own route. From Las Vegas, drive 68 miles north on Interstate 15, and exit at the Riverside/Bunkerville offramp (Exit 112). Drive three miles, passing Riverside and crossing the Virgin River to the Gold Butte Road. Turn south on the Gold Butte Road, and drive twenty miles to a fork at some fine Aztec sandstone outcroppings marking Whitney Pockets. Stay right and continue another 9.3 miles to a fork. The left fork heads to St. Thomas Gap in the Grand Wash country. Stay right and continue another 7.2 miles to a fork. Stay right again and in 2.6 miles you'll reach a road junction, and corral area that marks the site of Gold Butte (abandoned). *Route:* The peak is an easy scramble, although depending on your route, a little Class 3 bouldering may be encountered. The author climbed this peak from a rough road (but passable with a high clearance two-wheel drive vehicle) on the south side of the peak. The slopes were a bit loose, and dotted with pesky catclaw bushes that delighted in snagging a loose shirt sleeve, but the route was easily followed. Others have climbed the butte from mining trails on the north side of the mountain. Anticipate no more than three miles round trip and 1,000 feet of elevation gain round trip regardless of the route chosen.

### BONELLI PEAK (5,334 FT; 1,625.8 M)

The peak is named in honor of Daniel Bonelli, a noted early southern Nevada settler who discovered mica deposits in the area in 1873. Bonelli owned a large hay and vegetable ranch along the Virgin River, and is noted for bringing back vines from Europe and planting Nevada's first vineyard in Las Vegas. The views from this peak are among the finest of any desert peak in southern Nevada.

*Maps:* Jumbo Peak (NV) 7.5-minute (1:24,000 scale) topographic map; Lake Mead 1:100,000 scale metric topographic map; Automobile Club of Southern California (AAA) San Bernardino County map (Las Vegas area inset)

*Best Time to Climb:* November through April

*Approach:* Follow the directions to the junction at the site of Gold Butte as described for the Gold Butte climb. From the site of Gold Butte, head south on the Scanlon Road, staying on the main road, passing through a wash after 1.4 miles, and reaching a fork 3.5 miles from the Gold Butte junction. The right fork heads down Cataract Wash. Stay left, and continue another 5.3 miles to where a side road leaves the wash to the right. Take the right, lesser used road, that heads up Garnet Valley. For those who worry

Bonelli Peak from upper Garnet Valley. The principal route follows the ridge on the right. Alternate route heads up the steeper slope (east ridge) directly below the summit. Photo: Andy Zdon

about the paint on your car park here (about 3,165 ft). The road up Garnet Valley is narrow and overgrown by mesquite and catclaw bushes. Otherwise, continue up the canyon about a half mile and park.

*Route:* From a point where the Garnet Valley Road begins to head southeast, follow one of two canyons: either one that heads south or one that heads southwest. Follow these canyons until the north ridge of Bonelli can be reached and followed to the summit. Anticipate five miles round trip with about 2,200 feet of elevation gain.

*Alternate Approach and Route:* With determination, and some loud music or conversation to block out the sound of the bushes scratching the paint off your car, one can (with four-wheel drive) continue driving up Garnet Valley until reaching a point about due east of the peak (3,700 ft). The east ridge can then be climbed to the summit. Anticipate three miles round trip with 1,900 feet of elevation gain.

*With additional time, the dedicated summiteer will want to ascend several other named summits in the area including Mica Peak, Jumbo Peak, Powell Mountain, Gold Cross Peak, Gregg Peak, Garrett Butte and Rattlesnake Peak, all of which are in the Gold Butte area. They all will provide outstanding views of the Lake Mead and Gold Butte country. Mica Peak is most easily reached from the saddle between it and Gold Butte. The summit ridge of Jumbo Peak (5,763 ft) can easily be reached from either side. However, the summit block appears to be a very difficult rock climb. Additional maps that will be needed (in addition to those described for the other Virgin Mountain peaks described above) include the Garrett Butte and Hiller Mountains 7.5-minute topographic maps.*

# THE MUDDY MOUNTAINS

One of the most imposing ranges in southern Nevada, the Muddy Mountains, present numerous hiking and climbing possibilities. Besides the fine desert scenery, including the occasional sighting of bighorn sheep (as we were lucky enough to see) on the summit spire of Muddy Peak, the range is known as a classic Nevada geologic site. Similar to that of the Spring Mountains, the unique geologic feature is a thrust fault called the "Muddy Mountain Thrust." This fault is conspicuous in Hidden Valley where it has faulted older limestones (of which the summit block of Muddy Peak is comprised) on top of much younger, white to brilliant orange Aztec sandstone.

Campgrounds are available in the adjacent Valley of Fire State Park. Otherwise, camping is primitive and all minimum impact camping methods should be applied here. Supplies, gas, food and lodging are available in Las Vegas or Overton. For further information, contact the Bureau of Land Management office in Las Vegas.

### MUDDY PEAK (5,387 FT; 1,642 M)
*Maps:* Muddy Peak (NV) 7.5-minute (1:24,000 scale) topographic map; Lake Mead 1:100,000 scale metric topographic map; Automobile Club of Southern California (AAA) San Bernardino County map (Las Vegas area inset)
*Best Time to Climb:* November through April
*Approach:* From Las Vegas, drive north on Interstate 15 to Exit 75 (Valley of Fire exit). Exit the interstate and follow the road east toward Valley of Fire about three miles to where the road bends to the left. Continue straight 4.2 miles on the dirt road heading toward the Muddy Mountains (Bitter Springs Trail) to a fork. Follow the signs toward Buffington Pockets, continuing straight on the main dirt road another 6.2 miles to a dirt track heading west. Turn right (west), and drive about a mile to the road end at about 3,000 feet. This road should be passable to high clearance two-wheel drive vehicles. Make sure you have a good spare tire, as the limestone cobbles

Muddy Peak (tiny figure on summit is a hiker) . Photo: Andy Zdon

in the road can be rough on a set of tires.

*Route:* From the road end, hike west up the trail to a low saddle, then down into Hidden Valley. In Hidden Valley, head south to a prominent notch at the head of the valley. Upon reaching the notch and taking in the awesome views of Lovell Wash and out toward the Colorado River, turn left and climb the steep loose ridge which then levels out as it winds its way to the impressive summit block. Upon reaching the saddle before the summit block, Class 3 climbing will lead to the summit. A gully just west of the ridge goes well, although some will want the security of a rope. Anticipate 8.5 miles round trip with about 3,000 feet of elevation gain.

## BLACK MOUNTAINS

The Black Mountains are more noteworthy for the major portion of the range located across the Colorado River in Arizona. However, the section of the Black Mountains in Nevada, and within Lake Mead National Recreation Area, will provide many days of enjoyable desert mountaineering with excellent views of Lake Mead and surrounding desert ranges. Joseph Ives named the range in 1858 while exploring the Colorado River country. One of the best descriptions of the Black Mountains was given by McLane when he quoted J.S. Newberry, the geologist along on Ives' expedition:

*"The view of the western slope of the Black Mountains which we obtained from the summits bordering the canyon is scarcely equaled, in its wild savage grandeur, by any I have elsewhere seen. A thousand subordinate pinnacles spring from the mountain side, all displaying the ragged outlines which the materials composing them are so prone to assume, while their colors are as striking and varied as their forms. Not a particle of vegetation is visible in the landscape. Here and there a spiny cactus clings to the rocks, but its color blends with theirs, as its thorny and repulsive nature harmonizes with the forbidding features of the surrounding scenery. As the eye of the traveler sweeps over this wilderness of sunburnt summits, which stand so stark and still, glittering in the burning sunlight and yet so desolate, he shrinks from the unearthly scene with a feeling of depression which must be felt to be imagined."*

The modern traveler may experience much of these same feelings. However, the presence of the blue waters of Lake Mead, and the access that modern roads provide have made these mountains more friendly to the desert summiteer. Although only Hamblin Mountain is described below, the mountaineer will likely want to climb the other summits in the area including Bearing Peak (2,515 ft), and Pyramid Peak (3,069 ft). For further information on hiking in this area, contact the Lake Mead National Recreation Area. Supplies, food, gas and lodging are available in Boulder City and Las Vegas. There are several campgrounds in the area.

### HAMBLIN MOUNTAIN (3,310 FT; 1,008.9 M)

Hamblin Mountain is the remnant of an ancient volcano that has been displaced about 12 miles east due to faulting. The peak provides a spectacular view of the Lake Mead area.

*Maps:* Callville Bay and Boulder Canyon (NV) 7.5-minute (1:24,000) scale topographic maps; Lake Mead 1:100,000 scale metric topographic map; Automobile Club of Southern California (AAA) San Bernardino County map (Las Vegas area inset)

*Best Time to Climb:* November through April

*Approach:* From Boulder City, follow Highway 93 east to the junction with the North Shore Drive. The Alan Bible Visitor Center is here and should be visited for information, and browsing through their fine book selection. Turn onto the North Shore Drive and follow it 3.2 miles to a junction with Highway 147. Stay right and continue on the North Shore Drive to a sandy wash at milepost 18. Park along the highway at about 1,870 feet.

*Route:* From the highway, hike up the wash about one mile to Cottonwood Spring. The spring is sometimes dry, but when we visited the spring, animals had been smart enough to dig a few inches into the wash sands for water which was just below the surface. Either scramble up a short Class 3 section behind the spring, or bypass it to the right, to gain the wash above the spring. Here a wash takes off to the southwest to a saddle immediately northwest of Point 828 meters. From here, a variety of potential routes present themselves. One can climb along the ridge over Point 828 meters, gaining the northeast ridge of the peak, then southwest to the summit. Anticipate a lot of loose scree en route, and six miles round trip with 1,500 feet of elevation gain.

## RIVER MOUNTAINS

The River Mountains are a small range, the remnant of a fourteen million-year-old volcano that was detached from the rest of the volcano by a fault, and displaced (such as Hamblin Mtn.) about 12 miles west of its source. Outcrops of limestone are also present. Creosote scrub, typical of this region, sporadically covers the slopes. Between 1935 and 1937, the Civilian Conservation Corps built the River Mountain Trail, currently maintained by the Boulder City Recreation Department, Lake Mead National Recreation Area, the University of Nevada, Las Vegas, and volunteers. A lot of hard work goes into maintaining this trail. Minimum-impact hiking techniques apply here (as they should in all of nature's settings). The highpoint of the range is River Mountain (3,789 ft), but powerlines pass just to the south of the peak and detract from what would otherwise be fine views.

### BLACK MOUNTAIN (3,628 FT; 1,106 M)
The hike to Black Mountain is the closest thing to an "urban trail" described in this guide. Beginning at a housing development in Boulder City, the houses and man-made structures are soon left behind, and the route to the summit becomes a meandering desert trail hike with views of the Lake Mead region.
*Maps:* Boulder City and Boulder Beach (NV) 7.5-minute (1:24,000 scale) topographic maps; Lake Mead 1:100,000 scale metric topographic map; Automobile Club of Southern California (AAA) San Bernardino County map (Las Vegas area inset)

Cottonwood Spring in the Black Mountains. Photo: Andy Zdon

*Best Time to Climb:* November through April
*Approach:* From Boulder City, drive east on Highway 93 about a mile to a signed trailhead on the left for the River Mountain Trail. If you pass St. Jude's Ranch for Children on the left, you've gone too far. Park in the trailhead parking lot (about 2,400 ft).
*Route:* Follow the marked trail to the summit of Black Mountain Overlook (3,480 ft). There are interpretive markers along the way, and an accompanying pamphlet is available at the trailhead or at the Alan Bible Visitor Center just down the road. From the overlook, Black Mountain is a short scramble to the north. Anticipate five miles round trip with 1,300 feet of elevation gain.

# FRENCHMAN MOUNTAINS

The Frenchman Mountains are one of the most conspicuous ranges surrounding the Las Vegas metropolitan area. Although they are close to the action of the Las Vegas Strip, the highest slopes of the Frenchman Mountains are far above the excitement, a desert island of solitude. Other peaks that may be of interest, but not included here, are Sunrise Mountain (north of Frenchman Mountain), and Lava Butte, a popular local hike.

### FRENCHMAN MOUNTAIN (4,052 FT; 1,235 M)

Every major western city seems to have one mountain that stands as an iconic sentinel above the sprawl of city lights, and Las Vegas is no different. Charleston Peak is the highest; Potosi Mountain has the widest girth; Gass Peak looms to the north over the strip, but the honor of Las Vegas sentinel must go to Frenchman Mountain. In Las Vegas, those who are up just before dawn are treated to sunrise over Frenchman, and its neighbor Sunrise Mountain (aptly named). Surprisingly, the range and peak were not named in honor of a Frenchman. The peak was named after a local Belgian miner who everyone thought was French.
*Maps:* Frenchman Mountain (NV) 7.5-minute (1:24,000 scale) topographic map; Las Vegas 1:100,000 scale metric topographic map; Automobile Club of Southern California (AAA) San Bernardino County map (Las Vegas area inset)
*Best Time to Climb:* November through April
*Approach:* From Las Vegas, follow Lake Mead Boulevard east to Sunrise Pass (about 11.5 miles east of Interstate 15). Park here at about 2,400 feet.

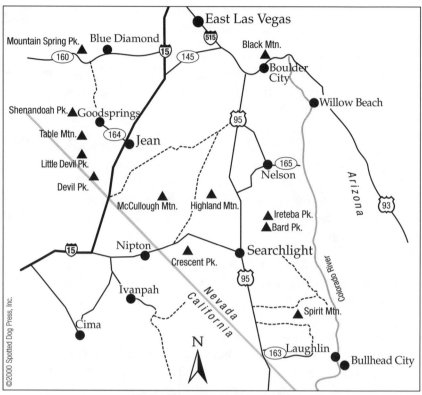

The Las Vegas area mountains (south)

Given its proximity to the Las Vegas urban area, and "civilization" be sure to lock your car at the pullout while you hike.

*Route:* From Sunrise Pass, follow the bulldozed track southward as it climbs to a pass near Frenchman's false north peak, then drops to a drainage and makes the final steep climb to the summit antennae. Anticipate four miles round trip with 1,900 feet of elevation gain.

## McCullough Range

Extending from just south of Henderson, Nevada, southward nearly 40 miles to the New York Mountains near the California border, the McCullough Range is one of the major desert ranges of southern Nevada. With over 5,000 feet of relief, but only visible from distant but frequently traveled highways, the McCullough Range does not present the desert hiker with the impressive appearance of the Clark Mountains, New York Mountains or other nearby ranges. However, a trip into the McCulloughs

Lava Butte (right foreground) and Lake Mead from the summit of Frenchman.  Photo: Andy Zdon

is highly worthwhile.

Geologically, the McCullough Range is more like two distinct ranges, that meld into one.  The northern half of the range is more rugged and of volcanic origin.  The southern half of the range presents a more friendly, and expansive character, the rocks present being Precambrian-age gneiss and schist. The usual creosote-blackbrush association occurs on the lower slopes of the range, but these species give way to a fine pinyon-juniper wood- land.  The Panamint rattlesnake and the southwestern speckled rattlesnake make this range home, and given the number of shady alcoves, and timber in the range, one should watch where they step and place their hands.

Camping in the McCullough Range is primitive and all minimum impact camping methods should be applied here.  Gas, food and lodging are available in Searchlight or State Line (Primm) Nevada.  For further information, contact the Bureau of Land Management office in Las Vegas.

## McCullough Mountain (7,026 ft; 2,142 m)

McCullough Mountain is the highpoint of the range, and provides impressive views of the immense surrounding territory. Both the east and west approaches provide many desert hiking opportunities.

*Maps:* McCullough Mountain (NV) 7.5-minute (1:24,000 scale) topographic map; Mesquite Lake 1:100,000 scale metric topographic map; Automobile Club of Southern California (AAA) San Bernardino County map

*Best Time to Climb:* October through May

*Approach:* From Baker, California drive 40 miles north on Interstate 15 to the Nipton Road exit. The Nipton Road exit can also be accessed by driving south on Interstate 15 from State Line (Primm) Nevada. Drive 18.1 miles east on Nipton Road, passing the world-famous lottery ticket store in Nipton and the Nevada State Line, to a dirt road on the north side of the road. Follow this dirt road north about a mile where it merges with a power line road. Head north on the power line road 3.9 miles to a junction and turn west on a rougher dirt road. Follow this dirt road 3.7 miles (staying right at a fork en route) and park at about 5,200 feet. Four-wheel drive is recommended for this route.

*Route:* Hike northwest over a hill and drop into a wash. Follow the curvy wash northwest about two miles (staying right at forks) to a saddle. At this point, it is a little disheartening to see how far away the summit looks–but this is deceiving–don't give up! Contour through pinyons along the northeast side of Point 6,425 feet to another saddle where the summit of McCullough becomes visible. Drop into a wash to the west, then follow that wash about a mile as it reaches the summit area from the east. Anticipate seven miles round trip with 2,300 feet of elevation gain. This route makes for a fine navigation challenge.

*Alternate Approach:* From State Line, Nevada, drive east past the Primadonna Casino. In 0.2 miles, continue east on a graded dirt road and follow it 0.8 miles to where it meets a power line road. Drive the dusty power line road two miles, crossing some railroad tracks en route, to a road fork. Head right and drive 5.4 miles to a microwave station road, and bear right, continuing another 2.2 miles to a dirt road at some corrals. Turn northeast and continue a quarter mile, then head south 5.2 miles to more corrals. Just before the corrals are reached, a road heads up a wash. Follow this road 3.6 miles (four-wheel drive required), staying on the main track to a cabin near Railroad Spring (5,240 ft).

*Alternate Route:* Head east, then northeast about a half mile up the canyon past Railroad Spring. From here head southeast gaining the peak's west slopes which are followed to the summit. Anticipate four miles round trip with about 2,000 feet of elevation gain round trip depending on your route.

## NEW YORK MOUNTAINS

The New York Mountains are primarily located in California, but the northeasternmost peak in the range, Crescent Peak, lies across the Nevada state line, hence its inclusion in this section. This portion of the New York Mountains is comprised of Precambrian-age metamorphic rocks. In days past, the Crescent Peak area has seen boom and bust for gold, turquoise, silver, and other minerals. Gold was the inspiration for the founding of the Crescent District in 1863, though Crescent's real boom came in 1894 when an Indian known as "Prospector Johnnie" discovered turquoise deposits. For the next ten years, the area was mined for its turquoise. As that excitement waned, silver was found. During 1905 to 1907, a vibrant mining camp, complete with hotels, saloons, restaurants, a newspaper, union hall, brothel and schools, provided all the amenities to an up and coming town. But by 1908, it was all over. The shops and restaurants closed. People moved on to more prosperous towns and camps. Only the Big Tiger Mine remained active during World War I. Today, there is some occasional mining activity so pay attention to the "No Trespassing" signs. Every now and then, an irate miner has been known to protect his claim.

Camping in the Crescent Peak area is primitive and minimum-impact camping methods should be observed. Gas, food and lodging are available in Searchlight or State Line (Primm) Nevada. Limited groceries are available at the store in Nipton. For further information, contact the Bureau of Land Management office in Las Vegas.

### CRESCENT PEAK (5,999 FT; 1,829 M)
*Maps:* Crescent Peak (NV-CA) 7.5-minute (1:24,000 scale) topographic map; Mesquite Lake 1:100,000 scale metric topographic map; Automobile Club of Southern California (AAA) San Bernardino County map
*Best Time to Climb:* November through April
*Approach:* From Las Vegas, drive south on Interstate 15, crossing the state line into California, and exit at Nipton Road (if you reach Mountain Pass you've gone too far). Head east on Nipton Road crossing back into Nevada,

passing through the town of Nipton (buy your California lottery ticket here) and turning south on a graded dirt road 14.8 miles from the interstate. Crescent Peak is the prominent pyramidal peak south of the Nipton Road and due east. The road crosses Big Tiger Wash, and heads generally east toward the peak about 3.5 miles from the Nipton Road. Once near the peak, use any of the mining roads in the area that head toward the peak to start your ascent.

*Route:* Once on the west or south side of the peak, park at a likely looking starting point, and follow your nose to the summit. All routes will work. The climb is likely to be a half-day hike. Due to the variety of starting points, no round trip mileage or elevation gain is provided.

## EL DORADO MOUNTAINS

The El Dorado Mountains loom over the Colorado River, and just east of Highway 95 between the towns of Boulder City and Searchlight, Nevada. Sparse creosote and blackbrush cover practically the entire range, giving the appearance, from a distance, of being somewhat void of vegetation. This is not at all the case. Besides having numerous species of plants, the desert bighorn sheep, and other hardy desert species, call this range home.

The El Dorado Mountains are within the Piute-El Dorado Area of Critical Environmental Concern. Camping in the El Dorado Mountains is primitive and all minimum impact camping methods should be observed. The campgrounds in the Boulder Basin area of Lake Mead National Recreation Area are a reasonable drive away, and one could camp there. Gas, food and lodging are available in Boulder City. For further information, contact the Bureau of Land Management office in Las Vegas.

### IRETEBA PEAK (5,060 FT; 1,542 M), "BARD PEAK" (4,969 FT; 1,515 M)

Ireteba Peak, the highpoint of the El Dorado Mountains, makes for a fine half-day climb and can be climbed in combination with the unofficially named Bard Peak (Point 4,969 ft on the map). The views eastward of the Colorado River between Lake Mead and Lake Mojave, and to the Highland Mountains and southwest to the East Mojave are superb. The peak is named for Ireteba, a Mojave Indian guide on the Whipple mapping expedition in the 1850's.

*Maps*: Ireteba Peaks (NV) 7.5-minute (1:24,000 scale) topographic map; Boulder City 1:100,000 scale metric topographic map; Automobile Club

The Colorado River from Ireteba Peak.  Photo: Andy Zdon

of Southern California (AAA) San Bernardino County map

*Best Time to Climb:* November through April

*Approach:* From Las Vegas, drive east toward Boulder City to the junction of Highways 93 and 95.  Head 26.8 miles south on Highway 95 to a dirt road heading east (at highway milepost 28).  If coming from the south, this road is approximately 7.5 miles north of the town of Searchlight. Follow the dirt road east two miles to a power line road.  Turn north (left) and follow the power line road 0.5 miles to a rough dirt road that heads east.  Follow the dirt road east (passable with high clearance two-wheel drive) 2.2 miles and park.  A wildlife guzzler is passed just before reaching the road end.

*Route:* Drop into the wash next to the road and follow it a short distance to Bard Peak's west ridge.  Follow this ridge to the summit.  Ireteba Peak is a short scramble to the north.  Anticipate 2.5 miles round trip with about 1,300 feet of elevation gain.

*Alternate Route:* One can also bypass Bard Peak, and head directly for the east ridge of Ireteba Peak which can be followed to the top.  This does not save much on distance or elevation gain, and the talus is more loose than on Bard's ridge. If climbing Bard and descending via this route be prepared for some sections with ball-bearing-like terrain, on which a slip is quite easy. Of course the terrain is relatively gentle and the only place you'll end up in a fall is on your derriere. However, the author managed a slip on easy terrain near the bottom resulting in a sprained foot, sprained ankle, and popping his knee out of joint!

# HIGHLAND SPRING RANGE

These short, rugged, volcanic mountains are a castellated mountain mass on the west side of El Dorado Valley. Camping in the Highland Spring Range is primitive and minimum impact camping methods should be observed. Camp at least 1/4 mile from any spring as human presence disrupts the wildlife. This is desert bighorn territory, and much of the range has been included within the Highland Range Crucial Bighorn Habitat Area. The campgrounds in the Boulder Basin area of Lake Mead National Recreation Area are a reasonable drive away, and one could camp there. Gas, food and lodging are available in Boulder City. For further information, contact the Bureau of Land Management office in Las Vegas.

HIGHLAND MOUNTAIN (4,960+ FT; 1,512+ M)
*Maps:* Highland Spring (NV) 7.5-minute (1:24,000 scale) topographic map; Mesquite Lake 1:100,000 scale metric topographic map; Automobile Club of Southern California (AAA) San Bernardino County map
*Best Time to Climb:* November through April
*Approach:* From Baker, California drive 40 miles north on Interstate 15 to the Nipton Road exit. If driving from Las Vegas, this exit is about ten miles south of State Line (Primm) Nevada. Drive 18.1 miles east on Nipton Road, passing the world-famous lottery ticket store in Nipton and the Nevada State Line, to a dirt road on the north side of the road. Follow this dirt road north about a mile where it merges with a power line road. Head north on the power line road 5.5 miles to a junction. Turn east on a rougher dirt road. Follow this dirt road as it curves past a corral, almost a mile to another track heading east. A high clearance two-wheel drive vehicle should be able to make it this far. Four-wheel drive vehicles can take the road heading east another 1.3 miles to a corral and park (about 4,250 ft).
*Route:* Continue up the road a few hundred feet to a wash. Follow the wash eastward a quarter- mile to Highland Spring, then another quarter-

mile north to the summit. A cliff is passed on the right. Anticipate one mile round trip with about 700 feet of elevation gain from the corral.

## NEWBERRY MOUNTAINS

The Newberry Mountains, topped by the granite alter of Spirit Mountain, tower above the Colorado River in the Lake Mojave area. The range was named in honor of J.S. Newberry, a geologist in Lieutenant Joseph Ives' expedition that explored the Colorado River. Newberry had previously visited this range in 1858, during which he ascended a minor peak northeast of Spirit Mountain.

Lower slopes are covered by creosote, giving way to blackbrush, scattered yucca, and Joshua tree woodlands on higher ridges. Scattered junipers and pinyons are found on the highest slopes of the range.

Although Spirit Mountain is within the Lake Mead National Recreation Area, much of the Newberry Mountains to the west is within the Piute-El Dorado Area of Critical Environmental Concern administered by the Bureau of Land Management. Camping in the Newberry Mountains is primitive and all minimum impact camping methods should be observed. A developed campground is available near Davis Dam at Laughlin, Nevada. Supplies, gas, food and lodging are available in the Laughlin-Bullhead City area. For further information, contact the Bureau of Land Management office in Las Vegas, or the Lake Mead National Recreation Area.

### SPIRIT MOUNTAIN (5,639 FT; 1,719 M)

This classic desert peak is of spiritual significance to the Chemehuevi Indians, who believed that the summit was the dwelling place of their departed tribal leaders. When we climbed this peak, a winter storm passed through during our ascent. First hail, then snow fell on us as we climbed up the slopes to the south ridge of the peak. The granite pinnacles passed along the route were dusted with newly fallen snow, giving this desert summit a truly alpine feel.

*Maps:* Spirit Mountain (NV) 7.5-minute (1:24,000 scale) topographic map; Davis Dam 1:100,000 scale metric topographic map; Automobile Club of Southern California (AAA) San Bernardino County map)

*Best Time to Climb*: November through April

*Approach:* From Searchlight, Nevada along Highway 95, drive 13.8 miles south on Highway 95, and turn east (left) on the well-graded dirt Christmas

The summit of Spirit Mountain on a stormy day. The wires and post are the remains of an old survey marker.
Photo: Wynne Benti

Tree Pass Road. This dirt road is 5.3 miles north of the junction of Highways 95 and 163 to Laughlin. Follow the Christmas Tree Pass Road 8.1 miles, crossing Christmas Tree Pass en route, to a faint track that heads north. Turn onto this road and follow it about 0.4 miles to a parking area (3,800 ft). All vehicles should be able to reach the road end. If unsure about driving the last 0.4 miles, park on the Christmas Tree Pass Road and walk in from there.

*Route:* Hike north about 0.4 miles, crossing a saddle and dropping about 150 feet on the other side. Head northeast toward the southwest face of the mountain, passing south and west of Point 4,280+ feet. Drop into the wash north of Point 4,280+ feet and follow it until dry waterfalls block further progress. At this point you are in prime desert country, granite faces and pinnacles extending west from Spirit Mountain takes one attention away from the steep climb. Exit north (left) onto easy slopes, and gain the south ridge of Spirit Mountain at about 5,400 feet. Follow the ridge north to the summit rocks which are Class 2-3. Anticipate five miles round-trip with 2,400 feet of elevation gain.

# Mojave National Preserve Area

When it comes to unique desert scenery, the Mojave National Preserve is truly magical country. Rugged limestone, volcanic, and granitic mountains, dry salt flats, sand dunes, dense Joshua tree forests, pinyon-juniper woodlands, scattered white fir groves, caves, old mining camps, and the occasional petroglyph panel are just a few of the desert features awaiting to be explored.

The plants, animals, rocks, historical objects, buildings, archeological artifacts and any other objects within the Mojave National Preserve are protected by law. Archaeological sites and artifacts are protected by the Antiquities Act of 1906 and the Archaeological Resources Act of 1979. Observe and enjoy the preserve but leave everything you find. Occasionally, private lands within the preserve will be encountered and should be respected. Pets are allowed within the preserve but must be leashed. The Mojave National Preserve covers more than 1.6 million acres, and has been referred to as the "Lonesome Triangle," although on a holiday weekend, one will likely encounter more people than expected.

The history of the region is tied closely to the two largest sources of water, the Colorado and Mojave Rivers. Native people are known to have inhabited the area as far back as 10,000 years ago, subsisting on the abundance of seeds and pinyon nuts in the area. About 700 years ago, Paiute-Shoshone people migrated to the region, and left behind evidence of their lifestyle through their ceremonial, camp, and village sites. The first known Europeans in the region were the Spanish explorers Juan Batista de Anza and Francisco Garces. They passed through the region during 1775 to 1776 via the Mojave River, passing by the Kelso Dunes and along

the Providence and New York Mountains. Garces described in his diary:
   "*I went four and one-half leagues to the east-southeast, having traveled through the big sand dunes and the Sierra de Santa Coleta.*"

The Sierra de Santa Coleta was the name used for the Providence Mountains. Garces' path probably took him through Cedar Canyon between the Mid Hills and Pinto Mountain. Fifty years passed before Jedediah Smith passed through the region on his way to southern California from the Rocky Mountains. John C. Fremont passed through the region in 1844 following the Spanish Trail which roughly followed the northern portion of the Mojave, and along the Mojave River. As early as 1846, Mormons on their way to southern California also used this route. A wagon route was established through the area in 1857, linking Prescott, Arizona with San Bernardino, California.

With the advent of this wagon road, prospecting in the region began in earnest. The late nineteenth century saw the establishment of many of the mining camps, that are today nothing but ghost towns or named sites marked upon a map. The first railroad to cross the Mojave did so in 1883. Soon, other rail lines crisscrossed the region. During the 1930's, bigger and better topographic maps of the area became available, and exploration of the area for minerals, water resources (tapping into the Colorado) and other resources began to increase. Today the region is crossed by interstate highways, and continues to be traversed by trains. What was once a remote place to be avoided is now a vacationer's paradise.

Throughout the region, the hiker will encounter three main rock types: Paleozoic and Mesozoic-age sedimentary rocks consisting of limestone, dolomite and sandstone (e.g., at Mitchell Peak in the Providence Mountains); granitic rocks of the Teutonia quartz monzonite (e.g., at Teutonia Peak, New York Mountain, and the Granite Mountains); and Tertiary-age volcanic rocks including basalt and rhyolite tuff (as at Pinto Mountain, the Woods Mountains, and Fountain and Edgar Peaks). The variety of these rock types leads to the wide range of scenery in the area. In the Marble Mountains, a green shale called the "Latham shale" is one of the most fossiliferous units in the Mojave with fine specimens of trilobites occurring in its thinly-bedded horizons. The author has observed trilobite cephalons (the head of the trilobite) up to four inches in diameter. It should be noted that the fossils are only casts of these creatures. The original material disappeared shortly after the demise of the trilobite.

The Mojave Desert is roughly bounded by the San Andreas and Garlock Faults, and is cut by a series of other faults. Some are roughly parallel to the San Andreas which runs northwest. Others, more typical of the Basin and Range, are range front faults that trend north-south. Others like the Garlock Fault, run east-west.

There are two developed campgrounds within the Preserve (not including the campground at Providence Mountains State Recreation Area, formerly known as Mitchell Caverns State Park). The first is Mid Hills Campground, a fine campground amid a pinyon-juniper woodland providing wind-sheltered and somewhat private campsites. Water is sometimes available at the campground but should not be depended on. Mid Hills is the superior campground to use if the weather is still warm, or during windy periods. Snow during the winter can sometimes make the road to the campground a muddy mess. The other campground is Hole in the Wall located northeast of Mitchell Caverns, and south of Mid Hills. The author remembers camping at Hole in the Wall when the camp consisted of sparse campsites with a few fire rings. With the creation of the national preserve, the facilities have been upgraded significantly. Whether this is good or bad, depends on your viewpoint! Regardless of the location of your campsite, if you plan on having a campfire, bring your own wood. Cutting or gathering wood in the preserve is prohibited.

Besides the campgrounds, primitive camping is permitted anywhere that appears to have been traditionally used for camping. Camping is prohibited within a quarter mile of any spring, well or other water source. Two of the finer primitive camping areas include Granite Cove (a useful campsite for climbing Granite Mountain, Van Winkle Mountain, or Providence Peak), and Carruthers Canyon (useful for climbing in the New York Mountains).

All camping in the area is first-come first-serve and there are no hotel accommodations within the preserve. The closest motels are in Baker or Needles, California, and State Line, Nevada. Plan on stocking up with supplies in Barstow, Baker, Searchlight, Needles or Las Vegas.

# Peaks Accessible from Interstate 15

### Little Cowhole Mountain (1,699 ft; 518 m)

*Maps:* Soda Lake North (CA) 7.5-minute (1:24,000 scale) topographic map; Soda Mountains 1:100,000 scale metric topographic map; Automobile Club of Southern California (AAA) San Bernardino County map

*Best Time to Climb:* November through April

*Approach:* From Baker, California, drive about one mile south on the paved Kelbaker Road to a triple junction. At this point, the paved Kelbaker Road heads to the left, a graded dirt road continues straight, and another graded dirt road turns right. Take the right-hand fork and continue another 1.3 miles to another fork. Turn left and drive 0.2 miles to a fork. Stay right, and continue 1.6 miles to a junction. Turn right and continue straight (south) 1.8 miles to a cattle watering hole (usually dry) on the west side of the road. From here, a poorer quality road heads east along the north side of Little Cowhole. One can park here (980 ft) and placidly walk down the desert road or drive the road until reaching a point due north of the peak (1,100 ft). These roads are generally passable to two-wheel drive vehicles with good clearance but watch for sand.

*Route:* From the point north of the peak, head south over easy terrain to the summit. Anticipate two miles round-trip with 600 feet of elevation gain. If hiking from the well, anticipate 4.5 miles round-trip with about 700 feet of elevation gain.

### Cowhole Mountain (2,252 ft; 680+ m)

*Maps:* Seventeenmile Point (CA) 7.5-minute (1:24,000 scale) topographic map; Ivanpah 1:100,000 scale metric topographic map; Automobile Club of Southern California (AAA) San Bernardino County map

*Best Time to Climb:* November through April

*Approach:* Follow the approach directions for Little Cowhole Mountain. From the watering place, continue south 2.6 miles, crossing the east end of Soda Lake (do not drive when wet) to another well on the south side of an intersection. Turn east onto the famed Mojave Road and continue a half mile to a junction. Turn south and continue a quarter mile and park at the marked wilderness boundary northwest of the peak (1,190 ft). These roads are generally passable to two-wheel drive vehicles with good clearance but watch for sand.

Arch along route to Kelso Peak. Photo: Andy Zdon

*Route:* Head southeast, climbing the peak via anyone of numerous potential routes. Anticipate six miles round-trip with 1,100 feet of elevation gain.

### KELSO PEAK (4,746 FT; 1,447 M)

This nicely located peak provides a central grandstand from which to view the Kelso Valley area. Of particular note is the view of Kelso Dunes to the south. Kelso Peak is comprised of Precambrian-age metamorphic rocks, although scattered outcrops of younger quartz monzonite are present. The slopes of the peak are covered with creosote, scattered yucca, cholla, and barrel cactus. The Kelso Mountains are frequented by the Old Dad Mountain herd of bighorn sheep, and on our ascent of this peak, as we reached the summit, we turned to the north just in time to see a herd of bighorn sheep heading northeast across our approach route. A peak west of Kelso Peak contains a road to the top along with some antennas and should not be confused with Kelso Peak.

*Maps:* Marl Mountains and Kelso (CA) 7.5-minute (1:24,000 scale) topographic maps; Ivanpah 1:100,000 scale metric topographic map; Automobile Club of Southern California (AAA) San Bernardino County map

*Best Time to Climb:* November through April

*Approach:* From Baker, drive 23.2 miles south on Kelbaker Road to where the road curves and passes under some powerlines. A dirt track heading due south toward Kelso Peak will come into view. Park at a pullout here (3,690 ft). The road is paved and passable to all cars.

*Route:* Follow the dirt track south as it heads to the peak, then follow a canyon south, possibly passing a curious granite arch depending on the chosen route, then southeast up a broad basin. Finally, the peak's northwest slopes are followed to the summit. Anticipate six miles round-trip with 1,100 feet of elevation gain.

### OLD DAD MOUNTAIN (4,252 FT; 1,295.9 M)

This prominent peak provides fine views of the Soda Lake and Kelso Valley region. Old Dad Mountain is permanent range for a herd of bighorn sheep, although their numbers are reported to be declining. Golden Eagles and Prairie Falcons forage in the area. The Old Dad Mountains are composed of Paleozoic and Mesozoic formations that have been faulted by the Playground thrust fault. This fault offsets the Paleozoic rocks eastward nearly two miles. This faulting occurred during a geologic event called the Sevier Orogeny which took place more than a hundred million years ago when the movement of the earth's plates was causing this part of the world to squeeze together. Geologists consider the fault inactive.

*Maps:* Old Dad Mountain (CA) 7.5-minute (1:24,000 scale) topographic map; Ivanpah 1:100,000 scale metric topographic map; Automobile Club of Southern California (AAA) San Bernardino County map

*Best Time to Climb:* November through April

*Approach:* From Baker, drive 19.5 miles south on the paved Kelbaker Road to a dirt road. This dirt road is also about 15 miles north of Kelso Depot. Turn southwest (right) and follow the dirt road to a junction. Stay right, and continue another 2.5 miles, bear right at another fork, and follow the road one mile to a road fork in a wash. Bear left and drive 1.3 miles (bearing right at a fork after 0.8 miles) to a junction. Park here at the wilderness boundary (2,300 ft, or 700 m). The road is passable to two wheel-drive vehicles with good clearance.

*Route:* Hike about 1.5 miles northwest up the wash toward the peak. Follow either the prominent drainage or the ridge to the north of the drainage, west to the summit area. Anticipate six miles round-trip with 2,000 feet of elevation gain.

Near the summit of Old Dad Mountain. Photo: Andy Zdon

### Teutonia Peak (5,753 ft; 1,754 m)

This granite peak, situated on the north slope of Cima Dome, catches the interest of most desert peak hikers that pass through this region. The broad dome of Cima was once thought to have resulted from the total erosion of a mountain mass, with Teutonia Peak merely sticking out as a final vestige of this former range. More recent investigations suggest that this is not the case. It is generally believed that Cima Dome formed as a result of up-warping of the area during emplacement of the granitic rocks. Volcanic rocks and sediments that formerly covered this highland eroded away exposing the domed granitic surface.

Teutonia Peak provides an excellent viewpoint of Cima Dome along with the neighboring Ivanpah, and New York Mountains. Dense stands of Joshua trees with an undergrowth of cholla are the most common vegetation encountered en route to the peak. The wildlife of most interest in this area are the birds: Golden Eagles, Swainson's Hawks, Gilded Flickers and Bendire's Thrashers can be observed here.

*Maps:* Cima Dome (CA) 7.5-minute (1:24,000 scale) topographic map; Ivanpah 1:100,000 scale metric topographic map; Automobile Club of Southern California (AAA) San Bernardino County map

*Best Time to Climb:* November through April

*Approach:* From Interstate 15, take the Cima Road off ramp, and drive about 12 miles south on the paved Cima Road to a trailhead on the west side of the road. The trailhead is near a very broad divide at 5,035 feet.

*Route:* A trail heads west through a fine stand of Joshua trees and yucca to the summit rocks. Scattered junipers are encountered as the summit is approached. The true summit block is a rock climb. Anticipate four miles round-trip with about 750 feet of elevation gain.

## Ivanpah Mountains and the Mescal Range

The Ivanpah Mountains and Mescal Range form a rounded mountain mass just south of Mountain Pass along Interstate 15. The numerous springs in the area were important to the native inhabitants here. In fact, the name "Ivanpah" is a Paiute word roughly meaning "a small spring coming from a white soil." These mountains are home to deer, coyote, and other mammals, along with a variety of birds, particularly near the several springs in the area. Of interest to the historically-minded, are the numerous old mining camps in the area.

Camping here is primitive so all minimum impact camping methods should be applied. The nearest supplies, gasoline, food and lodging are in State Line (Primm) Nevada to the north, Searchlight, Nevada to the east or Baker, California to the west. It is a fair distance to any of these places so come prepared. For further information, contact the Bureau of Land Management offices in Needles and Riverside.

### KESSLER PEAK (6,161 FT; 1,878.5 M)

This granitic peak, the highpoint of the Ivanpah Mountains, provides a fine view of Cima Dome and Teutonia Peak. The peak is named in honor of a settler, Dan Kessler, who was supposedly killed by Indians around 1890. One of the suspected Indians was tried and hanged from an oak tree at Kessler Spring, though it is not certain if the Indian was actually guilty.

*Maps:* Cima Dome (CA) 7.5-minute (1:24,000 scale) topographic map; Ivanpah 1:100,000 scale metric topographic map; Automobile Club of Southern California (AAA) San Bernardino County map

*Best Time to Climb:* November through April

*Approach:* Park at the Teutonia Peak trailhead.

*Route:* From the trailhead, Kessler Peak is the obvious mountain on the east side of the road. Hike east, crossing a dirt road, then climbing east-southeast up the steep ridge to the summit. Anticipate two miles round-trip with 1,150 feet of elevation gain.

### STRIPED MOUNTAIN (5,953 FT; 1,815 M)

*Maps:* Mescal Range (CA) 7.5-minute (1:24,000 scale) topographic map; Ivanpah 1:100,000 scale metric topographic map; Automobile Club of Southern California (AAA) San Bernardino County map

*Best Time to Climb:* November through April

*Approach:* From Interstate 15, take the Cima Road off ramp, and drive 7.2 miles south to a dirt road heading east toward the mountains. Take the dirt road east (there are some parallel routes here but all will work) about 2.6 miles to a junction. Turn left on a dirt road that heads northeast toward the east side of Striped Mountain. Continue 2.5 miles to a dirt track heading west toward the peak. Turn left, and follow the road about 0.4 miles to a turnaround and park (5,280 ft). The route is easily passable in two-wheel drive vehicles with good clearance. Low slung cars may need to park 0.4 miles east of the road end.

*Route:* Hike up a steep track that heads south to the ridge, then west up the ridge to the peak. Anticipate 1.5 miles round-trip with 800 feet of elevation gain.

### KOKOWEEF PEAK (6,088 FT; 1,840+ M)

Kokoweef Peak, the legendary site of the "Lost River of Gold" provides fine views of the surrounding eastern Mojave Desert. Kokoweef is another of those place names that is actually a misspelled version of another name, and where the misspelled version stuck. The correct name was "Kokoweep" meaning "canyon of wind" in the local Paiute dialect. Kokoweep was a reference to the valley where the peak is located. From a geologic perspective, the most interesting aspect of this peak is the presence of the Clark Mountain Fault that runs along the east side of the peak. This fault has uplifted Precambrian-age metamorphic rocks next to younger carbonate rocks of the Kaibab limestone, Bird Spring formation, Monte Cristo limestone, and the Goodsprings dolomite (at the summit).

*Maps:* Mineral Hill (CA) 7.5-minute (1:24,000 scale) topographic map; Ivanpah 1:100,000 scale metric topographic map; Automobile Club of Southern California (AAA) San Bernardino County map

*Best Time to Climb:* November through April

*Approach:* Exit Interstate 15 at the Bailey Road/Mountain Pass off ramp. Follow a paved frontage road east 0.7 miles to where it turns south (and becomes dirt) into the Ivanpah Mountains. Continue another 1.9 miles to a fork. Head southeast (left) 1.2 miles to a road junction at the base of Kokoweef Peak. Either park here (5,250 ft) or continue to the east side of Kokoweef Peak where an old mining track winds up to within a few hundred feet of the summit. This approach is passable to most cars.

*Route:* One can climb the north ridge directly, or up the east side of the peak. Either way, don't expect more than two miles round-trip with 800 feet of elevation gain.

### "MESCAL MOUNTAIN" (6,499 FT; 1,981 M)

This peak is the highpoint of the small Mescal Range and nearby Ivanpah Mountains. The range could be considered part of the Ivanpah Mountains.

*Maps:* Mescal Range (CA) 7.5-minute (1:24,000 scale) topographic map; Ivanpah 1:100,000 scale metric topographic map; Automobile Club of

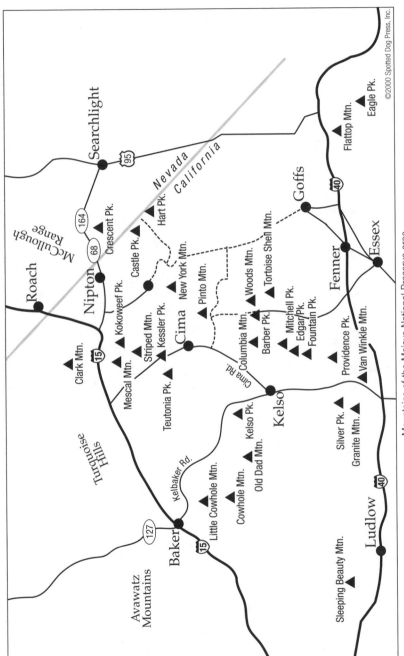

Mountains of the Mojave National Preserve area

©2000 Spotted Dog Press, Inc.

Southern California (AAA) San Bernardino County map
*Best Time to Climb:* November through April
*Approach:* Exit Interstate 15 at the Bailey Road/Mountain Pass off ramp. Follow a paved frontage road 0.7 miles east to where it turns south (and becomes dirt) into the Ivanpah Mountains. Continue another 1.9 miles to a fork. Stay right and continue another 1.1 miles south to another fork. Head west, and continue 0.9 miles to yet another fork. Turn right and continue a quarter mile to a parking area near the Iron Horse Mine (about 5,200 ft). Passable to two-wheel drive vehicles with good clearance.
*Route:* Continue up the road to a ridge line amid volcanic rock, then follow Mescal's northeast ridge southwest to the sedimentary rock-comprised summit, Anticipate three miles round-trip with 1,300 feet of elevation gain.

# NEW YORK MOUNTAINS

The New York Mountains rise as an imposing barrier above the south end of Ivanpah Valley. The range is something of an anomaly in this area, as it trends in a northeast direction, counter to the surrounding ranges that generally trend to the north, or even northwest. The entire New York Mountains, known as Avi Wacca in Mojave dialect, is an area of both sacred and mythological significance. The rugged, granitic ramparts of the range provide some of the most interesting mountaineering opportunities in the region from both a challenging aspect and from the surrounding scenery.

The New York Mountains rival the Kingston and Clark Ranges when it comes to biological diversity. Overall the vegetation is similar to Clark Mountain, and a small stand of about thirty white firs is present. Of particular interest is Carruthers Canyon where oak, holly, manzanita, pinyon and juniper are all present. The lower slopes of the range are generally covered by sagebrush, juniper and Joshua trees. A herd of about 30 bighorn sheep makes this range home, along with deer, mountain lion, and other animals. For the bird watcher, this area is a paradise. The New York Mountains provide one of only a few breeding localities for the Hepatic Tanager. The Gray Vireo, Yellow Warbler, Yellow-breasted Chat, and Golden Eagles are also present.

The northeastern portion of the range consists of a group of spires called the Castle Peaks, formerly known as the Castle Buttes. Although a part of the New York Mountains, the Castle Peaks area is an environment of its own, much different from the main body of the range. Portions of the

Castle Peaks area are covered by a combination of typical Mojavean plants, along with plant types more common in Arizona, and also hosting coastal chaparral (including California lilac) species. A small herd of bighorn sheep resides here, along with deer, moderate densities of desert tortoise, and the area also provides breeding habitat for Yellow Warblers, Golden Eagles and Prairie Falcons. The numerous mines in the area are interesting to visit from both geologic and historical perspectives. The first discovery of minerals in the New York Mountains was early in 1861.

Camping in the area is primitive so all minimum impact camping methods should be applied here. A developed campground within reasonably close proximity for climbing here is Mid Hills Campground. This campground is very convenient if intending to climb Pinto Mountain. The nearest gasoline, food, supplies and lodging are found at State Line (Primm) Nevada to the north, Searchlight, Nevada to the east or Baker, California to the west. It is a fair distance to any of these places so come prepared. The New York Mountains are within the Mojave National Preserve. For further information, contact the National Park Service office in Barstow, California, or the visitor centers in Baker or Needles.

### PINTO MOUNTAIN (6,142 FT; 1872.2 M)
A colorful, volcanic mesa, this mountain was a noted landmark along the old Mojave Road.

*Maps:* Mid Hills and Pinto Valley (CA) 7.5-minute (1:24,000 scale) topographic maps; Ivanpah 1:100,000 scale metric topographic map; Automobile Club of Southern California (AAA) San Bernardino County map

*Best Time to Climb:* November through April

*Approach:* From Interstate 15, take the Cima Road off ramp, and drive 12 miles south on the paved road to a junction. Turn south (right) and continue another 4.4 miles to the Cedar Canyon Road. Head 6.2 miles east on the Cedar Canyon Road (passable to all cars) to where the road crosses a wash just southwest of Pinto Mountain. Park here at about 5,100 feet.

*Route:* Hike 0.4 miles north to the mouth of the canyon, then continue north about another half mile to where the shallow canyon forks. Take the right fork, climbing out of the drainage and reaching a broad saddle to the east. The summit is visible from here. Anticipate 4.5 miles round-trip with 1,200 feet of elevation gain to the southeast.

## "NEW YORK MOUNTAIN" (7,530 FT; 2,295.8 M), "NORTH NEW YORK MOUNTAIN" (7,461 FT; 2,274.7 M)

New York Mountain (marked by a benchmark named New York Two), the highpoint of the range, is one of the more challenging peaks in the region. The views from its granitic summit block encompass the entire east Mojave and into western Arizona. Those who do not wish to tackle the Class 3 scramble up New York Mountain, may want to ascent North New York Mountain, an easy stroll from the saddle separating the two summits. Those climbing the rocky highpoint will also want to stroll over to North New York Mountain (marked by a benchmark named "New York") in order to gaze down at the impressive north slope of the range, a sight not readily appreciated from New York Mountain.

Seasonal stream in Carruthers Canyon near New York Mountain. Photo: Andy Zdon

*Maps:* Ivanpah and Pinto Valley (CA) 7.5-minute (1:24,000 scale) topographic maps; Ivanpah 1:100,000 scale metric topographic map; Automobile Club of Southern California San Bernardino County map
*Best Time to Climb:* October through May
*Approach:* From Baker, drive 40 miles north on Interstate 15 to the Nipton Road exit. Drive east on the Nipton Road 3.4 miles to the signed Ivanpah Road. Turn south (right) and follow the Ivanpah Road 11.9 miles, crossing

a set of railroad tracks, turning left and then right to where the road turns to dirt. Continue another six miles on a well-graded dirt road to a dirt road heading west (high clearance may be desirable). Follow the dirt road west 0.6 miles, bear right at a fork and continue another 1.8 miles, a good place for two-wheel drive vehicles to park. Four-wheel drive vehicles can bear left and continue another 0.7 miles up the canyon or as far as practicable. Note: The road conditions change drastically on this approach due to flash flooding and occasional road grading.

*Route:* Hike up the road to the right about a mile to a mine site. Climb southwest to a saddle at 2,060 meters (6,760 ft) via the steep slopes or the ridge to the right of the slope. Contour southwest, crossing the bottom of Carruthers Canyon, and up to the saddle north of the peak. Hike around to the north side of the summit block to reach its west side, and a Class 3 crack near the summit. The crack can then be climbed to the top. Some climbers may need a rope. The author and friends ascended the block from the west side. This route involved a "jump-across" move at an exposed spot and is not recommended. Anticipate five miles round-trip with 2,100 feet of elevation gain.

*Alternate Approach and Route 1:* Drive to the junction of the Nipton and Ivanpah Roads as for Route 1. Turn south (right) and follow the Ivanpah Road 11.9 miles, crossing a set of railroad tracks, turning left and then right to where the road turns to dirt. Continue another 12.3 miles on a well-graded dirt road to the signed New York Mountain Road heading west. Follow the New York Mountain Road west (high clearance may be desirable) 5.6 miles to its intersection with the Carruthers Canyon Road. Drive north on the Carruthers Canyon Road one mile to a fork and bear right. Staying right another 0.8 miles leads to the road end for most cars. There are excellent campsites amid pinyons and oak trees in the area. During spring, the wash bottom frequently contains running water, a prime water source for the area's wildlife. Hike up the road another 0.8 miles to the Giant Ledge Mine. Ascend a gully to the west-northwest, passing south of New York's prominent pinnacle. Once past the prominent pinnacle the summit rocks of New York will be visible. Climb around the south side of the summit rocks to the west side, and climb the crack described in Route 1. Anticipate four miles round-trip with 1,900 feet of elevation gain.

*Alternate Approach and Route 2:* In 1985, the author and some of his

Castle Peaks. Photo: Andy Zdon

buddies climbed the peak with a car shuttle from Fourth of July Canyon, camping on the small flat north of the summit block, and descending via Carruthers Canyon the following day. To reach Fourth of July Canyon, continue west on the New York Mountain Road past Carruthers Canyon to Pinto Valley where the New York Mountain Road turns sharply south. Instead of heading south, follow a dirt road north about two miles to the mouth of Fourth of July Canyon. At the time of that trip, there were some private lands in the area. Check with Mojave National Preserve regarding road access prior to doing this route.

### "Castle Peak" (5,834 ft; 1,778.7 m)

The high point of the Castle Peaks, marked with a benchmark named "Dove," Castle Peak is one of the most technically difficult peaks to climb in the Mojave region. Castle Peak and its finger-like neighbors are plainly visible when driving east on Interstate 15 from Mountain Pass. Their distinctive outlines somewhat resemble the skyscrapers of New York City, and being in close proximity to the New York Mountains, the name is fitting. Castle Peak is a technical Class 5 rock climb on volcanic rock and should only be attempted by climbers experienced in technical rock climbing.

*Maps:* Castle Peaks (CA) 7.5-minute (1:24,000 scale) topographic map; Ivanpah 1:100,000 scale metric topographic map; Automobile Club of Southern California (AAA) San Bernardino County map

*Best Time to Climb:* November through April

*Approach:* From Baker, California drive 40 miles north on Interstate 15

to the Nipton Road exit. If driving from Las Vegas, this exit is about ten miles south of State Line (Primm) Nevada. Drive 3.5 miles east on Nipton Road to the Ivanpah Road and turn right. Follow the Ivanpah Road 16.7 miles (becomes well-graded dirt after 11.9 miles) to the Hart Mine Road. Turn left on the Hart Mine Road and drive another 5.8 miles of well-graded dirt road to a fork. Turn north (left) and continue another 3.4 miles and park at the wilderness boundary. Two-wheel drive vehicles with good clearance are recommended.

*Route:* From the parking spot, continue hiking along tracks amid Joshua tree dotted hills, with the goal of reaching a saddle southwest of Castle Peaks, and shown on the topographic map between Point 1,665 meters and Point 1,661 meters. From the saddle, Castle Peak is the second pinnacle from the left. Head northeast, passing through, under or over a barbed wire fence and climb loose talus to a notch between Castle Peak and the pinnacle to its south. From the notch, hike around to the peak's east base where a Class 5 route ascends a crack to the right. Depending on where you park, you can anticipate four miles round-trip with between 1,000 and 1,500 feet of elevation gain.

### HART PEAK (5,542 FT; 1,689.5 M)

This sharp, volcanic peak is one of the more interesting in appearance within the region. Only sparse information is available on this peak.

*Maps:* Hart Peak (CA) 7.5-minute (1:24,000 scale) topographic map; Ivanpah 1:100,000 scale metric topographic map; Automobile Club of Southern California (AAA) San Bernardino County map

*Best Time to Climb:* November through April

*Approach:* From Baker, California drive 40 miles north on Interstate 15 to the Nipton Road exit. If driving from Las Vegas, this exit is about ten miles south of State Line (Primm) Nevada. Drive 3.5 miles east on Nipton Road to the Ivanpah Road and turn right. Follow the Ivanpah Road 16.7 miles (becomes well-graded dirt after 11.9 miles) to the Hart Mine Road. Turn left on the Hart Mine Road and drive 9.5 miles of well-graded dirt road to a junction. Turn right and continue about 1.2 miles and park at about 4,500 feet. Access to this route may change as a result of the mining operation in the area.

*Route:* From the parking area, hike east to the prominent saddle north of Hart Peak. The north slopes of Hart are reportedly Class 2-3.

# Peaks Accessible from Interstate 40

## Cady Mountains

The Cady Mountains rise as an extensive mountain range looming 3,000 feet over the Broadwell Basin and Mojave River Valley. The area is covered by the creosote scrub that is so common throughout the Mojave. A declining bighorn sheep herd roams the range. Golden Eagle and Prairie Falcon eyries have been noted here. The most interesting peak, Sleeping Beauty Mountain, is found at the southern end of the range. Sleeping Beauty was part of a volcano, and the area contains one of the thickest sections of Tertiary-age volcanic rocks in the region. The volcanic and sedimentary rocks of the Sleeping Beauty area are separated from the granite of the remaining Cady Mountains by a northeast-trending fault.

If planning on climbing this peak, supplies, gas, food and lodging are available at Barstow. Additionally, gas and food are available at Ludlow. Camping in the Cady Mountains is primitive, so minimum impact camping methods should be applied. Unfortunately, some campsites in the area show the impact of those who are not caring enough to apply these simple camping methods. For further information, contact the Barstow and Riverside offices of the Bureau of Land Management.

### Sleeping Beauty Mountain (3,980 ft; 1,213 m)

The author hiked this peak in October. The cool temperatures of late fall had not reached the desert and the ascent was nearly unbearable due to the triple-digit heat. Upon returning to the car (after having run out of water despite what seemed to be more than an ample supply at the beginning of the hike) about 48 ounces of water (about 32 of which were cloudy melted ice water in the cooler) were consumed with gusto. The peak has some of the sparsest vegetation of any range in the region. The Sleeping Beauty area is occasionally visited by the Cady Mountains herd of bighorn sheep although their numbers are declining and it is unclear how often this area is visited.

*Maps:* Sleeping Beauty (CA) 7.5-minute (1:24,000 scale) topographic map; Newberry Springs 1:100,000 scale metric topographic map; Automobile Club of Southern California San Bernardino County map

*Best Time to Climb:* November through April

*Approach:* From Barstow, drive 49 miles east on Interstate 40 to Ludlow.

Sleeping Beauty. Photo: Andy Zdon

Take the Ludlow off ramp and pass north under the freeway to the frontage road (the remains of old Route 66) that heads west. Drive 7.5 miles west on the frontage road to a dirt road heading north to Sleeping Beauty Mountain. Follow the dirt road north 1.8 miles to a gate. If access is not permitted beyond the gate, backtrack a quarter mile from the gate, then head east one mile to a dirt road heading north. Drive a quarter mile north to the mine area and park. Most cars should be able to reach the road end. *Route:* The route follows very loose ridges on volcanic rock that frequently have a surface that is seemingly covered by ball bearings. Only scattered creosote and a few other desert shrubs will bar the way on this peak. Anticipate four miles round-trip with about a thousand feet of elevation gain.

## GRANITE MOUNTAINS

The Granite Mountains are one of the dominant ranges of the Mojave Desert. Forming a granite barrier along the south end of the Kelso Valley, they stand guard over the extensive Kelso Dunes. The range's pinyon and juniper-covered ridges, and spring-fed canyons with cottonwood trees, yucca and cholla gardens provide some of the most interesting hiking opportunities in the California desert. The presence of a large number of springs, provides water to a rich fauna. A bighorn sheep herd of about 45 animals roams the boulder slopes of the range. Mule deer are common. Golden Eagles and Prairie Falcon eyries have been observed. Mountain lions are also present.

Many fine primitive campsites are available in the area. Granite Cove has long been a popular rock climbing spot. The closest gas and food can be found in Ludlow to the west or Needles to the east. If looking for lodging or supplies, one will have to drive long distances to either Needles, Barstow or Baker. The area is within the Mojave National Preserve, so for further information contact the National Park Service office in Barstow or the Visitor Centers in Baker and Needles.

### "Granite Mountain" (6,762 ft; 2,061 m)

The highpoint of the range, which towers above Kelso Dunes, Granite Mountain is unnamed on the topographic maps.

*Maps:* Bighorn Basin (CA) 7.5-minute (1:24,000 scale) topographic map; Amboy 1:100,000 scale metric topographic map; Automobile Club of Southern California (AAA) San Bernardino County map

*Best Time to Climb:* October through April

*Approach:* From Barstow, drive 78 miles east on Interstate 40, and exit on the Kelbaker Road off ramp. Turn north, and drive 9.4 miles on the

Cottonwood Spring, Granite Mountains. Photo: Andy Zdon

Kelbaker Road, crossing Granite Pass, to a dirt road heading southwest. Take this dirt road 1.7 miles to a junction. Park here at about 4,000 feet. Two-wheel drive vehicles with good clearance are recommended.

*Route:* From the road end, hike up the road a quarter mile to a junction. Bear right, and hike another quarter mile to a corral, then continuing straight on the track another 1.3 miles, always staying right at forks. From here, beautiful Cottonwood Spring is only a stone's throw away to the south. However, instead of wandering over to the spring, head southwest, following a boulder strewn wash, first through desert scrub, then through pinyon and juniper to the summit ridge just south of the summit. A short walk north leads to the summit

Granite Cove. Photo: Wynne Benti

with its expansive desert views. Anticipate seven miles round-trip with 2,600 feet of elevation gain.

### SILVER PEAK (6,300+ FT; 1,870+ M)
*Maps:* Bighorn Basin (CA) 7.5-minute (1:24,000 scale) topographic map; Amboy 1:100,000 scale metric topographic map; Automobile Club of Southern California (AAA) San Bernardino County map
*Best Time to Climb:* October through April
*Approach:* Follow the driving directions as for Granite Mountain.
*Route:* From the road end, follow the dirt track as it heads northwest across the basin and climbs up steep, rocky slopes to a ridge along the north slope of the range. Upon reaching the crest of the ridge, a climber's trail can be followed amid pinyon and juniper to the true summit. The summit provides a spectacular bird's-eye view of the Kelso Dunes. Anticipate eight to nine miles round trip with about 2,400 feet of elevation gain.

# PROVIDENCE MOUNTAINS

This rugged range, possibly the most scenic in the Mojave National Preserve, has four distinct sections: the southern granitic massif topped by Providence Peak, and separated from the rest of the range by Foshay Pass; the rugged volcanic section crowned by Fountain and Edgar Peaks; the limestone massif topped by Mitchell Peak; and the fourth more subdued terrain of which Columbia Mountain stands as the highpoint. Given the variety of terrains, and the large number of springs on their slopes, it is no wonder that these mountains are among the most visited in the area. It is the springs that led to the naming of the range. It was true providence to come across such fine watering places in such an arid region.

The upper slopes of the range are draped in pinyon-juniper woodlands that give way at lower elevations to yucca, Joshua trees, cactus, and a variety of desert shrubs. Bighorn sheep roam over the range, and are commonly found at the springs along the west range front. Deer, mountain lions, and bobcats are also present. The lower portions of the area have desert tortoise densities of up to 50 to 100 tortoises per square mile. Prairie Falcon and Golden Eagle eries have been noted here.

A trip to the Providence Mountains is not complete without a visit to Mitchell Caverns. These limestone caverns within the Paleozoic-age Bird Spring formation are not as spectacular as other well-known caves such as Mammoth Cave in Kentucky, Wind Cave in South Dakota, or Carlsbad Caverns in New Mexico, but they do contain a fascinating array of cave features. Developed campgrounds are available at Mitchell Caverns, and Hole In The Wall Campground. The campground at Mid Hills will be convenient if intending to hike up Columbia Mountain. Otherwise, primitive campsites can be found elsewhere. For further information, contact the National Park Service office in Barstow or the Visitor Centers in Baker and Needles.

### VAN WINKLE MOUNTAIN (4,595 FT; 1,401 M)
Although not part of the Providence Mountains proper, with a little imagination, this small peak could be lumped in with these mountains as an outlier. It does provide a fine viewpoint of the Granite Cove area.
*Maps:* Van Winkle Spring (CA) 7.5-minute (1:24,000 scale) topographic map; Amboy 1:100,000 scale metric topographic map; Automobile Club of Southern California (AAA) San Bernardino County map

*Best Time to Climb:* November through April

*Approach:* From Barstow, drive east on Interstate 40 and exit at Kelbaker Road. Drive about five miles north on Kelbaker Road, to a junction with a dirt road heading east, north of Van Winkle Mountain. Park near here at about 3,900 feet.

*Route:* Hike southeast up Van Winkle's northwest ridge to the summit. The final section is somewhat steep but passable. Anticipate three miles round-trip with 800 feet of elevation gain.

### "PROVIDENCE PEAK" (6,612 FT; 2,015.3 M)

Providence Peak, the highpoint of the Providence Mountains south of Foshay Pass, is a fine desert peak with expansive views of some of the best desert country in the southwestern U.S. The peak can be climbed from most any direction. Another interesting route not described below for those with four-wheel drive would be a ridge line route from Goldstone Spring, accessed from Foshay Pass (four-wheel drive required). Goldstone Spring has a pipe with running water, but the ground is covered with cattle dung, and I am unsure of the biological quality of the water. Boiling or filtering the water if you have to use it is recommended. There should be little reason to use this water as all the water you need should be stocked in your pack and in your vehicle, a short distance from the spring. Mule deer and bighorn sheep are commonly seen in this area due to the number of springs.

*Maps:* Van Winkle Spring and Fountain Peak (CA) 7.5-minute (1:24,000 scale) topographic maps; Amboy 1:100,000 scale metric topographic map; Automobile Club of Southern California (AAA) San Bernardino County map

*Best Time to Climb:* November through April

*Approach:* From Barstow, drive east on Interstate 40 and exit at Kelbaker Road. Drive about 9.2 miles north on Kelbaker Road, passing over Granite Pass, to a dirt road heading east. Follow the road 1.7 miles to the site of the old Pine Tree Ranch and Arroweed Spring (incorrectly named Arrowhead Spring on some Automobile Club of Southern California San Bernardino County road maps) and park (4,030 ft) here at the wilderness boundary. Two-wheel drive vehicles should have no problem with this approach.

*Route:* From Arroweed Spring, hike about a mile northeast along the base of the mountains, to a dirt track that heads up a canyon to the east. If all goes well, you should reach this road just east of Point 1,253

Goldstone Spring in the Providence Mountains. Photo: Andy Zdon

meters. The mile involves numerous wash crossings with anything but a level traverse. Hike up the track, and climb to the saddle at the head of the canyon, first following the wash, then on the surrounding ridges. From the saddle, climb northeast to a saddle just east of Point 1,956 meters, then head directly northeast toward the summit. Some minor elevation loss is encountered, but the going is easier than following the ridge line. Anticipate eight miles round-trip with about 3,600 feet of elevation gain.

### FOUNTAIN PEAK (6,988 FT; 2,130 M)

The views from this fine desert peak are astounding, particularly north along the crest of the range to Edgar and Mitchell Peaks. The peak is only climbed maybe once or twice a year. From the summit, we down-climbed the canyon directly below the peak and encountered dry waterfalls, other drop-offs, very unstable talus, and heavy growths of catclaw, prickly pear and cholla. This alternate route is not recommended.

*Maps:* Fountain Peak (CA) 7.5-minute (1:24,000 scale) topographic map; Amboy 1:100,000 scale metric topographic map; Automobile Club of Southern California (AAA) San Bernardino County map

*Best Time to Climb:* November through April

*Approach:* From Barstow, drive 109 miles east on Interstate 40 to the Essex Road off ramp. Turn left on Essex Road and drive 15.6 miles to the Mitchell Caverns Visitor Center and park (4,265 ft). The road is paved and accessible to all cars.

*Route:* Behind the visitor center, follow the delightful trail to Crystal Spring, surrounded by sage, cacti, and yuccas. Crystal Spring was used by Jack Mitchell as a water source for his settlement at Mitchell Caverns. From Crystal Spring, continue cross country up the canyon to a saddle. The brush and cholla of the lower canyon give way to scattered pinyon, juniper and oak higher up. Be wary of catclaw, cholla and yucca. The crest is then followed northward to the peak, generally staying west of the crest. Some easy Class 3 scrambling will be encountered. Return the same way. Anticipate four miles round-trip with 2,750 feet of elevation gain.

### EDGAR PEAK (7,162 FT; 2,183 M)

Edgar Peak, the highpoint of the Providence Mountains, is one of the outstanding peaks of the Mojave, particularly for the views from its rocky summit.

Edgar (right front) and Mitchell (left back) from the summit of Fountain Peak. Photo: Andy Zdon

*Maps:* Fountain Peak (CA) 7.5-minute (1:24,000 scale) topographic map; Amboy 1:100,000 scale metric topographic map; Automobile Club of Southern California (AAA) San Bernardino County map

*Best Time to Climb:* November through April

*Access:* From Barstow, drive 109 miles east on Interstate 40 to the Essex Road off ramp. Turn left on Essex Road and drive 15.6 miles to the Mitchell Caverns Visitor Center and park (4,265 ft). The road is paved and accessible to all cars.

*Route:* From the parking lot, follow the Mary Beal Nature Trail northwest about a half mile to its end, and continue west up the main canyon. At a fork in the canyon at 1,800 meters on the metric map (5,900 ft), head up the right fork and climb to a saddle a quarter mile south of the peak. Head north, following the rocky ridge to the top. Difficult false summits can be bypassed. Anticipate five miles round-trip with 2,900 feet of elevation gain.

*Alternate Approach and Route:* Drive to Mitchell Caverns as described above. Inquire at the visitor center regarding access and driving instructions to the Winding Stair Cave Road. If the road can be accessed, Edgar Peak can be climbed via Gilroy Canyon, and combined with Mitchell Peak as a loop trip with a descent via Mitchell's loose, ball-bearing gravel, cactus-filled southeast ridge. The total round-trip statistics for this loop are about six miles with 3,600 feet of elevation gain.

### "Mitchell Peak" (7,048 ft; 2,148.2 m)

This massive limestone peak, the most impressive of the Providence Mountains when viewed from Kelso Valley, is named for J.E. Mitchell, the developer of Mitchell Caverns on the range's east slope. The starting point of this hike, the site of Providence was a hub of activity during the 1870's and 1880's. The town was built to serve the richest mine in the area, the Bonanza King, that reportedly produced more than $1,000,000 during one eighteen month period.

*Maps:* Fountain Peak (CA) 7.5-minute (1:24,000 scale) topographic map; Amboy 1:100,000 scale metric topographic map; Automobile Club of Southern California (AAA) San Bernardino County map

*Best Time to Climb:* November through April

*Access:* From Barstow, drive 109 miles east on Interstate 40 to the Essex Road off ramp. Turn left on Essex Road and drive 10.6 miles to a graded dirt road heading northwest. This road has been signed "Blair Bros. 7IL Ranch." Take this graded but "washboard" dirt road 4.9 miles to a fork and turn left. Drive 0.8 miles to another fork. Bear right, and continue 2.3 miles to the remains of the town of Providence. Park here at about 3,800 feet.

*Route:* Head south up the road, over a saddle to some stone cabins (part of the ghost town). Hike southwest along the range front, then west up a slope to gain the east ridge of Mitchell Peak. Climb the east ridge to the summit. It will be necessary to bypass the sharp ridge line on its south side at one point.

*Alternate:* The peak can be combined with Edgar Peak as described for the Edgar Peak alternate route.

### Columbia Mountain (5,673 ft; 1,729.1 m)

This small, granitic mountain, provides fine views of the Kelso Valley and surrounding country.

*Maps:* Columbia Mountain (CA) 7.5-minute (1:24,000 scale) topographic map; Ivanpah 1:100,000 scale metric topographic map; Automobile Club of Southern California (AAA) San Bernardino County map

*Best Time to Climb:* November through April

Mitchell Caverns. Photo: Andy Zdon

*Approach:* From Barstow, drive 109 miles east on Interstate 40 to the Essex Road off ramp. Turn left on Essex Road and drive 9.7 miles northwest to the junction with the Black Canyon Road (Hole In The Wall Road). Turn north onto the Black Canyon Road, and continue another nine miles to the Wildhorse Canyon Road (good dirt) that heads west, just south of Hole In The Wall Campground. Follow the Wildhorse Canyon Road northwest 5.9 miles to a poor dirt road that heads west down the wash of upper Macedonia Canyon. Two-wheel drive vehicles should park here (4,946 ft). The road down Macedonia Canyon is accessible to four-wheel drive vehicles but can become very sandy.

*Route:* From the Wildhorse Canyon Road, hike down the Macedonia Canyon road about 0.6 miles, then climb Columbia's southeast slopes to the summit. There is no need to follow the track that loops around to the north ridge of the peak. If hiking from Wildhorse Canyon Road, anticipate 2.5 miles round-trip with 900 feet of elevation gain.

# PEAKS AROUND LANFAIR VALLEY

Lanfair Valley, in the Mojave National Preserve, is south of the New York Mountains, north of Interstate 40, and west of the Piute Range. For years, standing in the middle of this vast desert valley was a lone pay phone, a fabulous surrealistic connection with the outside world. People came from all over the planet to use the phone and have their picture taken next to it. The humble pay phone saved more than one near-stranded life. Sadly, just before press time, CNN reported the phone, now considered an environmental blight upon the desert, was being removed.

## "BARBER PEAK" (5,504 FT; 1,677.5 M)

This irregular mesa provides a fine view of Gold Valley and a view of the Providence Mountains reminiscent of the Colorado Plateau. When the author climbed this peak in 1982, very few ascents had been previously recorded. With the new campground, the peak may become more popular. The summit is marked by a benchmark named "Barber."

*Maps:* Columbia Mountain (CA) 7.5-minute (1:24,000 scale) topographic map; Ivanpah 1:100,000 scale metric topographic map; Automobile Club of Southern California (AAA) San Bernardino County map

*Best Time to Climb:* November through April

*Approach:* Drive to Hole In The Wall Campground (4,265 ft) as described for Columbia Mountain.

*Route:* From the campground, hike north along the base of the mesa, until a shallow draw is reached that cuts through the rim of the mesa. Follow the draw to the summit plateau, then stroll along the mesa, amid a few particularly photogenic junipers and pinyons, to the summit, the farthest point west. The flatness of Table Mountain's summit is striking from this vantage point. Anticipate three miles round-trip with 1,000 feet of elevation gain.

## TABLE MOUNTAIN (ALSO KNOWN AS TABLE TOP) (6,178 FT; 1,883 M)

This volcanic mesa is a prominent landmark, clearly visible from Interstate 40 east of the Providence Mountains, as a flat mesa on the northern skyline. Vegetation varies from sagebrush around the base of the mountain, to pinyon and juniper with increasing elevation. Upon reaching the summit, a circumnavigation of the mesa rim is a fine addition to the ascent.

*Maps:* Columbia Mountain and Woods Mountain (CA) 7.5-minute (1:24,000 scale) topographic maps; Ivanpah 1:100,000 scale metric topographic

Russ White and Dave Clegg along the rim of Table Mountain. Photo: Andy Zdon

map; Automobile Club of Southern California (AAA) San Bernardino County map

*Best Time to Climb:* November through April

*Approach:* Drive to Hole In The Wall Campground as described for Columbia Mountain. From Hole In The Wall Campground, continue 3.4 miles north on the Black Canyon Road to a dirt road heading northeast. Leave the Black Canyon Road, and continue along the dirt track northeast about 1.5 miles to a mine shaft. Park here. The road is accessible to most vehicles.

*Route:* Hike northeast to a small drainage that cuts the south side of the mountain. Scramble up along this drainage, making your way through a break in the cliffs to the summit plateau. The summit is marked with a wood surveyor's marker. Anticipate 5.5 miles round-trip with 1,000 feet of elevation gain if starting from the end of the road.

*Alternate Approach and Route:* One can climb Table Mountain by parking along the Black Canyon Road where it meets Table Mountain's west ridge. Hike along the southern base of the mountain until a suitable route can be followed up a pinyon-juniper dotted draw toward the summit plateau. This route has only minor additional mileage and elevation gain.

# WOODS MOUNTAINS

This small but colorful range east of Hole In The Wall Campground provides excellent flora-related photographic opportunities. Cactus gardens of prickly pear, cholla, barrel cactus, and very large yuccas are scattered throughout the range, which also supports a wide variety of bird and mammal species.

The Woods Mountains and neighboring Hackberry Mountain are the remnants of an eleven million year old volcanic center. Some of the volcanic activity may even have been as old as eighteen million years. The results of the eruptive events that took place here can be seen in the many layered volcanic buttes and mesas, both within the Woods and Hackberry Mountains, and beyond, including Barber Peak, Table Mountain and Pinto Mountain. The famous "Hole In The Wall" is the result of erosional processes taking place on these volcanic rocks.

### "WOODS MOUNTAIN" (5,589 FT; 1,704 M)

The highpoint of the Woods Mountains, Woods Mountain is unnamed on the topographic map. Woods Mountain can be dayhiked from Hole In The Wall Campground. It is possible to drive closer to the peak if so desired.
*Maps:* Columbia Mountain and Woods Mountain (CA) 7.5-minute (1:24,000 scale) topographic maps; Ivanpah 1:100,000 scale metric topographic map; Automobile Club of Southern California (AAA) San Bernardino County Map
*Best Time to Climb:* November through April
*Approach:* Drive to Hole In The Wall Campground (4,265 ft) as described for Columbia Mountain.
*Route:* From the campground, hike due east toward Black Canyon Wash. Hike north up the wash, staying right where the wash forks, until east or northeast of the summit. One can climb directly to the summit or up to the mountain's northwest ridge which can then be followed to the summit. Anticipate six miles round-trip with 1,250 feet of elevation gain.

### TORTOISE SHELL MOUNTAIN (4,601 FT; 1,400+ M)

*Maps:* Columbia Mountain and Woods Mountain (CA) 7.5-minute (1:24,000 scale) topographic maps; Ivanpah 1:100,000 scale metric topographic map; Automobile Club of Southern California (AAA) San Bernardino County map
*Best Time to Climb:* November through April

*Approach:* Drive to Hole In The Wall Campground (4,265 ft) as described for Columbia Mountain.

*Route:* Although roads can be used to get closer to the summit, the campground makes a fine place to leave your car while on this hike. From the campground, hike due east toward the Woods Mountains, meeting Black Canyon Wash at the base of the mountains. Hike about 1.7 miles southeast along the wash, passing south of Rustler Canyon and Grass Canyon until at a point just south of Point 1,247 meters. Leave the wash here and head east-northeast, crossing the wash coming down from Burro Canyon, and climbing northeast up the broad ridge that curves southeast to the summit. Anticipate 7.5 miles round-trip with 1,300 feet of elevation gain.

## PEAKS SOUTH OF INTERSTATE 40

This section includes those peaks south of Interstate 40, and north of Highway 62. All of these ranges are outside the boundary of Mojave National Preserve, and regulations typical of desert Bureau of Land Management lands apply.

## ORD MOUNTAINS

This range is composed primarily of volcanic rocks including andesite, dacite, and tuff known to geologists as the "Sidewinder Volcanic Series." Granitic rocks are also present. Copper, gold and silver have been mined in these mountains since the 1870's. In fact, the name of the range came from a group of mining claims staked here in 1876, named in honor of a General O.C. Ord, under whom the prospector served. Ord was the leader of the first official survey of Los Angeles. Covered by creosote scrub, there are few if any "desert trees" in the range. Supplies, gas, food and lodging are available in Victorville and Barstow. Camping in the area is primitive so minimum impact camping methods apply. For further information, contact the Bureau of Land Management offices in Barstow and Riverside.

### WEST ORD MOUNTAIN (5,525 FT; 1,684 M)

*Maps:* Ord Mountain, Grand View Mine, Fry Mountains, and Camp Rock Mine (CA) 7.5-minute (1:24,000 scale) topographic maps; Newberry Springs 1:100,000 scale metric topographic map; Automobile Club of Southern California (AAA) San Bernardino County map

*Best Time to Climb:* November through April

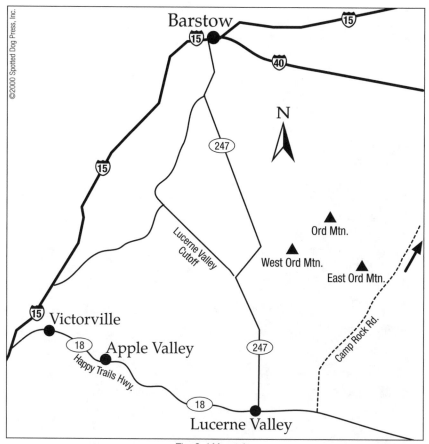

The Ord Mountains

*Approach:* From Interstate 15 in Victorville, take the "D Street" (Highway 18) offramp to Apple Valley. Drive 23 miles east on Highway 18 (named the "Happy Trails Highway" in honor of Roy Rogers) to the junction of Highways 18 and 247 (Barstow Road). Turn left (north) on Highway 247 and continue about 14 miles to where the paved road curves to the left. From the curve, multiple dirt roads continue straight northeast up the valley toward the peak. Follow any of the dirt roads northeast about a mile to near Taylor Spring, and park at about 4,000 feet. This route is accessible to all cars.

*Route:* Climb a ridge eastward to the summit ridge. Anticipate 2.5 miles round-trip with 1,600 feet of elevation gain.

Heading up East Ord.  Photo: Wynne Benti

## ORD MOUNTAIN (6,309 FT; 1,923 M)

*Maps:* Ord Mountain, Grand View Mine, Fry Mountains, and Camp Rock Mine (CA) 7.5-minute (1:24,000 scale) topographic maps; Newberry Springs 1:100,000 scale metric topographic map; Automobile Club of Southern California (AAA) San Bernardino County map

*Best Time to Climb:* November through April

*Approach:* From Interstate 15 in Victorville, take the "D Street" (Highway 18) offramp to Apple Valley. Drive 23 miles east on Highway 18 to the junction of Highways 18 and 247. Head east on Highway 247 five miles to the Camp Rock Road. Turn north, driving four miles to a fork. Stay left and continue another 8.8 miles on a graded dirt road to a junction. Turn east (right) and drive 0.4 miles to another junction. Turn left and continue about three miles to a saddle at the north end of Tyler Valley, and west of the peak (about 4,500 ft). Four-wheel drive is recommended.

*Route:* From the saddle head east-northeast up a ridge that leads to the summit plateau. The highpoint is on the northeast side of the plateau. Anticipate five miles round-trip with 1,800 feet of elevation gain.

## EAST ORD MOUNTAIN (6,168 FT; 1,880 M)

East Ord Mountain is the most prominent, though not the highest peak in the range (Ord Mountain). The route meanders through creosote scrub and other Mojave shrubs and grasses.

*Maps:* Ord Mountain, Grand View Mine, Fry Mountains, and Camp Rock Mine (CA) 7.5-minute (1:24,000 scale) topographic maps; Newberry Springs 1:100,000 scale metric topographic map; Automobile Club of Southern California (AAA) San Bernardino County map

*Best Time to Climb:* November through April

*Approach:* Interstate 15 in Victorville, take the "D Street" (Highway 18) offramp to Apple Valley. Drive 23 miles east on Highway 18 to the junction of Highways 18 and 247. Head east on Highway 247 five miles to the Camp Rock Road. Turn north, driving four miles to a fork. Bear right, and continue another 9.1 miles to a dirt road that heads northwest to the peak. Turn left, and drive 0.5 miles, crossing a power line road, to a junction. Turn right and continue 0.9 miles to a fork, bearing right and continuing another 0.7 miles to some ruins. Park here. Four-wheel drive vehicles could continue another 0.4 miles to a guzzler at 4,100 feet, but it is best to not park near desert wildlife watering places such as this, as it tends to scare

Sheephole Mountain crest.  Photo: Wynne Benti

the wildlife away from them.

*Route:* Hike up the road to the guzzler, then up the rocky, scrub-filled wash about a quarter mile to a fork. Take the right fork of the wash, and follow the wash, or the ridge to east, to the summit rocks. Anticipate three miles round-trip with 2,200 feet of elevation gain.

## SHEEPHOLE MOUNTAINS

The Sheephole Mountains dominate the northeastern skyline when viewed from most any high summit in Joshua Tree National Park. The Sheepholes' rugged skyline, impressive-looking from surrounding valleys, is even more spectacular when experienced firsthand by those who brave the steep, boulder-laden slopes. A small herd of bighorn sheep roams these rugged mountains, and are only occasionally seen.

The highpoint of the range, Sheephole Mountain, is within the 175,000-acre Sheephole Valley Wilderness. Camping in the area is primitive. This peak can be easily climbed in one day from a campsite at the north end of Joshua Tree National Park, such as Jumbo Rock. Supplies, gas, food and lodging are available in Twentynine Palms or Yucca Valley. For further information, contact the Bureau of Land Management offices in Needles and Riverside.

### SHEEPHOLE MOUNTAIN (4,613 FT; 1,400+ M)

*Maps:* Dale Lake (CA) 7.5-minute (1:24,000 scale) topographic map; Sheep Hole Mountains 1:100,000 scale metric topographic map; Automobile Club of Southern California (AAA) San Bernardino County map

*Best Time to Climb:* November through April

*Approach:* From the main intersection in Twentynine Palms, California, turn north, leaving Highway 62, and drive two miles to the paved Amboy Road heading east. Follow the Amboy Road about 25 miles to the summit of Sheephole Pass. A dirt road heads east about a quarter mile to a microwave relay station. Park here at about 2,430 feet. This approach is passable to all cars.

*Route:* From the microwave relay station, hike east-southeast up a steep draw that heads up to the north-south trending crest just south of Point 1,310+ meters. From the ridge, the summit of Sheephole looks jagged and impressive. The views to the east from atop the range's steep slopes gives pause to the hiker, a great spot for a rest. The ridge is then followed, skirting the actual crest on a use trail until the summit rocks of the peak are reached and climbed from the southwest. Anticipate four miles round-trip with 2,300 feet of elevation gain.

# IRON MOUNTAINS

The Iron Mountains rise nearly 3,000 feet above the Ward and Cadiz Valleys, and are a northward extension of the Granite Mountains to the south. The mountains are covered by creosote and other desert shrubs. Camping in the area is primitive so all minimum impact camping methods apply. Supplies, gas, food and lodging are available in Twentynine Palms. For further information, contact the Bureau of Land Management offices in Needles and Riverside.

### IRON MOUNTAIN (3,330 FT; 1,015 M)

With grand views of the Cadiz and Ward Valleys from the summit, Iron Mountain has an odd distinction. The Colorado River Aqueduct's Iron Mountain Tunnel passes through it, nearly 2,400 feet beneath the summit. *Maps:* Iron Mountains and Granite Pass (CA) 7.5-minute (1:24,000 scale) topographic maps; Sheep Hole Mountains 1:100,000 scale metric topographic map; Automobile Club of Southern California (AAA) San Bernardino County map

*Best Time to Climb:* November through April

*Approach:* From Twentynine Palms, drive 51 miles east on Highway 62 to its junction with Highway 177. This junction can also be reached from Desert Center along Interstate 10, by driving 27 miles north on Highway 177 to its junction with Highway 62. From the junction of Highways 62 and 177, drive one mile east on Highway 62 to a power line road. A sign states, "Private Right of Way–any person entering thereon does so at his own risk–Permission to pass is revocable at any time–Metropolitan Water District of Southern California." Turn left, and follow the power line road 6.7 miles to a dirt road on the left. Turn north and follow the dirt road to a borrow pit. The dirt roads on this route are of generally excellent quality, and should be passable to almost all vehicles.

*Route:* Head south-southwest to a large northwest-trending canyon. The canyon has two forks, so take the left (more westerly) fork up the canyon to another fork. Bear left and follow the wash until a chute is climbed to the southeast ridge of the peak. Upon reaching the ridge crest, head northwest to the summit. Anticipate six miles round-trip with about 2,200 feet of elevation gain.

## MARBLE MOUNTAINS

The Marble Mountains are defined by a long northwest-trending ridge. Vegetation is sparse on the slopes, but dense creosote grows on the alluvial fans surrounding the range. The opportunities for solitude are great, and a climb of Castle Peak is likely to be a quiet one. Bighorn sheep herds roam the range.

The portion of the Marble Mountains in the Castle Peak area consists of volcanic rocks overlying granitic and Cambrian-age sedimentary rocks. Castle Peak, the highpoint of the range, is within the 31,000-acre Trilobite Wilderness, named for the classic fossils that can be found in the green Latham shale. For those who hike in the Grand Canyon, this shale is correlative to the Bright Angel shale in the Canyon.

Camping in the area is primitive so all minimum impact camping methods apply. The nearest supplies, gas, food and lodging are 50 miles west in Needles. Additionally, there is lodging in Amboy at the little motel that has been used in countless movies and commercials. For further information, contact the Bureau of Land Management offices in Needles and Riverside.

## "CASTLE PEAK" (3,842 FT; 1,171 M)

This peak is marked by a benchmark named "Castle" on the topo map.
*Maps:* Van Winkle Wash (CA) 7.5-minute (1:24,000 scale) topographic map;
Amboy 1:100,000 scale metric topographic map; Automobile Club of
Southern California (AAA) San Bernardino County map
*Best Time to Climb:* November through April
*Approach:* From Barstow, California drive east on Interstate 40 and exit at
Kelbaker Road. Drive about 1.5 miles south on Kelbaker Road to a dirt
pipeline road heading east. Follow the rough pipeline road (four-wheel
drive recommended) about 3.2 miles east over a divide, to a fork. Take the
right fork as far as practicable and park. The end of the road is about 0.8
miles from the pipeline road (2,820 ft).
*Route:* From the road end, follow the wash south, then up a broad ridge to
a draw on the north side of the peak. Follow the draw to the summit area.
Anticipate three miles round-trip with about 1,100 feet of elevation gain.

# OLD WOMAN MOUNTAINS

The Old Woman Mountains are a large and diverse range offering an
array of climbing, from easy dayhikes to a technical climb of Old Woman
Statue. Rising steeply from the surrounding valleys, deep canyons cut
across the range. Gentle slopes quickly become jagged and spire-like.
Vegetation in the range includes creosote, yucca, nolina, barrel cactus, with
scattered junipers and pinyon on the highest slopes. There are numerous
springs, which are the main water source for a herd of about forty-five
bighorn sheep that have made the Old Woman Mountains their permanent range. Desert tortoises are also found in the area. The Chemehuevi,
Mohave, and Panamint Shoshone traditionally hunted here.

Routes on the two principal summits in the range are described below.
These peaks are within the 146,000-acre Old Woman Mountains Wilderness.
Other peaks in the range offering hiking opportunities are Carbonate Peak
and Mercury Mountain. Routes on those peaks are fairly obvious and
will be left to the hiker to identify. Camping in the area is primitive and
all minimum impact camping methods should be observed. The nearest
supplies, gas, food and lodging are in Needles, about 35 miles northeast.
There are private lands within the wilderness so please respect the
rights of the landowners and do not use their lands without permission.
For further information, contact the Bureau of Land Management offices
in Needles and Riverside.

## "OLD WOMAN MOUNTAIN" (5,325 FT; 1,623 M)

It is not until reaching the summit of this, the highpoint of the Old Woman Mountains, that the vastness of the range can be fully appreciated. The route to the summit is steep but stable through yucca, juniper and a few scattered pinyon pine. The summit is marked by a benchmark named "Woman."

*Maps:* Old Woman Statue (CA) 7.5-minute (1:24,000 scale) topographic map; Amboy 1:100,000 scale metric topographic map; Automobile Club of Southern California (AAA) San Bernardino County map

*Best Time to Climb:* November through April

*Approach:* From Barstow, California drive 52 miles east on Interstate 40 to Ludlow. In Ludlow, continue east on old Route 66, the National Trails Highway. Follow Route 66 about 53 miles, passing through Amboy to the Danby Road. Turn southeast onto the dirt Danby Road, and follow it 8.7 miles, crossing a set of railroad tracks, to the Florence Mine (1,720 ft). There are some rough areas between the tracks and the mine, and a vehicle with high clearance is recommended.

*Route:* From the Florence Mine, head south up a gully to a saddle. Contour south on a climbers' path to a wash that is followed to the northwest ridge of Old Woman Mountain. Follow the ridge southeast to the summit. On the way up, a rocky spur ridge with jagged pinnacles provides interesting scenery. From the summit, the views of the entire East Mojave are spectacular, and plan on spending at least an hour to take in the full panorama. The view south along the crest of the range reveals just how extensive this otherwise unknown desert range is. Anticipate three miles round-trip with 2,300 feet of elevation gain.

*Alternate Route:* This peak has also been climbed via the south and southeast slopes from Carbonate Gulch. The route is approximately the same length, but given the much rougher roads for the Carbonate Gulch approach, this route is not recommended, unless planning to climb other peaks in the area.

## OLD WOMAN STATUE (5,105 FT; 1,556 M)

*Maps:* Old Woman Statue and Painted Rock Wash (CA) 7.5-minute (1:24,000 scale) topographic maps; Amboy 1:100,000 scale metric topographic map; Automobile Club of Southern California (AAA) San Bernardino County map

*Best Time to Climb:* November through April

*Approach:* From Barstow, California drive about a hundred miles east on

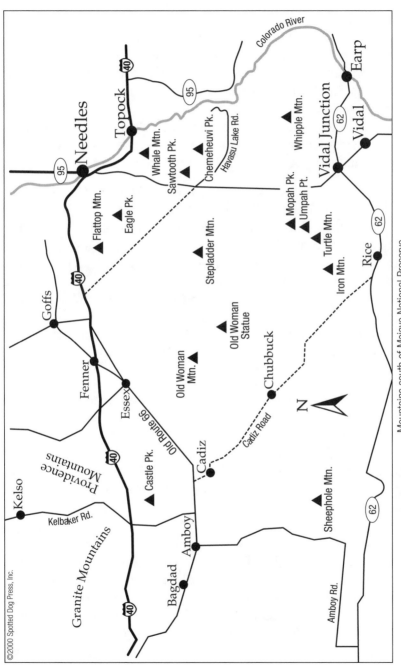

Mountains south of Mojave National Preserve

©2000 Spotted Dog Press, Inc.

Interstate 40 to the Essex turnoff, and drive south to the "town" of Essex (no services). From Essex, take a dirt road that crosses the railroad tracks and heads southeast 19 miles to a junction. Take the newer right-hand road to Weaver's Well. Take the left-hand fork at Weaver's Well, then south on the Painted Rock Road, to the actual well. Four-wheel drive is recommended for this route.

*Route:* From the well, hike northwest to a saddle at 4,400 feet, then continue to the west side of the summit block. A third class move over a chockstone leads to a mid-to-upper Class 5 rock climb to the summit.

## SACRAMENTO MOUNTAINS

Against a cloudless sky, the silhouette of the Sacramento Mountains, rising above the Colorado River Valley, is quietly subdued, lacking the dramatic pinnacles and jagged edges of neighboring ranges. Creosote is the dominant desert shrub in the area. Other vegetation types include blackbrush, brittlebrush, desert holly, cholla and bursage. The two rather short hikes described here offer secluded, but convenient hiking close to the town of Needles. Supplies, gas, food and lodging are all available in Needles. For further information regarding the Sacramento Mountains, contact the Bureau of Land Management offices in Needles and Riverside.

### FLATTOP MOUNTAIN (3,029 FT; 923 M)

This dark brown, truncated cone is a noteworthy landmark in the region. Expect to encounter loose talus on the way to the summit and its fine views of the Colorado River Valley.

*Maps:* West of Flattop Mountain and Flattop Mountain (CA) 7.5-minute (1:24,000 scale) topographic maps; Needles 1:100,000 scale metric topographic map; Automobile Club of Southern California (AAA) San Bernardino County map

*Best Time to Climb:* November through April

*Approach:* From Barstow, California drive about 129 miles east on Interstate 40 and exit at the Water Road off-ramp. This is about 4.8 miles west of Mountain Springs Summit, and about 22 miles west of Needles. On the south side of the power substation, two dirt roads stretch out in front of you. Take the left road (marked "to Highway 95" on a stake) as it heads east, then southeast 4.9 miles on a graded dirt power line road to a junction. Turn east (left) and continue 3.8 miles to a junction. Park here at about

2,300 feet. Two-wheel drive vehicles with high clearance recommended. When driving the power line road, don't let the well-graded nature of the road lead you to complacency. Some ruts that are nearly invisible until you reach them could lead to a bent rim if approached too quickly.

*Route:* From the parking spot, the peak is directly ahead of you to the east. Follow any likely looking route to the summit. Some steep, loose talus is unavoidable. Anticipate three miles round-trip with 750 feet of elevation gain.

### EAGLE PEAK (3,308 FT; 1,008 M)

*Maps:* Flattop Mountain and Needles SW (CA) 7.5-minute (1:24,000 scale) topographic maps; Needles 1:100,000 scale metric topographic maps; Automobile Club of Southern California (AAA) San Bernardino County map

*Best Time to Climb:* November through April

*Approach:* Follow the route to the Flattop turnoff on the power line road described above. Continue on the power line road another 4.4 miles to a junction. Turn left on the Eagle Pass Road which is followed east to Eagle Pass along the crest of the range at about 1,800 feet. Four-wheel drive vehicles are recommended to the pass.

*Route:* The peak is due north. Anticipate two miles round-trip with 1,500 feet of elevation gain.

## STEPLADDER MOUNTAINS

A low but rugged range, the Stepladder Mountains provide outstanding desert hiking country. Stepladder Mountain is one of the author's favorites. Crossing the gently sloping bahada on the east side of the range in spring, one will pass scattered ocotillo in full bright red bloom, Mojave yucca, creosote, and other desert shrubs. The Stepladder Mountains were once a viable bighorn sheep habitat, but they have all but disappeared from the range. Stepladder Mountain is the highpoint of the range and is within the 82,000-acre Stepladder Mountains Wilderness. Camping in the area is primitive so all the usual minimum impact camping methods are observed. The nearest supplies, gas, food and lodging are in Needles, about 15 miles to the northeast. For further information, contact the Bureau of Land Management offices in Needles and Riverside.

## "Stepladder Mountain" (2,927 ft; 892 m)

From a distance, the ascent of Stepladder Mountain, on the north end of the Chemeheuvi Valley, looks more difficult than it really is. Stands of ocotillo, creosote scrub, cholla, yucca, and catclaw sweep across the gently rolling desert terrain before the steepest part of the hike is reached. Typical of most desert plants, these are packed with thorns and spines and seem to want to leap on to anything passing by too closely. There are fine views from the small, rocky summit.

*Map:* Stepladder Mountains (CA) 7.5-minute (1:24,000 scale) topographic map; Needles 1:100,000 scale metric topographic map; Automobile Club of Southern California (AAA) San Bernardino County map

*Best Time to Climb:* November through April

*Approach:* From Needles, California on Interstate 40, drive 11.4 miles south on Highway 95 to a pipe line road marked by a stop sign. Turn west, and drive 8.4 miles to its junction with a Metropolitan Water District power line road. Continue another 0.6 miles past the power line to a faint, dirt road heading south down the Chemehuevi Valley. This road is recommended for four-wheel drive vehicles only. Follow this road 4.7 miles south to a marker designating the Stepladder Wilderness boundary (approximately 1,840 ft).

*Route:* From the road head, continue hiking south along the dirt road about two miles. From here, the peak looks like serious business. Hike two miles west to a wash, and follow this wash toward the mountains about a half mile. Head west-northwest over some low hills to a saddle 0.3 miles northeast of the peak. As you approach the peak, the idea that the route is on the impressive northeast face makes one wonder what they're getting into. Honest, its only Class 2! Climb to the base of the cliffs and a large gully that leads up to the summit area. When practicable, exit onto easy ledges on the northeast face of the peak. These ledges lead to the summit rocks. The northern pinnacle, comprised of a volcanic breccia, is the summit. Anticipate 13 miles round-trip with 1,800 feet of elevation gain.

# Chemehuevi Mountains

The Chemehuevi Mountains stand above the Colorado River as a rugged, oval-shaped, granitic range topped by a few volcanic spires. Smoke trees and mesquite grow in the broad, scenic sandy washes on the way to the peak. To the west is the vast Chemehuevi Valley. Creosote is the domi-

Wynne Benti on the impressive volcanic breccia comprising the summit of Stepladder.
Photo: Andy Zdon

nant plant species, although dense thickets of cholla, barrel cactus and ocotillo are also numerous. A small herd of about twenty-five bighorn sheep are present, along with the occasional deer, wild burros, and desert tortoise. Several Native American cultures have hunted here and used the range as a backdrop for traditional ceremonies. Chemehuevi Peak, the highpoint of the range, is inside the 64,000-acre Chemehuevi Mountains Wilderness. Whale Mountain (2,775 ft), at the north end of the range, is another objective, and is most accessible from the pipeline road that forms the northern boundary of the wilderness.

The nearest supplies, gas, food and lodging are in the town of Needles, California, about 12 miles to the northwest. The area is managed by the Bureau of Land Management district offices in Needles, Riverside and Yuma.

### CHEMEHUEVI PEAK (3,694 FT; 1,126 M)

This summit of this peak probably provides a great view of the Lake Havasu area and the surrounding desert ranges. When the author climbed this peak after a winter storm, the summit was completely enshrouded in dense cloud cover, with visibility of about 100 feet. Regardless, the hike to its summit was an enjoyable desert scramble.

*Maps:* Chemehuevi Peak (CA) 7.5-minute (1:24,000 scale) topographic map; Needles 1:100,000 scale metric topographic map; Automobile Club of Southern California (AAA) San Bernardino County map

*Best Time to Climb:* November through April

*Approach:* From Needles, California on Interstate 40, drive about 20 miles south on Highway 95. Just before the Lake Havasu Road, turn east onto a power line road. Drive 4.2 miles along this road and park (1,700 ft). All cars should be able to reach the starting point.

*Route:* Hike northeast across the broad alluvial fan to a large embayment in the mountain front. At the north end of the embayment, a beautiful and rocky, but easily-traveled, canyon heads northwest then north to a saddle at approximately 3,120 feet. From the saddle, climb Chemehuevi's north-west ridge to the summit. Anticipate eight miles round-trip with 2,000 feet of elevation gain.

### SAWTOOTH MOUNTAIN (2,324 FT; 708 M)

Sawtooth Mountain is the highpoint of the diminutive Sawtooth Range, southwest of the Chemehuevi Mountains. When approaching from the south along Highway 95, the range is difficult to see as it blends to the like-colored Chemehuevi Mountains behind.

*Maps:* Chemehuevi Peak (CA) 7.5-minute (1:24,000 scale) topographic map; Needles 1:100,000 scale metric topographic map; Automobile Club of Southern California (AAA) San Bernardino County map

*Best Time to Climb:* November through April

*Approach:* From Needles, California on Interstate 40, drive about 20 miles south on Highway 95. Just before the Lake Havasu Road, turn east onto a power line road. Drive two miles along this road and park.

*Route:* Hike a quarter mile northeast to a dirt road heading north. Follow the dirt road about 0.7 miles then east to the peak. Class 2 slopes lead to the summit (the south peak). Anticipate four miles round-trip with 700 feet of elevation gain.

## THE TURTLE MOUNTAINS

The Turtle Mountains are one of the most visually spectacular desert ranges described in this book. It is a diverse landscape, where plateaus and uniquely-shaped mountains, give way to vast, open valleys punctuated by reddish, steep 15-20 million year old volcanic spires. Creosote, cactus, and other shrubs are common throughout the area. Canyons and washes contain palo verde, acacia and other vegetation commonly found in desert washes. A small cluster of native palm trees, the northernmost occurrence of fan palms, is found at the oasis of Mopah Springs. Wildlife includes the Turtle Mountain herd of bighorn sheep, desert tortoises, and other varied mammals. Prairie Falcon and Golden Eagle build their eyries high in the range.

The Turtle Mountains are important from a cultural and historic perspective. The northern portion of the range was the location of a Chemehuevi village and several ceremonial sites. The Chemehuevi Trail, a main trading trail, cuts across the northern end of the range in an east-west direction.

All of the peaks described below fall within the 144,500-acre Turtle Mountains Wilderness. Camping in the area is primitive. Observe minimum impact camping methods. Gasoline and a small coffee shop are located at Vidal Junction. For more serious supplies, food, and lodging, Needles or Blythe are your best bets . For further information, contact the Bureau of Land Management offices in Needles and Riverside.

## "Turtle Mountain" (4,313 ft; 1,310+ m)

Turtle Mountain's excellent view of the Mopah Peaks area is certainly worth the long, rough approach route. To the southwest is "Horn Peak" (3,864 ft), unnamed on the topo, that can be climbed from the same road end as Turtle.

*Maps:* Mopah Peaks and Horn Spring (CA) 7.5-minute (1:24,000) scale topographic maps; Parker 1:100,000 scale metric topographic map; Automobile Club of Southern California (AAA) San Bernardino County map

*Best Time to Climb:* November through April

*Approach:* From Twentynine Palms, California on State Highway 62, drive 83 miles east on Highway 62 to a dirt road 0.7 miles east of milepost 117 (beyond a railroad crossing). This turnoff is also 8.1 miles west of Vidal

On the summit of Turtle Mountain.
Photo: Wynne Benti

Junction. Follow this dirt road 0.2 miles crossing the Metropolitan Water District Aqueduct then turn left on a dirt road 1.8 miles to a junction. If driving into the area at night, it is recommended that you stop and camp here for the evening. The rest of the road is nearly impossible to follow at night, and four-wheel drive is required from this point on. Head northwest, continuing 5.2 miles to a faint road to the right. Turn southeast onto this road and follow it 0.3 miles into a wash. Follow the road through the wash 0.1 miles where it exits the east edge of the wash and heads north. Continue another 4.7 miles, bearing left at a fork and driving another 0.5 miles. Park just before the road enters a sandy wash at 2,330 feet.

*Route:* Hike generally northwest along the wash 1.3 miles to a broad low saddle. Turtle Mountain, and much of the northern peaks of the Turtle Mountains will come into view here. Head generally west-northwest, gradually gaining elevation and crossing numerous washes en route until

Heading back down Mopah, just below the short section of third class. Photo: Wynne Benti

east of the peak. Head west up Turtle's east ridge to a point just south of the summit, then north a short distance to the summit. The views of Umpah and Mopah from the route, will inspire the occasional, well-earned rest stop. Anticipate seven miles round-trip with 2,100 feet of elevation gain.

### "MOPAH PEAK" (3,530 FT; 1,076 M)

This spire-like peak, along with its neighbor Umpah, is one of the most impressive summits in the Mojave Desert region.

*Maps:* Mopah Peaks and Savahia Peak SW (CA) 7.5-minute (1:24,000) scale topographic maps; Parker 1:100,000 scale metric topographic map; Automobile Club of Southern California (AAA) San Bernardino County map

*Best Time to Climb:* November through April

*Approach:* From Vidal Junction (junction of Highways 95 and 62), drive 12.1 miles north on U.S. Highway 95. Turn left on a good dirt road heading west. Follow this dirt road 4.4 miles to its end at the wilderness boundary. The road is passable to two-wheel drive vehicles with high clearance. Initially the road is smooth; it deteriorates as it approaches the trailhead.

*Route:* Hike along the road about 0.8 miles to a wash near some ruins. Follow the wash about 1.8 miles to where you'll see a notch in the base of Mopah's east face. Head south toward this notch, climbing through it, and continuing along the base of the cliffs to yet another notch. Climb through the notch, then up a chute until cliffs bar progress. At this point go right toward an overhanging cliff with a small "cave" below it. Go to the cave and climb a short section of Class 3 rock to the slope above. Follow this slope to a narrow chute leading to a notch at its top. After reaching this notch, drop down about ten feet on the other side to a small platform. Here lies the rub! Make sure you have good holds on this crumby volcanic rock, as a short but awkward Class 3-4 move diagonals up to the right to a ledge which is followed to easy slopes leading to the summit. A rope is recommended. Anticipate eight miles round-trip with about 2,200 feet of elevation gain.

### "UMPAH POINT" (3,553 FT; 1,083 M)

This is the highpoint of the Mopah Group of the Turtle Mountains. Both Mopah and Umpah have been climbed together in one day.

*Maps:* Mopah Peaks and Savahia Peak SW (CA) 7.5-minute (1:24,000 scale) topographic maps; Parker 1:100,000 scale metric topographic map; Automobile Club of Southern California (AAA) San Bernardino County map

*Best Time to Climb:* November through April

*Approach:* Follow the approach directions for Mopah Point

*Route:* The peak is approximately one mile south of Mopah Point. To climb it, climb the gully on the north side of the peak, climbing the tougher looking rock on the right. Continue up the slopes to the left of the cliffs, reaching the eastern ridge. Cross over the ridge, dropping down the south side to easy slopes that lead to the summit. Climbing the east ridge direct is also reportedly Class 3 to 4. Class 2 to 3 routes can be found up the summit rocks. Anticipate ten to eleven miles round-trip with about 2,300 feet of elevation gain if climbed alone.

Umpah Point. Photo: Wynne Benti

## WHIPPLE MOUNTAINS

When it comes to desert mountain ranges frequented by geologists and geology students, the Whipple Mountains probably take the prize. The geological aspects of the range are so fascinating and unique, that they are a complete distraction from the physical exertion needed to reach its summits. The west and east portions of the range are very different in character. A low angle fault called a "detachment fault" runs through the Whipples, separating the light-colored rocks on the west from the stark, red volcanic rocks on the east. This striking contact is visible in several areas of the range.

Steep red mountains, and deep narrow canyons are tempered by creosote, brittle bush, foxtail cactus, Bigelow cholla, and Mojave prickly-pear. On the east side of the range, one can even occasionally spot that tall sentinel of the desert, the Saguaro. Palo verde, mesquite, smoke tree and ironwood trees are encountered in the washes. Bighorn sheep roamed the Whipple Mountains, but they have vanished from this once permanent habitat, and are rarely seen passing through to other range lands.

The Whipple Mountains contain numerous cultural sites that are of significance to the Chemehuevi, Mojave, and Halchidhoma tribes. Due to the presence of these sites, a portion of the range has been designated an area of critical environmental concern by the Bureau of Land Management.

Whipple Mountain, the highpoint of the range is within the 77,000-acre Whipple Mountains Wilderness. Southwest of the main mass of the Whipples is the impressive, wedge-shaped Savahia Peak, providing a striking example of the Whipple Mountains detachment fault. Because of the fault and the ensuing gold mining that took place here (the Bailey Mine), a number of old mining roads constructed along the fault reach the base of the west side of the peak from which a route is likely. This is based on the review of an oblique aerial photograph of the mountain, and not on the author's experience. The road to the Bailey Mine heads north from Highway 62 about four miles east of Vidal Junction, crosses the aqueduct, then heads back west about 1.5 miles, then north about six miles to the mine. Four-wheel drive will probably be needed. Another climbing possibility is Monument Peak, which looms over the Copper Basin Reservoir, in the heart of the eastern Whipples.

Camping in the area is primitive so all minimum impact camping methods should be applied here. One could also camp at Lake Havasu State Park, across the border in Arizona if more developed campsites are desired. The nearest supplies, gas, food and lodging are in Parker, about ten miles to the south. For further information, contact the Bureau of Land Management offices in Needles, Riverside and Yuma, Arizona.

### "WHIPPLE MOUNTAIN" (4,130 FT; 1,259 M)

The summit of this peak is marked by a benchmark named "Axtel."
*Maps:* Whipple Mountains SW (CA) 7.5-minute (1:24,000 scale) topographic map; Parker 1:100,000 scale metric topographic map; Automobile Club of Southern California (AAA) San Bernardino County map
*Best Time to Climb:* November through April
*Approach:* From Vidal Junction (the junction of Highways 95 and 62), drive 13.8 miles east on Highway 62, and turn left on a well-graded dirt road. Drive north 4.2 miles on this dirt road, crossing the Colorado River Aqueduct. From here on good clearance is recommended. Continue 1.8 miles northwest on a rough dirt road and bear left at a fork. Continue 1.9 miles, staying left at a fork, and continuing another 1.5 miles to a mine site. Park here (1,835 ft).
*Route:* Follow the road northwest a quarter mile to a saddle and drop into

the large wash heading north. Hike up this wash 2.5 miles, staying right at all forks until just past a prominent rock outcrop on the right side of the wash. From here, turn west up a ridge following it to near Point 4,092 feet.

Up the main route to Whipple. Photo: Wynne Benti

Bypass Point 4,092 feet to the east and head northeast to the summit. Anticipate nine miles round-trip with 2,500 feet of elevation gain.

*Alternate Approach and Route:* This alternate approach route is not quite as rough as that for the primary route, and is recommended for those with two-wheel drive vehicles. From Vidal Junction, drive 27.8 miles north on Highway 95 to the Lake Havasu Road. Turn east on the Lake Havasu Road and drive 9.7 miles to a well-graded power line road. Turn southeast, and follow the road 6.8 miles to its junction with another dirt road heading south-southwest. Turn right and drive 3.9 miles to a junction and stay left. Continue another 1.9 miles to the War Eagle No. 1 Mine. Hike about 0.8 miles south-southeast in the wash to a fork. From here one can either stay right and continue south in the wash passing just east of Point 1,806 feet, and follow the wash all the way to Whipple's southwest ridge, or, one can bear left and walk about 1.5 miles to the wash immediately west of Point 2,005 feet, and following this wash about one mile to the 2,400 foot level. From there climb a ridge that leads to just southwest of the summit. Either of these routes is approximately nine miles round-trip with 2,700 feet of elevation gain.

# Joshua Tree
# National Park Area

Known all over the world for its excellent rock climbing, Joshua Tree National Park is only about a two and a half hour drive from Los Angeles. Routes up the area's mountains range in difficulty, from easy half-day hikes to a full day's workout. This beautiful area of remote mountains, huge granite boulders, volcanic outcrops, joshua trees, and cholla gardens has something for everyone. There are trails up many of Joshua Tree's desert mountains, while others have no trails, requiring those wishing to stand on their summits to embark on challenging cross-country adventures across a wide variety of desert landscapes.

When hiking in the Joshua Tree area, you are likely to encounter three general types of rocks: older metamorphic rocks, somewhat younger granitic rocks, and even younger volcanic rocks. The older metamorphic rocks are largely crystalline rocks that have been altered over the hundreds of millions of years since they were formed and bear slight, if any, resemblance to their original form. As you stroll near the summit of Ryan Mountain, you will encounter these older rocks. The granitic rocks are still in the hundred million year-old range, considered young when evaluating life at the pace of rocks! The granitic rocks are the large rounded boulder outcrops found throughout the national park. Camping within these magnificent formations at Hidden Valley Campground or at Jumbo Rocks will place you in the midst of a rock type termed "quartz monzonite" by geologists, the rock that draws rock climbers from around the world. Volcanic rocks are more dispersed, but can be seen when hiking in the Lost Horse Mountain area or along the Geology Tour Road.

Joshua Tree. Photo: Andy Zdon

The geology of the Joshua Tree area is strongly influenced by the presence of the San Andreas Fault. To the south, the San Andreas runs northwest through the Salton Basin, and makes a bend to the west, where it continues along the southern slope of the San Bernardino Mountains. This bend has caused the San Andreas to "lock up" in this area. The Landers earthquakes of the 1990's were likely the result of a release of stress caused by this lock up. The earthquakes that occur along the faults in the Little San Bernardino Mountains area are roughly parallel to a line that could be drawn if the San Andreas Fault continued northwest instead of bending to the west.

Large animals most often encountered in the park include the coyote, an occasional deer and the rare bighorn sheep. This is also mountain lion habitat. Often one spends the evening camped out in Joshua Tree listening to the yips of coyotes on their nightly hunt. Deer are most commonly found in the mountainous areas of the national park, and those who venture out into the backcountry are more likely to observe them than those who drive through the park in the comfort of their cars.

Several thousand years ago, the Pinto people, a prehistoric culture, lived in the sprawling basin beneath Pinto Mountain. Joshua Tree was not as arid then as it is now. Water was more plentiful in the Pinto Basin enabling humans to carve out a niche for themselves there. The Pinto people were hunter-gatherers and were known for using the atlatl for hunting.

Long after the Pinto people, the Serrano and Chemehuevi Indians moved into the area. By 1850, Joshua Tree saw its first mining activity when prospectors wandered into the country with their burros in tow. Serious mining activity didn't begin until the 1870's, and the Lost Horse Mine, the old abandoned mine workings passed on the way to the mountain of the same name, is an example of one of the more serious mining endeavors. Between the 1890's and 1920's, mining activity continued to grow as promising prospects were located in the Pinto and Hexie Mountains.

It was an unusual form of mining, the gathering of desert plants, that resulted in the eventual creation of Joshua Tree National Monument (later Park). During the 1920's and 1930's, entrepreneurs tapped into the rich biological resource of the area by digging up Joshua trees, cholla, ocotillo, and other unusual desert cacti, shrubs and trees to sell for commercial landscaping. Joshua Tree National Monument was created in 1935 to protect the area's unique plant resources. More than half a century later,

Bouldering at Joshua Tree. Photo: Wynne Benti

passage of the California Desert Protection Act changed the park's status from monument to national park, significantly enlarging the area managed by the National Park Service.

Hiking in the Joshua Tree region during the spring wildflower bloom greatly enhances the routes described in this section from an aesthetic perspective. For the latest wildflower bloom information contact the Living Desert (760)346-5694 or Anza-Borrego (760)767-4684 wildflower hotlines.

For those peaks described within Joshua Tree National Park, a few regulations that need to be observed when traveling and hiking include:

• Campfires are not allowed in the backcountry, only in campgrounds (bring your own wood)

• Off-road driving is prohibited (that includes mountain bikes)

• Pets are prohibited on the trails

• Drilling of rocks for installation of bolts for technical rock climbs is prohibited within the park boundary

• Use of bolts is not allowed in park wilderness areas. Replacement of existing, but otherwise unsafe bolts in non-wilderness areas is possible with permission from the national park.

• All the minimum impact camping and backcountry travel methods described earlier should be adhered to in this area.

# BIGHORN MOUNTAINS

The Bighorn Mountains rise as the northernmost extension of the Little San Bernardino Mountains. The range is home to a wide variety of vegetation types including yucca, cactus, creosote, pinyon-juniper woodlands, and scattered ponderosa pine. Some of the world's largest Joshua trees grow here. A portion of the range has desert tortoise concentrations ranging from twenty to fifty tortoises per square mile. Mule deer, mountain lion, and bobcat are also present. The Bighorn Mountains, as their name suggests, were once the range of a large herd of bighorn sheep. They have now completely vanished from the area, an occurrence of rather recent origin.

The highpoint of the range, Bighorn Mountain, is within the 39,000-acre Bighorn Mountains Wilderness. The area is managed by the Bureau of Land Management offices in Barstow and Riverside. Supplies, food, lodging and gasoline are all available in nearby Yucca Valley. There is primitive camping in the area, although the campgrounds in the northern portion of Joshua Tree National Park are also within an easy drive from the area.

### "BIGHORN MOUNTAIN" (5,894 FT; 1,797 M)

The hike up Bighorn Mountain is a delightful stroll amid pinyon and Joshua trees. The mountain is unnamed on the topographic map.

*Maps:* Rattlesnake Canyon and Bighorn Canyon (CA) 7.5-minute (1:24,000 scale) topographic maps; Big Bear Lake 1:100,000 scale metric topographic map; Automobile Club of Southern California (AAA) San Bernardino County map

*Best Time to Climb:* November through April

*Approach:* From Yucca Mountain, California leave Highway 62 at the signed Highway 247/Joshua Lane intersection. Head 11.5 miles north on Highway 247 to New Dixie Mine Road (well-graded dirt) and head west. Follow the New Dixie Mine Road 9.2 miles (staying right at forks). A triple-junction is reached and the right-hand (northward) road is followed another 1.6 miles to a parking area (5,300 ft). Two-wheel drive vehicles with good clearance are recommended, as the New Dixie Mine Road can be alternating rough washboard dirt and sandy. There are many roads criss-crossing the area, and a wrong turn or two can be expected.

*Route:* Follow the old, eroded jeep trail as it winds its way to the summit area. Anticipate five miles round-trip with 700 feet of elevation gain.

# LITTLE SAN BERNARDINO MOUNTAINS

The Little San Bernardino Mountains are the highest mountains in Joshua Tree National Park and form the park's western boundary. The range extends northwestward with several peaks located outside the park boundary. Quail Mountain is the highpoint of Joshua Tree National Park. Meeks Mountain, Black Mountain, Chaparosa Peak, and South Park Peak are all north of the National Park boundary. Supplies, gas, food and lodging can be obtained north of the park in the towns of Yucca Valley, Joshua Tree and Twentynine Palms. Several campgrounds are available within the park in close proximity to the range. If climbing Warren Peak and the peaks north of the park, there is camping at Black Rock Canyon Campground (see trailhead for Warren Peak). For the remaining peaks in the range, the closest campgrounds in the park are Hidden Valley, Sheep Pass and Jumbo Rocks. For further information regarding these peaks, contact the Riverside office of the Bureau of Land Management. Otherwise, information about the Little San Bernardino Mountains can be obtained from the Joshua Tree National Park office in Twentynine Palms.

## MEEKS MOUNTAIN (6,277 FT; 1,913 M)

This peak provides a pleasant, very short ascent. Unfortunately, the area has been impacted by off-road enthusiasts.

*Maps:* Rattlesnake Canyon and Bighorn Canyon (CA) 7.5-minute (1:24,000 scale) topographic maps; Big Bear Lake 1:100,000 scale metric topographic map; Automobile Club of Southern California (AAA) San Bernardino County map

*Best Time to Climb:* November through April

*Approach:* From Yucca Mountain, California leave Highway 62 at the signed Highway 247/Joshua Lane intersection. Head 11.5 miles north on Highway 247 to New Dixie Mine Road (well-graded dirt) and head west. Follow the New Dixie Mine Road 9.2 miles (staying right at forks). A triple-junction is reached and the left-hand (southwest) road is followed another 0.9 miles to an old cabin site (no longer standing) at 5,360 feet. High clearance vehicles with two-wheel drive are recommended.

*Route:* Follow an old track that heads southwest from the cabin site, then leave the track and scramble up Meeks' pinyon-covered northeast slopes to the summit. Anticipate two miles round-trip with 940 feet of elevation gain.

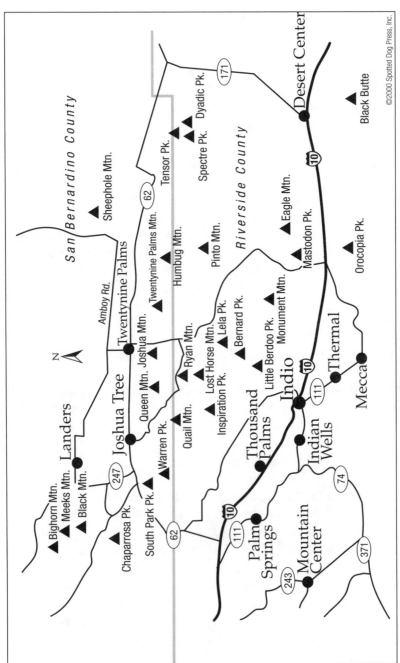

Joshua Tree National Park area peaks

©2000 Spotted Dog Press, Inc.

## BLACK MOUNTAIN (6,149 FT; 1,874 M)

The route to this peak follows desert washes and highlands, replete with a variety of desert flora, to the summit area.

*Maps:* Rimrock (CA) 7.5-minute (1:24,000 scale) topographic map; Big Bear Lake 1:100,000 scale metric topographic map; Automobile Club of Southern California (AAA) San Bernardino County map

*Best Time to Climb:* November through April

*Approach:* From Yucca Mountain, California leave Highway 62 at the signed Highway 247/Joshua Lane intersection. Head 5.5 miles north on Highway 247 to Pipes Canyon Road (well-graded dirt) and head west. Follow the Pipes Canyon Road 4.1 miles to Gamma Gulch Road. Head northwest on Gamma Gulch Road two miles, then stay left and continue another 1.7 miles to another fork. Take the right fork, continuing about 0.2 miles to a parking area (4,800 ft). The peak is visible to the northwest. When we hiked up this peak, some folks were living in a tepee along the road. Two-wheel drive vehicles with good clearance will have no problem on these roads.

*Route:* From the road end, hike north over a small hump into a large dry wash (Antelope Creek). Follow Antelope Creek about a quarter-mile to a fork. Follow the right hand (north) wash as it heads up between scattered pinyon and juniper toward the peak. The route to the summit is obvious from here. Anticipate five miles round-trip with 1,500 feet of elevation gain round-trip.

## CHAPARROSA PEAK (5,541 FT; 1,689 M)

This pleasant desert peak is a good conditioner, and provides good desert views. The peak is likely named for the desert shrub "chuparosa" that grows in the area. The chuparosa's beautiful red flowers that appear during late winter and early spring, contain nectar that attracts hummingbirds.

*Maps:* Rimrock (CA) 7.5-minute (1:24,000 scale) topographic map; Big Bear Lake 1:100,000 scale metric topographic map; Automobile Club of Southern California (AAA) San Bernardino County map

*Best Time to Climb:* November through April

*Approach:* From Yucca Valley, California leave Highway 62 at Pioneertown Road and head 7.3 miles north to Pipes Canyon Road. Head west on Pipes Canyon Road about a half mile to a fork. Take the left fork and continue another quarter-mile to a parking area at the location marked "The Pipes"

on the map (4,460 ft). The road is accessible to all cars.

*Route:* Hike up the jeep road that heads south then southwest up Chaparrosa's northeast ridge. At about 4,900 feet, leave the jeep trail and continue southwest to the summit. The upper part of the ridge can be followed over a couple of false summits, or they can be bypassed on the north. Hikers' use trails are generally available over the entire route. Anticipate five miles round-trip with 1,100 feet of elevation gain.

### SOUTH PARK PEAK (4,395 FT; 1,340 M)

*Maps:* Yucca Valley South (CA) 7.5-minute (1:24,000 scale) topographic map; Big Bear Lake 1:100,000 scale metric topographic map; Automobile Club of Southern California (AAA) San Bernardino County map

*Best Time to Climb:* November through April

*Approach:* From Yucca Mountain, California leave Highway 62 at the signed Highway 247 (Old Woman Springs Road)-Joshua Lane intersection. Drive about five miles south on Joshua Lane to the Black Rock Canyon Campground. At the campground entrance, head 0.7 miles west on a dirt road past a horse camp and a fire house to a trailhead among joshua trees that provides shaded parking (4,120 ft). The road is accessible to all cars.

*Route:* From the picnic area, an interpretive trail climbs to the summit, where a park bench has been mounted on the summit. From this fine vantage point, much of the Yucca Valley-Black Rock Canyon area can be viewed. Anticipate less than a mile round-trip with a mere 275 feet of elevation gain.

### "WARREN PEAK" (5,103 FT; 1,555 M)

The ascent of Warren Peak is a hike up sandy desert washes to a pinyon-juniper dotted highland south of the peak, then up easy slopes to the summit. There are great views from the summit, especially in the late afternoon light. The summit of this peak is marked by a benchmark named "Warren."

*Maps:* Yucca Valley South (CA) 7.5-minute (1:24,000 scale) topographic map; Big Bear Lake 1:100,000 scale metric topographic map; Automobile Club of Southern California (AAA) San Bernardino County map

*Best Time to Climb:* November through April

*Approach:* From Yucca Mountain, California leave Highway 62 at the signed Highway 247 (Old Woman Springs Road)-Joshua Lane intersection. Drive about five miles south on Joshua Lane to the Black Rock Canyon Campground. Enter the campground and park at the Black Rock Campground

Ruins of the Johnny Lang Mine on the route to Quail. Photo: Wynne Benti

Visitor Center (4,040 ft). The paved road is accessible to all cars.

*Route:* From the visitor center, head south through the campground then up the sandy wash of Black Rock Canyon about 0.8 miles. Head southwest up a rocky side canyon amid open pinyon, juniper, oak and joshua tree woodlands about 0.6 miles to Black Rock Spring (usually dry). At the spring head southwest, passing north of Point 4,751 feet, then up Warren's southeast ridge to its rocky summit. Anticipate four miles and 1,100 feet of elevation gain round-trip.

### QUAIL MOUNTAIN (5,813 FT; 1,772 M)

The ascent of Quail Mountain, the highpoint of Joshua Tree National Park, is a fine desert hike through a scenic desert wash, passing a key historical site, and up to one of the best viewpoints in the park. En route, the hiker will pass through Johnny Lang Canyon, and visit the Johnny Lang Mine. Johnny Lang was a former area prospector who founded the Lost Horse Mine, and eventually settled in the canyon that now bears his name. The remains of his shack and mine are still present. In 1926, Lang put a sign on the door of his cabin saying he was off to get supplies. Months later, while working on the road to what is now Keys View,

Bill Keys (a pioneer of the area) found Lang's body, with only meager provisions and wrapped in canvas. Lang was buried on the spot, and his grave can be visited along the Keys View Road.

*Maps:* Indian Cove and Joshua Tree South (CA) 7.5-minute (1:24,000 scale) topographic maps; Big Bear Lake 1:100,000 scale metric topographic map; Automobile Club of Southern California (AAA) San Bernardino County map

*Best Time to Climb:* November through April

*Approach:* From the town of Joshua Tree, California head about 11 miles south on the Joshua Tree National Park road to the Quail Springs Picnic Area (3,979 ft). The road is paved and accessible to all cars.

*Route:* From the picnic area, hike west along a dirt road about two miles to Johnny Lang Canyon. Follow Johnny Lang Canyon south, and at a major fork in the canyon, climb the ridge to the south, passing by the Lang Mine, then southwest along the ridge to the summit, marked by a very large rock cairn. Anticipate 13 miles and 2,400 feet of elevation gain round-trip.

### "INSPIRATION PEAK" (5,575 FT; 1,699 M)

This peak is unnamed on the topographic map, and is marked with a benchmark named "Inspiration."

*Maps:* Keys View (CA) 7.5-minute (1:24,000 scale) topographic map; Palm Springs 1:100,000 scale metric topographic map; Automobile Club of Southern California (AAA) San Bernardino County or Riverside County maps

*Best Time to Climb:* November through April

*Approach:* From the town of Joshua Tree, California leave Highway 62 at the signed Joshua Tree National Park turnoff. Drive south 16 miles to the Loop Road-Keys View Road junction. Follow the Keys View Road to the Keys View parking lot (5,193 ft). The road is paved to the trailhead and is accessible to all cars.

*Route:* From the parking area, follow the ridge northwest to the summit-passing a false summit en route. On a clear spring day, the view of the snowcapped San Jacinto and San Bernardino Mountains is wonderful. Anticipate 1.5 miles and 1,100 feet of elevation gain round-trip.

View from Inspiration Peak. Photo: Andy Zdon

## "LITTLE BERDOO PEAK" (5,440+ FT; 1,658+ M), "BERNARD PEAK" (5,375 FT; 1,638 M)

These remote peaks are usually combined as a single trip due to their proximity to each other. The view of the escarpment of the Little San Bernardino Mountains from the summit of Little Berdoo is singularly impressive. The summits of these two peaks are marked by benchmarks with their respective unofficial names. On our ascent, we were harassed by numerous bees.

*Maps:* Rockhouse Canyon (CA) 7.5-minute (1:24,000 scale) topographic map; Palm Springs 1:100,000 scale metric topographic map; Automobile Club of Southern California (AAA) San Bernardino County or Riverside County maps

*Best Time to Climb:* November through April

*Approach:* From the town of Joshua Tree, California leave Highway 62 at the signed Joshua Tree National Park turnoff. Drive 16 miles south to the Loop Road-Keys View Road junction. Drive 5.3 miles east on the Loop Road to the Geology Tour Road. Drive 5.5 miles south on the graded dirt geology road, passing Squaw Tank, to a fork. Stay left and continue another 2.3 miles to a fork. Head south, following the road that crosses the dry lake (only attempt if dry), and continue another five miles to the marked national park boundary. If the dry lake is muddy, that section of road can be bypassed on dirt roads to the east. The roads are recommended for two-wheel drives with good clearance.

*Route:* From the park boundary, head west until a major wash is reached. Follow the wash northwest about 1.5 miles to a fork. Follow the ridge heading north then northwest to the summit of Bernard Peak. Little Berdoo Peak is reached by following the easy ridge less than one mile southwest. Heading back, bypass Bernard Peak by heading directly southeast down the ridge from Little Berdoo, intersecting the wash at the fork. Anticipate six miles and 1,800 feet of elevation gain round-trip.

## LOST HORSE MOUNTAINS

This small desert range, located entirely within the Joshua Tree National Park, provides fine vistas over the central portion of the national park, along with opportunities to explore some of the more historic sites of the region such as the Lost Horse Mine. Supplies, gas, food and lodging can be obtained north of the park in the towns of Yucca Valley, Joshua Tree and Twentynine Palms. Several campgrounds are available within the park in close proximity to the range including Hidden Valley, Sheep Pass and Jumbo Rocks. For further information regarding these peaks, contact the Joshua Tree National Park office in Twentynine Palms.

### RYAN MOUNTAIN (5,457 FT; 1,663 M)

This centrally located peak provides outstanding views of the entire national park. The mountain is named for the operators of the Lost Horse Mine, Thomas and Jep Ryan.

*Maps:* Keys View (CA) 7.5-minute (1:24,000 scale) topographic map; Palm Springs 1:100,000 scale metric topographic map; Automobile Club of Southern California (AAA) San Bernardino County or Riverside County maps

*Best Time to Climb:* November through April

*Approach:* From the town of Joshua Tree, California leave Highway 62 at the signed Joshua Tree National Park turnoff. Drive 16 miles south to the Loop Road-Keys View Road junction. Drive two miles east on the Loop Road to a large parking area (4,400 ft).

*Route:* From the parking area, a well-graded trail leads to the summit amid

Lost Horse Mine. Photo: Andy Zdon

fine rock outcrops, scattered joshua trees and desert shrubs, and ever-changing desert vistas. Anticipate three miles round-trip with 1,100 feet of elevation gain.

### LOST HORSE MOUNTAIN (5,313 FT; 1,619 M)

*Maps:* Keys View (CA) 7.5-minute (1:24,000 scale) topographic map; Palm Springs 1:100,000 scale metric topographic map; Automobile Club of Southern California (AAA) San Bernardino County or Riverside County maps

*Best Time to Climb:* November through April

*Approach:* From the town of Joshua Tree, California leave Highway 62 at the signed Joshua Tree National Park turnoff. Drive 16 miles south to the Loop Road-Keys View Road junction. Follow the Keys View Road 2.5 miles south to the Lost Horse Mine Road. Follow this good dirt road about a mile east to the road end (4,560 ft).

*Route:* Follow the Lost Horse Mine Trail southeast to the Lost Horse Mine, and to a saddle south of the mine. The summit is a short scramble southwest. Anticipate five miles round-trip with 900 feet of elevation gain.

# PINTO MOUNTAINS

A widespread, dispersed mountain range, the Pinto Mountains actually make up a cluster of individual ridges, mountains, and hills that can be lumped together into somewhat of an east-west trend. The most famous peak in the range, Pinto Mountain, is far from being the highest peak in the range, but it does provide one of the finest hikes in Joshua Tree National Park. Most of the area is covered by creosote, and colorful cacti grow on the rocky ridges of the peaks. Washes commonly contain smoke trees, and higher valleys contain Mojave yuccas.

Supplies, gas, food and lodging can be obtained north of the park in the towns of Yucca Valley, Joshua Tree and Twentynine Palms. Several campgrounds are available within the park in close proximity to the range including Hidden Valley, Sheep Pass and Jumbo Rocks for the peaks in the Queen Mountain-Twentynine Palms area, or Cottonwood Campground for Pinto Mountain. For further information regarding these peaks, contact the Joshua Tree National Park office in Twentynine Palms.

### QUEEN MOUNTAIN (5,687 FT; 1,733 M)

This peak, the highpoint of the range, provides a fine half-day ascent, leading to grand views of the Wonderland of Rocks.

*Maps:* Queen Mountain (CA) 7.5-minute (1:24,000 scale) topographic map; Big Bear Lake 1:100,000 scale metric topographic map; Automobile Club of Southern California (AAA) San Bernardino County map

*Best Time to Climb:* November through April

*Approach:* From the town of Joshua Tree, California leave Highway 62 at the signed Joshua Tree National Park turnoff, and follow the road 16 miles south to an intersection with the Loop Road and the Keys View Road. Follow the Loop Road 4.5 miles to a dirt road heading northwest. Follow the dirt road 2.8 miles straight toward Queen Mountain to a turnaround. Two-wheel drive vehicles may not be able to reach the road end, but should be able to get to within a mile or so.

*Route:* Head east, then northeast, gradually climbing around a ridge and into a brushy draw that leads up to a saddle between Queen Mountain (to the west) and Point 5,677 feet. The peak is an easy scramble on granite slabs from the saddle. Anticipate four miles round-trip with 1,000 feet of elevation gain round-trip from the road end.

## JOSHUA MOUNTAIN (3,746 FT; 1,142 M)

*Maps:* Queen Mountain (CA) 7.5-minute (1:24,000 scale) topographic map; Big Bear Lake 1:100,000 scale metric topographic map; Automobile Club of Southern California (AAA) San Bernardino County map

*Best Time to Climb:* November through April

*Approach:* From Twentynine Palms, California leave Highway 62 at the signed Joshua Tree National Park turnoff (Utah Trail). Drive south on Utah Trail, 2.5 miles past the National Park Visitor Center, parking on the sandy shoulder of the road. If in a two-wheel drive vehicle, and getting stuck in the sand is a concern, try exiting the shoulder in a downhill direction. For example, if parked on the west side of the road, try backing off the shoulder.

*Route:* Climb the steep gully to the west directly toward the peak. Climb the final summit monolith on the north side. Anticipate some Class 3 scrambling en route. Three miles round-trip with 1,200 feet of elevation gain.

## TWENTYNINE PALMS MOUNTAIN (4,562 FT; 1,391 M)

*Maps:* Twentynine Palms Mountain (CA) 7.5-minute (1:24,000 scale) topographic map; Sheep Hole Mountains 1:100,000 scale metric topographic map; Automobile Club of Southern California (AAA) San Bernardino County map

*Best Time to Climb:* November through April

*Approach:* From Twentynine Palms, California leave Highway 62 at the signed Joshua Tree National Park turnoff (Utah Trail). Drive 1.7 miles south on Utah Trail to Morning Drive. Turn east (left) on Morning Drive, and drive 0.6 miles east to Sahara Avenue and turn right on a dirt road heading north. Although the road is an easy drive the first couple of miles, put your vehicle into four-wheel drive here as you will need it later on. Continue on the dirt road, ignoring side roads, 2.6 miles to a stake marking the National Park boundary. At times the road is sandy, the canyon becomes narrow, and the backroad traveler is glad that four-wheel drive is engaged. In another 0.8 miles (3.4 miles from Morning Drive) you'll encounter another stake indicating that you're leaving the National Park. At 4.7 miles from Morning Drive, you'll encounter the first of many abandoned mining operations that marked the old Gold Park District. Continuing up the wash, at 7.1 miles from Morning Drive, the canyon begins to open up and a fork is reached. A right turn heads to a Bureau of Land

Joshua Mountain. Photo: Andy Zdon

Management Information Outpost, that is occasionally occupied. When occupied, the normal open hours are from 8 to 5 daily. Stay left at the fork, passing many sideroads to mine diggings, heading over a low group of hills, and dropping back into another wash. At 8.7 miles from Morning Drive (1.6 miles from the BLM Outpost turnoff), exit the wash and begin driving south down lonely Music Valley. The road becomes rough and narrow, with the occasional creosote bush rubbing along the outside of your vehicle (if the occasional paint scratch on your vehicle is a serious concern, you might consider climbing another peak). Heading down Music Valley, the bladed track heading up Twentynine Palms Mountain becomes more and more visible, and about 2.7 miles after leaving the wash (11.1 miles from Morning Drive), a fork is reached. Make a sharp right and continue a quarter mile and park. (3,080 ft).

*Route:* Follow the bulldozed track as it climbs the ridge until it leaves the ridge crest and reaches the south end of a saddle. Leave the track, climbing east to the main ridge. Upon gaining the ridge crest, follow the winding ridge southward to the summit, bypassing Point 1,354 meters en route. The summit is the southernmost high point marked by a bench-mark named "Twenty Nine." An antennae installation is present on the lower northern summit of the mountain. Anticipate five miles round-trip with 2,200 feet of elevation gain.

### HUMBUG MOUNTAIN (2,260 FT, 689 M)

The term "humbug" was a prospector's term for a claim that did not yield as anticipated. The mines found in the area were probably a disappointment. The scramble up this peak will not be a humbug! Many routes are possible for this mountain. That given below is a pleasant loop hike that the author recommends.

*Maps:* Twentynine Palms Mountain and Humbug Mountain (CA) 7.5-minute (1:24,000 scale) topographic maps; Sheep Hole Mountains 1:100,000 scale metric topographic map; Automobile Club of Southern California (AAA) San Bernardino County map

*Best Time to Climb:* November through April

*Approach:* From Twentynine Palms, California drive 14.2 miles east of the signed Joshua Tree National Park turnoff (Utah Trail) on Highway 62 to the dirt Gold Crown Road heading south across the desert. Follow this rough dirt road (two-wheel drive vehicles with good clearance are okay) 3.7 miles to a junction. Stay right and engage four-wheel drive here. Continue another 0.6 miles, dropping into a wash at a sandy spot that has metal runners to drive on in the sand to keep your car from bogging down, to a fork in the wash. Stay right and continue another 0.4 miles, leaving the wash and reaching a sign that states "160-acre Claim." Stay left, and left again in a few hundred yards where the road drops back into the wash. The road winds in and out of the wash the next mile, finally reaching a barren alluvial terrace. When the author visited here, he drove another quarter mile and parked here (about 1,800 feet or 550 meters). One could continue around to the southwest side of Humbug to the Imperial Mine and climb from there (a shorter hike), but the drive is hardly worth it. Besides, this fine loop hike with ever-expansive views is charming and barely a half-day hike.

*Route:* From the parking area, hike northwest across the wash to an obvious, brown alluvial fan to the northwest. Hike up the alluvial fan to it's host canyon (between Points 595 meters and 598 meters on the topographic map), and at a fork in the canyon, head up an easy ridge that heads northwest gaining a significant north-south ridge. Upon reaching the ridge crest, Humbug Mountain is directly west across a broad valley. The peak looks farther away than it is. Follow the pleasant, undulating ridge, with wide open desert vistas as it heads north. An obvious ridge heading south-

Humbug Mountain. Photo: Andy Zdon

west is then followed over to Humbug's summit (shown as Point 689 meters northeast of the Imperial Mine on the map). A look into the summit register will show that this peak is rarely ascended. After taking in the wide open views, head south down the ridge, then southwest into the valley bottom. The wash can be followed southward, then east back toward the car. It is best to exit south out of the wash back onto the alluvial terrace in order not to pass up your vehicle on the return trip! The total round-trip loop hike is about three miles and 1,500 feet of elevation gain. If hiking from the end of the two-wheel drive portion of road anticipate eight-miles round-trip

### Pinto Mountain (3,983 ft; 1,214 m)

Although this peak looks like an easy walk from the parking area, it is one of the longer summit hikes in the area. The views from the summit across the vast Pinto Basin are spectacular, and distant canyons invite further exploration.

*Maps:* Pinto Mountain (CA) 7.5-minute (1:24,000 scale) topographic map; Eagle Mountains 1:100,000 scale metric topographic map; Automobile Club of Southern California (AAA) San Bernardino County or Riverside County maps

Crossing the sand dunes to Pinto Mountain (background).  Photo: Wynne Benti

*Best Time to Climb:* November through April

*Approach:* From Twentynine Palms, California leave Highway 62 at the signed Joshua Tree National Park turnoff (Utah Trail). Drive 8.8 miles south on Utah Trail, and continue straight on the Pinto Basin Road at the road junction. This junction can also be reached via a paved road from the town of Joshua Tree. Drive about 16.5 miles south to a large turnoff on the north side of the road just past highway marker 16. If driving in from the south park entrance, exit Interstate 10 at the Mecca-Twentynine Palms exit, turning left on the Cottonwood Springs Road. Drive about 14.5 miles north to the parking area described above.

*Route:* Head northeast directly toward the peak crossing the large alluvial valley, about a 2.5 mile walk. As you approach the mountain front, a ridge bisecting two prominent washes (on the northeast) is followed to the summit. This ridge can be followed on the return. The more adventuresome might want to return by a different route, making a nice loop trip.

As you stand on the summit and look back at the highway, you'll see to your right (southwest), a ridge leaving the summit. A very old footpath follows this ridge to its end. This route is pretty obvious, and when one walks it, it is not difficult to imagine that this was once a trail used by prehistoric people, perhaps even the Pinto people. At the end of the ridge, you'll have to scamble down some steep stuff to get back to the flats. Anticipate nine miles round-trip with 2,400 feet of gain.

## HEXIE MOUNTAINS

The Hexie Mountains are a small, compact group of desert mountains, entirely within Joshua Tree National Park. Monument Mountain is the highpoint of the range, and stands nearly 3,000 feet above the Pinto Basin to the northeast. The remainder of the range is surrounded by desert canyons with large desert washes named Fried Liver, Washington, Porcupine, and Pinkham. The west end of the range near Lela Peak, overlooks a small but scenic area called Pleasant Valley. A variety of desert shrubs and grasses cover the range, and in the west, a few Joshua trees dot its open slopes. If climbing Monument Mountain, the nearest place to camp is Cottonwood Campground. If climbing Lela, the Hidden Valley, Sheep Pass, and Jumbo Rocks campgrounds are your best bets.

## "LELA PEAK" (4,747 FT; 1,447 M)

Lela Peak is the highpoint of the western portion of the Hexie Mountains, resulting in fine distant views of the surrounding area amid desert scrub and a few Joshua trees. The peak is not officially named. The summit is marked with a named benchmark "Lela."

*Maps:* Queen Mountain (CA) 7.5-minute (1:24,000 scale) topographic map; Big Bear Lake 1:100,000 scale metric topographic map; Automobile Club of Southern California (AAA) San Bernardino County or Riverside County maps

*Best Time to Climb:* November through April

*Approach:* From the town of Joshua Tree, California leave Highway 62 at the signed Joshua Tree National Park turnoff. Drive 16 miles south to the Loop Road - Keys View Road junction. Drive 5.3 miles east on the Loop Road to the Geology Tour Road. Drive 5.5 miles south on the graded dirt geology road to the Squaw Tank parking area (3,580 ft). The road is sandy in places but Squaw Tank should be reachable in most cars.

*Route:* From Squaw Tank, head along the north base of the east-west ridge toward the peak. Pass north of Point 4,255 feet, and up to a saddle between Points 4,255 feet and 4,278 feet. Ascend Point 4,278 feet, then down to a saddle over to some flats west of the peak. Finally, ascend the northwest ridge. The route is straightforward; the peak is the second plateau that will be reached. Anticipate five miles round-trip with about 1,400 feet of elevation gain.

## MONUMENT MOUNTAIN (4,834 FT; 1,473 M)

The highpoint of the Hexie Mountains, Monument Mountain also has some of the most far-ranging views within the Park.

*Maps:* Washington Wash and Porcupine Wash (CA) 7.5-minute (1:24,000 scale) topographic maps; Eagle Mountains 1:100,000 scale metric topographic map; Automobile Club of Southern California (AAA) Riverside County map

*Best Time to Climb:* November through April

*Approach:* From the Interstate 10 turnoff described above for Pinto Mountain, drive north on the park road toward the Cottonwood Visitor Center / Campground area. Just south of the visitor center, a dirt road (Pinkham Road) heads north then forks after about a mile. Take the left fork west as it turns into a rough, four-wheel drive road following Smoke Tree Wash

Little San Bernardino Mountains from Lela Peak.  Photo: Andy Zdon

to a point south of Monument Mountain, 4.2 miles from the fork (3,250 ft). *Route:* Cross Smoke Tree Wash, and follow the southeast ridge of Monument Mountain to the summit.  Anticipate five miles round-trip with 1,700 feet of elevation gain round-trip.

## EAGLE MOUNTAINS

This east-west trending mountain range, rises above the Haystack and Chuckwalla Valleys to the south and east, and above the Pinto Basin to the north. The Eagle Mountains mark the transition from the Mojave Desert to the north and the Colorado Desert to the south.  This transition is striking in that plant species from these two very different environments appear side by side in this range.  Here, palm trees typical of the Colorado Desert grow side by side with such high desert species as the juniper.  The Eagle Mountain area is a microcosm of the life zones represented throughout the entire national park.

Supplies, gas, food and lodging are available in the Indio-Palm Springs area or north of the park.  Lodging at either of these locations would lead to a lengthy drive into the road end for Eagle Mountain.  Therefore, camping at Cottonwood Campground is your best bet.  Have all the supplies, food and gas you will need for your trip in this area.  It's a fairly long drive to get supplies.  The hike to Eagle Mountain is entirely within the national park, so for further information contact the Joshua Tree National Park office in Twentynine Palms.

### MASTODON PEAK (3,371 FT; 1,027 M)

This small peak is more of a boulder outcrop than a true mountain. Nonetheless, it is a pleasant hike, alive with the sounds of desert birds, particularly at the site of Winona and at Cottonwood Spring.

*Maps:* Cottonwood Spring (CA) 7.5-minute (1:24,000 scale) topographic map; Eagle Mountains 1:100,000 scale metric topographic map; Automobile Club of Southern California (AAA) Riverside County map

*Best Time to Climb:* November through April

*Approach:* From the Interstate 10 turnoff described above for Pinto Mountain, drive north on the park road toward the Cottonwood Visitor Center/ Campground area. Just south of the visitor center, follow the road that passes along the south side of the campground to the Cottonwood Springs Oasis trailhead.

*Route:* From the trailhead, follow the north Mastodon Loop Trail, passing the 1920's-vintage mining camp site of Winona to the peak. A path leaves the main trail heading for the peak, an interesting boulder outcrop. Some easy scrambling will be needed to reach the summit. On the return, continue on the loop trail to Cottonwood Springs and back to the car. Anticipate three miles round-trip with about 450 feet of elevation gain.

### EAGLE MOUNTAIN (5,350 FT; 1,631 M)

*Maps:* Porcupine Wash, Cottonwood Spring, Hayfield, and Conejo Well (CA) 7.5-minute (1:24,000 scale) topographic maps; Eagle Mountains 1:100,000 scale metric topographic map; Automobile Club of Southern California (AAA) Riverside County map

*Best Time to Climb:* November through April

*Approach:* From the Interstate 10 turnoff described above for Pinto Mountain, drive 9.4 miles north to a dirt road that turns off to the northeast. Follow the dirt road to its end in a few yards, or park along the paved Pinto Basin Road (3,125 ft).

*Route:* From the end of the dirt road, head southeast to a large boulder outcrop at the base of the mountains, about 2.5 miles. These boulders mark the entrance to a large canyon which is followed eastward, and eventually up to a notch at approximately 5,040 feet. The summit is about one mile east along the ridge. Anticipate nine miles round-trip with 2,400 feet of elevation gain.

Spectre Peak summit area.  Photo: Andy Zdon

## COXCOMB MOUNTAINS

Mysterious and rugged, with classic desert washes, the Coxcomb Mountains are captivating as they rise up abruptly from the Ward and Sheephole Valleys, and above the Pinto Basin.  Vegetation is sparse, but when it is present, it's the ubiquitous creosote.  Twenty years ago, the Coxcomb bighorn sheep herd was counted at ten animals and declining. It is unclear how many exist here now.  The Coxcombs were formerly used by the Pinto Mountain bighorn herd, but sadly that herd has also disappeared.  The Coxcomb Mountains were added to Joshua Tree National Park as part of the Desert Protection Act.  For information on this fine desert range, contact the Joshua Tree National Park office in Twentynine Palms.

**"SPECTRE PEAK" (4,260+ FT; 1,300+ M, AS SHOWN ON CADIZ VALLEY SW MAP)**
Spectre Peak is the principal peak climbed in the Coxcomb Mountains. However, it is unclear whether its harder rival, Dyadic, is actually the high-point of the range.  This peak which is clearly higher than its neighbor Tensor shows up on the topographic map as a lower peak.  Hopefully, this will be corrected in later versions of the Cadiz Valley SW topographic map. *Maps:* Cadiz Valley SW (CA) 7.5-minute (1:24,000 scale) topographic map; Sheep Hole Mountains 1:100,000 scale metric topographic map; Automobile

Club of Southern California (AAA) San Bernardino County map
*Best Time to Climb:* November through April
*Approach:* From Twentynine Palms, California drive 40 miles east on Highway 62, continuing 0.8 miles past milepost 72 to a gated, sandy road heading southeast toward the mountains. The gate marks the boundary of the Joshua Tree Wilderness. Park here along the highway.
*Route:* Hike along the former sandy dirt road about four miles to a significant canyon that drains the area north of Spectre Peak. A predawn start is recommended for this hike. As you approach the canyon where the climbing begins in earnest, the dawn light on the jagged peaks and desert vegetation is guaranteed to provide an inspirational, desert experience. At about a point in the canyon between Points 1,016 meters and 908 meters (on the topographic map), head up the steep wash to the south, following it to a saddle. Drop about 100 feet then bear southwest (right) up a boulder-filled wash (the author encountered a rattlesnake here) to a second saddle just west of benchmark Aqua (also known as Tensor Peak or Tensor Point). A fine view of Spectre Peak is had from here. Gain the northeast ridge of Spectre, and follow it to the top, staying left to avoid getting stuck in high boulders. Anticipate 13 miles round-trip with 3,300 feet of elevation gain.
*Alternate Route:* For those wishing a kinder and gentler pedestrian route (even though it is longer), instead of leaving the canyon four miles from the highway, continue southeast up the sandy wash 1.1 miles to a saddle at about 925 meters as shown on the metric map. Continue southeast down the wash 0.4 miles to a broad wash heading up a canyon to the southwest. This canyon can then be followed to the summit area. Anticipate 14 miles round-trip with 3,800 feet of elevation gain.

## TENSOR PEAK (4,417 FT; 1,346.5 M)
This peak appears on the topographic map as a point with a benchmark named "Aqua." This is the lowest of the trio of Spectre, Tensor and Dyadic. Oddly enough, the topographic map presents Tensor as the highest summit. This puzzling situation points out that U.S.G.S. topographic maps are fallible!
*Maps:* Cadiz Valley SW (CA) 7.5-minute (1:24,000 scale) topographic map; Sheep Hole Mountains 1:100,000 scale metric topographic map; Automobile Club of Southern California (AAA) San Bernardino County map
*Best Time to Climb:* November through April

High in the Coxcomb Mountains, near Spectre Peak.  Photo: Andy Zdon

*Approach:* Same approach as for Spectre Peak.

*Route:* Follow the route for Spectre Peak to the second saddle just west of Tensor. The peak is an easy scramble from here. Anticipate 13.5 miles round-trip with 3,200 feet of elevation gain.

**"DYADIC PEAK" (4,362+ FT, OR 1,330+ M AS SHOWN ON CADIZ VALLEY SW MAP)**

*Maps:* Cadiz Valley SW (CA) 7.5-minute (1:24,000 scale) topographic map; Sheep Hole Mountains 1:100,000 scale metric topographic map; Automobile Club of Southern California (AAA) San Bernardino County map

*Best Time to Climb:* November through April

*Approach:* Same approach as for Spectre Peak.

*Route:* From the small basin surrounded by Spectre, Dyadic and Tensor, the climb of Dyadic will require some rock work, and has been rated as Class 5.1 to 5.4.

# South and East of Joshua Tree National Park

### Orocopia Mountains

Looking north from the Salton Sea and Coachella Valley, the north scarp of the Orocopia Mountains is jagged and sheer, while the southern slope of the range is rolling and highly colorful, with a badland-like topography resulting from the range front's proximity to the San Andreas Fault. The oldest rocks in the range consist of Precambrian-age metamorphic rocks. This is not to say that all the metamorphic rocks in the Orocopias are that old. The Orocopia Schist, once thought to be Precambrian in age, is essentially the same rock formation as the Pelona Schist in the San Gabriel Mountains north of Los Angeles, making it hundreds of millions of years younger then previously thought. The duplication of these rocks in the Orocopias and the San Gabriels is no accident. The outcrops of this singular schist in these two places, are on opposite sides of the San Andreas Fault, and provide further evidence (with other similar occurrences elsewhere along the fault), that about 130 miles of displacement has occurred along the San Andreas Fault.

From the north, the Orocopias' gentle aspect is observed, appearing as low desert hills when viewed from Interstate 10, hiding the grand vista to the south from the unsuspecting traveler. Vegetation in the Orocopias is sparse but variable. Creosote and ironwood are found in the open valleys of the range, while ocotillo are found on hilly slopes. About 40 bighorn sheep roam these open slopes, along with deer, desert tortoise and a host of small mammals. Prairie Falcon build their eyries in the range.

The highpoint of the range is within the 41,000-acre Orocopia Mountains Wilderness. Camping in the area is primitive, although one can easily drive north into Joshua Tree National Park and camp at Cottonwood

Campground. The nearest supplies, gas, food and lodging are in the Indio-Palm Springs area to the west. For further information, contact the Bureau of Land Management offices in Palm Springs and Riverside.

### "Orocopia Mountain" (3,815 ft; 1,163 m)

Climb Orocopia Mountain during the spring when the ocotillo and other wildflowers in the area are in their colorful spring bloom. When we climbed Orocopia, the mountain was alive with tiny horned lizards. The summit provides great views of the Salton Sea and the Coachella Valley, and is a great place for the geologically-oriented to submit fellow hikers to arm-waving lectures concerning the San Andreas Fault System, one of the prominent features seen from here. This, the highpoint of the range, is unnamed on the topographic map.

*Maps:* Orocopia Canyon (CA) 7.5-minute (1:24,000 scale) topographic map; Eagle Mountains 1:100,000 scale metric topographic map; Automobile Club of Southern California (AAA) Riverside County map

*Best Time to Climb:* November through April

*Approach:* From the Interstate 10 turnoff described for Pinto Mountain, turn south and drive about 0.3 miles to the paved Pinto Road. Head east and drive 0.6 miles to a dirt road heading south toward the Orocopia Mountains. Follow this dirt road 3.8 miles, to a junction (always staying left). Two-wheel drive cars should park here. Those with four-wheel drive can turn left up a hill and continue another 0.7 miles to a gully and park (2,700 feet).

*Route:* From the four-wheel drive road end, cross the gully, and follow the wash south about 1.3 miles to a junction with another large wash. Climb the ridge directly ahead and follow the ridge line to the peak. Anticipate five miles round-trip with about 1,500 feet of elevation from the two-wheel drive road end.

*Alternate Approach and Route:* From Indio, California follow State Highway 111 southeast to Parkside Drive opposite the Salton Sea Visitor Center. Follow Parkside drive east 1.7 miles, then left on Desert Aire Road to its end at an aqueduct. Head east along the aqueduct road 3.5 miles to Siphon 28, then left on a four-wheel drive road about 2.7 miles and park. Hike east up the ridge to Point 1,890 feet. From Point 1,890 feet, head north then northeast to the summit. Anticipate 5.5 miles and 2,700 feet of elevation gain round-trip.

## CHUCKWALLA AND
## LITTLE CHUCKWALLA MOUNTAINS

These two ranges form one continuous mountain mass, extending roughly east-west, similar to the Orocopias. The westernmost range, the Chuckwalla Mountains, is capped by Black Butte. The oldest rocks in these ranges consist of Precambrian-age metamorphic rocks.

The Chuckwalla Mountains consist of rugged mountains cut by washes frequently containing ironwood trees. Clusters of ocotillo, cholla, yucca, creosote, barrel cactus, foxtail cactus and nolina denote that this range marks the boundary between the Colorado and Mojave Deserts. The area also has relatively large populations of bighorn sheep, deer, raptors, coyotes, fox, and desert tortoise. The Chuckwalla Mountains are of Native American cultural importance, and numerous rock art, ritualistic sites, rock shelters, camp sites, trails, and village sites are present throughout the range. Corn Springs is a Cahuilla sacred site and is marked by petroglyphs, pictographs, and intaglios, and was a known trading center. The Little Chuckwalla Mountains, with their highpoint Chuckwalla Mountain, is similar in nature to the Chuckwallas. Of note is that Native American sites are almost entirely lacking in this range, just a short distance east from one of the richest cultural areas in the California desert.

J. Smeaton Chase wrote about his moonlit ascent over the Chuckwallas in his classic book *California Desert Trails*. The Chuckwallas are a pleasant, even friendly, range to hike in during the day, but the character of the range was transformed during his evening trip. He described the views:

"*. . .sufficiently weird. To the right was a mesa of the curious mosaic-like character that I have described elsewhere: to the left was the deep barranca on the brink of which ran the track (his trail). The moon shone clearly down on the gleaming black floor, which might have been the pavement of some ruined city of antiquity. At intervals stood great ocotillos whose gaunt arms waved aloft in sinister contortions, while here and there a dead one lay bleached to the hue of bone. Looking down into the ravine I could make out dark forms of palo verde and ironwood, or gray smoketrees, like ghosts, outlined on the pallid sand of the bottom. The only sound was that of Kaweah's hoofs hoarsely rattling the gravel of the track. Close ahead rose the black wall of the Chuckwallas, with here and there some bolt of rock taking questionable shape under the eerie touches of the moon. The total impression was freakish and unearthly: it was a place nor* *uninformed with phantasy–and looks that threaten the profane."*

Black Butte, the highpoint of the Chuckwalla Mountains, is within the 81,000-acre Chuckwalla Mountains Wilderness. After climbing Black Butte, one may want to climb Pilot Mountain (4,215 feet) from Corn Springs. Chuckwalla Mountain, the highpoint of the Little Chuckwallas, is within the neighboring 30,000-acre Little Chuckwalla Mountains Wilderness. A developed campground can be found in the Chuckwalla Mountains at Corn Springs. Otherwise, camping in the area is primitive and all minimum impact camping methods apply. The closest place to get supplies, food and lodging are in Blythe, California, about 25 to 40 miles to the east. For further information, contact the Bureau of Land Management offices in Palm Springs and Riverside.

### BLACK BUTTE (4,504 FT; 1,373 M)
*Maps:* Pilot Mountain (CA) 7.5-minute (1:24,000 scale) topographic map; Eagle Mountains 1:100,000 scale metric topographic map; Automobile Club of Southern California (AAA) Riverside County map

*Best Time to Climb:* November through April

*Approach:* From Chiriaco Summit on Interstate 10, continue nine miles east to the Red Cloud Road off ramp. Head 1.2 miles south on a well-graded dirt road to a fork. Stay right as the road quality decreases, and in about 0.9 miles bear left at another fork. Continue another 1.1 miles (taking the high road - you'll know it when you see it), then right another 0.9 miles to a gas line road. Follow the gas line road (BLM Road J3724) 7.7 miles south to the Bradshaw Trail National Back Country Byway. Head 6.8 miles east on the Bradshaw Trail Road to a dirt track that heads north toward the peak. Follow this road 2.4 miles and park. If driving in a two-wheel drive vehicle, you will need to park here at about 2,680 feet. If driving in a four-wheel drive, you should be able to drive another 0.8 miles to Gulliday Well at about 2,840 feet.

*Route:* From the road end, cross a wash and follow the rough track up the canyon about 1.8 miles. This may be passable to four-wheel drive vehicles, but can get washed out during the summer monsoon season. From this point, a canyon heads northeast directly toward Black Butte. Some dry waterfalls along the route are easily surmounted. From the two-wheel drive road end, anticipate 6.5 miles round-trip with 1,850 feet of elevation gain round-trip.

Chuckwalla Mountain from the south.   Photo: Andy Zdon

## "CHUCKWALLA MOUNTAIN" (3,446 FT; 1,050 M)

The summit of this peak is marked by a benchmark named "Bunch."
*Maps:* Chuckwalla Spring (CA) 7.5-minute (1:24,000 scale) topographic map; Eagle Mountains and Salton Sea 1:100,000 scale metric topographic maps; Automobile Club of Southern California (AAA) Riverside County map
*Best Time to Climb:* November through April
*Approach:* From the town of Desert Center along Interstate 10, drive 9.3 miles east on Interstate 10, exiting at the signed Corn Springs Road off-ramp. Turn south then east onto the Chuckwalla Road and continue 13 miles to the well-graded Graham Pass Road (BLM Road C081). Head 15.4 miles south on the Graham Pass Road (staying left at a fork about midway along the road) to a faint track heading northwest. If you reach the Bradshaw Trail, you've gone too far. Follow the faint road 1.5 miles and park. Four-wheel drives can continue a bit further but it is hardly worth the effort. Best to let the desert reclaim this short portion of the road.
*Route:* Faint climbers' paths lead to the summit, clearly visible to the north-east. Anticipate three miles round-trip with 1,600 feet of elevation gain.
*Alternate Approach:* Many desert climbers combine Black Butte and Chuckwalla Mountain on the same trip. If this is desired, it is not neces-sary to drive all the way back to the Interstate. From the Bradshaw Trail turnoff for Black Butte, continue another 14.5 miles along the Bradshaw

Trail Road to the Graham Pass Road. Head north, and the dirt road turnoff is reached in about a quarter mile.

## GRANITE MOUNTAINS

North of the Palen Mountains, the Granite Mountains consist of rugged, granitic peaks rising above the Ward and Chuckwalla Valleys. At the north end of the range, the mountains drop to Granite Pass, crossed by Highway 62, separating the Granite Mountains from the Iron Mountains. Vegetation is sparse, consisting primarily of creosote and brittle bushes. The small Granite Mountain bighorn sheep herd roams the rugged crest of the range. Other animals in the area include deer, coyote, bobcat, gray fox and mountain lion.

The highpoint of the range, Granite Mountain, is within the 270,000-acre Palen-McCoy Wilderness. Camping in the area is primitive, and all minimum impact camping methods should be applied here. The nearest supplies, gas, food and lodging are in Blythe, about 25 miles to the southeast. For further information, contact the Bureau of Land Management offices in Palm Springs and Riverside.

### "GRANITE MOUNTAIN" (4,331+ FT; 1,320+ M)

This peak is recommended for those with four-wheel drive vehicles only due to the sandy areas encountered en route. The summit is marked by a benchmark named "Granite."

*Maps:* Palen Pass (CA) 7.5-minute (1:24,000 scale) topographic map; Eagle Mountains 1:100,000 scale metric topographic map; Automobile Club of Southern California (AAA) Riverside County or San Bernardino County map

*Best Time to Climb:* November through April

*Approach:* From the town of Desert Center along Interstate 10, drive 17 miles north on Highway 177 to the Palen Pass dirt road. Follow the Palen Pass Road (BLM Road P172) 11 miles east to a bend in the road. Turn left and head north on a rough four-wheel drive road 1.5 miles to the road end at about 1,500 feet.

*Route:* Hike due north up the alluvial fan toward the peak which is visible from here. You will be hiking between two major dry washes that, at the base of the mountains, are separated by a north-trending ridge. Follow this ridge northward to the peak's west ridge. The west ridge is then

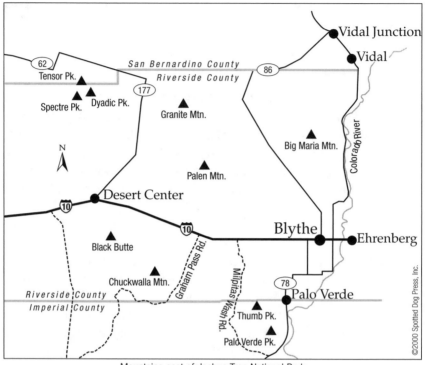

Mountains east of Joshua Tree National Park

followed to the summit. Anticipate six miles round-trip with 2,900 feet of elevation gain.

*Alternate Approach:* Drive to the Palen Pass Road as described above. Follow the Palen Pass Road 13.4 miles east to the pass. This is lonely country, and two-wheel drive vehicles should be careful not to get stuck in the sand. Continue another mile east of the pass to a dirt road heading north. Follow this road, bearing left at a fork in a few hundred feet, and continue 0.9 miles to where the road drops into a wash. Drive in the wash about 300 yards (bypassing an extremely rough road that exits the wash) to an easier road that leaves the wash to the left. Continue another 0.4 miles and park. The road end also makes a fine desert camp. From here, the northward-trending ridge can be reached via a northwest traverse along the base of the mountains.

*Alternate Route:* Instead of following the ridge, the dry wash to the east of the ridge can be followed, generally staying left at all major wash forks until at an elevation of approximately 980 meters on the metric map, where a steep gully is followed to the summit ridge. A dry waterfall en route can be bypassed. This route is roughly the same length and elevation gain as the primary route.

## PALEN MOUNTAINS

The Palen Mountains consist of a relatively low, but rugged complex of sedimentary and volcanic rocks. They rise above the Palen and Chuckwalla Valleys on the west, south and east. Looking down from Palen Mountain, one sees the extent of Palen Dry Lake, the largest playa in the Colorado Desert. To the north, the range drops down to Palen Pass. Palen Pass separates the Palen Mountains from the neighboring Granite Mountains. Vegetation is sparse, consisting primarily of creosote and brittle bush. The Granite Mountain bighorn sheep herd occasionally visits the Palen Mountains. However, the Palens do not provide any permanent range for that herd. Other animals in the area include deer, coyote, bobcat, gray fox and mountain lion.

The highpoint of the range, Palen Mountain, is within the Palen-McCoy Wilderness. Camping in the area is primitive, and all minimum impact camping methods should be applied here. The nearest supplies, gas, food and lodging are in Blythe, about 25 miles to the southeast. For further information, contact the Bureau of Land Management offices in Palm Springs and Riverside.

### "PALEN MOUNTAIN" (3,848 FT; 1,173 M)

The summit of this peak is marked by a benchmark named "Red Top."
*Maps:* Palen Mountains (CA) 7.5-minute (1:24,000 scale) topographic map; Eagle Mountains 1:100,000 scale metric topographic map; Automobile Club of Southern California (AAA) Riverside County or San Bernardino County map
*Best Time to Climb:* November through April
*Approach:* Due to the rather convoluted approach to this peak, a detailed road description is in order. Four-wheel drive is generally recommended although high-clearance two-wheel drives should have little problem with the route. Exit Interstate 10 in Blythe at the Lovekin Boulevard off ramp. Follow Lovekin Boulevard five miles north to some railroad tracks, and continue another 12.1 miles (Lovekin Boulevard becomes Midland Road) to a boulder on the west side of the road marking a good dirt road to Inca. Follow the "Inca Road" 0.4 miles west to the railroad tracks that are crossed

and bear left toward a small abandoned settlement about 200 yards away, then right onto the main dirt road (Arlington Mine Road). Stay on the Arlington Mine Road four miles, bear left at a fork, and continue another 3.4 miles to a second fork. Stay left, following BLM Road P172 1.4 miles to a fork and bear left (leaving P172) and drive 0.2 miles to another fork. Stay right and drive 2.7 miles on a rougher road, bear right at yet another fork, and continue 1.4 miles to a junction. Continue straight 0.4 miles to a fork in a wash. Bear right, and drive 0.6 miles to another fork. Bear right and continue 0.2 miles to a large wash. With a four-wheel drive, you could drive a little further but it is hardly worth the effort, and after all this you're ready to start walking anyway.

*Route:* Hike west up the road 0.4 miles, then continue west up the canyon a half mile to a fork. Bear right and hike another half mile to a second fork. Bear right again and follow this canyon to a saddle about 500 feet northeast of Point 964 meters on the metric topographic map. From the saddle, head northeast to the rocky summit. Anticipate five miles round-trip with 2,600 feet of elevation gain.

## BIG MARIA MOUNTAINS

This rugged, and relatively undisturbed range stands guard 3,000 feet above the Colorado River near Blythe. The range is surrounded by the broad desert valleys of the Parker Valley (along the Colorado River) to the east, Rice Valley to the north, Palo Verde Valley to the south, and McCoy Wash to the west and southwest. Vegetation in the canyons of the range includes palo verde, ironwood and acacia trees, along with the typical creosote and other shrubs. Foxtail and barrel cactus dot the range's slopes. Deer inhabit the range, primarily on the east slope closer to the Colorado River. For bat enthusiasts, there are known Yuma myotis and western pipistrelle roosts. The Brazilian free-tailed bat has been sighted here.

Big Maria Mountain, the highpoint of the range, is within the 47,000-acre Big Maria Mountains Wilderness. Supplies, food, lodging, and gasoline are available in Blythe, about ten miles to the south. Camping in the area is primitive, and all minimum impact camping methods should be applied here. For further information, contact the Bureau of Land Management, Palm Springs, Riverside and Yuma offices.

Julie Rush and Pete Doggett on Big Maria. Photo: Wynne Benti

## "Big Maria Mountain" (3,381 ft; 1,031 m)

The summit of this peak is unnamed on the topographic map.

*Maps:* Big Maria Mountains SW (CA) 7.5-minute (1:24,000 scale) topographic map; Blythe 1:100,000 scale metric topographic map; Automobile Club of Southern California (AAA) Riverside County map

*Best Time to Climb:* November through April

*Approach:* Exit Interstate 10 in Blythe at the Lovekin Boulevard off ramp. Follow Lovekin Boulevard five miles north to some railroad tracks, and continue another 8.5 miles to a dirt power line road. Turn north onto the power line road (BLM Road P3020) and follow it four miles to power pole #48-1. Two-wheel drives and four-wheel drives not wishing to leave their undercarriage in the middle of the desert can park here. Adventurous four-wheelers can continue another 1.7 miles along the road over progressively more vehicle-abusing ruts to the "official" road end at pole 46-3.

*Route:* From the "official" road end, head east up a large wash about one mile, then north to a saddle just east of Point 2,546 feet. From the saddle, head east up the ridge to Big Maria's southwest ridge, then northeast to the summit. Anticipate 4.5 miles round-trip and 2,300 feet of elevation gain from the "official" road end. From pole 48-1, anticipate eight miles round-trip and 2,500 feet of elevation gain.

# PALO VERDE MOUNTAINS

This range, named for the small tree with green bark that occurs in the area, is a fine little desert range, but with very rugged and colorful peaks, sheer cliffs, and a few small arches. The range overlooks the Palo Verde Valley and the Colorado River to the east. A climb in this range can be accompanied by a visit to a noted geode collecting area west of Milpitas Wash and roughly due west of Thumb Peak. The oldest rocks in the area consist of Precambrian-age metamorphic rocks, however, the range is dominated by three volcanic rock units that comprise the plugs and domes that are of interest to desert mountaineers.

Vegetation is sparse (creosote-dominant), although ironwood is plentiful in the washes that cut the range, including a large stand in Milpitas Wash. A palm oasis exists at Clapp Spring. A herd of bighorn sheep is present in these mountains, as are deer, coyotes, bobcats, and desert tortoises. The Palo Verde Mountains contain known ritual and mythological association localities for several tribes including the Quechan, Cocopa, Maricopa, Halchidoma, Chemehuevi, and Mojave.

Palo Verde Peak, the highpoint of the range, is within the 32,000-acre Palo Verde Mountains Wilderness. Camping in the area is primitive, so please apply all minimum impact camping methods. The nearest supplies, gas, food and lodging are in Blythe, about 18 miles to the northeast. For further information, contact the Bureau of Land Management offices in El Centro and Riverside.

### Palo Verde Peak (1,795 ft; 547 m)

*Maps:* Palo Verde Peak (CA) 7.5-minute (1:24,000 scale) topographic map; Trigo Mountains 1:100,000 scale metric topographic map; Automobile Club of Southern California (AAA) Imperial County map

*Best Time to Climb:* November through April

*Approach:* From the intersection of Interstate 10 and Highway 78 near Blythe, California, drive south on Highway 78, passing through Palo Verde, to a junction with the Milpitas Wash Road, 12 miles south of Palo Verde. Drive about a mile west along the Milpitas Wash Road to the Palo Verde Road. Turn north (right) and continue another 3.7 miles to where a drainage leads toward the peak.

*Route:* Climb southeast to the summit ridge, then north to the summit. The route is somewhat exposed but is Class 2. This is a short scramble with less than two miles round-trip and 1,000 feet of elevation gain, respectively.

### Thumb Peak (1,375 ft; 419 m)

*Maps:* Wiley Well (CA) 7.5-minute (1:24,000 scale) topographic map; Trigo Mountains 1:100,000 scale metric topographic map; Automobile Club of Southern California (AAA) Riverside County or Imperial County map

*Best Time to Climb:* November through April

*Approach:* From the junction of Interstate 10 and Highway 78 near Blythe, California, drive about 14 miles east on Interstate 10 to the Wileys Well Road. Follow the Wileys Well Road 8.7 miles south to the Bradshaw Trail. At this point, Wileys Well Road becomes the Milpitas Wash Road. Follow the Milpitas Wash Road another six miles and park.

*Route:* The peak is about two miles to the east. If climbing this peak, be prepared for Class 5 climbing. Anticipate four miles round-trip with about 1,000 feet of elevation gain.

# Anza-Borrego Desert State Park Area

The Anza-Borrego Region provides desert scenery, totally unique to anywhere else described in this guide. From the pine-forested Santa Rosa Mountains, to the stark Carrizo Badlands and Yuha Desert; from lush, hidden palm oases to dry, mud hills , the Anza-Borrego region has it all. Of course, that is the impression that modern desert travelers of the area will have. Early travelers, such as the trapper James Ohio Pattie, referred to the area as *"a more fitting abode for fiends than any living things that belong to our world."* Of course, the principal area of interest, is the Anza-Borrego Desert State Park, itself. At more than 600,000 acres, Anza-Borrego is California's largest state park.

Native people are known to have inhabited the region for more than 20,000 years. Over that time, four distinct cultures existed: San Dieguito (from more than 10,000 years ago to about 9,000 years ago), Pinto Basin (about 5,000 to 2,000 years ago), prehistoric Yuman and Shoshonean (beginning about 1,000 years ago), and the modern Native Americans encountered by the European travelers through the region.

The first Europeans to explore this region were probably a Spanish party under the leadership of Captain Pedro Fages, who passed through Borrego Valley and Coyote Canyon in pursuit of deserters from the presidio at San Diego. Later, Juan Batista de Anza, and his party including Francisco Garces, Juan Diaz, and an Indian guide named Sebastion Tarabal, passed through the area. Their party traveled through this region during the spring of 1773, and their first night's camp was probably close to today's dirt road heading north to the Painted Gorge, south of Carrizo Mountain. Later they passed along the south slope of Borrego Mountain, and entered the Borrego Valley. They continued up Coyote Creek, then west to the Mission San Gabriel. Anza followed that trip, with another, much larger expedition during 1775 and 1776. Occasional Spanish forays into the area continued for the next 50 years. Possibly the first "Euro-American" to visit this land was Thomas "Pegleg" Smith, a ne'er-do-well who passed through here during the 1830's and claimed to find gold near Borrego Springs. Later, during the nineteenth century, the region provided a main route to reach southern California from the Colorado River. In 1849 a stage route passed through this region along today's Road S-2. For a thorough discussion regarding the history of the Anza-Borrego region, the reader is referred to the book, *Our Historic Desert: The Story of the Anza-Borrego Desert* by Diana Lindsay.

There is no way to adequately describe the geology of this region in one or two paragraphs. However, to get a sense of what the montains in Anza-Borrego are like, a few words are in order. The mountains of Anza-Borrego have been extensively influenced in form by the San Andreas Fault, with many of the ranges running parallel to this important geologic feature. The oldest rocks consist of metamorphic rocks that were at one time deposited in a marine environment. The granitic rocks were emplaced hundreds of millions of years later. About four to five million years ago, the Salton Trough was filled by a large sea, and the associated sediments from this feature contain numerous fossils. Later, as the mountains to the west were uplifted, a rain-shadow effect was created and the area became the desert we see today. For more detailed information, refer to the book, *Geology of Anza-Borrego: Edge of Creation* by Paul Remeika and Lowell Lindsay.

Wildlife and vegetation in the region are highly diverse. Bighorn sheep roam over many of the ranges in the area along with coyote, mountain lion, and many other mammals, reptiles and birds. In fact, the name "Borrego" is the Spanish word for mountain sheep. As diverse as the wildlife, trees present in the region include fir, pine, palm, and the unique elephant tree. A November through April climbing season is recommended for the majority of the peaks listed in this section of the book. However, this region is noted for its spectacular spring wildflower displays, and hikers may want to take advantage of this season when scheduling their ascents.

For those who would like to conduct their desert mountaineering during the spring wildflower season, the park has set up a wildflower hotline that can be called to receive a report on current bloom conditions. The wildflower hotline number is (760)767-4684. A park use permit is currently required before driving, parking, camping or using the established dirt roads in the park. The permit can be acquired for a fee at the park visitor center, campgrounds, or any of the numerous self-service pay stations scattered throughout the park. A permit is not required to simply drive through the park on any of the paved highways. A few regulations that need to be followed when visiting Anza-Borrego Desert State Park include all vehicles must remain on established roads; hunting and shooting are not allowed and all firearms must be unloaded, inoperative and in a case; all campfires must be built in a metal container above the ground (no ground fires); all natural, cultural and historic features are fully protected (including wildlife); and collecting plants, rocks, fossils or Indian artifacts is prohibited. Dogs are not allowed on park trails or in any part of Anza-Borrego's backcountry. Outside of Anza-Borrego (for example on Santa Rosa Mountain), dogs are allowed.

The region is accessible by three interstate highways, Interstate 10 on the north, Interstate 15/215 on the west, and Interstate 8 on the south. Numerous fine paved highways crisscross the region making this area the most easily accessible area in this guide. There are numerous campgrounds in the state park, and opportunities for primitive camping on public lands outside of the park. Supplies, food, and lodging are available in towns along the Interstates, as well as in small towns scattered throughout the region.

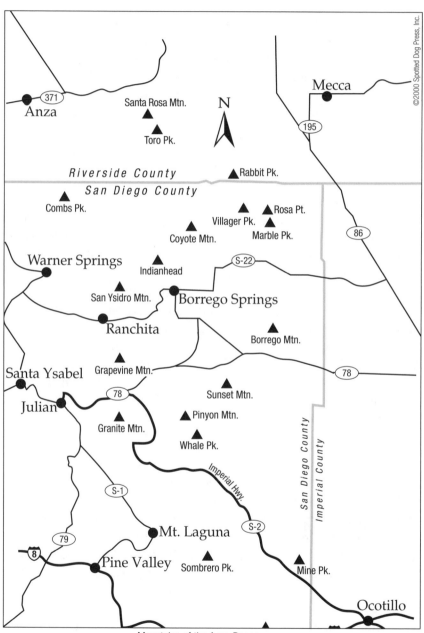

Mecca

Anza

371

Santa Rosa Mtn.

N

Toro Pk.

195

*Riverside County*

Rabbit Pk.

*San Diego County*

Combs Pk.

Villager Pk.

Rosa Pt.

Coyote Mtn.

Marble Pk.

86

Warner Springs

Indianhead

S-22

San Ysidro Mtn.

Borrego Springs

Ranchita

Borrego Mtn.

Grapevine Mtn.

78

Santa Ysabel

78

Sunset Mtn.

Julian

Pinyon Mtn.

Granite Mtn.

Whale Pk.

*San Diego County*

*Imperial County*

*Imperial Hwy.*

S-1

Mt. Laguna

S-2

79

8

Pine Valley

Sombrero Pk.

Mine Pk.

Ocotillo

Mountains of the Anza-Borrego area

# SANTA ROSA MOUNTAINS

Rising more than 8,000 feet above the south end of the Coachella Valley, the Santa Rosa Mountains are a varied, and interesting desert range. From the pine and fir-covered slopes of Santa Rosa and Toro, to the dry, sparsely vegetated lower slopes of the range, the Santa Rosas hold fine scenery that will suit most anyone's taste. The most infamous of the range's peaks, Rabbit Peak, lies within the 84,500-acre Santa Rosa Wilderness. This rarely visited wilderness is home to bighorn sheep (one of the largest herds in the state), mule deer, mountain lions, coyotes, and ringtails. The ridges and canyons are covered by a somewhat sparse flora of pinyon and juniper along the highest ridges, with creosote, agave, ocotillo and a host of cacti and other desert shrubs lower down. Beyond the peaks listed here, several unofficially named peaks such as Dawn's Peak, and Pyramid Peak, among others can be climbed. The peaks listed below are simply the primary mountain objectives for this range.

Camping is available in the Santa Rosa Mountain area, in forest service campgrounds in the nearby San Jacinto Mountains, and in nearby Anza-Borrego Desert State Park. Food, gas and lodging are nearby in Borrego Springs, Palm Springs, Idyllwild and Hemet. Much of the Santa Rosa Mountains are within the Santa Rosa Mountains National Scenic Area administered by the San Bernardino National Forest. Additionally, some lands, such as the summit of Toro Peak, are within the Santa Rosa Indian Reservation, and access can be revoked at any time.

### SANTA ROSA MOUNTAIN (8,070 FT; 2,460 M)

This forested mountain provides some nice views of the Coachella Valley and north to the Little San Bernardino Mountains. The former log cabin of Desert Steve Ragsdale is found on the summit. Desert Steve was a crusty character who wandered this area extensively. An example of his character is in his epitaph: *"Desert Steve - Worked like hell to be an honest American citizen, Loved his fellow men and served them, Hated Booze Guzzling, Hated War, Hated Dirty Deal Damn Fool Politicians. Hopes a guy named Ragsdale will ever serve humanity at Desert Center. He dug his own grave. Here are his bones. I put this damn thing up before I kicked off. Nuff said - Steve."*

*Maps:* Toro Peak and Butterfly Peak (CA) 7.5-minute (1:24,000 scale) topographic maps; Palm Springs 1:100,000 scale metric topographic map; Automobile Club of Southern California (AAA) Riverside County map

Desert Steve Ragsdale's cabin on the summit of Santa Rosa Mountain.  Photo: Andy Zdon

*Best Time to Hike:* June through October

*Approach:* From Interstate 10 in the Palm Springs area, take the Highway 111 off ramp to Palm Springs.  Follow Highway 111, as it passes through Palm Springs, Cathedral City and Rancho Mirage to Palm Desert and the junction with Highway 74.  Drive 18.5 miles south on Highway 74 to the Santa Rosa Mountain Road (Forest Service Road 7S02).  This road can be accessed via a variety of routes from the west including a route from Interstate 215 by driving 46 miles east on Highway 74 (passing through Hemet) to the Santa Rosa Mountain Road.  From Highway 74, follow the Santa Rosa Mountain Road 8.5 miles to a fork, passing a campground shortly before the junction.  Stay right at the fork, and continue another 1.3 miles to a sharp turn to the right.  Stay right and continue on to the summit of Santa Rosa Mountain.  With care, most cars should be able to drive very close to the summit area.  A two-wheel drive with high clearance should have little problem reaching the summit.

### Toro Peak (8,716 ft; 2,657 m)

This is the highpoint of the Santa Rosa Mountains. There is an installation on its summit.

*Maps:* Toro Peak (CA) 7.5-minute (1:24,000 scale) topographic map; Palm Springs 1:100,000 scale metric topographic map; Automobile Club of Southern California (AAA) Riverside County map

*Best Time to Hike:* June through October

*Approach:* Follow the route to Santa Rosa Mountain to a point at the sharp turn to the summit. Instead of heading right to the summit of Santa Rosa, stay left, and continue along the wooded, north slope of the range until below Toro Peak which is visible en route.

*Route:* One can easily scramble up to the summit from the road. This route is on the Santa Rosa Indian Reservation and access can be revoked at any time.

### Rabbit Peak (6,623 ft; 2,019 m)

This peak, the legendary long slog known to desert mountaineers, has no "easy" way up. All routes involve more than 6,000 feet of elevation gain in largely shadeless, dry country. This peak is only for those in excellent physical condition. En route to Rabbit, and its neighbor Villager, you will pass through creosote bush, ocotillo, agave and a host of cacti. Keep a watchful eye out for bighorn sheep.

*Maps:* Rabbit Peak and Fonts Point (CA) 7.5-minute (1:24,000 scale) topographic maps; Borrego Valley 1:100,000 scale metric topographic map; Automobile Club of Southern California (AAA) Riverside County map

*Best Time to Hike:* November through April

*Approach:* This is the traditional route up Rabbit, and has the most clearly followed track up the mountain. From Interstate 10 at Indio, take the Dillon Road off ramp and drive a mile southwest to the junction of Highways 86 and 111. Drive 15 miles south on Highway 86 to the Avenue 74-Fillmore Road junction. Drive 2.5 miles south on Fillmore Road to the road end and park (about 80 feet below sea level).

*Route:* From the road end, hike south over the levee and into a sandy wash. Head about a half mile west in the wash to a dirt road. Head south on the dirt road a short distance to another levee. Follow this second levee west about a quarter mile to a dirt track that is followed about a half mile southwest to the beginning of a trail. Follow the ducked trail three miles

Twenty-five miles and 13,000+ feet of loss. Along the Santa Rosa Mountains crest from Toro Peak, to Rabbit, Villager, and the end of the crest in Anza Borrego.  Photo: Wynne Benti

to the ridge separating the smaller drainage south of Sheep Canyon from Barton Canyon, and continuing up the ridge crest to a flat area.  Head west up the ridge to the summit.  Rocky sections can be bypassed.  Anticipate 16 miles round-trip with 6,700 feet of elevation gain.

*Alternate Approach and Route:* Climb Villager Peak as described below. From Villager Peak, continue north along the crest of the Santa Rosas to the summit of Rabbit.  Anticipate 21 miles round-trip with 6,800 feet of elevation gain.  An overnight bivouac is recommended for this route.

*Alternate Approach and Route #2:* Rabbit Peak has been climbed as a two-day trek along the crest of the Santa Rosa Mountains from Toro Peak to the Villager Peak parking area.  It requires a long car shuttle, leaving one car near the top of Toro Peak and a vehicle at the Villager parking area. This route is only recommended for experienced desert climbers in outstanding physical condition.  The route is a waterless, rugged, cross-country backpack that can be completed comfortably in three to four days, or in two days by experienced desert hikers in excellent condition.  The route is approximately 25 miles long with 13,000+ feet of elevation loss and 6,200 feet of gain.

### VILLAGER PEAK (5,756 FT; 1,754 M)

*Maps:* Rabbit Peak and Fonts Point (CA) 7.5-minute (1:24,000 scale) topographic map; Borrego Valley 1:100,000 scale metric topographic map; Automobile Club of Southern California (AAA) San Diego County map
*Best Time to Hike:* November through April
*Approach:* From Interstate 10 in Indio, take the Dillon Road off ramp and drive a mile southwest to the junction of Highways 86 and 111. Drive south on Highway 86 along the west shore of the Salton Sea to Salton City. From Salton City, head 14.5 miles west on Road S22-the Borrego Salton Seaway, to the Thimble Jeep Trail on the south side of the road. Park at the parking area (at a call-box) on the north side of the road (900 ft). If reaching this point from Borrego Valley, this parking area is 12.8 miles east on Road S22. The road is paved and accessible to all cars. Be sure your car is secured here. The author knows one climber who returned from the hike of Villager and Rabbit only to find that his car had been stolen.
*Route:* Hike north to the broad ridge on the west side of Rattlesnake Canyon. Climb this ridge to the summit. Point 5,640 feet is bypassed to the east. Anticipate 14 miles round-trip with 4,800 feet of elevation gain.

### "ROSA POINT" (5,000+ FT; 1,524+ M); "MARBLE PEAK" (4,257 FT; 1,298 M)

*Maps:* Fonts Point (CA) 7.5-minute (1:24,000 scale) topographic map; Borrego Valley 1:100,000 scale metric topographic map; Automobile Club of Southern California (AAA) San Diego County map
*Best Time to Hike:* November through April
*Approach:* Same as for Villager Peak.
*Route:* From the parking area, hike northeast up the alluvial fan to the mouth of Palo Verde Canyon, and hike about 1.5 miles up the canyon (to 1,900 ft). Scramble west to the ridge line, then north on a climber's path to the summit. At about 3,400 feet, a couple of routes will present themselves. Once can either head northeast back into the head of Palo Verde Canyon then up Rosa's south ridge or one can continue north, climbing over Point 3,680+ feet and Marble Peak (Point 4,237 ft) to the summit. Anticipate 12 miles round-trip with 4,800 feet of elevation gain.

### COYOTE MOUNTAIN (3,192 FT; 973 M)

Clark Lake, the starting point for this climb, is named for two brothers, Fred and Frank Clark. In 1891, after securing the property in the area, they dug Clark's Well, and developed a cattle ranch here. The Clark Lake area provides one of the finest views of the 6,000-foot scarp of the Santa Rosa Mountains. This scarp formed along the San Jacinto Fault (one of the most active faults in California) that runs along the base of the range.

*Maps:* Clark Lake (CA) 7.5-minute (1:24,000 scale) topographic map; Borrego Valley 1:100,000 scale metric topographic map; Automobile Club of Southern California (AAA) San Diego County map

*Best Time to Hike:* November through April

*Approach:* From Interstate 10 in Indio, take the Dillon Road off ramp and drive a mile southwest to the junction of Highways 86 and 111. Drive south on Highway 86 along the west shore of the Salton Sea to Salton City. From Salton City, head 21 miles west on Road S22-the Borrego Salton Seaway, to the Clark Lake Road (signed "Rockhouse Canyon"), and continue 1.5 miles on the well-graded dirt road to a fork. Stay left, and continue another 1.9 miles on the dirt road to the west side of Clark Lake and a yellow hopper (560 ft). If reaching this point from Borrego Springs, the Clark Lake Road is 7.3 miles east on Road S22. This approach should be accessible to most cars.

*Route:* Head southwest gaining the ridge just north of a prominent wash, then climb the ridge directly to the summit over somewhat loose slopes. Anticipate four miles round-trip with 2,650 feet of elevation gain.

## THE WEST BOUNDARY PEAKS
### COMBS PEAK (6,193 FT; 888 M)

This peak, the highpoint of Bucksnort Mountain, is barely within the northwest corner of Anza-Borrego Desert State Park, but is the highest peak within the park.

*Maps:* Beauty Mountain, Bucksnort Mountain, and Hot Springs Mountain (CA) 7.5- minute (1:24,000 scale) topographic maps; Borrego Valley 1:100,000 scale metric topographic map; Automobile Club of Southern California (AAA) San Diego County map

*Best Time to Hike:* November through April

*Approach:* From Interstate 15 in Temecula, drive 17 miles east on Highway 74 to Aguanga, then 16.4 miles northeast on Highway 371 to Kirby Road, just before reaching the town of Anza. Drive one mile south on Kirby Road to Wellman Road. Head east one mile on Wellman Road to Terwilliger Road. Continue 3.8 miles southeast on Terwilliger Road to Ramsey Road.

Head a few hundred feet west on Ramsey Road, to the Tule Canyon South Truck Trail heading south. Follow the dirt Tule Canyon South Truck Trail 2.8 miles to a junction with the Rim Rock Canyon Road. Turn east onto the Rim Rock Canyon Road, and continue one mile to a fork and stay right. Continue another mile and stay right. After a quarter-mile, the road forks and continues straight. A few hundred feet up the road, park at the parking area on the right side of the road at about 4,600 feet. Two-wheel drive vehicles with good clearance should not experience any problems on this approach. With care, most cars should be able to reach the parking area. *Route:* This roundabout route is mostly on a trail. From the parking area, head south down the road a few hundred feet to where a trail heads east. Follow the trail about 0.4 miles to a gate. Go through the gate, and continue another quarter mile to a junction with the Pacific Crest Trail. Head south on the Pacific Crest Trail about 300 yards to a trail junction. Stay right on the Pacific Crest Trail another three miles to the east ridge of Combs. Bushwhack west through dense chaparral to the summit. Long pants and sleeves should be worn on this hike. Anticipate nine miles round-trip with about 2,000 feet of elevation gain. Check for ticks back at the car.

### INDIANHEAD (3,960+ FT; 1,207 M)

This rugged peak provides a fitting trademark for the conspicuous San Ysidro Mountains. Visible from throughout much of the Borrego Valley, this peak will certainly "pique" the interest of the desert mountaineer. When hiking up Borrego Palm Canyon, keep an eye out for the diverse wildlife that lives here including the bighorn sheep, and a host of birds including quail, roadrunners, Canyon Wrens and orioles.

*Maps:* Borrego Palm Canyon (CA) 7.5-minute (1:24,000 scale) topographic map; Borrego Valley 1:100,000 scale metric topographic map; Automobile Club of Southern California (AAA) San Diego County map

*Best Time to Hike:* November through April

*Approach:* From Borrego Springs, California drive two miles west on Palm Canyon Road, then right to the Borrego Palm Canyon Campground. Continue through the campground to the day use parking area at about 800 feet.

*Route:* Although twice as long as the alternate, this route provides a far more interesting desert experience, reaching a large palm oasis deep in Borrego Palm Canyon. From the parking area, follow the nature trail, heading 2.5 miles northwest up Borrego Palm Canyon (passing the large palm oasis after 1.5 miles) to just below a fork in the canyon at 1,800 feet. The hike along Borrego Palm Canyon is particularly scenic soon after a rainfall when the ocotillo blooms a scarlet red, contrasting with its rich green leaves. The leaves fall off after about a month of dry weather. Once past the palms, the wash will provide an opportunity to practice your boulder-hopping skills. Head north, then northeast, up a ridge to a saddle northwest of Indianhead. Follow the ridge southeast to the summit. Anticipate eight miles round-trip with 3,200 feet of elevation gain.

*Alternate Route:* Follow the nature trail into Borrego Palm Canyon to where a prominent drainage heads up to the north. Climb up this drainage to the saddle just east of the peak, then west to the summit. Anticipate four miles round-trip with 3,200 feet of elevation gain.

## San Ysidro Mountain (6,147 ft; 1,874 m)

This peak, the highpoint of the San Ysidro Mountains, will test out your bushwhacking skills, and wearing long pants and a long-sleeved shirt are recommended. The mountain and range are named for a former local rancho that was named for the Spanish Saint Isidore the Plowman. Although the route to the summit of San Ysidro Mountain traverses relatively gentle terrain, the tremendously rugged, east scarp of the mountain rises above the Borrego Valley, giving anyone who views it from this angle a true appreciation for the immensity of this desert mountain.

*Maps:* Hot Springs Mountain, Borrego Palm Canyon, Ranchita and Tubb Canyon (CA) 7.5-minute (1:24,000 scale) topographic maps; Borrego Valley 1:100,000 scale metric topographic map; Automobile Club of Southern California (AAA) San Diego County map

*Best Time to Hike:* November through April

*Approach:* From Interstate 15 in Temecula, drive 37 miles east on Highway 79 to Warner Springs. From Warner Springs, continue another 3.3 miles south to the San Felipe Road (Road S2) on the left. Follow the San Felipe Road 4.7 miles to the Montezuma Valley Road (Road S22). Turn left onto the Montezuma Valley Road, and continue 6.6 miles to the Anza-Borrego Desert State Park boundary at a pass and park (4,200 ft).

*Route:* From the road, hike along the fence on the north side of the road, then head north, generally following the fence line on its east side. The brushy route (watch for cholla) follows the broad ridge (with some minor

Granite Mountain looms above Earthquake Valley.   Photo: Andy Zdon

ups and downs) passing east of Chimney Rock, passing over Point 5,326 feet, and east of the granite pinnacle called "The Thimble." Once past The Thimble, the route heads northwest to the summit marked by a bench-mark named Ysidro.  Anticipate seven miles round-trip with 2,100 feet of elevation gain.

### GRAPEVINE MOUNTAIN (3,810 FT; 1,161 M)
*Maps:* Tubb Canyon and Earthquake Valley (CA) 7.5-minute (1:24,000 scale) topographic maps; Borrego Valley 1:100,000 scale metric topographic map; Automobile Club of Southern California (AAA) San Diego County map
*Best Time to Hike:* November through April
*Approach:* From Interstate 15 in Temecula, drive 37 miles east on Highway 79 to Warner Springs.  From Warner Springs, continue another 3.3 miles south to the San Felipe Road (Road S2) on the left.  Follow the San Felipe Road 16.9 miles to Highway 78.  Turn left, and follow Highway 78 through Senetac Canyon four miles to a dirt road heading north. If San Felipe Creek is running, it may be necessary to park here. If San Felipe Creek is flooding, save this peak for another day. Otherwise continue 1.3 miles northwest on the dirt road to a pull out and park (at about 1,400 ft).
*Route:* This cholla-infested hike should be hiked with caution, and with

a pair of needle-nosed pliers for pulling out cholla clumps. Climb southwest up a wash, then right to a saddle east of Point 2,620 feet. From the saddle head south, through junipers, to the summit. Anticipate six miles round-trip with 2,400 feet of elevation gain.

### GRANITE MOUNTAIN (5,633 FT; 1,717 M)

*Maps:* Earthquake Valley (CA) 7.5-minute (1:24,000 scale) topographic map; Borrego Valley 1:100,000 scale metric topographic map; Automobile Club of Southern California (AAA) San Diego County map

*Best Time to Hike:* November through April

*Approach:* From Interstate 15 in Temecula, drive 37 miles east on Highway 79 to Warner Springs. From Warner Springs, continue another 3.3 miles south to the San Felipe Road (Road S2) on the left. Follow the San Felipe Road 16.9 miles to Highway 78. Turn right for a quarter mile, then south 9.8 miles on Road S2 to Vallecito Wash. Road S2 follows the Great Overland Stagecoach Route of 1849. This route is also accessible from Borrego Springs, by driving a quarter-mile west up the wash to a fork and turning right. Another 1.8 miles leads you to yet another fork. Stay right toward Rodriguez Canyon, and continue a quarter mile to where a dirt track heads off to the right at 2,520 feet.

*Route:* Hike up the dirt track as it climbs the ridge to the north, eventually reaching some mine workings at about 3,500 feet. From the mine workings, head northeast to the ridge line, then northwest to Granite's southwest ridge. Climb northeast to the summit. Anticipate seven miles round-trip with 3,100 feet of elevation gain.

## BORREGO MOUNTAIN

Borrego Mountain is actually a very small desert range consisting of two distinct peaks...the West and East Buttes. The higher West Butte is of particular interest. When hiking up this peak and meeting a fellow hiker en route, an appropriate greeting is "What's shakin'?" Why you ask? In 1968, a magnitude 6.4 earthquake (called the Borrego Mountain Earthquake) occurred along the Coyote Creek Fault that runs along the eastern base of the mountain. Ground surface rupture occurred over 30 miles of the fault trace. The earthquake occured when the stresses that built up beneath the surface overcame the frictional forces along the fault plane, and the earthquake ensued.

Borrego Mountain from along the ridge leading to the summit.    Photo: Andy Zdon

### WEST BUTTE (1,207 FT; 368 M)

This granitic summit, the highpoint of Borrego Mountain, provides a classic desert panorama of the surrounding country including the Borrego Badlands and the Salton Sea region.

*Maps:* Borrego Mountain (CA) 7.5-minute (1:24,000 scale) topographic map; Borrego Valley 1:100,000 scale metric topographic map; Automobile Club of Southern California (AAA) San Diego County map

*Best Time to Hike:* November through April

*Approach:* From Borrego Springs, follow the Borrego Springs Road 5.8 miles southeast to an intersection with Road S3, the Yaqui Pass Road. Continue straight on the Borrego Springs Road another 6.2 miles to Highway 78. Head 1.5 miles east on Highway 78 to the marked Buttes Pass Road. Follow the Buttes Pass Road one mile north to a junction and stay left. Drive another 0.9 miles to the Slot Lookout. Park here at about 800 feet.

*Route:* From the parking spot, follow the track east to a ridge line, then follow the ridge through thin-stalked ocotillo on a well-worn path northeast to the summit. Anticipate two miles round-trip with about 600 feet of elevation gain.

## PINYON AND VALLECITO MOUNTAINS

As with most of the "ranges" in the Anza-Borrego Region, the Pinyon and Vallecito Mountains are relatively small and compact. Their location in the central portion of the state park leads to fine views of the entire park region from their summits. These mountains provide excellent opportunities to view wildlife. A small herd of bighorn sheep makes the Pinyon Mountains their home.

### SUNSET MOUNTAIN (3,657 FT; 1,115 M)

This peak provides fine views of the Salton Sea.

*Maps:* Whale Peak (CA) 7.5-minute (1:24,000 scale) topographic map; Borrego Valley 1:100,000 scale metric topographic map; Automobile Club of Southern California (AAA) San Diego County map

*Best Time to Hike:* November through April

*Approach:* From Borrego Springs, drive 5.3 miles south on Borrego Springs Road to Yaqui Pass Road (Road S3). Follow the Yaqui Pass Road 6.9 miles south to Highway 78. Turn east on Highway 78, and continue four miles east to the Pinyon Wash Jeep Road.  Head south up Pinyon Wash to the junction with Nolina Wash and park at about 1,450 feet. This route is accessible to most vehicles. With a four-wheel drive, one could continue another mile up the canyon.  The Pinyon Wash Jeep Road can also be reached by driving 37 miles east on Highway 79 from Interstate 15 in Temecula to Warner Springs.  From Warner Springs, continue another 3.3 miles south to the San Felipe Road (Road S2) on the left.  Follow the San Felipe Road 16.9 miles to Highway 78. Turn east on Highway 78 and follow it 11 miles to the jeep road. If driving from the east, Pinyon Wash is 4.6 miles west of the Borrego Springs Road-Highway 78 junction.

*Route:* From the two-wheel drive parking spot, follow the Pinyon Wash Jeep Road southeast about a mile to where the west side of Sunset Mountain comes into view.  Hike west up Sunset's east ridge to the summit. Anticipate six miles round-trip with 2,200 feet of elevation gain.

### Whale Peak (5,349 ft; 1,630 m)

This gentle desert peak supports a diverse flora including pinyon, oak, manzanita and nolina on its higher slopes.  At lower elevations, creosote, jojoba, catclaw, agave and many other desert shrubs predominate.  This peak is reportedly one of the most frequently climbed desert summits in Anza-Borrego Desert State Park.

*Maps:* Whale Peak (CA) 7.5-minute (1:24,000 scale) topographic map; Borrego Valley 1:100,000 scale metric topographic map; Automobile Club of Southern California (AAA) San Diego County map

*Best Time to Hike:* November through April

*Approach:* From Interstate 15 in Temecula, drive 37 miles east on Highway 79 to Warner Springs.  From Warner Springs, continue another 3.3 miles south to the San Felipe Road (Road S2) on the left.  Follow the San Felipe Road 16.9 miles to Highway 78.  Turn right for a quarter mile, then south 4.1 miles to the Pinyon Mountain Road on the left.  About 500 feet up the Pinyon Mountain Road you'll reach a fork.  Stay right, and continue about 3.6 miles to a narrow spot in the canyon.  Two-wheel drive vehicles may desire to park here.  With a four-wheel drive vehicle, continue another 2.1 miles to a fork. Stay right and continue another 0.3 miles to the mouth of a canyon. Park here at 4,080 feet. The Pinyon Mountain Road is also reached from Borrego Springs by driving 5.3 miles south on Borrego Springs Road to Yaqui Pass Road (Road S3).  Follow the Yaqui Pass Road 6.9 miles south to Highway 78.  Head west on Highway 78 seven miles to Road S2 heading south through Earthquake Valley (part of the Elsinore Fault Zone), then south 4.1 miles to the Pinyon Mountain Road on the left.

*Route:* Hike south up the canyon to where the grade lessens, then head southeast along the base of the ridge about a quarter mile, then south again up a draw to another flat area.  From here, head south-southeast over undulating terrain until Whale's northwest slopes are reached and are followed to the summit. Anticipate five miles round-trip with 1,400 feet of elevation gain.  From the two-wheel drive parking spot, anticipate ten miles round-trip with 2,000 feet of elevation gain.

*Alternate Approach and Route:* This route is recommended for those who don't mind some additional mileage and elevation gain in order to view some pictographs.  From the junction of Road S2 and Highway 78, drive six miles south on Road S2 to the dirt Blair Valley Road on the left.  Follow the Blair Valley Road 3.9 miles, following signs to the "pictographs" and reaching the site of Mortreros, an ancient Indian village.  Continue another 1.4 miles to the pictograph trailhead (about 3,040 ft).  Follow the trail east about one mile to the pictographs.  Head north up a draw about 1.5 miles as it winds around Whale's broad southwest ridge, then northeast up toward the peak.  At about 4,400 feet, climb southeast to a flat area at 5,000 feet, and head east to the summit. Anticipate eight miles round-trip with 2,400 feet of elevation gain.

### Pinyon Mountain (4,492 ft; 1,369 m)

*Maps:* Whale Peak (CA) 7.5-minute (1:24,000 scale) topographic map; Borrego Valley 1:100,000 scale metric topographic map; Automobile Club of Southern California (AAA) San Diego County map

*Best Time to Hike:* November through April

*Approach:* Drive to the Pinyon Mountain Road as described for Whale Peak. About 500 feet up the Pinyon Mountain Road you'll reach a fork. Stay left, and continue about 5.7 miles to a pass at 3,980 feet. Park here. Two-wheel drive vehicles with high clearance are recommended.

*Route:* The summit is a short scramble to the northwest. Anticipate two miles round-trip with 500 feet of elevation gain.

On the route to Sombrero.  Photo: Wynne Benti

# IN-KO-PAH AND JACUMBA MOUNTAINS

These two small, compact desert ranges, include two of the finer desert peaks in the Anza-Borrego country.

### SOMBRERO PEAK (4,229 FT, 1,289 M)

*Maps:* Sombrero Peak (CA) 7.5-minute (1:24,000 scale) topographic map; El Cajon 1:100,000 scale metric topographic map; Automobile Club of Southern California (AAA) San Diego County map

*Best Time to Hike:* November through April

*Approach:* From Interstate 15 in Temecula, drive 37 miles east on Highway 79 to Warner Springs. From Warner Springs, continue another 3.3 miles south to the San Felipe Road (Road S2) on the left. Follow the San Felipe Road 16.9 miles to Highway 78. Turn right for a quarter mile, then south 29.3 miles to the Indian Valley Road (dirt). To access the Indian Valley Road from Borrego Springs, drive 5.3 miles south on Borrego Springs Road to Yaqui Pass Road (Road S3). Drive west to the junction with Road S2, then south 29.3 miles to the Indian Valley Road. Follow the Indian Valley Road southwest about 2.5 miles to a fork. Stay left, and continue 2.8 miles to a grove of palm trees and park (2,240 ft). This road is accessible to two-wheel drive vehicles with good clearance. Additionally, Road S2 can be accessed from Interstate 8 on the south.

*Route:* Climb southwest up a steep chute to where the grade lessens, then continue southwest up the bouldery slopes, passing over Point 3,840+ feet en route. Anticipate three miles round-trip with 2,100 feet of elevation gain.

### JACUMBA MOUNTAIN (4,512 FT; 1,375 M)

Both routes on this peak have significant pluses. On one hand the primary route is much shorter. On the other hand, the alternate route starts out at a nice grove of palm trees. If you only have two-wheel drive, your decision is made up for you; choose the alternate route. The summit provides a fine view toward the Carrizo Gorge. The name is derived from the name of the former Rancheria named Jacom, and is probably of Diegueno origin. The Jacumba Mountains were recorded as "la sierra de Jacum" in an 1841 report.

*Maps:* Jacumba (CA) 7.5-minute (1:24,000 scale) topographic map; El Cajon 1:100,000 scale metric topographic map; Automobile Club of Southern California (AAA) San Diego County map

*Best Time to Hike:* November through April

*Approach:* From El Cajon along Interstate 8, drive about 50 miles east and leave the Interstate at the In-Ko-Pah off ramp. Follow the Carrizo Gorge Road south 1.1 miles to a junction with Highway 80. Head 1.7 east miles on Highway 80 to a dirt road heading back to the Interstate. Follow this dirt road a half mile north. Turn right and continue about a hundred yards then north 0.4 miles, passing under the Interstate en route, to a fork. Stay left for a few hundred feet, then bear right. Passing the Mica Gem Mine, continue two miles to a point near a radio repeater. Continue along the east side of a hill with a second repeater to a junction. Turn left, and follow the road 1.7 miles to a fork. Bear left at the fork, and drive a few hundred feet to a parking spot at about 3,485 feet. Four-wheel drive vehicles are recommended.

*Route:* The peak is an easy scramble to the north. Anticipate three miles round-trip with 1,200 feet of elevation gain.

*Alternate Approach and Route:* From Ocotillo along Interstate 8, drive nine miles north on Road S2, entering Anza-Borrego Desert State Park, to a dirt road heading southwest. Follow the dirt road four miles to the railroad tracks at Dos Cabezas. Turn south at the tracks, and drive 1.5 miles to where they can be crossed. Cross over the tracks, and follow the road 1.7 miles to a fork, bearing left at the fork and continuing another 0.4 miles to Mortrero Palms at 2,000 feet. From Mortrero Palms, hike southwest, gaining the crest of Jacumba's north ridge at its far northern end, then south to the summit. Anticipate five miles round-trip with 2,600 feet of elevation gain.

## Coyote Mountains

These low, sparse, but colorful desert hills are the southernmost range described in this book, and provide distant views across the border into Mexico. Their metamorphic core is overlain by marine deposits containing extensive fossil horizons. The photographer who is present at sunrise or sunset will be treated to fine opportunities to apply his craft. The lack of water in the area, serves to severely limit the wildlife that inhabits these mountains other than the occasional coyote. Sparse creosote with a sprinkling of agave makes up the flora.

Mine Peak lies within the 17,000-acre Coyote Wilderness. Primitive camping along the roads surrounding the wilderness is available and all

Old mill site ruins at the Dolomite Mine.    Photo: Andy Zdon

minimum impact camping methods should be applied here.  The closest supplies, gas, food and lodging can be obtained in several towns along Interstate 8.  For further information concerning this area, contact the Bureau of Land Management office in El Centro.

Carrizo Mountain, the highpoint of the range is accessible from Painted Gorge, south of Anza-Borrego Desert State Park.  Unfortunately, off-road vehicle use has heavily impacted that area and the route is not recommended.

## "Mine Peak" (1,850 ft; 564 m)

This peak provides fine views of the surrounding desert country, particularly of the Carrizo Badlands, Salton Sea and Yuha Desert. The summit marked by the benchmark "Mine."

*Maps:* Sweeney Pass (CA) 7.5-minute (1:24,000 scale) topographic map; El Cajon 1:100,000 scale metric topographic map; Automobile Club of Southern California (AAA) San Diego County map

*Best Time to Hike:* November through April

*Approach:* From Interstate 15 in Temecula, drive 37 miles east on Highway 79 to Warner Springs. From Warner Springs, continue another 3.3 miles south to the San Felipe Road (Road S2) on the left. Follow the San Felipe Road 16.9 miles to Highway 78. Turn right for a quarter mile, then south 35 miles, crossing Sweeney Pass, to West Dolomite Mine Trail. Follow the West Dolomite Mine Trail 0.7 miles east to a fork. Turn left and continue a few hundred yards and park at about 1,150 feet. Two-wheel drive vehicles with high clearance should be able to drive the road. From Interstate 8, the West Dolomite Mine Trail is about 11.5 miles north of the town of Ocotillo. Additionally, Road S2 can be accessed from Interstate 8 on the south. The West Dolomite Mine Trail turnoff is about 17 miles south of Aqua Caliente Springs.

*Route:* From the road end, the peak is a short scramble to the north. Anticipate two miles round-trip with 800 feet of elevation gain.

# Important Addresses and Phone Numbers

**Anza-Borrego Desert State Park**
200 Palm Canyon Drive
Borrego Springs, California 92004
Phone (760)767-5311
Wildflower Recorded Message (760)767-4684
Web Site - www.cal-parks.ca.gov/DISTRICTS/
colorado/abdsp622.htm

**Anza-Borrego Desert Natural History Association**
P.O. Box 310
Borrego Springs, California 92004-0310
Phone (760)767-3052
Fax (760)767-3099
Web Site - www.california-desert.org

**Bodie State Historic Park**
P.O. Box 515
Bridgeport, California 93517
Phone (760)647-6445
Fax (760)647-6486
Web Site - www.parks.ca.gov/DISTRICTS/sierra/
bodie/bshp324.htm

**Bureau of Land Management,**
**Barstow Field Office**
2601 Barstow Road
Barstow, California 92311
Phone (760)252-6000
Fax (760)252-6099
Web Site - www.ca.blm.gov/barstow

**Bureau of Land Management,**
**Bishop Field Office**
785 N. Main Street, Suite E
Bishop, California 93514
Phone (760)872-4881
Fax (760)872-2894
Web Site - www.ca.blm.gov/bishop

**Bureau of Land Management,**
**El Centro Field Office**
1661 S. 4th Street
El Centro, California 92243
Phone (760)337-4400
Web Site - www.ca.blm.gov/elcentro

**Bureau of Land Management,**
**Las Vegas Field Office**
4765 W. Vegas Drive
Las Vegas, Nevada 89108-2135
Phone (702)647-5000
Fax (702)647-5023
Web Site - www.nv.blm.gov/vegas

**Bureau of Land Management,**
**Needles Field Office**
101 W. Spikes Road
Needles, California 92363
Phone (760)326-7000
Fax (760)326-7099
Web Site - www.ca.blm.gov/needles

**Bureau of Land Management,**
**Palm Springs South Coast Field Office**
690 Garnet Avenue, P.O. Box 1260
Palm Springs, California 92258
Phone (760)251-4800
Fax (760)251-4899
Web Site - www.ca.blm.gov/palmsprings

**Bureau of Land Management,**
**Ridgecrest Field Office**
300 S. Richmond Road
Ridgecrest, California 93555
Phone (760)384-5400
Fax (760)384-5499
Web Site - www.ca.blm.gov/ridgecrest

**Bureau of Land Management,**
**California Desert District Office**
6221 Box Springs Boulevard
Riverside, California 92507
Phone (909)697-5200
Fax (909)697-5299
Web Site - www.ca.blm.gov/cdd

**Bureau of Land Management,**
**Tonopah Field Station**
1553 S. Main Street
Tonopah, Nevada 89049-0911
Phone (775)482-7800
Fax (775)482-7810

**Bureau of Land Management,**
**Yuma Field Office**
2555 East Gila Ridge Road
Yuma, Arizona 85365-2240
Phone (520)317-3200
Fax (520)317-3250
Web Site - www.yuma.az.blm.gov/yumahome.html

**Death Valley Natural History Association**
P.O. Box 188
Death Valley, California 92328-0579
Phone (760)786-3285
Fax (760)786-2236
Web Site - www.nps.gov/deva/nathist.htm

**Death Valley National Park**
P.O. Box 579
Death Valley, California 92328-0579
Phone (760)786-2331
Web Site - www.nps.gov/deva

**Desert National Wildlife Range**
c/o Desert Complex
1500 N. Decatur Boulevard
Las Vegas, Nevada 89108
Phone (702)646-3401

**Eastern Sierra Interpretive Association**
190 E. Yaney Street
Bishop, California 93514
(760)873-2411
Web Site- access through Inyo National Forest
web site and click on bookstore

**Inyo National Forest - White Mountain Ranger District**
873 N. Main Street
Bishop, California 93514
Phone (760)873-2400
Web Site - www.r5.fs.fed.us/inyo

**Joshua Tree National Park**
74485 National Park Drive
Twentynine Palms, California 92277
Phone (760)367-7511
Fax (760)367-6392
Web Site - www.nps.gov/jotr

**Joshua Tree National Park Association**
74485 National Park Drive
Twentynine Palms, California 92277
Phone (760)367-5525
Fax (760)367-5583
Web Site - www.joshuatree.org

**Lake Mead National Recreation Area**
601 Nevada Highway
Boulder City, Nevada 89005
Phone (702)293-8907
Web Site - www.nps.gov/lame

**Mono Basin Scenic Area Visitor Center**
Hwy. 395, Lee Vining, California (760)647-3045

**Mojave National Preserve**
222 E. Main Street, Suite 202
Barstow, California 92311
Phone (760)255-8801
Web Site - www.nps.gov/moja

**Mojave National Preserve Baker Information Center**
75157 Baker Boulevard, P.O. Box 241
Baker, California 92309
Phone (760)733-4040

**Mojave National Preserve Needles Information Center**
707 W. Broadway
Needles, California 92363
Phone (760)326-6322

**Providence Mountains State Recreation Area**
Essex, California
Phone (760)928-2586
Web Site - www.parks.ca.gov/DISTRICTS/angeles/pmsra538.htm

**Red Rock Canyon National Conservation Area**
HCR 33, Box 5500
Las Vegas, Nevada 89124
Phone (702)363-1921
Web Site - www.redrockcanyon.blm.gov

**San Bernardino National Forest-**
**San Jacinto Ranger District**
P.O. Box 518
Idyllwild, California 92549
Phone (909)659-2117
WebSite - www.fs.fed.us/recreation/forest_descr/
ca_r5_sanbernardino.html

**Toiyabe National Forest-**
**Bridgeport Ranger District**
P.O. Box 595
Bridgeport, California 93517
Phone (760)932-7070
Web Site - www.fs.fed.us/htnf

**Toiyabe National Forest-**
**Spring Mountains National Recreation Area**
2881 Valley View Boulevard, Suite #16
Las Vegas, Nevada 89102
Phone (702)873-8800
Web Site - www.fs.fed.us/htnf

**Valley of Fire State Park**
P.O. Box 515
Overton, Nevada 89040
Phone (702)397-2088

## The Basic Essentials

Every daypack packed for desert hiking should include a basic list of items:
- Map (7.5 minute USGS topographic maps for specific area)
- Compass
- Sunglasses (and a spare pair)
- Sunscreen
- Hat (brimmed, light-colored to reflect the sun)
- Water (at least 2-4 liters minimum) with electrolyte replacement powder and energy food/snacks/lunch
- Clothing. Dress in layers. Include lightweight rain jacket/pants that can double as a windbreaker; lightweight polypropylene or other synthetic underwear, tops and bottoms; synthetic or wool sweater
- Pocket knife
- Matches in a waterproof container or plastic baggie
- Flashlight
- First-aid kit with the following basic items:
    - Waterproof tape (good for wrapping heels and toes to prevent blisters)
    - Moleskin (good for wrapping heels and toes to prevent blisters)
    - Neosporin (anti-bacterial ointment)
    - Alcohol pads
    - Blistex (or other anti-chapping ointment)
    - Small bottle of bug repellent
    - Tweezers (for removing cactus spines)
    - Needle-nose pliers (for removing cholla spines)
    - Roll of gauze/gauze pads; ace bandage (for sprains)
    - Band-aids
    - Whistle
    - Aspirin (or acetaminophen for high altitude–not as apt to cause stomach upset)
    - Antacid for stomach upset (for high-altitude)
- Sturdy boots with insoles
- Cell phone

### Basics for the car (refer to "Desert Roads" on page 33 for additional information):
- Road map (AAA maps or DeLorme Atlas & Gazetteer maps)
- Water (at least six to eight gallons, in separate containers, for two people on one waterless weekend)
- Tire jack, spare tire, lug wrench, tool kit, battery jumper cables, roll of duct tape, tow-rope
- Can of puncture seal (for emergency flats when the spare has been used)
- Cooler (with fruit juices, soda, preferably with sugar, sports drink like Gatorade)
- 2 two to three foot long two by four boards (for tires that get stuck in sand)
- Small shovel

### Basics for the overnight car camp:
- Water (extra containers)
- Roll-away camp table
- Camp stove
- Lawn chairs
- Ground cloth
- Sleeping bags (good for wrapping cooler during day to insulate and keep cool in car from sun)
- Sleeping pads
- Firewood & metal tub or garbage can lid (for campfires where permitted)
- Tent

## Geologic Time Scale

Frequently in the text of this guide, the age of rocks are described by using odd-sounding geologic terms such as Cambrian or Mesozoic. The geologic time scale presented below attaches numerical ages to these terms.

| ERA | PERIOD | EPOCH | YEARS |
|-----|--------|-------|-------|
| **Cenozoic (Age of Mammals)** | Quaternary | Holocene | |
| | | | 10,000 |
| | | Pleistocene | |
| | | | 2-3 million |
| | Tertiary | Pliocene | |
| | | | 12 million |
| | | Miocene | |
| | | | 26 million |
| | | Oligocene | |
| | | | 37-38 million |
| | | Eocene | |
| | | | 53-54 million |
| | | Paleocene | |
| | | | 65 million |
| **Mesozoic (Age of Reptiles)** | Cretaceous | | |
| | | | 136 million |
| | Jurassic | | |
| | | | 190-195 million |
| | Triassic | | |
| | | | 225 million |
| **Paleozoic (Age of Fishes)** | Permian | | |
| | | | 280 million |
| | Pennsylvanian | | |
| | | | 320 million |
| | Mississippian | | |
| | | | 345 million |
| | Devonian | | |
| | | | 395 million |
| | Silurian | | |
| | | | 430-440 million |
| | Ordovician | | |
| | | | 500 million |
| | Cambrian | | |
| | | | 570 million |
| **Precambrian** | | | |
| | Origin of the Earth | | 4.6 billion |

# References

Adrian, Mark, 1998. Thumb Peak a.k.a. BM Butte 2, March 27, 1998. The Desert Sage, Desert Peaks Section of the Sierra Club, May/June 1998, #255.

Adrian, Mark, 1998. Bridge Mountain, Wilson Peak (Nevada), June 13. The Desert Sage, Desert Peaks Section of the Sierra Club, July/Aug., #256.

Albers, J.P., and J.H. Stewart, 1972. Geology and Mineral Deposits of Esmeralda County, Nevada. Nevada Bureau of Mines and Geology Bulletin 78. 80 pp.

Arno, Stephen F., and Ramona P. Hammerly, 1984. Timberline: Mountain and Arctic Forest Frontiers. The Mountaineers, Seattle, Washington. 304 pp.

Austin, Mary, 1903. The Land of Little Rain. Houghton Mifflin and Co., Boston and New York.

Bailey, Roy A., 1989. Geologic Map of the Long Valley Caldera, Mono-Inyo Craters Volcanic Chain and Vicinity, Eastern California. U.S. Geological Survey Miscellaneous Investigations Series Map I-933.

Bear, Doug, 1998. Dry Mountain & Saline Peak, April 25-26, 1998, Private Trip. The Desert Sage, Desert Peaks Section of the Sierra Club, May/June 1998, #255.

Belden, L. Burr, 1956. Goodbye Death Valley. Death Valley 49ers, Death Valley.

Benti, Wynne, "Dangers In and Around Mines," Death Valley to Yosemite: Frontier Mining Camps and Ghost Towns, Spotted Dog Press, 1998

Bowers, Janice Emily, 1993. Shrubs and Trees of the Southwestern Deserts. Southwest Parks and Monuments Association, Tucson, Arizona. 140 pp.

Brasket, Ted and Jean Vincent, 1999. Rainbow Mountain 6,924' - Sep./Oct 98: Mount Wilson 7,070' - Oct. 97/Jan98, Red Rocks (Nevada). The Desert Sage, Desert Peaks Section of the Sierra Club, July, #262.

Bureau of Land Management, 1980. Final Environmental Impact Statement and Proposed Plan; Appendix, Volume B, Appendix III: Wilderness, California Desert Conservation Area. September. 684 pp.

Bureau of Land Management, 1995. BLM Wilderness Areas, National Parks and Preserve: Maps and Information. 149 pp.

Bureau of Land Management, (no date). Rand Mountain Management Area Visitor Information and Trail Map.

Cain, Ella M., 1961. The Story of Early Mono County. Fearon Publishers, San Francisco, California. 166 pp.

Calhoun, Margaret, 1984. Pioneers of Mono Basin. Artemisia Press, Lee Vining, California. 172 pp.

California State Mining Bureau, 1917. Mines and Mineral Resources of Alpine County / Inyo County / Mono County. California State Printing Office, Sacramento, California, 1917.

Carey, Richard L., 1994. Mormon Peak: 24-Nov-94 (private trip). Desert Peaks Section archives.

Carruthers, William, 1951. Loafing Along Death Valley Trails. Death Valley Publishing Company, Ontario.

Cates, Robert, 1984. Joshua Tree National Monument: A Visitor's Guide. Live Oak Press, Chatsworth, California. 100 pp.

Chalfant, W.A., 1933. The Story of Inyo. Chalfant Press, Bishop, California

Chalfant, W.A., 1939. Death Valley: The Facts. Stanford University Press.

Charlet, David A., 1998. Atlas of Nevada Mountain Ranges: Vegetation. Biological Resources Research Center, University of Nevada, Reno and Community College Southern Nevada, Department of Science, North Las Vegas. BRRC Web Site.

Chase, J. Smeaton, 1919. California Desert Trails. Houghton and Mifflin, Boston. 387 pp.

China Lake Branch of the American Association of University Women, 1960. Indian Wells Valley Handbook. China Lake, California.

Clark, Ginny, 1992. Guide to Highway 395: Los Angeles to Reno. Western Trails, San Luis Obispo, California. 207 pp.

Clark, William B., 1980. Gold In The California Desert, in Geology and Mineral Wealth of the California Desert. South Coast Geological Society - Dibblee Volume. Pp. 128-139.

Cleland, Robert Glass, 1944. From Wilderness to Empire: A History of California 1542 to 1900. Knopf, New York. 388 pp.

Cronkhite, Daniel, 1981. Death Valley's Victims: A Descriptive Chronology 1849-1980. Sagebrush Press, Morongo Valley, California. 77 pp.

D'Azevedo, Warren L., Great Basin, Handbook of North American Indians, Volume 11, Smithsonian Institution, Washington 1986.

DeLorme, 1986. Southern California Atlas & Gazetteer. DeLorme Publishing Company, Freeport, Maine.

DeLorme, 1995. Northern California Atlas & Gazetteer. DeLorme, Freeport, Maine.

DeLorme, 1996. Nevada Atlas & Gazetteer. DeLorme, Freeport, Maine.

Desert Peaks Section, Sierra Club, 1992. Road and Peak Guide.

Dibblee Jr., Thomas W., 1967. Areal Geology of the Western Mojave Desert, California. U.S. Geological Survey Professional Paper 522, 153 pp.

Digonnet, Michel, 1999. Hiking Death Valley: A Guide To Its Natural Wonders and Mining Past. Michel Digonnet, Palo Alto, California. 542 pp.

Dokka, R.K., and A.F. Glazner, 1982. Field Trip Roadlog: Late Cenozoic Tectonic and Magmatic Evolution of the Central Mojave Desert, California, in Geologic Excursions in the Mojave Desert, Geological Society of America Cordilleran Section Volume and Guidebook. Pp 1-30.

Elliott, Russell R., 1966. Nevada's Twentieth Century Mining Boom. University of Nevada Press, Reno, 1966.

Faye, Ted, 2000. Of Myths and Men: Separating Fact from Fiction in the Twenty-Mule Team Story, in Proceedings: Fifth Death Valley Conference on History and Prehistory, March 4-7, 1999. Pp 145-162.

Federal Writers' Project, 1939. Death Valley, A Guide. Houghton Mifflin, Boston.

Ferguson, Tom, 1985. Old Woman Statue. The Desert Sage, Desert Peaks Section of the Sierra Club, Aug./Oct, #180.

Frost, E.G., Donna L. Martin, and T.E. Cameron, 1982. Comparison of Mesozoic Compressional Tectonics with Mid-Tertiary Detachment Faulting in the Colorado River Area, California, Arizona and Nevada, in Geologic Excursions in the Mojave Desert, Geological Society of America Cordilleran Section Volume and Guidebook. Pp 113-159.

Furbush, Patty A., 1987. On Foot In Joshua Tree National Monument: A Comprehensive Guide to Walking, Hiking and Backpacking. Second edition, M.I. Adventure Publications, West Lebanon. 122pp.

Ganci, Dave, 1983. Desert Hiking. Wilderness Press, Berkeley, California, 178 pp.

Gath, Eldon M., Gregory, Jennifer L., Sheehan, Jack R., Baldwin, E. Joan, and J. Kirk Hardy, 1987. Owens Valley Field Trip Road Log, in Geology and Mineral Wealth of the Owens Valley Region, California. South Coast Geological Society Annual Field Trip Guidebook #15. Pp. 1- 32.

Glasscock, C.B., 1940. Here's Death Valley. Grosset and Dunlap, New York.

Glazner, Allen F., 1980. Geology of the Sleeping Beauty Area, Southeastern Cady Mountains, in Geology and Mineral Wealth of the California Desert. South Coast Geological Society - Dibblee Volume. Pp. 249-255.

Grayson, Donald K., 1993. The Desert's Past: A Natural Prehistory of the Great Basin. Smithsonian Institution Press, Washington D.C. 356 pp.

Gudde, Erwin G., 1949. California Place Names. University of California Press, Berkeley, California. 431 pp.

Hall, Wayne E., and E.M. MacKevett, 1958. Economic Geology of the Darwin Quadrangle, Inyo County, California. Division of Mines, San Francisco, California.

Hanson, Herschelle and Genevieve, 1972. The Unsung Heroes of Esmeralda. Johnson and Hanson Publishers, Fish Lake Valley, Tonopah, Nevada. 53 pp.

Hare, Trevor, 1995. Poisonous Dwellers of the Desert: Description-Habitat-Prevention- Treatment. Southwest Parks and Monuments Association, Tucson, Arizona. 32 pp.

Hart, John, 1981. Hiking the Great Basin: The Desert Country of California, Oregon, Nevada, and Utah. Sierra Club, San Francisco. 371 pp.

Hewett, D.F., 1931. Geology and Ore Deposits of the Goodsprings Quadrangle, Nevada. U.S. Geological Survey Professional Paper 275. 171 pp.

Hewett, D.F., 1956. Geology and Mineral Resources of the Ivanpah Quadrangle, California and Nevada. U.S. Geological Survey Professional Paper 275. 172 pp.

Hill, Mason, 1980. History of Geologic Explorations in the Deserts of Southern California, in Geology and Mineral Wealth of the California Desert. South Coast Geological Society - Dibblee Volume.

Houston, Charles, 1998. Going Higher: Oxygen, Man and Mountains. The Mountaineers, Seattle, Washington. 272 pp.

Houston, Charles, 1993. High Altitude Illness and Wellness. ICS Books. 72 pp.

Hundred Peaks Section, Sierra Club, 1990. Peak Guide.

Jaeger, Edmund, 1957. The North American Deserts. Stanford University Press, Stanford, California. 308 pp.

Johnson, Leroy and Jean, 1987. Cartographical Confusion - or - The Case of the Leaping Landmarks, in Proceedings: First Death Valley Conference on History and Prehistory, February 8-11, 1987. Pp. 86-97.Jurasevich, Dave, 1993. Iron Mountain, 3330 Feet Elevation. The Desert Sage, Desert Peaks Section of the Sierra Club, March, #224.

Jurasevich, Dave, 1994. Castle Peaks, Desert Peaks Section of the Sierra Club Archives.

Jurasevich, Dave, 1994. Mormon Peak (BM "North Mormon"). The Desert Sage, Desert Peaks Section of the Sierra Club, July, #232.

Jurasevich, Dave, 1995. Mesquite Mtns HP (5151 feet); Mescal Mtns HP (6499 feet); Sawtooth Range HP (2324 feet). The Desert Sage, Desert Peaks Section of the Sierra Club, May, #237.

Jurasevich, Dave, 1995. Highland Mtns Highpoint (No Benchmark). The Desert Sage, Desert Peaks Section of the Sierra Club, November 1995, #240.

Kirk, Ruth, 1959. Exploring Death Valley. Stanford University Press, Stanford.

Knopf, Adolph, 1918. The Geological Reconnaissance of the Inyo Range and the Eastern Slope of the Southern Sierra. Government Printing Office, Washington D.C.

Lawlor, Florine, 1999. Out From Las Vegas. Spotted Dog Press, Bishop.

Lindsay, Diana Elaine, 1973. Our Historic Desert: The Story of the Anza-Borrego Desert. Copley, San Diego. 144 pp.

Lingenfelter, Richard E., 1986. Death Valley & The Amargosa: A Land of Illusion. University of California Press, Berkeley, California. 664 pp.

Long, Margaret, 1950. The Shadow of the Arrow. Caxton Printers, Caldwell, Idaho. 354 pp.

Loose, Warren, 1971. Bodie Bonanza. Exposition Press, Jericho. 246 pp.

Madison, Cheri C. and Howard Booth, 1992. Red Rock Canyon Trail Guide. Red Rock Canyon Interpretive Association, Las Vegas, Nevada. 38 pp.

Manly, William Lewis, 1949. Death Valley in '49. Borden Publishing Company, Los Angeles, California.

Martineau, LaVan, 1992. Southern Paiutes: Legends, Lore, Language and Lineage. KC Publications, Las Vegas, Nevada. 312 pp.

McCurry, Michael, 1980. A Preliminary Report of a Large Silicic Volcanic Center in the Eastern Mojave Desert, San Bernardino County, California, in Geology and Mineral Wealth in the California Desert. South Coast Geologic Society - Dibblee Volume. Pp. 242-248.

McLane, Alvin R., 1978. Silent Cordilleras: The Mountain Ranges of Nevada. Camp Nevada Monograph No. 4. 118 pp.

Merriam, C.W., 1963. Geology of the Cerro Gordo Mining District, Inyo County, California. U.S. Geological Survey Professional Paper 408. 83 pp.

Michael, Bob, 1997. Rambles In A Blank Spot On The Map, The Nevada Strip, February 1997. The Desert Sage, Desert Peaks Section of the Sierra Club, July 1997, #250.

Michael, Bob, 1998. Bare Mountain, Nevada (6,317'). The Desert Sage, Desert Peaks Section of the Sierra Club, May/June 1998, #255.

Michael, Bob, 1998. McFarland Peak (10,745'), Spring Mountains, Nevada. The Desert Sage, Desert Peaks Section of the Sierra Club, Nov/Dec, #258.

Miller, Ronald Dean, 1985. Mines of the High Desert. La Siesta Press, California. 72 pp.

Miller, Ron & Peggy, 1975. Mines of the Mojave. La Siesta Press, Glendale, California.

Miller, William J., 1957. California Through the Ages. Westernlore Press, Los Angeles, California.

Mitchell, Roger, 1990. Exploring Joshua Tree. La Siesta Press, Glendale, California. 48 pp.

Mitchell, Roger, 1975. Western Nevada Jeep Trails. La Siesta Press, Glendale, California.

Murbarger, Nell, 1956. Ghosts of the Glory Trail. Desert Magazine, Palm Desert, California.

Nadeau, Remi, 1948. The City-Makers. Doubleday & Company, Inc., Garden City.

Nadeau, Remi, 1965. Ghost Towns and Mining Camps of California. Ward Ritchie Press, Los Angeles. 278 pp.

Nielson, Jane and Ryan D. Turner, 1986. Miocene Rocks of the Northern Turtle Mountains, San Bernardino County, California, in Cenozoic Stratigraphy, Structure and Mineralization in the Mojave Desert. Geological Society of America Cordilleran Section Guidebook and Volume - Trips 5 and 6. Pp. 25-32.

Norris, Robert M., and Robert W. Webb, 1976. Geology of California. John Wiley & Sons, New York. 365 pp.

Noyce, Wilfred, 1950. Scholar Mountaineers: Pioneers of Parnassus. Roy Publishers, New York. 164 pp.

Paher, Stanley W., 1971. Las Vegas: As It Began - As It Grew. Nevada Publications, Las Vegas, Nevada. 181 pp.

Paher, Stanley W., 1984. Nevada Ghost Towns and Mining Camps. Nevada Publications, Las Vegas, Nevada. 492 pp.

Palmer, T.S., 1980. Place Names of the Death Valley Region in California and Nevada. Sagebrush Press, Morongo Valley, California. 80 pp.

Pepper, Choral, 1973. Guidebook to the Colorado Desert of California. Ward Ritchie Press, Los Angeles. 128 pp.

Perkins, Edna Brush, 1922. The White Heart of Mojave. Boni and Liveright Publishers, New York. 229 pp.

Pipkin, George C., 1982. Pete Aguereberry: Death Valley Prospector & Gold Miner. Murchison Publications, Trona, California. 159 pp.

Purkey, Becky W., Ernest M. Duebendorfer, Eugene I. Smith, Jonathon G. Price, and Stephen B. Castor, 1994. Geologic Tours in the Las Vegas Area. Nevada Bureau of Mines and Geology Special Publication 16. 156 pp.

Reid, Harry, 1998. Searchlight: The Camp That Didn't Fail. University of Nevada Press, Reno, Nevada. 223 pp.

Remeika, Paul and Lowell Lindsay, 1992. Geology of Anza-Borrego: Edge of Creation. Sunbelt Publications, El Cajon. 208 pp.

Rinehart, C. Dean and Donald C. Ross, 1956. Economic Geology of the Casa Diablo Mountain Quadrangle, California. Division of Mines, San Francisco, California.

Russell, Israel, 1889. Quaternary History of Mono Valley, California. U.S. Geological Survey Eighth Annual Report, Pp. 267-394.

Schad, Jerry, 1986. Afoot and Afield in San Diego County. Wilderness Press, Berkeley, California. 290 pp.

Shumacher, Genny, 1959. Mammoth Lakes Sierra. Sierra Club, San Francisco, California.

Shumacher, Genny, 1963. Deepest Valley: Guide to Owens Valley and its Mountain Lakes, Roadsides and Trails. Sierra Club, San Francisco, California. 208 pp.

Spurr, Josiah Edward, 1903. Descriptive Geology of Nevada, South of the Fortieth Parallel and Adjacent Portions of California. Government Printing Office, Washington D.C.

Stone, Paul and Calvin H. Stevens, 1986. Triassic Marine Section at Union Wash, Inyo Mountains, California, in Mesozoic and Cenozoic Structural Evolution of Selected Areas, East- Central California, Geological Society of America Cordilleran Section Guidebook and Volume. Pp. 45-51.

Taylor, Gary C., and Stephen E. Joseph, 1988. Mineral Land Classification of the Eureka-Saline Valley Area. California Division of Mines and Geology Open File Report 88-2.

Tierney, Timothy, 1997. Geology of the Mono Basin. Kutsavi Press, Mono Lake Committee, Lee Vining, California. 73 pp.

Troxel, Bennie W., 1974. Geologic Guide to the Death Valley Region, California and Nevada, in Guidebook: Death Valley Region, California and Nevada. Geological Society of America Cordilleran Section. Pp. 2-16.

Troxel, Bennie W., 1982. Description of the Uppermost Part of the Kingston Peak Formation, Amargosa Rim Canyon, Death Valley Region, California, in Geology of Selected Areas in the San Bernardino Mountains, Western Mojave Desert, and Southern Great Basin, California. Geological Society of America Cordilleran Section Volume and Guidebook. Pp. 61-73.

Troxel, Bennie W., and John D. Cooper, 1982. Geologic Road Guide, Day 3, Segment B - Shoshone to Northern Nopah Range, in Geology of Selected Areas in the San Bernardino Mountains, Western Mojave Desert, and Southern Great Basin, California. Geological Society of America Cordilleran Section Volume and Guidebook. Pp. 89-90.

Wernicke, B.P., Hodges, K.V. and J.D. Walker, 1982. Geological Setting of the Tucki Mountain Area, Death Valley National Monument, California, in Mesozoic and Cenozoic Structural Evolution of Selected Areas, East-Central California, Geological Society of America Cordilleran Section Guidebook and Volume. Pp. 67-80.

Wheelock, Walt, 1971. Desert Peaks Guide, Part 1. La Siesta Press, Glendale, California.

Wheelock, Walt, 1975. Desert Peaks Guide, Part 2. La Siesta Press, Glendale, California.

Woodward, Arthur, 1961. Camels and Surveyors in Death Valley: The Nevada-California Border Survey of 1861. Death Valley 49ers Publication No. 7. 73 pp.

Wuerthner, George, 1998. California's Wilderness Areas: The Complete Guide - Volume 2 - The Deserts. Westcliffe Publishers, Englewood. 320 pp.

Wynn, Marcia Rittenhouse, 1963. Desert Bonanza: Early Randsburg - Mojave Desert Mining Camp. Arthur H. Clark, Glendale, California. 275 pp.

Zdon, Andy and Jack Kepper, 1991. Geology of the Las Vegas Region. American Institute of Professional Geologists, Nevada Section Field Trip Guidebook.

# About the Author

Andy Zdon at the Moki Dugway near Natural Bridges National Monument in Utah.
Photo: Wynne Benti

Andy Zdon climbed his first desert peak, Telescope, in the winter of 1981, and has been climbing desert peaks ever since. His work as a hydrogeologist has taken him to many of the desert locations described in this book, including the Inyo Mountains, Providence Mountains, New York Mountains, Lanfair Valley, and the Lower Virgin River Valley.

A graduate in geology of Northern Arizona University in Flagstaff, Arizona, Andy is a passionate collector of books on mountaineering and the history of the desert southwest. Andy lives and works in the Owens Valley.

## Design / Photographs

Born in a small Indiana farm town on the Wabash River, Wynne Benti climbed her first mountain in 1985, and her first desert peak, Tin Mountain, the same year.

Ruby and Wynne Benti
Photo: Andy Zdon

A graduate of the University of California at Davis, Wynne coauthored the Spotted Dog Press book, *Climbing Mt. Whitney*. She designed the cover, text pages, maps, and produced the index for *Desert Summits*. Wynne has hiked to the summits of more than 400 desert mountains, and lives at the foot of White Mountain Peak, the highest desert peak in the United States.

FOR MORE INFORMATION ON BOOKS BY
SPOTTED DOG PRESS, PLEASE VISIT:

**WWW.SPOTTEDDOGPRESS.COM**